Selected Readings on Marriage and the Family: A Global Perspective

The publication of this book is sponsored by:

Asian Programs, University of Indianapolis

Association of Chinese Social Scientists in North America

Selected Readings on Marriage and the Family: A Global Perspective

Edited by

Phylis Lan Lin
University of Indianapolis

Wen-hui Tsai
Indiana University—Purdue University at Fort Wayne

University of Indianapolis Press
1995

University of Indianapolis Press

Address for publication correspondence and orders
Phylis Lan Lin, Director
Asian Programs
University of Indianapolis
Indianapolis, Indiana 46227-3697
317-788–3264 or 317-788-3275 (Fax)

Design, layout, and typesetting: Rosalie Fletcher
Technical assistance: Bradley D. Bishop, Mujib Lodhi, and Rauf Khalid
Cover design: Rolf-Peter Noot

98 97 96 3 2 1

Library of Congress Catalog Card Number 94-61127
ISBN 1-880938-013

Previous editions of the following articles have appeared in *Families: East and West*, Volumn 1 (no longer in print) edited by Phylis Lan Lin, Winston Y. Chao, Terri L. Johnson, Joan Persell & Afred Tsang (Library of Congress Catalog Card Number 92-60088, ISBN: 1-880938-00-6) and *Marriage and the Familiy in Chinese Societies: Selected Readings* edited by Phylis Lan Lin, Ko-wang Mei & Hui-chen Peng (Library of Congress Catalog Card Number 94-060460, ISBN: 1-880938-010) under 1992 and 1994 copy rights and published by the University of Indianapolis Press: "Characteristics of A Healthy Family" by Phylis Lan Lin; "Division of Labor in Household Tasks Among Korean Immigrant Families" by Shin Kim; "My Choice or My Obligation?" by Chid-duen C. (Painyon) Tse; "Marital Violence in Taiwan: A Cultural Perspective" by Rita Jing-Ann Chou; and "Why Are U.S. and Japanese Divorce So Different? An Aggregate-level Analysis" by Lynn K. White & Yuko Matsumoto.

Cover Source: Painting by Master Au Ho-nien.

Printed in the United States of America

Contents

Foreword

More than a phrase in the title of a book, "a global perspective," describes the goal of the University of Indianapolis in all its programming and activities. Just a short distance from my office, in the entry hall to our university library fly the flags of 37 countries representing the homelands of our international students. In those flags and in the faces of our students daily we see beyond the horizon of Indianapolis, the world which is our campus, a world made up of many families and traditions.

In addition to our international student population at our home campus, we are also actively engaged in international programming in Cyprus, Greece, Taiwan, and Mainland China. Our formal academic programs are complemented by academic conferences held on our home campus to which colleagues from around the world are invited. One such conference is the *International Symposium on Families: East and West* which has been held in 1991 and 1993. In these symposia scholars from many countries have gathered to present papers and to discuss similarities and differences in the tradition of the family in different cultures. Although there are a number of similarities and a number of differences in the development and understanding of the family and individual roles (parental, children, and gender), one conviction permeated all the discussions: the family is the core of the society and upon its health, societal health is finally dependent. The facts that family traditions are the subject of frequent attacks and that the sanctity of family is eroding and changing in various places in the world are compelling reasons to understand what has been and what is happening in order to strengthen the institution of the family and the values that are inherent therein around the globe.

In order to share the works of the scholars who have gathered for these discussions, thereby to further extend the understanding of the problems facing the families of the world, and to provide resources which will further the discussion and share the knowledge present in these symposia, we have published some of the papers from the 1991 and 1993 conferences. The titles of these volumes are *Families: East and West* and *Marriage and the Family in Chinese Societies: Selected Readings.* This is the third volume of this series.

As we have learned from others, so also we are seeking to reciprocate by returning what we have gained. The University of Indianapolis Press is one means whereby we can reach out to our interdependent society and affirm our common membership in the human family. With the able direction of Dr. Phylis Lan Lin, this is the fifth book in four years under the sponsorship of our Asian Programs area.

Modern communication and transportation have reduced our planet to a global village. The families of the world, with their traditions, move from place to place with relative ease. It is our hope that this series of books will assist the readers in understanding these families, and in creating around the world an environment in which the family, as the bedrock of our society, can be strengthened and we can learn to celebrate both the differences and the similarities which are found within the greater global human family.

G. Benjamin Lantz, Jr.
President
University of Indianapolis

Acknowledgment

No one can accomplish a project such as this one single-handed. I have been most fortunate to have all sorts of help from various sectors in and outside my university.

Beginning with my student assistant Kathy Munsch, who worked with me throughout the hot summer months and the Fall semester while carrying full-load. We worked at regular and odd hours. For a young student who bore with me on this tedious project with perseverance, I commend her for her intellectual capability and delightful personality. I am proud to have been asked to sponsor her membership to a national honor society, Alpha Chi, in October, 1994. I sincerely thank Kathy for being a most effective and efficient helper.

My relationship with the Publications Office at the University of Indianapolis has been particularly gratifying because of the professional assistance I received from Peter Noot and Rosalie Fletcher. Peter designed the cover and Rosalie did the layout and typesetting the manuscript. She patiently worked through the tedious task of seven drafts without a single complaint--she always got the corrections done in time for me to move on to the next draft. She is extremely efficient and precise, a fine professional who deserves special thanks. Producing a book with state-of-the-art technology requires technical assistance from a professional staff. Brad D. Bishop, Mujib Lodhi, and Rauf Khalid of our Data Processing Center have given me timely assistance. I am indebted to them.

Thanks goes to Dr. Carl Stockton, Professor of History and Dean for Extended and Special Programs, and a prose laureate, for writing the insightful *Afterword* for the book. I am also very grateful to Professor Emeritus Dr. Earning Peterson for proof-reading the final draft. Thanks also go to our department secretary, Sandra Baughn, who has given me invaluable "first class" secretarial help, including typing part of the second draft of the subject index. Finally, I am very grateful to many colleagues at the University of Indianapolis who have given me expressive support throughout the years in all my academic endeavors. I would like to specially mention my deep gratitude to Dr. Lynn Youngblood, Dr. Mary Moore, Dr. Greg Reinhardt, Dr. Pat Cook, Dr. Nancy O'Dell, Dr. Bob Vernon, Dr. Victoria Bedford, Dr. Robin Livesay, Dr. Gerry Speth, Dr. Tim Maher, Linda Dye, Kathy Koval, Christi Guyonneau, Mimi Chase, among others.

Since I teach full-time, direct the Asian Programs, do research, and perform the usual services at the university and the community, the immense amount of time dedicated to this project was often taken from my own family life. I wish to acknowledge my husband, Leon, daughter, Toni, and my parents for their continuing support and understanding throughout my academic life. As a career woman, a wife, a mother, and a daughter, I am most fortunate to have my family's blessing.

It has been a unique privilege to share the editing of this book with Dr. Wen-hui Tsai. A senior sociologist and internationally renowned theorist, researcher, and author of 20 books, Dr. Tsai, who specializes in Chinese studies, social change, marriage and the family, and gerontology, is well respected and recognized by scholars and students both in the United States and abroad. I have known Dr. Tsai for many years and shared the same membership in several professional organizations. It was Dr. Tsai's idea that we expand this volume from a mere conference proceedings to include papers that were not presented at the conference to attract a broader readership and to be suitable for classroom use as a supplement to conventional textbooks on marriage and family. As sociology today is giving more attention to the global society, I share with Dr. Tsai's conviction that American students need to be aware of variations in norms and values in different societies and cultures. This volume thus represents our efforts in promoting cross-cultural studies in sociology in general and in the field of marriage and family in particular.

Special thanks are due Alfred Tsang, the former Attorney General of the State of Indiana. Since his retirement in 1992, he has provided his volunteer services to the community and to junior colleagues in various fields. Many people benefit from his wisdom. I am one of the most fortunate. In the course of preparing this book, he generously contributed his volunteer time in assisting us in numerous ways, including the review of the first draft and working on the first draft of the subject index. He is most humble, yet I see him as my mentor without an official title. His wife, Buzzy Tsang, who has been Alfred's good companion for 42 years, has always played a supportive role to Alfred's volunteer services. I wish to express my special thanks to Buzzy.

Since the publication of the 1st volume (*Families: East and West*) and the 2nd volume (*Marriage and the Family in Chinese Societies: A Selected Reading*) of this series, many students in my classes and readers around the globe have given me the benefit of their thoughtful encouragements and suggestions. I am looking forward to hearing from them again. There is a Chinese saying, "as we are teaching, we are taught." As I have learned a lot from them, I expect to learn more from them again.

Many people made this book possible. Most of all, I wish to thank the authors for their contribution of articles in this anthology.

Also, my deepest gratitude must be expressed to the internationally famed painter, Master Au Ho-nien, for his generous permission to use his painting for the cover graphic

On behalf of my co-editor, we wish to express our deep appreciation to the Association of Chinese Social Scientists in North America for providing us a special research grant for partial sponsorship of the publication of this book. A special thanks must be addressed to Dr. George Chen, Executive Secretary of the Association, for his instrumental assistance in procuring the grant for us. The major (95%) funding for this book was sponsored by the Asian Programs, University of Indianapolis.

Finally, on behalf of those who worked on this project, I wish to once again express our deepest gratitude to President Lantz for his vision in the promotion of family studies at the University. His leadership has been inspirational to us all.

Phylis Lan Lin
University of Indianapolis

Introduction

Phylis Lan Lin
Wen-Hui Tsai

> *The family, a cultural universal, is considered the foundation of a society. We are born into families, grow up in families, and create new families for future generations. The family is the corner stone for personal growth and national development.*
>
> Phylis Lan Lin, "Preamble to International symposium on Families: East and West" (1991)

The family provides the continuity of the society. It links humankind from generation to generation. We descend from our ancestors, and in turn, our progeny succeed us. Societies do not exist without families; and they exist for families. Without the family, there is neither history of, nor the future for, the society. We are the product and participants of the socio-biological-economic-psychological function called family. Our basic personal well-being depends on healthiness of the family. The society is served when the family is served.

This is the third volume in a series of collections of papers presented in the first two conferences of International Symposium on Families: East and West, held at the University of Indianapolis in 1991 and 1993. The first, under the title of *Families: East and West*, was published in 1992, the second, *Marriage and the Family in Chinese Societies: Selected Readings*, was published in the Fall of 1994. Not all the papers accepted for the conferences were published. A few invited papers, that were not presented at the symposium, were included in these volumes.

The aim of the symposium was to provide a forum for the exchange of research and study on the family, with the objective that public policies and programs on the family would evolve from our work. The publication of these volumes preserves the data and analysis for further research, and seeks to stimulate interest in the study of family as a career.

By means of advanced communication and transportation technologies, and unabated fertility growth, people of the world are brought closer. Where it used to take days and months for people to reach another country, now is matter of hours and minutes to travel, and nanoseconds to see and hear. Pizza, tofu, KFC chicken, tortillas, pitas, and foods of all ethnic origins from different corners of the world are popularly consumed worldwide.

Linguistically, some non-alphabetical languages are now Romanized, as is the computer keyboard. The Hindu-Arabic numeral system is the universal method of counting and numbering no matter what spoken language. The measurement of time based on the Greenwich Observatory in England and Gregorian calendar, based on the sun and the birth of Jesus Christ, is commonly used for international commerce and diplomacy.

Notwithstanding the slowness of the United States in joining the rest of the world in the metric system of measurement, and the ethnic strife in the Balkans, central Africa, and other parts, people of different races, ethnic origin and creed are permanently residing in parts of the world not of their ancestry. People of mixed background intermarry and many alternative family forms are receiving acceptance by both the public and the law.

Surely and gradually, political and economical boundaries are being dismantled as we see the emergence of a united European Community and a North American trade bloc that will expand and merge in time. The wide, wide world is but a global village, and people are but passengers in a space ship called earth.

In order to know and understand the family, we must view it from a global perspective. The entire human race, whoever and wherever we are, is driven by the same impulse for survival and propagation. The family is our first and last resort to look to in order to sustain our existence.

We have come a long way from the primitive period when our immediate surroundings dictated how we lived and survived. To a larger extent, the local climate and weather are no longer of great concern to most individuals. We no longer depend on what we can gather and hunt for food, fiber, and fuel to live on as we advance in agriculture and manufacturing.

When we study the family from the global perspective, the experience encountered by the families under a given social/economical/political setting may be applied to the families in other parts of the world. Thus we may learn from the lessons experienced by people in one society for the benefit of others.

Even though cultural diversity rooted in a long history of tradition will remain, certain customs and practices of local origin tend to spread at more rapid rates. We have seen the trend in the change of household structure from the extended family to nuclear family in parallel with industrialization and economic development. A counter trend is found as grandparents fill in the breach for the families of single parents. Unlike the traditional extended family, centered on elderly authority, this new multi-generational family functions as a primary care giver for the elderly. The nuclear family of the American television Ozzie and Harriet Show is not necessarily the only bi-generational family model. There are families whose members are not biologically linked. There are households of half or step siblings, adopted children by parents with and without partner or even parents of the same sex. They may not be viewed as the most ideal or "deviant", but the children are mostly better off than living with mismatched biological parents in a tension filled household. Many of the famous and accomplished are brought up under such settings.

Since the ending of cold war, regional armed conflicts are occurring in the major continents. Families are taking on the global perspective as they seek refuge in other lands and orphaned children are adopted in unfamiliar settings.

In this United Nations' International Year of the Family, we see the family as an international entity. Except for the few aborigine peoples, most people or their ancestors migrated from other regions of the earth. Nations and empires rose and fell. Marriages transcend national boundaries. In the universal context, all earthlings of the world are indigenous of this planet. Are we not members of the same extended kinship descended from Adam and Eve?

The conjugal intimacy, being the biological fulfillment for the formation and continuation of the family, differentiates the male from the female, not only the reproductive roles, but the household division of labor as well. Industrialization and medical advances have altered the balance on the rights and burden of the members of the family. the transition from dependence to independence toward interdependence is examined in Part II and IV.

Beyond the spousal relationship are those between parents and children, kin folks, and by affinity. The dynamics of the family web in changing societies are analyzed in Part III and VII.

Coupled with reduction in childbirth risks and infant mortality, people are living longer. Nuclearization of the family, advanced by industrialization and requiring political and social solutions is the topic discussed in Part V and VII.

At the opposite extreme, and counter-paradigmatic of a healthy family, is a family in conflict, and severed. The much hushed marital violence is now in the open. The rising trend in divorce rates has moved from the West to the society of other cultures. Part VI and VIII discuss the development of the troubling conditions, and how they are dealt with.

If the families of the world were functioning at their potentials, there wouldn't be any book to write about the subject. The society would be in total harmony. The aim of marriage and family study is to seek ways to help it work for its members. It is not realistic that every family can be prosperous and healthy at all times. An ideal family protects its members against stresses and adverse conditions. This is the point of departure where this volume begins (Part 1).

Marriage and Family in Global Perspective

Part I

Article 1

Characteristics of a Healthy Family

Phylis Lan Lin

Introduction

The search for self-actualization and self-fulfillment has become one of the cultural mainstreams in modern societies. This has had profound influence on the quality of individual growth, family life, and community mental health. In addition, contemporary families have been affected by significant social, economic, and moral changes. We have evidenced increasing divorce rates, heartbreaking parent-child conflicts and worsening problems of juvenile delinquency. Many social researchers have wished to delineate a typology of an ideal family and to identify the image of a healthy family. In other words, recent studies have switched the focus from identifying the characteristics of a dysfunctional and broken family to identifying the characteristics of a healthy and happy family. The reason for studying the characteristics of a healthy family is to encourage and strengthen the family to move toward an enriched family life by using these characteristics as bench marks. In today's changing society, most families need to put forth extra efforts in order to just survive.

There are many words that have been used to describe the characteristics of a healthy family. "Family strengths" has been used to describe the family resource of adaptability and integration, which denotes a happy, successful and stable family. "Happy family" refers to a healthy, comfortable, intimate, harmonious, warm and well-balanced family life. These two labels may be used interchangeably. "Healthy" is not limited to the narrow medical definition. Instead, it encompasses a much broader meaning regarding the harmonious relations and successful functioning so that both the individual and the family's needs can be met. Every family has problems, including healthy families. Those families who are able to cope and adjust well in daily life demands are termed "healthy families." Therefore, the definition of a healthy family is not based solely on the structure of the family, hence, even a single parent family can be considered a healthy family as long as that family's needs are met and stresses are managed through positive mechanisms. A healthy family is a stress effective family in that such a family is able to function at its fullest capacity, and is able to cope with daily life demands (Chen & Lin, 1991; Curran, 1983; Lin, 1987a, 1987b, 1992, 1993; Lin et al., 1992).

In the introduction to *Building Family Strengths: Blueprints for Action*, Nick Stinnett defined family strengths as "those relationship patterns, interpersonal skills and competencies, and social and psychological characteristics which create a sense of positive family identity, promote satisfying and fulfilling interacting among family members, encourage the development of the potential of the family's stability to deal effectively with stress and crises" (Stinnett et al., 1979, p. 2). Therefore, "healthy family" is not only a concept, but can be operationalized, observed and measured; i.e., the positive dynamic human relations within a family (namely, characteristics of a healthy family) can be studied empirically. This concept focuses more on the interactions between and among family members than on the structure of the family.

A hundred years ago, Leo Tolstoy said, "Every happy family has similar characteristics; but all the unhappy families have their own reasons" (Lin, 1987b). If this is so, what is the image of a healthy family? A few years ago, Professor Jeaw-mei Chen of the National Cheng-chi University in Taiwan and I studied over 600 college students in Taiwan and the United States on the perception of a healthy family (Lin & Chen, 1987). Our findings supported the studies of Curren (1985), Stinnett (1985), and others.

The following section will integrate the findings of these studies, using the six characteristics of a healthy family as identified by Stinnett (1985) as the headings for further discussion on the essence of a healthy family.

Commitment

A family is like an organism, with life and vitality. It is made of many interdependent parts. For the family to survive, those interdependent parts (different roles in the family) must work, coordinate, and be supportive of each other. Building a family is not an easy chore. In addition to family members' mutual support and cooperation, it is most important that family members have commitments to each other. They must "put family life ahead of every thing else" (1)*, including sacrificing individual hobbies, reducing work hours, etc. in order to maintain family wellness. Self is a miniature of the family. The Chinese denote this spirit of self-sacrifice for the fulfillment of the family as "sacrificing small self for the big self" (2). In a healthy family, members agree on family goals, and are willing to work toward these short- or long-term goals. It is most important that family members understand the meaning of those goals and how they might affect their family life.

The family is the smallest unit of a social organization. It must respond to the demands from within and from the outside environment. Through family members' mutual commitment to each other, a solid foundation can be built. A healthy family's goals are set with flexibility and room for modification. When family members have opportunities to participate in goal-setting and the implementation of family goals, those family members are interacting, coordinating and working together as a team. A long-term mutual support by team members is a special kind of commitment. Every successful family must make certain investments in time, energy, and compassion in each other. There is another type of investment called commitment which simply says that marriage and the family receive top priority.

---

*Chinese inserts at the end of this article.

Healthy families focus on the long-term perspective. "Without a long-term perspective on marriage and family, we simply cannot endure or sustain the inevitable rigors, struggles, and challenges. With a long-term perspective, where there is a will, there is a way" (Covy, 1994, pp. 130-131). It takes a strong and lifetime commitment to develop a long-term perspective. After all, presumably, family relationships are lifelong relationships. Commitment also implies the transmission of family heritage, and abiding by family rules and regulations. In a healthy family, members are proud of their family heritage and lineage.

In a healthy family, commitment and fidelity are closely related. The couple mutually respects and trusts each other, and is honest with each other. Trust and commitment are inseparable. If the trust is low, communication between family members is exhausting, ineffective, difficult, and the passage of the message becomes meaningless and in vain. In the occurrence of an extramarital affair, the individual demonstrates his or her lack of commitment to his or her marriage and family. It permits a threat to the couple's intimate relations. An extramarital affair is a threat to the spouse's self esteem and dignity. It implies that the spouse can be replaced. In a happy marriage, both spouses see the other as "indispensable."

Togetherness

Professor Stinnett asked 1,500 children, "What is a happy family?" They did not list money, car, or big house. What they really looked for was the family spending time together in such activities as: playing games, taking family vacations, and celebrating birthdays together. This finding is in accord with a study of elementary students in Taipei, Taiwan, who also emphasized how much they are longing for family togetherness.

Regardless of how busy its members are, a healthy family learns to control time and is not controlled by time. Most importantly, they know how to arrange family time together. Family togetherness does not take place incidentally. It must be planned to allow it to happen. Activities such as attending church, community potluck lunches, cooking, cleaning yards, family trips, game playing, or shopping are frequently shared by healthy families. What is important is not what you do, but doing it together.

Recently, Lucy Alexander of the Family Wellness Center at Tunghai University in Taiwan designed the **Appreciation Game**. The game not only creates happy times, but also, through playing together, family members are able to interact in a nonthreatening atmosphere. Through playing together, family members are able to share their values, thoughts, needs and appreciation. Family games are becoming a very popular pastime in Taiwan. I am intrigued by observing families as they play the game, recognizing their attachment to each other, and revealing more and more of themselves. They break through the traditional Chinese authoritarian parent-child relations in a relaxed and "democratic" environment. Since playing games is not a part of the traditional Chinese family pastime, family members actually have to make an effort and a commitment to engage in this activity. Those families who have played this game have benefited by a commitment to each other in time, and sharing of needs and expectations, hopes and dreams. Commitment of self and expectation of others are two sides of the same coin. In a healthy family, members are seen as a unit, as a "coin." For, only through commitment and being together, can unity be brought about.

Healthy families provide their members emotional support and a sense of security. "Security represents our sense of worth, identity, emotional anchorage, self-esteem, and personal strength" (Covy, 1992, p. 22). When family members are all together, the individual's loneliness is reduced to its lowest level.

Meal times are one of the best times for family gathering, especially around the Chinese round table that symbolizes balance, harmony, and allows equal communication. Meal time not only allows family members to pour out their life experience of the day, it also provides a good time for family socialization. A lot of family life education takes place during meal times. Today many families exploit this hour for family togetherness by having meals while watching television, focusing their attention on the TV programs instead of interacting with family members. Not long ago in Taiwan there was a "Daddy, come home for dinner!" campaign, broadcast on TV to promote the whole idea of family togetherness.

Family-time provides a good opportunity to observe family dynamics. In some families, meal time looks like "wartime," with fussing and attacking each other. In other families there is peace with expression of mutual affection and caring. Meal times quite often reflect family traditions, such as respect for the elderly, good manners, and orderliness. In Japanese families, before meals they would say "Itadakimas"—please start your meal with appreciation for the service. In a healthy family, meal times are usually good times. In religious families, prayers before meals express mutual appreciation as well as appreciation to the Creator. Healthy families use meal time as a time for family togetherness and also to show appreciation to the providers, i.e., God, the meal preparer, and the bread earners.

One of the foundations for a happy family is that family members admire and appreciate each other. Today, both parents and children are busy doing their own things. It seems that everybody is always in a hurry. We don't take time to really sit down and have a good meal with family members and have good conversations.

How about the quality of time together? Healthy families know that their time together must be of high quality. However, providing adequate time together is important. It is hard to imagine providing a high quality of interaction in less than ten minutes of togetherness. This argument of quality versus quantity of time together has brought some ambiguities particularly to working parents. In the case of single-parent, working mother, dual career, and commuter families, parents are hard put to have adequate time for themselves or for their children. Spending time together with the family really takes extra commitment to make it happen. There is always a debate of whether quantity and quality are equated. We are sure that insufficient time makes it difficult to provide quality time. However, many parents make high commitment to their children even though they spend very little physical time together. Yet they appear to have a high degree of cohesiveness. For example, a very busy working mother tells her children, "In case of emergency, make sure to drag me out of my meeting, whether it is an important meeting or not. I will be right back because you are more important than my job." With this kind of reassurance to her children, the quantity time has been compensated. In the case that frequent face-to-face interaction with family members is impossible, for instance, in a commuting marriage, commitment is crucial for family solidarity.

Appreciation

One of the basic human needs is to be appreciated and admired by other human beings. Studies show that there is a high degree of mutual admiration and appreciation between members of healthy families. When parents kiss their children goodnight, it says to their child, "You have been a good kid and we love you very much." This statement at bedtime is one of the best reassurances to the child of affirmation of their good behavior during the day. It is also a very subtle way for parents to express to the young child, "My goodness, thank God, you have been such a good kid." In the traditional, relatively authoritarian Chinese family, it is very unusual for parents to express their appreciation to children. Chinese parents, by and large, have high expectations of their children's academic achievements. When their children reach parents' expectation, many parents keep their joy and contentment inside and seldom express directly their pride and "appreciation" to their children. Children want to be appreciated too! It is even more so when children feel, "Ma and Pa, I am doing this for you!"

Chinese people are relatively reserved in expressing appreciation, and showing mutual affection in public is almost a taboo. Recently a number of Couple Growth workshops were introduced through family life education programs in Taiwan. Many participants responded that through this experiential training they realized that "Appreciation is the best lubricant for marriage" and "One can bring happiness through the spouses' strength." Therefore, a happy couple would frequently say to each other, "I appreciate your hard work."

Good Communication

Good communication creates a sense of belonging, reduces frustration, and enhances marital relations. One must deliberately practice good communication, including becoming a good listener. It takes practice. This is one of the most important units in family life education.

In a healthy family, communication avoids redundancy. If the same message has to be repeated, they try to use different phrases and words. Concentrating on listening to the other is an important self-discipline. In an unhealthy family, bad communication quite often has been equated with "tossing pearls before swine" or in Chinese saying, "playing the piano to a cow," (3) or "go in the right ear and out the left ear" (4).

This means that the listener is not paying attention to the speaker. The first step to becoming a good listener is to show respect and attentiveness to the speaker.

It doesn't mean a healthy family does not have conflict, argument or rivalry. The difference between a healthy and unhealthy family is that a healthy family's solution to conflict is not to push the other into a corner. They would use creative or constructive solutions to their conflict. They do not attack, but focus on a solution. Good communication is problem solving not conflict creating.

A sense of humor is important to good communication. It brings a relaxed atmosphere. It releases tension in conflict. When a family enjoys humor together, it reflects the family's harmonious rapport and encourages a democratic spirit. A family's communication style reflects the power structure in the family.

A healthy family stresses egalitarian relations between husband and wife. When we ask a child, "who is the boss?" the child will reply, "sometimes my father makes the decision; sometimes my mother does." In a healthy family, we tend to find the division of labor at home is more equal and the decision-making process is more rational and considerate. In some harmonious traditional families, we find the father is obviously the head of the household. However, if we do a more careful observation, it will not be too difficult to find that although the wife or the mother is not the commander, she, nevertheless, exercises her influence in a subtle way. In a healthy family, the husband respects the wife, accepts her opinion. This has been evident in many traditional Chinese families, where father is the authority figure, but mother has her influence as well. There is a saying, "In the traditional Chinese family, father is on the throne, whereas mother is the power behind the throne." In fact, Chinese women might have more "power" in the family than they thought they had.

Television is the best and the worst enemy. It transforms family life style. It transmits many values to children. A family therapist pointed out humorously that his clients complain that the soap operas and football games are the main reasons for their broken marriage. The couple spends more time with TV than with each other. Not only does TV time affect family relations, but the selection of programs often becomes the focus of family conflicts.

Healthy families avoid becoming slaves to the television. They try to control the time and programs that their family watches. They see the positive function of TV. For example, some parents accompany the young child watching TV and use the program as a topic of conversation. They may ask what the child has learned from the program, and how was the dramatized story related to the real world. TV may become a tool for good communication if used properly.

Good communication not only delivers the message, but responds to the message. It includes verbal and nonverbal messages. Family members are free to express their emotions and feelings. Although "silent communications " (5) may describe the love and affection in a couple's heart, we must be aware that at times silence may also mean resentment, protest, or anger. In traditional Chinese families the approach is, "Children have ears but no mouth"

(6). In other words, children should listen without expressing their opinions. This traditional approach has its own merit. Yet, in dealing with adolescents, it is very important that we should try to understand their feelings through direct expression. Especially for Chinese American parents, open communication with their American born children is very important because they have to break two barriers: culture and generation. In a healthy family, members are allowed to freely express their opinions and not to put down one another. In addition, communication in a healthy family pays attention to clarifying messages. "What you said is not what I heard" (7) is a sign of a communication problem. Feedback between encounters reconfirms the exchange of messages. Therefore, in addition to learning good communication skills, you must also learn good self-communication. Try to understand yourself before you try to understand another. A disciple asked the most popular and well-respected Buddhist Priestess in Taiwan, Priestess Cheng-Yen, "What is communication? How can I communicate? Can people with different backgrounds, habits and levels of education communicate with each other?" She replied, "In reality, it will be easier for people with similar habits, goals, etc. to communicate. However, the individual is very important. One must listen well and not be afraid to express one's own opinion. One should have the wisdom and humility to accept your encounter's ideas. Therefore, do not ask others to communicate with you, instead, ask yourself to communicate with others. If I insist to put my opinion forward, that is not communication—that is persuasion. If I step back a step for you, that is communication" (Buddhist Priestess Cheng-Yen's Meditations, 1990, p. 256).

For those who are married or planning to be married, ask yourself this fundamental question: Do I want to marry myself? This question has several meanings. Before we try to communicate with others, we should first evaluate and know ourselves. In a happy marriage, couples are relatively objective, and can listen and give feedback to the message from the other. They are courteous to each other (8).

Spiritual Well-Being

We know that not all healthy families have religious beliefs. However, studies show that high religiosity and happy family are positively correlated (Stinnett & Defrain, 1994). High religiosity does not mean actively participating in attending church or temple services. It refers to a spiritual aspect of the family life-style. When family members share a common faith, it reassures their mutual support. Religious families tend to be more patient, forgiving, and broadly accepting of each other. Our differences in faith create distance between people. Those couples who share common religious faith (beliefs and activities) tend to have a higher degree of emotional intimacy. Spiritual well-being not only provides family members a common value orientation, but also provides similar life goals, mission and meaning. A recent Gallop poll in America showed that 63% of the surveyed public indicated that religion strengthened their family relations. In the Western society, religion becomes part of the social norm.

Religion is a social force which binds people together. Many family traditions are transmitted through religious rituals. Faith promotes family members' mutual dependency and cohesiveness; a common fate ties people together. The traditional Chinese Confucianism is a social and family religion. It binds people together and defines proper social conducts and interpersonal relations in the family through the practice of filial piety (Lin & Lin, 1994). Phrases such as "Do not travel far while parents are still living"(9); "Being a friendly older brother and a respectful younger brother;" (10); "Obedience to your parents" (11); "Benevolence is the foundation of human nature and to be human is to be benevolent" (12) illustrate common practices of filial piety in Chinese families. Intimately connected with the practice of filial piety is the "cult of ancestor worship" which ensures the stability of the family. Chai and Chai (1969, p. 84) pointed out that "Ancestor worship, which binds one to all the preceding generations, has been used by Confucianism as one of the means to integrate the kinship group. The secular function of ancestor worship is to cultivate kinship values, such as filial piety, family loyalty, and continuity of the family lineage." The practices of filial piety and ancestor worship are the most significant Confucian teachings that are considered pillars of a healthy family and hence the foundation of a strong community. These practices and ideas also set the foundation for the family support system which is so important and rooted in enhancing resiliency among Chinese families.

Spiritual well-being does not necessarily mean active participation in religious activities. Volunteer work and any philanthropy, or humanitarian activities are included in the broad definition of spiritual well-being. Healthy families stress spiritual well-being and work toward a common mission. Healthy families know their family mission, know their family values, know what they are all about, and know their reason for being. They are able to put their moral values into action. They are not only concerned about their own family's well-being, but also the welfare of the community where they live.

Coping with Crisis and Stress

The Chinese have a saying: "Every family has complaints" (13). The healthy family is no exception. Healthy families may face many problems as well. The difference is that members of healthy families are able to face the reality and creatively, systematically and rationally cope with the crises together. In certain difficult times, family members must extend each other's mutual trust and interdependence. However, they are able to solve their problems effectively, as Curran (1985) calls a healthy family, the "crisis effective family."

Then what are some of the mechanisms of coping used by healthy families? In addition to effective use of general coping skills for stress (Lin, 1983; McCubbin et al., 1980), the following are some of the common coping strategies healthy families adapt:

1. Make good use of support systems, including seeking help from the extended family system, friends, and community resources. In fact, regardless of the trend toward

the nuclear family, the extended family support system is still very functional in Chinese society today.

2. Develop new family rules, such as prioritizing of family budget, taking turns doing family chores, and alternating family roles.
3. Take a resilient and flexible attitude. Everyone in the family is willing to be "re-socialized" and adapt to a "paradigm shift" when necessary. They are not ashamed of lower standards in household chores. For example, a family put a sign in the kitchen which read, "My house is clean enough to be healthy and dirty enough to be happy."
4. Develop and strengthen good communication skills.
5. Focus on solutions rather than circulating conflicting issues.
6. Reevaluate the congruence between expectations and commitment of both family and marital roles.
7. Recognize that stress is inevitable but surmountable and controllable in daily life.
8. Avoid creating unnecessary stress for oneself or family members.
9. Recognize each other's special needs, especially teenager's developmental needs.
10. In summary, healthy families are able to effectively and efficiently manage a crisis situation. These families are able to discover problems early and are able to develop alternate strategies and very decisively take action to avoid larger crises.

In a healthy family, parents are willing to ask for help from professionals. They are not embarrassed to share their "family ugliness to outsiders" (14). They do not use sarcastic attitudes in analyzing the weakness of the family. Instead, through objectivity, they are able to recognize and evaluate family strengths. The most important characteristic of a healthy family is its willingness to change and make changes. It does not mean healthy families do not have problems. Members of healthy families are able to endure together their hardships in life.

A recent public opinion poll in the United States reaffirms that, in times of economic depression, unemployment or other difficult times, middle income families welcome a real harbor. People are reaffirming the importance of family, whether in the West or in the East. Family, indeed, is the most secure and stable source of strength for those who are facing challenges in the work place. According to Mutual Life's 1980 survey, 42% of those studied believed that "Family is the foundation for transmitting basic values of society." That percentage has increased to 84% in the 1990 survey. Those 1,200 surveyed, indicated that the family more than the government, schools, employers, or religious institutions, was able to transmit social cultural values. They recognized that only if we have a solid family can we create a solid community. A recent survey in Taiwan showed similar findings. Facing rapid social change and increasing social problems, family values are re-recognized. We must create healthy families. Family life must be enriched for it is the cornerstone of our nation. This thought is as old as Confucius' Cannon (Lin & Lin, in press).

References

Buddhist Priestess Cheng-Yen. (1990). Buddhist priestess Cheng-Yen's meditations. Taipei: Geou-ko Publishing Company.

Chai, C., & Chai, W. (1969). *The changing society of China*. New York: Mentor Book.

Chen, J., & Lin, P. L. (1991). Daily life demands, stress, social support and life satisfaction: A comparative study of working women and housewives in Taiwan. In *Selected papers of conference on gender studies in Chinese societies* (pp. 99–118). Hong Kong: Hong Kong Institute of Asia-Pacific Studies and the Chinese University of Hong Kong.

Covy, S. R. (1992). *Principle-centered leadership*. New York: Fireside.

Curran, D. (1983). *Traits of a healthy family*. Minneapolis: Winston.

Curran, D. (1985). *Stress and the healthy family*. San Francisco: Harper & Row.

Lin, P. L. (1985). *Stress and coping*. Taipei: Young Lion Publishing (In Chinese).

Lin, P. L. (1987a). *Healthy family and family strengths*. Taiwan: Training Center for Social Welfare Workers, Taiwan Provincial Government. (In Chinese).

Lin, P. L. (1987b). Characteristics of a healthy family and family strengths: A cross-cultural study. In H. R. Lingren, L. Kimmons, P. Lee, G. Rowe, L. Rothmann & L. Schwab (Eds.) *Family strengths 8-9: Pathways to well-being*. Lincoln, Nebraska: University of Nebraska. pp. 143–164.

Lin, P. L. (Feb. 18-19, 1992.) Roots of family life education. Paper presented at the 2nd International Conference on Family Life Education, Taiwan. (pp. 143-164). (In Chinese).

Lin, P. L. (August 1-4, 1993.) The modernization of family organization. Paper presented at the International Conference on China Modernization, Taiwan. (In Chinese).

Lin, P. L. Chao, W. Y., Johnson, T. L., Persell, J., & Tsang, A. (Eds.) (1992) *Families: East and West*. Indianapolis: University of Indianapolis Press.

Lin, P. L. & Chen, J. M. (1987). Characteristics of a healthy family and family strengths: Cross-cultural study. *Journal of Educational Psychology, 10*(8), 199-222.

Lin, P. L. & Lin, L. (in press). The Family System in Taiwan. In K. Altergott (Ed.). *International handbook on marriage and the family*. New York: Greenwood Publishers.

McCubbin, H., Joy, C., Cauble, A., Patterson, J., & Needle, R. (1980). Family stress and coping: A decade review. *Journal of Marriage and the Family*, *42*, 855–871.

Stinnett, N. (1985). Six qualities that make families strong. In G. Rekers (Ed.). *Family building*. Ventura, Ca: Regal, pp. 35–50.

Stinnett, N., Chesser, B., & DeFrain, J. (Eds.). (1979). *Building family strengths: Blueprints for action*. Lincoln, Nebraska: University of Nebraska.

Stinnett, N., & DeFrain, J. (1989). The healthy family: Is it possible? In M. Fine (Ed.). *The second handbook on parent education* (2nd ed., pp. 53–74). New York: Academic Press.

Note

A portion of this paper was derived from a speech made by the author at the 2nd Family Life Education Conference in Taiwan, in February, 1990. The title of the speech was "Roots of Family Life Education." The speech was delivered in Chinese. The Chinese manuscript and the videotape were published by the Family Wellness Center at Tunghai University in Taichung, Taiwan.

Chinese Inserts

1. 家庭至上
2. 犧牲小我，完成大我
3. 對牛彈琴
4. 右耳進，左耳出
5. 無聲勝有聲
6. 小孩有耳無嘴
7. 言者無心聽者有意
8. 相敬如賓
9. 父母在不遠行
10. 兄友弟恭
11. 唯命是從
12. 仁者人也
13. 家家有本難唸的經
14. 家醜不可外揚

Article 2

Modern Family Life and the Significance of Values

Vera S. Maass

The structure of family life is changing drastically and rapidly. World wide social changes as well as changes in values and attitudes toward human sexuality, marriage and family life have contributed to the development of different family systems.

The shift from traditional to modern type marriages in western societies has been well documented. But similar changes have been reported from other parts of the world. In Japan, the marriage process has undergone a major transformation from the traditional system of arranged mate selection to one based on free choice of mates (Goldman, 1993). Traditional Chinese marriages also were arranged, and the main functions of a marriage were those of procreation, heritage, economic production, family alliance, adult identity and legitimate sexual activities. As institutional marriage gives way to a more modern or companionship style of marriage, a strong emphasis is placed on personal fulfillment and a flexibility of roles arranged through negotiation and consensus. Additionally, in many parts of the world nuclear families have replaced the larger multi-generational or extended family systems of earlier generations.

A sobering aspect of changing family life is the increase in development of single-parent families and families blended by divorce and remarriage. In Hong Kong, marital separations and divorce in Chinese marriages have increased steadily over the last decade. The number of separated or divorced persons has increased from 24,300 in 1981 to 42,700 in 1986, resulting in about 36,500 single parent families (Yeung, 1992). Rising divorce rates in Singapore generate 3000 new single-parent families each year. As Thailand is undergoing a transition from a basically agricultural to an industrial society, Thailand's divorce rate, 8.5 divorces per 1,000 existing marriages in the late 1980s, has been steadily increasing (Thailand Ministry of the Interior, 1988).

In the United States single-parent households increased by 14.8 percent from 1985 to 1989. In 1989 there were nearly 8.6 million households with children younger than age 18 that were headed by a single parent. One out of four families is missing either a father or a mother in the home. Due to high divorce rates and increasing numbers of births by unwed mothers, almost half of the children born in the past ten to twenty years in America will be living in single-mother households, at least during part of their childhood (Bumpass & Sweet, 1989).

In the past, much attention was given to the difficulties inherent in single-parent families, especially female-headed families (Garfinkel & McLanahan, 1986; McLanahan & Bumpass,

1988). Theoretical sociologists and clinical psychologists seem to accept the notion that divorce and remarriage have long lasting negative effects on the children's emotional well-being and that the living arrangements after a divorce are less healthy than they had been prior to separation or divorce (Baydar, 1988).

Although there are disadvantages and risks that children of divorce are exposed to, the expectations of traumatic effects on children in single-parent households may turn into self-fulfilling prophecies. If teachers, social workers, psychologists, and parents expect these children to have more difficulties, they may treat them in such a way that it will exacerbate or generate these expected difficulties (Amato, 1991).

Earlier studies concerned with the social and psychological development of children in single-parent homes in relation to parental sex have not shown significant differences (Santrock & Warshock, 1979; Rosen, 1979). Risman & Park (1988) did not find an association between parental sex and parenting behaviors and concluded that the skills necessary for functioning as a primary care giver can be developed by female or male single parents.

Despite increasing popularity of fathers seeking joint or outright custody of their children at time of divorce and the more recently expressed sentiments that children in single-parent households may be better off living with the same-sex parent (Downey & Powell, 1993), mothers emerge as the custodial parent in the majority of divorces. As diverse as single-parent families may be, if they are headed by single mothers, most of them have one thing in common: their economic situation is unstable. This is partly because their fathers pay little or no child support (Garfinkel & McLanahan, 1986). According to Duncan and Hoffman (1985), the income of single-mother families one year after divorce was only 67 percent of their pre-divorce income. Yet the income of divorced men is about 90 percent of their income prior to the divorce (Weitzman, 1985).

When studying adjustment to divorce and a new lifestyle, Spanier and Fleer (1979) found that economic adjustment was the only area with significant sex differences. Most men reported that they were as well or better off than before the divorce, while economic problems affected their whole adjustment for most women. Many women had been out of the work force for a long time or had few marketable skills. With the presence of young children, the situation was even worse for those who had to find baby-sitters in order to hold a job. Often the baby-sitters' wages swallowed a significant part of their incomes. Yet, if they did not have custody of their children, they experienced more public censure than fathers who did not get custody of their children (Neely, 1992).

Federal and state government agencies have initiated programs to help single mothers improve their economic situation by providing opportunities for training and education. However, these programs have not been as successful as had been expected. Indeed, it has been argued that some of these projects may succeed only in converting the welfare poor into the working poor. Although the average educational attainment of welfare mothers is higher than generally believed, their scores on tests are distressingly low. It is interesting to note that about one third of welfare mothers have negative views about mothers working outside the home. This view is shared by economically stressed mothers who do not receive public assistance and who hold similarly traditional attitudes about women with children working outside the home (Maass, 1992).

Taking a historical view, social changes may be precipitated and maintained by crises or economical hardships, such as World War II and the Great Depression. However, as the general culture supported by the socializing institutions may undergo relatively rapid change, we forget that individuals may change at a much slower rate. For instance, the appropriateness of women working outside the home has become a relatively enduring social value which can be passed on from one generation to the next (Elder & Runck, 1979). In traditional attitudes, the appropriateness of women in the work force was seen as temporary or as "helping out" or supplementing a husband's income. However, in general, jobs performed by women are seldom thought of as careers. In dual-worker families, wives often continue to see the home rather than the workplace as central to their identity and are unwilling to part with the homemaker role (Lein & Blehar, 1979).

Individuals conform to a given role as the result of approval expressed by other individuals, usually parents or teachers. Perhaps the most important aspect in the child-raising process is the transmission of values and attitudes. According to "structural location" theory, the family is the location within the social structure where the individual is exposed to particular rewards which reinforce behaviors valued by the family. Parents in their own educational and occupational experiences learn and accept certain values which, in turn, significantly influence the strategies they use to socialize their children and communicate their expectations for them (Farmer, 1985; Peterson, Rollins, Thomas, & Heaps, 1982). The attitudes of parents, especially mothers, form the basis for the children's attitudes and values in adulthood (Acock & Bengtson, 1978; Jennings & Niemi, 1982; Smith, 1983). Thus mothers teach their daughters to display subordinate behaviors by approving of these as role-appropriate. This is not necessarily because they fear that their daughters will be punished by the male-dominated society for any insubordination, but because they themselves have been socialized (Connell, 1985).

Another theory, based on "psychosocial mediation," maintains that values become internalized during a person's development. As values are learned in early childhood through modeling, reinforcement, and role-taking, they become lasting qualities in the person's value system. Still, others consider a more comprehensive framework, such as a "psycho-structural perspective". Ranges of structural factors, such as a person's social class, generation, and the person's sex constitute possible bases for values. Individual differences within these ranges affect the person's values (Langman, Block, & Yahraes, 1979). Luster, Rhoades, and Haas (1989) concluded that differences in parenting behavior are closely linked to differences in parental values, and these values, are related to social class.

Thus, the values and attitudes of this generation's women are still being shaped through the influences of traditional sex role models of past generations as long-established attitudes and values are passed on—even though social institutions may already have made substantial changes.

Although values are among the most powerful behavioral determinants, and value considerations are prominent across a broad spectrum of disciplines, most theorists practically ignore modifying values as part of the psychotherapy process (Maass & Featherstonaugh, 1981). As long ago as 1973 Rokeach emphasized the significance of values in counseling when he stated that "values, attitudes, and behavior can undergo lasting change when people become aware of certain contradictions within themselves" (p. 330).

According to Rokeach (1968), values "may be consciously conceived or unconsciously held, and must be inferred from what a person says or does." Although operating values can be a source of distress, they can be quite obscure and unrecognized by the individual. Usually people are sincerely committed to their values; they become stable, sacred entities that are not subject to investigation or change, even though they may be quite self-defeating and unrealistic. Although individual values remain quite stable over the person's lifetime, the order of priority of individual values may change at different stages of a person's life. For instance, in younger years the value of freedom may have great importance to an individual, but as he grows older, security may replace freedom in the hierarchy of values with freedom being of lesser significance. Thus the place that an individual value occupies within the hierarchy or constellation of values may change as a function of the person's stage in his life cycle.

In noting the difference between actions that lead to individual and those that lead to social goals, Adkins (1960) distinguished between activities in which personal success is of paramount importance and those that are characteristic in a partnership or a social contract. Courage, forcefulness, or aggressiveness are often commended when success is achieved in a hotly contested situation. Fairness, or a similar measure, is the basis for estimating interpersonal behavior. Adkins (1960) proposed the dimensions "competitive" and "cooperative" to distinguish between individual excellence and relationship oriented values.

In a therapeutic setting it is useful to describe values as having most of the characteristics of beliefs and attitudes. Values are broad conceptualizations about how a person ought to behave in attaining individual and social goals. While beliefs may be relatively neutral, values usually include strongly held positive or negative emotional components. In contrast to attitudes, which are usually situation specific, Rokeach (1968) defined values as abstract modes of conduct and terminal goals not tied to a specific object or situation.

Distorted value conceptualization, unrealistic hierarchies in the value system, and imbalance in the cooperative—competitive continuum may result in self-hate, pervasive guilt, and crippling avoidance which, in turn, may lead to missed opportunities and lowered motivation to achieve one's goal. Individuals who submerge a balancing competitive value, such as personal freedom, while overtly demonstrating a dominating cooperative value, are likely to react as if they were deprived of the submerged value. In stereotypical homemakers, we would expect behaviors indicating that their responsibility to the family (cooperative value) dominates any personal achievement or freedom (competitive value). Acting primarily on this type of cooperative value can be appropriate for a woman while she is in the protection and security of an intact marriage. However, for a female head of household this would seem to be a poor basis for decision making.

A good example can be seen in a young divorced woman who came into therapy with the presenting problem that she was unable to divorce herself emotionally from her former husband—even though she was quite certain that she did not love him anymore.

Kathy met her husband in high school. They dated off and on until they both went to different colleges. But over the years they returned to their hometown for holidays and became more seriously involved. When Ray entered medical school he suggested they get married right away even though Kathy was about 35 credits short of her Bachelor's degree. Kathy gave in, thinking that Ray needed her, and dropped out of college. While Ray attended medical school Kathy worked as a secretary to help with their finances. Their first son was born when Ray was at the end of medical school, and their daughter came along during Ray's internship.

As soon as their financial situation allowed it, Kathy changed to part-time work, so she could devote more time to her children. And when Ray found a desirable position at a local hospital she quit working altogether to take care of their nice new home and the family. In time, Ray became somewhat bored with family life and gave in to the seductions of a much younger woman. It was more exciting to take this pretty young girl on trips to professional conferences than to bother with the family. Ray changed his wardrobe to a more youthful yuppie style, treated himself to a new, bright red sports car, and left the old family station wagon to Kathy.

Ray's next step was to buy a second home close to the hospital. This made it more convenient when he needed to be available for medical emergencies. It also made it more convenient to entertain his girlfriend whenever he wanted to. Although Ray did not want a divorce, he made it clear that he did not find family life interesting enough for him. Kathy initiated divorce proceedings and Ray found himself an experienced divorce lawyer who specialized in helping prosperous spouses obtain favorable divorce settlements which left few financial resources to their soon to be ex-spouses.

Kathy found a part-time job and returned to college to finish her degree. Whenever the children were to visit their father, she delivered and picked them up because Ray was much too busy to do that. He reminded her that she initiated the divorce and it was her fault that the children had to be carted back and forth. Often while in Ray's place Kathy helped clean the house and prepare meals for the children and their father. During visitation periods Kathy could not plan any significant activities for herself since she never knew how Ray would cooperate. At the least interruption, Ray would not hesitate to ask Kathy to come and pick up the children. If Ray needed work done on his home, he expected Kathy to do it for him or to babysit the place while professionals did the work.

Kathy realized that she allowed Ray to continue to take advantage of her. She had learned how to say No! in assertiveness workshops, but she couldn't say No! to Ray. In therapy, it became clear that Kathy was still operating under her old value system. Although her life situation changed drastically, her value priorities remained the same. The value of commitment, found by Swensen and Moore (1979) to be the value most consistently related to longevity of a marriage, was still on the top of Kathy's list of values. Kathy was able to realize that she was committed to something that did not exist in her marriage to Ray. It was time to reorganize her attitudes, beliefs and values in ways that were more appropriate to her new lifestyle.

Independence, responsibility, decision making, and other more competitive values would be more beneficial for Kathy's new situation. But these changes are not easy to accomplish—especially if they are to be of a long-lasting nature.

How did Kathy come to hold on so strongly to her cooperative value of commitment? She really did not have an answer beyond, "I always thought this was the way to be."

Exploring her background history, Kathy reported that she grew up in a very gentle and loving home environment. Her father was a school teacher and she remembered her mother reminding Kathy and her older brother not to be too noisy while playing in the late afternoons or early evenings because her father was correcting papers or working on the lesson plan for the next day. Kathy described her father as a very kind man. Neither she nor her brother were afraid of him. It just was the way of life in the house when her father was around. Actually, her father never reprimanded the children for being noisy, it was their mother who gently reminded them of the fact that their father had important work to do and that the children needed to respect that.

Kathy's mother grew up as one of three children in a minister's family. Kathy's grandfather was very well respected in every congregation he ever served. Kathy remembered her mother talking about the grandmother's beautiful voice. As the daughter of a pastor, Kathy's grandmother had learned to play the piano and organ. In addition, she had a very soft and clear, yet powerful voice. She never used these talents for her own aggrandizement but devoted her life and her musical skills to her husband's calling and to rearing her children according to the values she had been exposed to.

Kathy's mother did not inherit musical talents but she certainly had learned to assist her husband in his profession by protecting him from any kind of stress in the home. Kathy also remembered that when she started school her mother found a part time job during the hours that Kathy was in school. On one of the first days of school, Kathy came home a little earlier than usual and found her mother gone. She felt abandoned and started crying. When her mother finally returned home after about 10 or 15 minutes, Kathy was still crying. Her mother quit her job the next day.

It is interesting to note that while Kathy's brother always knew that he would become a teacher, Kathy did not have any specific career goals as she grew up.

Thus Kathy followed in the footsteps of generations of middle- and upper-class American women who until very recently had been required to function as backup persons to their husbands' careers. The wife's emotional support and contribution to her husband's career, required by many corporations and governmental agencies, became the involvement of two persons in a single career. The actual work of these women was largely invisible because it was mostly performed behind the scenes. Womanhood in America was believed to influence society in indirect ways. The woman's sphere was defined to be a place for emotional support and for healing the wounds inflicted upon husband and children by the outside world. This ideology of society's two spheres served to hide the contributions and achievements made by women in the support of their husband's careers while at the same time keeping women away from the powerful world outside of the home (Lopata, 1993).

For the smooth functioning of this "two spheres" world, it was advantageous to socialize women to embrace a larger percentage of cooperative values (as compared to competitive values) in their value and belief systems while men were encouraged to acquire a large proportion of competitive values. Today, women need to find their rightful place in society, but with traditional upbringing, females are ill equipped for this situation.

What does society do to help prepare single mothers for their responsibilities? We have raised a generation or two by preparing women for a life style that has been obsolete for a large portion of them. Opening up opportunities—as valuable as this is—is not enough. Lopata (1993) contends that American women have changed in recent years and, through increased education, have overcome many barriers to social involvement. To the superficial observer, the relatively high number of women on the nation's college and university campuses may indicate that women finally are actively involved in shaping their own destiny. However, for many women the changes in roles are only skin deep. Increased education most often is still seen as something to fill the time until marriage—even if employment follows the educational process. Or college is regarded as the most effective environment for finding a suitable husband (Wilson, Peterson, & Wilson, 1993).

While some (Lopata, 1993) have given credit to the feminist movement for changes in women's views of themselves and their increased participation in occupational and political roles, others have argued that by portraying women as victims the feminists have preserved these victim conditions and have fostered resignation (Westkott, 1979). If women continue to regard themselves as victims, the best they can ever hope to achieve is graduation to the level of survivor.

The alternative is to retrain young women for their independence by helping them explore their value systems and modify individual beliefs and values that are hindering them in their attainment of mental, emotional and financial independence. Women need to understand how oppression evolved in their families of origin, how it continued during the years of their schooling and in work situations, and how it may now be practiced within their own marriages. Women also need to understand the part they play in their own oppression by over emphasizing values and beliefs that foster dependence and subservience (Wilson, Peterson, & Wilson, 1993).

In order to prepare for the changes that accompany family modernization, the most important step is to help women reconceptualize values that are not working, and establish behavior patterns that are congruent with new, balanced value systems.

References

Acock, A. C., & Bengtson, V. L. (1978). On the relative influence of mothers and fathers: A covariance analysis of political and religious socialization. *Journal of Marriage and the Family, 40*, 519-530.

Adkins, A. W. H. (1960). *Merit and responsibility*. London: Oxford University Press.

Amato, P. R. (1991). The 'child of divorce' as a person prototype: Bias in the recall of information about children in divorced families. *Journal of Marriage and the Family, 53,* 59-69.

Baydar, N. (1988). Effects of parental separation and reentry into union on the emotional well-being of children. *Journal of Marriage and the Family, 50,* 967-981.

Bumpass, L. L., & Sweet, J. A. (1989). Children's experience in single parent families: Implications of cohabitation and marital transitions. *Family Planning Perspectives, 21,* 256-260.

Connell, R. W. (1985). Theorizing gender. *Sociology, 19,* 260-272.

Downey, D. B., & Powell, B.(1993). Do children in single-parent households fare better living with same-sex parents? *Journal of Marriage and the Family, 55,* 55-71.

Duncan, G. J., & Hoffman, S. D. (1985). A reconsideration of the economic consequences of marital disruption. *Demography, 22,* 485-498.

Elder, G. H., & Runck, B. (1979). Families in hard times–a legacy. In E.Corfman (Ed.), *Families today* (Science Monographs,Vol. 1, pp. 29-65). Rockville, Md: National Institute of Mental Health.

Farmer, H. S. (1985). Model of career and achievement motivation for women and men. *Journal of Counseling Psychology, 32,* 363-390.

Garfinkel, I., & McLanahan, S. S. (1986). *Single mothers and their children: A new American dilemma*. Washington, DC: Urban Institute Press.

Goldman, N. (1993). The perils of single life in contemporary Japan. *Journal of Marriage and the Family, 55,* 191-204.

Jennings, M. K., & Niemi, R. (1982). *Generations and politics: A panel study of young adults and their parents.* Princeton: Princeton University Press.

Langman, L., Block, R., & Yahraes, H. (1979). Transmission of parental values. In E. Corfman (Ed.), *Families today,* (Science Monographs,Vol. 1, pp. 129-142). Rockville, Md.: National Institute of Mental Health.

Lein, L., & Blehar, M. C. (1979). Working couples as parents. In E. Corfman (Ed.), *Families today,* (Science Monographs, Vol. 1, pp. 299-321). Rockville, Md.: National Institute of Mental Health.

Lopata, H. Z. (1993). The interweave of public and private: Women's challenge to American society. *Journal of Marriage and the Family, 55,* 176-190.

Luster, T., Rhoades, K., & Haas, B. (1989). The relation between parental values and parenting behavior: A test of the Kohn Hypothesis. *Journal of Marriage and the Family, 51,* 139-147.

Maass, V. S. (1992). *The effects of values on the self-sufficiency of single-parent families.* Third International Conference–Counseling in the 21st Century, Singapore.

Maass, V. S., & Featherstonaugh, H. G. (1981). *Conflicting motivators in Cognitive Behavioral Therapy.* First European Meeting on Cognitive-Behavrioural Therapies, Lisbon, Portugal.

McLanahan, S. S., & Bumpass, L. (1988). Intergenerational consequences of family disruption. *American Journal of Sociology, 94,* 130-152.

Neely, M. A. (1992). *Single parents and family dynamics.* Third International Conference-Counseling in the 21st Century, Singapore.

Peterson, G. W., Rollins, B. R., Thomas, D. L., & Heaps, L. K. (1982). Social placement of adolescents: Sex-role influences on family decisions regarding the careers of youth. *Journal of Marriage and the Family, 44,* 647-661.

Risman, B. J., & Park, K. (1988). Just the two of us: Parent-child relationships in single-parent homes. *Journal of Marriage and the Family, 50,* 1049-1062.

Rokeach, M. (1968). *Beliefs, attitudes and values.* San Francisco: Jossey-Bass, Inc.

Rokeach, M. (1973). *The nature of human values.* New York: The Free Press.

Rosen, R. (1979). Some crucial issues concerning children of divorce. *Journal of Divorce, 3,* 19-25.

Santrock, J. W., & Warshock, R. A. (1979). Father custody and social development in boys and girls. *Journal of Social Issues, 35,* 112-125.

Smith, T. E. (1983). Parental influence: A review of the evidence of influence and theoretical model of the parental influence process. In A. C. Kerckshoff (Ed.), *Research in sociology of education and socialization,* (Vol.4, pp. 13-45). Greenwich, CT.

Spanier, G., & Fleer, B. (1979). Factors sustaining marriage; factors in adjusting to divorce. In E. Corfman (Ed.), *Families today,* (Science Monographs, Vol. 1, pp. 205-231). Rockville, Md.: National Institute of Mental Health.

Swensen, C., & Moore, C. D. (1979). Marriages that endure. In E.Corfman (Ed.), *Families today,* (Science Monographs, Vol. 1, pp. 249-286). Rockville, Md.: National Institute of Mental Health.

Thailand Ministry of the Interior (1988). *Registered divorces.* Bankok: Thailand.

Weitzman, L. J. (1985). *The divorce revolution: The unexpected social and economic consequences for women and children in America.* New York: Free Press.

Westkott, M. (1979). Feminist criticism of the social sciences. *Harvard Educational Review, 49,* 422-430.

Yeung, C. S. (1992). *Changes in marriage patterns in Hong Kong: Implications for counselling.* Third International Conference-Counseling in the 21st Century. Singapore.

Article 3

Chaos Theory and Family Behavior: A Convergence of Eastern and Western Thought

Sal Imbrogno

Introduction

Changes in family systems are dynamic, exceedingly turbulent, leaving in their wake ambiguity and indeterminate policies. This is the case irrespective of eastern and/or western socio-cultural orientations to family structure. It is a fundamental proposition of the I Ching. There is nothing that does not change, no less in family systems. There are only degrees, directions and types of change (Wilhelm, 1973, pp. 3-10). Change is ubiquitous. To unravel the complexities of these propositions as it specifically relates to family behavior, it is vital to understand the implications of chaos and transformation theory as a western perspective that integrates an eastern perspective in the book of changes. Is family life, structure and policy evolving in random behavior or is it deterministic and purposeful?

Let us begin by accepting the proposition that the common core to policy deals with a problem of choice. In addition to a behavioral dimension, there exist the normative and structural dimensions which taken together comprise the key information components necessary in understanding these complex family systems. If the behavioral dimension analyzes the choices individuals make and the reasons for their selection of particular options, then the structural dimension considers choices in patterns and relations of social action, the relationships within a family and between family systems. The normative dimension deals with the values and norms influencing choices that ought to be made.

Contemporary social policies have generally reflected the structural dimensions of adjusting family institutions, social programs and projects as a response to problematic situations. Remediations through incremental change in the organization of social patterns and relations has had a minor impact upon the normative dimension that undergirds family behavioral changes. Nor, for that matter, is it discernible how the daily choices made by families in the selection among alternatives presented by the other two dimensions impact upon social policy.

When individual and family choices are made in a structural and normative dimensions and are integrated in the behavior of families, the interrelated and interdependent connections produce unexpected results; namely, chaos. By applying a chaos theory to a multidimensional conception of a family system, an unusual reality emerges: family behavior can never be viewed as orderly, stable and equilbrial but rather as a fluctuating, dynamic system in a process of continuous change. Change processes can be characterized as linear only in the short run, as in the progression of time during the day (Glass & Mackey, 1988).

If it is accepted that a multidimensional analysis is a closer approximation of reality, then a search for a linear, analytical and causal explanation for changes in a family system is futile. Policies that are reactive to external perturbations by introducing adjustments to existing structural arrangements might explain the traditional family and even strive toward its maintenance and preservation, but reveal little about contemporary changing family values. Hence, the integration of cultural values and norms; social institutional arrangements and adaptation and the behavioral and motivational processes of families in their daily lives, must be placed in the center of policy analysis. The behavioral dimension is selected as the catalyst in transforming the normative and structural dimensions to family systems.

The basic concepts derived from chaos and transformation theory provides remarkable insights into the key role the behavioral dimension plays in family systems. For example, chaos theory would have us view changing family choices in "life style" as purposeful and structured instead of extrinsic, accidental aberrations (Poole, 1989, p. 26). Family behavior with all of its external idiosyncrasies, is deterministic. It arises from intrinsic causes and not randomness in what is too often perceived on the surface as irregular pathological and unpredictable behavior. Chaos theory conceptualizes changes in family systems as "deterministic-randomness"; an unusual idea that requires further explanation. Briefly, family systems are structurally stable while simultaneously undergoing change.

Transformation is defined as a forming over, a restructuring. In policy analytical terms this means converting a "wicked" policy problem into new terms (synectics) so that it can be solved. Transformation is a process that makes the strange familiar (disorder to order) and makes the familiar strange (order to disorder). The idea of redesigning a family system is to infuse it with innovative, creative and novel thinking. Moving from being to becoming is a process of transformation.

On a more practical level, the primary focus of family policy is to transform and not reform. This orientation views the deterministic- randomness of families as order and not disorder (Gleick, 1987). Hence, a discussion follows on how chaotic behavior introduces a new dimension to the meaning of change in non-equilibrium systems. In contrast to the equilibration of deterministic-randomness, random behavior is manifested in states of disequilibrium.

From within this perspective, chaos theory and eastern Asian philosophy, namely I Ching, have many points in common. For example, in addition to the view that change is constant, natural and consistent, opposing perspectives generated by change between existing and emerging family structure are viewed as harmonious complementary (i.e. yin and yang) and mutually inclusive; all social and family system levels are interdependent, homologous in structure, and corresponding; any system is a dynamically changing web of interdependent parts and the system is a sui generis reality that cannot be understood correctly by reductionist analysis alone (Imbrogno & Canda, 1988).

Changes in the Family System From a Policy Perspective

Family behavior is deterministic in "deep structure" yet so complex as to seem random. It is familiar scene to social policy analysts who can readily describe the structural requisites necessary for family maintenance and development but who encounter difficulties explaining the complex variations manifested in family behavior. Multiple and random variables (i.e., non-controllable and intervening) present wicked problems for mainstream policy research. It is difficult to describe, no less explain, and then predict policy outcomes for family behavior in transition.

Changes discerned in "inexplicable behavior" is neither negative nor positive but an inevitable outcome of families in transformation: that is, moving toward greater complexity. Hence, the random variations that give license to various causal explanations are, in reality, family systems in transition moving hopefully in a bifurcation, toward growth and development. Deterministic-randomness can be conceived as a stable family structure confronted with external fluctuations. These fluctuation must be integrated within the changing normative and behavioral manifestations of the family system.

The burgeoning literature in the human services addressing the "changing family life cycle" allude to the possibility of a social transformation. A healthy family alters its patterns under the impact of change and becomes stable between transitional periods. Ideas of a normal life cycle can lead to serious misunderstanding, if deviation from the family "norms" is perceived as pathological (Carter & McGoldrick, 1989, p. 4).

The basic postulates undergirding chaos and transformation theory offer both causal explanations in a deterministic realization of being (stability), while in finality an explanation is found for the functional outcomes intrinsic to random events and occurrences of becoming (changing). Hence, families can be stabilized under changing conditions. This is a crucial explanation for stability in treatment of families and the inevitability of changes in family structure and policy. Understanding family behavior is always enhanced by converging diverse perspectives; in this case, stability and change.

Concepts of a Family System in Transformation

Let us examine the sets of postulates from an I Ching perspective of change, chaos and transformation theory that have been explicated for the purpose of unraveling the complexity of family behavior:

1. Families in fluctuations:

A family system can comprise an individual as a member of nuclear family, part of an extended family; and families in a wider community. Each can be viewed as a system or as a sub-system to a larger system. A family system therefore, has two integrative tendencies: a part of a larger whole and a self assertive tendency to preserve its autonomy (Koesler, 1978, p. 35). Given the mutual interactive processes of systems, a family is continually in a state of fluctuation from the environmental inputs. Choices made in direction change make impact on the structural and normative dimensions.

The fluctuations within and between family sub-systems generate powerful positive feedback so as to shatter the pre-existing family structure. This radical change is referred to as a "bifurcation"; a splitting. Hence, fluctuations, necessary for the continuance of family life, create over a time a series of bifurcations. It is impossible to determine in advance in what direction change will occur. For example, how will a family system behave if its structure is radically impacted upon? Will it disintegrate or leap to a new, richer and higher order? In a viable family system, one or a series of fluctuations will transform disorder into a new order.

The critical knowledge skill for a policy analyst is to be able to anticipate and recognize when these bifurcations are creating a problematic situation. As will be noted, this is a formidable task in structuring policy problems.

It is axiomatic that family systems are always turbulent and policy is always in a state of flux. Both processes can only be sustained through a constant flow of energy—hopefully, in responding to a bifurcation that leads to continuous life cycle of complex development. Complexity conceived in transformation theory should not be confused with complication or quantification. Rather the elements of the old patterns come into contact with each other in new ways and make new connections.

The multidimensions that comprise a family system are reorganized into a new whole. The system has escaped into a higher order. For example, childless couples, professional parents, serial and contract marriages, open marriages, group marriages, one parent families, reconstructed families, two sets of grandparents, gay families, are new and complex family forms.

2. Families as dissipative structures:

It is also axiomatic that family systems cannot function without a continuous exchange of social and human energy with the external environment. For example, families take in energy from other families, the social, religious and educational institutions. Enlightened families transform this energy by becoming more responsive, knowledgeable and informative citizenry. As a result, these families return the energy to the system: families affect and are affected by the system. There is no internal transformation of energy, a fact that should not be lost in an analysis "of and for" policy (Prigogine, 1984, p. 12).

A family system responding to a positive feedback in a bifurcation, is open to new inputs, and therefore change. That is, their structure is maintained by a continuous dissipation of energy. A family therefore is a highly self-organizing body in a deterministic way, but subject to change in a developmental process. The more complex the family system becomes (i.e., its dissipative structure) the more energy is needed to maintain all the interactions and interrelations established with the environment. Hence, an open family system that encourages a free and mutual interactive process with the environment is subject to fluctuations; changing disorder into order.

In sum, a fluctuation that produces a bifurcation falls within the purview of dissipative structures. This same fluctuation resulting from a social perturbation produces a non-equilibrium state. Unexpected social perturbations precipitate unpredictable behavior in family systems and are therefore far from equilibrium (Imber-Black, 1989). Non-equilibrium states are healthy phenomena. Families suffer from policies that strive for stability in system maintenance and preservation. Accepting equilibrium (i.e., status quo) as a desirable terminal goal state produces a false sense of balance and security. Instability is key to transformation.

3. Family perturbations:

The idea of creating new family structure by reason of perturbations seems outrageous on a micro-level of practice. From a macro-level policy planning perspective, it means that families have a self-organizing capability and opportunity to adapt and change their external environments.

A bifurcation resulting from fluctuations inevitably creates problematic situations: they perturb the system. In turn, these perturbations increase the number of novel interactions (i.e., various forms of family constellations) within it. The elements of the old family patterns come into contact with each other in new ways and make new connections. The parts reorganize into a new whole. The family system moves into a new and higher order of complexity. Hence, the more complex or coherent the family structure, the more complex the next level of development. This is what is meant by the transformation of the whole.

In family systems as dissipative structures, a final state is not unequivocally determined by the initial conditions. A final state may be reached from different initial conditions in different ways. The final outcome of a systems behavior is different from that of each family members behavior taken independently: the "whole is different from its parts".

4. Family and equifinality:

A concept of equifinality discloses some interesting observations for policymaking: a family sub-system exhibiting similar chaotic behavior with others reaches the same final state from along several different and independent causal trajectories. In relation to the "instability" of family structure, no deterministic inference can be made regarding the cause of that conclusion. The final state of any one stage in the family cycle cannot be determined by the preceding initial conditions from which families evolved. This is not to suggest that family systems evolve in an irreversible process. Only when a family system behaves in a sufficiently random way, do the differences between past and future, and therefore irreversibly, enter into the prescription for change.

What are the implications of chaos and transformation theory on structuring policy problems? It reaffirms a systems conception and specification on structuring policy problems heretofore reliant upon traditional world views associated with social problem identification and definition. A social problem is not the same as a structuring policy problem. Policy problems cannot be decomposed into independent, discrete and autonomous categories. A "system of problems" views the whole as greater, and qualitatively different from, an aggregate of its parts.

Family systems are in transition evolving from a complex array of internal fluctuations precipitated by external events and occurrences. It is indeed a deterministic-randomness. A family is a sub-system in continuous exchange of information and energy within and between other social systems. As a result, family systems are in continuous transition. Social perturbations are incentives, a motivating factor toward an increase in complexity.

A social perturbation that generates family stress, strain and tension (fluctuations) creates a bifurcation in two possible directions: a state of disequilibrium (i.e., decay and death) or if engaged in a mutual interactive process with the environment, a state of equilibration (i.e. growth and development).

Systems of Inquiry and Structuring Policy Problems

There are at least four ways in which to conceptualize and structure policy problems: well-structured problems (means/ends both known; subject to probability equations); ill-structured problems (means known; ends unknown or in disagreement); moderately structured problems (means unknown; ends known); and non-structured policy problems (means/ends are in a mutual interactive process of exchanging information).

As in the case of non-equilibrium (equilibration), non-structured does not mean "having no structure," but rather that the interactive process intrinsic to transforming a problem from a given state (means) to a goal state (ends) changes the original structure of the problem to a new and more complex form (structuration). In the mainstream structuring of policy problems, a primary focus is on retrospective analysis: knowing what happened as a means toward realizing a terminal goal state. In non-equilibrium systems, time/space relation is viewed quite differently. A policy problem is concurrently reversible and prospective: knowing what will happen. In this later state, knowing what to do involves transforming an original problem to a purposeful goal state.

Let us examine alternative systems of inquiry in structuring policy problems: There is a propensity to adapt a scientific inquiry into structuring problems in analytical reductionistic models. The component parts to problems in families can be broken down into simple units for analysis. Logic and rationality leads to an analytical simplification in the specification of the parts that comprise a problematic situation. A linear causal explanation of the relationship between variables (dependent and independent) creates the conditions for replicating and predictions. This leads to an irreversible deterministic solution to a well-structured problem. Probability equations account for variability. If rules of logic and rationality are followed, then the ends of the inquiry guarantee the means, as the means guarantee the ends.

1. Logic of well-structured policy problems:

The scientific precision intrinsic to policies that advocate planned short term service (PSTS) selects one isolated component part to a problematic situation, designates it for treatment and specifies the time frame for resolution. Similarly in policy, social problems become discrete entities: poverty is treated separately from housing, health and education. In this well structured model, an analyst is a technician. It is a skillful parcelling of a presenting problem and request by a family. "Check-off" line items in family impact analysis comprise the informational components of a family structure. It produces in aggregate the "scientific" data upon which policymaking or program evaluation is conducted (Ooms & Preister, 1988).

2. Consensus in ill-structured policy problems:

In ill-structured problems, the desired state of a problematic situation is unknown or in disagreement. Policy is formulated to mediate/facilitate a solution. Policy becomes a remedial pursuit for social adjustment of differences. Models of problem resolution focus upon the "...here-and-now problems as undermine or constrict their personal satisfaction and social adequacy" (Perlman, 1986, p. 262). Policies designed for a social adjustment mode of intervention try to resolve, remedy and restore a family to its previous level of functioning.

A mediating/facilitating mode of intervention designed to enable a family to "fit into" a social system suppresses random behavior as an aberration and hence, minimizes, if not omits, behavioral choices that are not marginal and dependent upon the existing values. The diagnostic and treatment strategy of task centered social work is embedded with problem resolution (i.e., equilibrium) as a desirable goal state (Reid, 1986, p. 271). Its greatest failure is that it eliminates the need for anticipating, recognizing and integrating randomness in the treatment process.

While the first problem solving approach produces a professional practitioner in scientific and technical problem solving in relatively "perceived" stable systems, the second approach produces a professional mediator striving for problem resolution through social adjustments. In both cases, problems "in and about" family are identified as social perturbations to a well being state of equilibrium. A problem goal state is to remedy, restore or resolve to initial conditions. In non- structuring problem models, change is conceived as ubiquitous, requiring not only technical problem solving skills and skills in the social groups dynamics for resolution, but also skills in anticipating, recognizing and integrating a complex array of problematic situations in a family (Mitroff & Kilmann, 1978).

3. Chaos in non-structured policy problems:

A non-structured perspective of family problems in a state of equilibration explains chaotic fluctuations. As noted, fluctuations reflect the external interactive process leading to greater complexity as new ideas, information and experiences are generated in family development. The functional outcome of this process is a transformation of the family system. Does chaotic theory provide a conceptual framework for policy analysis of these fluctuations in non-structured policy problematic situations? Let us see:

A. interdependence of problems: "system of problems" exist in families experiencing difficulties (i.e., marital discords are reflected in child care problems). This position would hold that problems cannot be analytically broken down into its component parts; family behavior cannot be separated from the environment in which it functions nor can any one family problem be distinguished from other sets of problems.

B. problems have no beginning or end, but are continuously evolving toward a more advanced, higher and richer level of complex problematic situations. Problems "in and about" family, its norms, structure and behavior, are a continuous life long activity with impending flows of energy.

C. acting upon a policy problem in process occurs under turbulent conditions, in which case the family system is in transition emerging into a new form. The family, as well as the policy system, strives to maintain and preserve its stability under changing conditions.

Hence, the complex interactions of the normative, structural configurations and behavioral activity in family life are in a state of chaos: a process often mistakenly characterized as erratic, disorganized and in disarray. As a result, policy analysts must become problem integrators to augment their technical skills: anticipating problematic situations as they emerge in development with a recognition that the original problem changes its configuration as a family advances to a higher level of complexity.

The critical factor in structuring policy problems is to ensure a congruence between a conceptualization and specification of a problem and the original problematic situation (i.e., is the world view family disorganization and deterioration or growth and development). Critical questions arise regarding the contemporary conceptions to problem solving. How can policy avoid errors of the first, second and third kind:

1. Errors of the first kind: policymakers selecting the wrong world-view when the right one should have been chosen;
2. Errors of the second kind: policymakers choosing the wrong specification of the problem when the right one should have been chosen and finally,
3. Errors of the third kind: choosing the wrong problem to solve when the right one should have been chosen.

By considering the implications of chaos and transformation theory to a non-structured system of inquiry, errors of the first, second and third kind can be avoided, if not eliminated.

Implications for Social Policy Practices

An inquiry comprising a "system of problems" exists to structuring policy problems. Problems are interrelated within a family and interdependent with larger systems in which they evolve. The total functional outcome of a family system is different from an analysis of independent outputs taken separately by family members or even in aggregate. This advances a position that social policy theory and practice must broaden its perspective to integrate causality and finality: an approach that concentrates on the benefits to be derived from equifinality in family policy.

Non-structured problematic situations in states of equilibration mean that problems have no beginning or end but are deterministic and random. They are continuously being transformed to higher levels of complexity. The technical problem solving skills of social policymakers need to be matched with the capability of recognizing, anticipating and integrating problems in a non-structured conceptualization of a continuous state of non-equilibrium.

Initial conditions that give rise to a problematic situation will markedly change with an interchange of expected and unexpected value inputs. Hence, projections based on extrapolation of past events in the family policy into the future, and predictions based on theoretical assumptions derived from linear causal explanations of problematic situations in families, have minimal value in planning for random behavior.

Random behavior, a source of concern in making predictions and developing projections, can be anticipated and recognized based on conjectures of subjective judgments about future states of family. Unexpected random changes, it is anticipated, will occur in development generating parallel changes in the direction of the conjectured goals. It would require a system design, sufficiently flexible to cope with random behavior, while it pursues, and if necessary changes, the original image of an hypothesized family structure.

One of the greatest difficulties facing social policymakers is deciding precisely where, when and how to intervene when a problematic situation arises. Well-structured problems that mathematically account for their variations can use logic to guarantee goal achievement with certainty. The mode of intervention is precise and highly scientific in its effectiveness and efficiency. It offers little however, in goal setting, goal seeking and goal direction.

Modes of intervention are also in place for the mediation of problems where opposition exists over the preferred desired ends, in which case the practitioner facilitates resolution either through advocacy or coalition formations. A pluralistic process of consensus leads to reconciliation. If however, the structure of a problem and the behavioral processes associated with it are in transition, constantly fluctuating in a state of chaotic equilibration, then a mode of intervention must be designed that can more appropriately respond to a family in transformation.

A critical social policy function is to create conditions for sustaining and maintaining stability under changing conditions. That is, a system is to be designed that is inherently self-organizing, self-regulating and self-modifying as new information is generated from the anticipated chaotic behavior of a system. This means a mode of intervention that is goal direction; capable of changing in development while it is concurrently meeting the needs and requirements of families.

An understanding of the convergent and harmonious properties of chaos; with its relativeness to stability and change coupled with its reciprocity in multi-levels of human and social behavior, enables the process for family participation and contribution to be open and not coerced. This entails reshaping the classical human service modes of intervention in education/research, mediation/ facilitation, advocacy, broker and social action for constituency involvement within the context of chaos theory and chaotic behavior (Connaway & Gentry, 1988; Loye & Eisler, 1987).

Summary

It is through a transformation process that order gives way to chaos and where chaotic behavior once again leads to order—a process that can be characterized as a harmonious complementary. Hence, transformation theory offers an advanced perspective for explaining movement over time while chaos theory provides an explanation for the determinism in "deep" family structure that, in a "surface" structure, experiences random behavior. I Ching offers critical insights into the meaning given to the interpretation of change as natural, desirable and inevitable processes.

Let us recapitulate this idea of the internal and external transfer of information and harmonious flow of social and human energy in an emergence of a new family system:

1. Chaotic systems move from the initial conditions of analytical simplification quite amenable to deterministic equations, to synthesis complexity in which the final outcome lies in its transformation to a new configuration quite different from the independent parts taken independently.

2. A flow of energy (i.e., ideas, values, interest, beliefs etc.) into the family system results in fluctuations that increase the interactions to new and higher levels of intercourse through new informational networks. This is a self-organizing system: parts are reorganized into new wholes. A family system can become highly organized (i.e., deterministic) but always in an unpredictable final process, that if properly understood, can lead to higher levels of problem solving.

3. A family system can only be sustained through a continuous flow of information (i.e., inputs). The more coherent the structure (i.e., equilibrium) the more unstable it is. Instability is what is meant by transformation. Dissipative energy in the family structure creates the conditions for reordering

4. The fluctuations discerned in the dynamics of a turbulent process are relative to time and place leaving open the possibility that the randomness behavior associated with chaos theory, if observed at the moment, represents an important piece of reality.

If these basic and derived concepts are accepted as a reasonable explanation for contemporary developments in family behavior and structure, then social policies must adapt analytical frameworks, and professionals incorporate practice methods and techniques reflective of families in transition, entering a stage of social transformation. In this view, ideals intrinsic to policy planning and development are in a harmonious complementary with the daily realities of family structure and behavior.

References

Carter, B., & McGoldrick, M. (1989). *The changing family life cycle.* Boston, MA.: Allyn and Bacon.

Connaway, R., & Gentry, M. (1988). *Social work practice.* New York: Prentice Hall.

Glass, L., & Mackey, M. (1988). *From clocks to chaos.* Princeton, N.J.: Princeton University Press.

Gleick, J. (1987). *Chaos: Making a new science.* New York: Penquin Books.

Imber-Black, E. (1989). *Families and larger systems.* New York: Guilford Press.

Imbrogno, S., & Canda, E. (1988 April). General systems theory and the book of changes: Toward a convergence of western and eastern thought. *The Journal of Eastern Studies, 22*, pp. 203-218.

Koesler, A. (1978). *Janus.* London: Hutchinson.

Loye, D., & Eisler, R. (1987). Chaos and transformation: Implications of non-equilibrium theory for social science and society. *Behavioral Science, 32,* 53-65.

Ooms, T., & Preister, S. (1988). *A strategy for strengthening families: Using family criteria in policymaking and program evaluation*. A report of the family criteria task force. Washington, DC: Government Printing.

Mitroff, I., & Kilmann, R. (1978). *Methodological approaches to social sciences*. San Francisco, CA.: Jossey-Bass Publishers.

Perlman, H. (1977). Social casework: The problem solving approach. *Encyclopedia of Social Work.* New York: National Association of Social Workers, *2,* 1290-1300.

Pool, R. (1989). Is it healthy to be chaotic? *Science, 243,* 604-606.

Prigogine, I. (1984). *Order and of chaos*. New York: Bantam Books.

Reid, W. (1986) Task-centered social work. In F. Turner, *Social work treatment* (pp. 267-295). New York: The Free Press.

Wilhelm, H. (1973). *Change: Eight lectures on the I Ching*. Princeton; N.J.: Princeton University Press.

Gender Roles

Part II

Article 4

The Effects of Gender and Ethnicity on Sex Role Attitudes: A Comparison Among Caucasian-Americans, Japanese-Americans, and Chinese-Americans

Tsun-yin Luo

Introduction

This study was conducted to examine the effects of gender and ethnicity on sex role attitudes among university students. Sex role attitudes have been a major focus among studies on gender issues. Nevertheless, little attention has been directed towards ethnic variations, particularly among Asian-Americans, on the attitudes towards sex roles (Engel, 1985; Engel & Dickson, 1985). The number of Asian Americans more than doubled during the 1980's and, as the fastest-growing minority in the States, account for almost half of all immigration to the United States (Winnick, 1990). Nevertheless, Chinese and Japanese Americans, as the longest-established and two of the largest categories within the Asian-American population, have received little research attention on their attitudes towards sex roles. As sex role attitudes represent cultural characteristics in gender socialization, this study considered it imperative to explore ethnic variations on sex role attitudes among Chinese, Japanese and Caucasian Americans for a better understanding of ethnic and cultural diversities in the United States.

The literature has suggested gender difference on sex role attitudes among the general public: women were found to be less sex role stereotyped than men (Burt, 1978; Field, 1978; Hawley & Even, 1982). Nevertheless, a study on sex role attitudes among residents of six states (N = 3,639) reported that male attitudes were significantly more stereotyped than female unless they were college educated (Hawley & Even, 1982).

However, a bulk of studies on college students suggest that women held more liberal and more egalitarian attitudes towards sex roles than males (Hartman & Hartman, 1983; Marrone & Rutnik, 1987; Nelson, 1988; Silver, 1988). Although both college men and women were relatively liberal, women generally expressed more egalitarian attitudes than men (Marrone & Rutnik, 1987). Compared to their male counterparts, female students scored higher than male students on five domains of sex role egalitarianism (Beere et al., 1984) and were less sex role stereotyped in their evaluation of wife, mother and father roles (Rao & Rao, 1985b). A cross-cultural study indicates that, among American and Indian students, women were less traditional in sex role attitudes than men (Rao & Rao, 1985a).

Gender difference on sex role attitudes could be traced back to the adolescent age: female adolescents were found to be less sex role stereotyped than males. A study on adolescent sex role attitudes among a national probability sample (N = 1,626) reported that female respondents held a less traditional sex role attitude than the males (Canter & Ageton, 1984). A study comparing attitudes of adolescents towards sex role stereotyping in 1956 and 1982 indicated boys still emphasized both sex role differentiations and symbols of male dominance and female subordination more than girls (Lewin & Tragos, 1987).

The literature is in disagreement concerning the effects of race/ethnicity on sex role attitudes: some studies reported significant ethnic differences on sex role attitudes (e.g., Arafat & Yorburg, 1976; Belk et al., 1989; Canter & Ageton, 1984; Fischer, 1987; Seginer et al., 1990; Williams & Holmes, 1982) while others observed no relationship between ethnicity and sex role attitudes (e.g., Bonner, 1974; Brown, Perry & Harburg, 1977; Hershey, 1978; Grimes, Hansen & Page, 1982).

Among studies suggesting ethnic differences on sex role attitudes, no clear direction on the differences has yet emerged. For example, previous studies reveal that, although caucasians and blacks differed significantly on sex role attitudes, the difference was by no means conclusive. Some studies comparing Caucasian and Black women reported that caucasians were less traditional than blacks on sex role attitudes (Beale, 1970; Cade, 1970; Cole, 1975; Epstein, 1973; Franklin & Walum, 1972; Gump, 1975; Hays & Mindel, 1973; Jackson, 1971; Nobles, 1974; Rosen, 1978; Stack, 1974; Williams & Holmes, 1982; Young, 1970). However, other studies observed the opposite: Caucasian women were found to be more traditional towards sex role attitudes than Black women (Arafat &Yorburg; 1976; Scanzoni, 1975; Williams & Holmes, 1982).

Nevertheless, caucasians were found to be less sex role stereotyped than ethnic minority groups. Compared to caucasians, minority respondents (e.g., Hispanic, Asian, etc.) held more traditional attitudes towards sex roles (Belk et al., 1989; Braun & Chao, 1978; Canter & Ageton, 1984; Fischer, 1987; Williams & Holmes, 1982); and Japanese-Americans differed significantly from Caucasian-Americans on specific aspects of sex roles (Arkoff, Meredith & Iwahara, 1964; Engel, 1985).

Regarding sex role attitudes among Asian minorities, Chinese men were more traditional than Japanese men, and Japanese women were relatively more traditional than the Chinese women (Engel & Dickson, 1985).

Nationality differences were observed, where women from the United States expressed stronger rejection of traditional views about women than women from Mexico; and American college students were less traditional in their sex role attitudes than their Indian counterparts (Belk et al., 1989; Gonzalez, 1982; Rao & Rao, 1985a).

Among studies reporting no significant racial/ethnic differences on sex role attitudes (Bonner, 1974; Brown et al., 1977; Lyson, 1986; Rao & Rao, 1985b; Scanzoni, 1975; Silver, 1988), a majority concern themselves with racial differences between the Caucasians and the

Blacks; Caucasians were found to be no different from Blacks on sex role attitudes (Bonner, 1974; Brown et al., 1977; Lyson, 1986; Rao & Rao, 1985b; Scanzoni, 1975).

The sex role literature presents an extensive research on the attitudinal differences between Caucasian and Black but has paid little attention to other ethnic groups, particularly Asian groups, such as Japanese and Chinese. Thus, the literature has not yet established the ethnic pattern among Asians towards sex role attitudes. As Asian immigrants have become the fast growing minorities in the past decade, it is imperative to direct more research attention to attitudinal and behavioral patterns among Asian communities in the States. This study took advantage of the ethnic diversity in the state of Hawaii to include Caucasian, Japanese, and Chinese students in the study sample to examine ethnic effects on sex role attitudes.

Research Method

Survey Instrument

The literature has suggested a multi-dimensional structure of sex role attitudes (Beere et al., 1984; Belk & Snell, 1986; Belt et al., 1989; Brown, Perry & Harburg, 1977). Brown et al., (1977) identified three factors in sex role attitudes: 1) women in the home, 2) traditional family roles, and 3) job inequality. Studies on sex role attitudes specified traditional roles for father, mother, wife and husband, respectively, to solicit responses (e.g., Rao & Rao, 1985; Scanzoni, 1975). The sex-role egalitarianism scale represented five domains of adult living: marital roles, parental roles, employee roles, social-interpersonal-heterosexual roles, and educational roles (Beere et al., 1984). Hatchet & Quick (1983) focused on three dimensions in sex role attitudes: attitudes towards familial division of labor, perceptions of the consequences of women working, and attitudes towards motherhood.

To reflect the multi-dimensional structure of sex role attitudes, this study includes five dimensions of sex role stereotypes to solicit evaluations on the appropriate roles for men and women. The five dimensions are: 1) traditional gender role prescription in the context of family and marriage, 2) double standards on deviant behaviors, 3) gender equality in economic, social and sexual freedom, 4) traditional courtship norms for men and women, and 5) women's autonomy in social life.

Sex role attitude scale was composed of 20 survey items covering stereotyped role prescriptions on the five dimensions of adult life (Alpha = .87). All items on the attitudinal scales were written in a five-point Likert format, ranging from 1 "Strongly Disagree" to 5 "Strongly Agree," with 3 as "Neutral/Unsure."

Study Sample

Men and women at a metropolitan state university were sampled to collect data for this study. Stratified by class size, disciplines and academic classifications, 43 classes at University of Hawaii-Manoa were selected by the study and approved by the respective instructors to be surveyed. The questionnaire survey was conducted in the month of April, 1990, and 827 usable surveys were included in the analysis. The study sample is representative of the UHM student population on ethnic background[1], but the sample contained slightly more female and undergraduate students than the student population (Table 1).

Table 1—Demographic Characteristics of Study Sample (N= 827)

Demographic Variables	N	%*
Sex		
Male	321	39.0
Female	502	61.0
Age		
21 and under	231	29.1
22–25	286	36.0
26–30	129	16.2
31 and over	148	18.6
Ethnicity		
Caucasian	297	35.9
Japanese	387	46.8
Chinese	143	17.3
Academic Cllassification		
Freshman	75	9.2
Sophomore	122	15.0
Junior	153	18.9
Master Program Student	174	21.5
PhD Student	34	4.2
Other Post-Graduate	35	4.3
Marital Status		
Never Married	606	73.5
Cohabiting	43	5.2
Married	142	17.2
Separated/Divorced	25	3.0
Other	8	1.0

*The distribution is based on valid percentage.

Data Analysis

A factor analysis [2] was employed to extract a five-factor solution on the 20-item sex role attitude scale (Table 2). These five factors, accounting for 56% of total variance, were labeled "Gender Roles in Family/Marriage," "Double Standards in Deviant Behaviors," "Gender Inequality," "Courtship Norms," and "Women's Autonomy" with an eigenvalue of 5.63, 1.62, 1.53, 1.37 and 1.03, respectively.

The factor of "Gender Roles in Family and Marriage" refers to traditional role prescriptions for men and women in the context of marriage, parenting, and family obligations. Scale items include: "A woman's place is in the home looking after her family, rather than following a career of her own," "Women should worry less about being equal with men and more about becoming good wives and mothers," and "Women should give higher priority to marriage or family over a career."

The factor labeled "Double Standards" refers to the double standard on deviant behaviors for men and women. Scale items include: "It's less acceptable for a single women to have multiple sexual partners simultaneously than single men," "It's less acceptable for the wife to engage in extramarital affairs than for the husband," and "It's worse to see a drunken woman than a drunken man."

The factor of "Gender Equality" addresses gender equality on social, economic, and sexual freedom. Scale items include: "Women should be able to go wherever men go and to do whatever men do," and "Women should have completely equal opportunities as men in getting jobs and promotions."

The "Courtship Norms" factor focuses on men and women's behavioral norms in courtship interaction. Scale items include: "The initiative in dating should come from the man," and "The initiative in sex should come from the man."

The fifth factor touches upon women's autonomy in social life. Scale items include: "A woman—whether she is married or not has a right to control her own body and to decide whether or not to have a child," and "Women earning as much as their male dates should share expenses equally when they go out together."

The results of the factor analysis support the study contention that sex role attitudes are composed of multiple specific dimensions on gender ideologies and stereotypes. For each of the dimensions, the lower the mean score, the stronger the rejection of the corresponding sex role stereotype.

The surveyed students most strongly rejected gender inequality in social, economic and sexual freedom (Mean = 1.75, S.D. = .76), followed by traditional gender roles in family and marriage (Mean = 1.89, S.D. = .71), women's autonomy (Mean = 2.01, S.D. = .66), double standards in deviant behaviors (Mean = 2.20, S.D. = 1.0), and least strongly rejected traditional courtship norms (Mean = 2.36, S.D. = .93).

Table 2—Oblique Rotated Factor Structure of Attitudes towards Sex Roles Scale with Factor Loadings on Scale Items

Loading	Item Number	Content
Factor 1—Gender Roles in family and Marriage (Eigenvalue = 5.63)		
.76	8.	Women's place in the home.
.69	9.	Becoming good wives/mothers should be women's major concern.
.67	2.	Women should give higher priority to marriage/family.
.64	10.	Father should have more authority in bringing up the children.
.59	3.	Husband should have more financial responsibility than wife.
.54	14.	Sons should be more encouraged to go to college than daughter.
.45	12	Men should give higher priority to career.
Factor 2—Double Standards on Deviant Behaviors (Eigenvalue =1.62)		
.86	18.	It's less acceptable for single women to have multiple partners simultaneously than single men.
.82	17.	It's less acceptable for the wife to engage in extramarital affairs than for the husband.
.72	19.	It's worse to see a drunken woman than a drunken man.
.62	20.	It's all right for men to tell dirty jokes but not for women.
Factor 3—Gender Inequality (Eigenvalue = 1.53)		
.71	*4.	Women should be able to go wherever men go, and to do whatever men do.
.66	*7.	Women should have equal opportunities as men in getting jobs.
.62	*5.	Women should be as free as men to propose marriage.
.61	*11.	Women should have as much sexual freedom as men.
Factor 4—Traditional courtship (Eigenvalue = 1.37)		
.77	1.	The initiative in dating should come from the men.
.66	16.	The initiative in sex should come from the men.
Factor 5—Women Independence (Eigenvalue = 1.37)		
.60	*15.	Women earning as much as their date should share the expenses.
.56	*13.	Women have the right to control their own bodies in reproduction.
.43	*6.	Economic/social freedom is worth far more to women than acceptance of the ideal of femininity.

Note: Each item is scored 1 to 5, with 1 = "Strongly disagree," 2 = "Disagree," 3 = "Neutral/Unsure," 4 = "Agree," and 5 = "Strongly Agree," except for item marked * where the score is reversed.

Table 3 presents significant main effects of gender and ethnicity, but no significant interaction effect, on the five dimensions of sex role attitudes. In general, female students indicated stronger rejection than male students towards sex role stereotypes; Caucasian students most strongly rejected sex role stereotypes, followed by Japanese and Chinese students.

As shown in Table 3, the ANOVA reported significant gender effect on attitudes towards family/marriage obligation, double standards on deviant behaviors, gender inequality in social/economic freedom, and women's autonomy. Female students indicated stronger rejection than male students on all dimensions of sex role stereotypes except for the courtship norms.

Table 3—The Effects of Gender and Ethnicity on Attitudes towards SexRoles: ANOVA with F-value and Mean (N = 872)

	Family Roles	Double Std.	Gender Equality	Courting Norms	Female Autonomy
Main effects	58.39	35.64	27.29	20.44	11.16
Combined	1.89	2.20	1.75	2.36	2.01
Gender	105.81	42.91	18.81	n.s.	22.26
Male (319)	2.19	2.48	1.91	2.17	
Female (498)	1.69	2.02	1.65	1.90	
Ethnicity	31.53	29.05	29.29	15.62	4.58*
Caucasian (294)	1.69	1.87	1.47	2.11	1.90
Japanese (385)	1.90	2.30	1.86	2.45	2.06
Chinese (142)	2.26	2.62	2.02	2.64	2.08
Gender x Ethn.	n.s.	n.s.	n.s.	n.s.	n.s.

a. All significant at $p < .001$, except otherwise specified; * $p > .05$.

b. Each item is scored 1 to 5, with 1 = "Strongly Disagree," 2 = "Disagree," 3 = "Neutral/Unsure," 4 = "Agree," and 5 ="Strongly Agree." Thus, the lower the mean score, the less acceptance of the corresponding factor.

c. Item scores of this particular factor were reversed.

The ANOVA also indicated significant ethnicity effect on attitudes towards family/marriage obligation, double standards on deviant behaviors, gender inequality in social/economic freedom, courtship norms, and women's autonomy. Consistently, Caucasian students expressed the strongest rejection of all dimensions of sex role stereotypes, followed by Japanese students, with Chinese students expressed the least rejection towards sex role stereotypes.

Discussion and Conclusion

The study was conducted to examine the effects of gender and ethnicity on sex role attitudes among university students. The study findings indicated significant effects of gender and ethnicity on sex role attitudes: female students indicated stronger rejection than male students towards sex role stereotypes; Caucasian students indicated the strongest rejection towards sex role stereotypes, followed by Japanese and Chinese students. Contrasted to one previous study on Asian Americans (Engel & Dickson, 1985), this study found no significant interaction effect between gender and ethnicity on sex role attitudes.

The study finding on gender effects is consistent with previous studies. The literature has consistently suggested that women hold more liberal attitudes than men towards various dimensions of sex roles (Lin et al., 1994). This phenomenon is intuitively understandable. Traditional sex roles have benefited men more than women by attaching prestige and power to male roles in the society. Under the prescription of traditional sex roles, men often enjoy prestige and power while women are often deprived of resources, power and even autonomy. As historical victims of institutionalized sex roles, women have become more conscious than men of gender inequality in various social arrangements, and thus tend to express stronger rejections towards traditional sex roles than their male counterparts, as indicated in the study findings.

The findings on the effects of ethnicity are also consistent with the literature. Although ethnicity effect is inconclusive among previous studies, the majority of the literature suggests that Caucasians are less supportive of sex role stereotypes than non-Caucasian minorities (Belk et al., 1989; Canter & Ageton, 1984; Field, 1978; Fischer, 1987; Williams & Holmes, 1982). Empirical findings of this study lend support to this theory as Caucasian students were found to express stronger rejection of sex role stereotypes than both Japanese and Chinese students.

American society witnessed the sexual revolution in the sixties and the feminist movement in the seventies. Both social movements have challenged traditional sex roles in various aspects of social life, and have advocated for gender equality in the economic and social arena, and women's autonomy in sexuality and reproduction.

As a racial majority in American society, the Caucasians have exercised more influence on the making of American culture, and consequently, have been more integrated into the major social movements. Thus, it is reasonable to expect that the Caucasians are influenced by the ideas of the gender revolution and feminist movement to a greater degree than ethnic minorities, such as the Asians.

In addition, Asian culture is characterized with Confucian-patriarchy which stresses male-domination and female-submission (Stacey, 1983). Students with Asian ancestry have been socialized in this unique cultural content and may therefore acquire more traditional attitudes towards sex roles. The differentiation in socialization between Western and Asian culture may provide some explanation to the finding that Caucasian students hold more liberal attitudes towards sex roles than both Japanese and Chinese students, as indicated by the study findings.

Nevertheless, the Asian culture is not homogeneous. The study found a consistent ethnic pattern on sex role attitudes within Asian students: the Japanese were found to be more liberal than the Chinese towards all of the five dimension on sex role attitudes. In interpreting the attitudinal difference between Japanese and Chinese students towards sex roles, the study considers the following factors relevant:

1) Population size: The state of Hawaii is unique in its ethnic composition. As Chinese Americans represent the major Asian group in the US mainland, Japanese Americans constitute the largest Asian community in Hawaii, while Chinese are the smallest.[3] (Char et al., 1980). As group cohesiveness decreases as the group size increases (Wicker, 1969), the Japanese community may display more diversified attitudes than the smaller Chinese community in Hawaii. In contrast, the small size of the Chinese community may facilitate tighter social control over individual members on their social attitudes, and thus better preserve the Confucian patriarchal tradition than in the Japanese community.
2) Cultural assimilation: Better equipped with knowledge about the United States before arrival, the Japanese immigrants were assimilated into American culture to a greater degree than the Chinese immigrants. In addition, Japanese immigrants have achieved higher upward social mobility than their Chinese counterparts, which better encourages cultural assimilation (Fugita & O'Brien, 1985). As a matter of fact, the Japanese in Hawaii have assimilated with the mainstream culture to the extent that Americans of Japanese ancestry are considered intensely American middle-class (Rogers & Izutsu, 1980). The effect of cultural assimilation is reflected in the liberal attitudes towards sex roles among Japanese students in this particular study. In contrast, the Chinese community in Hawaii is characterized by new immigrants from Taiwan and Hong-Kong. These recently-arrived Chinese immigrants tend to be less assimilated into mainstream culture and thus better preserve traditional Asian culture (Char et al., 1980), including stereotyped attitudes towards sex roles, as indicated by the study findings.

Endnotes

[1] Based on self-reported primary and secondary ethnic backgrounds, the study classified ethnicity into three categories: Caucasian (N = 294), Japanese (N = 384), and Chinese (N = 143).
[2] Both orthogonal and oblique rotations employed in the factor analysis create same grouping among the scale items. As expectations among factors are expected the study adopts oblique rotation and the final analysis.
[3] Japanese Americans represent 34% of the state population and Chinese Americans represent only 4% (State of Hawaii Data Book 1990).

References

Arafat, I., & Yorburg, B. (1976). *The new women: Attitudes, behavior and self-image*. Columbus, OH: Charles Merrill.

Arkoff, A., Meredith, G., & Iwahara, S. (1964). Male-dominant and equalitarian attitudes in Japanese, Japanese-American, and Caucasian-American students. *Journal of Social Psychology, 64*, 225-229.

Beale, F. (1970). Double jeopardy: To be Black and female. In T. Cade (Ed.), *The Black women* (pp. 90-100). New York: Mentor.

Beere, A., Carike, D., King, W., Beer, D. B., & King, L. A. (1984). The sex-role egalitarianism scale: A measure of attitudes toward equality between the sexes. *Sex Roles*, *10*(7/8), 563-576.

Belk, S. S., & Snell, W. E., Jr. (1984). Beliefs about women: Components and correlates. *Personality and Social Psychology Bulletin, 12*(4), 403-413.

Belk, S. S., Snell, W. E., Jr., Holtzman, W. H., Jr., Hernandez, J. E., & Garcia-Falconi, R. (1989). The impact of ethnicity, nationality, counseling orientation and mental health standards on stereotypical beliefs about women: A pilot study. *Sex Roles, 21*(9/10), 671-695.

Bonner, F. B. (1974). Black women and white women: A comparative analysis of perceptions of sex roles for self, ideal-self, and the ideal-male. *Journal of Afro-American Issues*, *2*, 234-247.

Braun, S. J., & Chao, H. M. (1978). Attitudes towards women: A comparasion of Asian-born Chinese and American Caucasians. *Psychology of Women Quarterly*, *2*(3),195-201.

Brown, P., Perry, L., & Harburg, E. (1977). Attitudes towards women: A comparison of Asian-born Chinese and American Caucasians. *Psychology of Women Quarterly*, *2*(3), 195-201.

Burt, M. R. (1978). Attitudes supportive of rape in American culture. In House committee on Science and Technology. Subcommittee on Domestic and International Scientific Planning, Analysis, and Cooperation. *Research into violent behavior: Sexual assault* (Hearing 95th congress, 2nd session, January 10-12, 1978), pp. 277-322. Washington, DC: Government Printing Office.

Burt, M. R. (1980). Cultural myths and supports for rape. *Journal of Personality and Social Psychology, 3*, 217-230.

Cade, T. (1970). *The Black women*. New York: Mentor.

Canter, R. J., & Ageton, S. S. (1984). The epistemology of adolescent sex-role attitudes. *Sex Roles, 11*(7/8), 657-676.

Char, F. W., Tseng, W. S., Lum, K. Y., & Hsu, J. (1980). The Chinese. In J. F. McDermott, Jr., W. S. Tseng, & T. W. Maretzki (Eds.), *People and cultures of Hawaii: A psychocultural profile* (pp. 54-72). Honolulu, HI: University of Hawaii Press.

Cole, D. J. (1975). Assessment of the organization of sex role stereotypes among minority male and female. Paper presented at the conference on Empirical Research in Black Psychology, New York.

Engel, J. W. (1985, November 4-8). Male/female role values: A comparison of Caucasian and Japanese American college students. Paper presented at the annual meeting of the National Council on Family Relations, Dallas, TX.

Engel, J. W. & Dickson, C. A. (1985). Chinese and Japanese American students attitudes towards male/female roles. *Family Perspective, 20*(3), 197-206.

Epstein, C. F. (1973). Black and female: The double whammy. *Psychology Today, 89*, 68-71.

Field, H. S. (1978). Attitudes toward rape: A comparative analysis of police, rapists, crisis counsellors, and citizens. *Journal of Personality and Social Psychology, 36*, 156-179.

Fischer, G. J. (1987). Hispanic and majority student attitudes toward forcible date rape as a function of differences in attitudes toward women. *Sex Roles, 17*(1/2), 93-101.

Franklin, C. W., & Walum, L. R. (1972). Toward a paradigm of substructural relations: An application to sex and race in the United States. *Phylon, 33*, 242-259.

Fugita, S. S., & O'Brian, D. J. (1985). Structural assimilation, ethnic group membership, and political participation among Japanese Americans: A research note. *Social Forces, 6*, (4), 986-995.

Gonzales, A. (1982). Sex role of the traditional Mexican family: A comparison of Chicano and Anglo students' attitudes. *Journal of Cross-Cultural Psychology, 13*, 330-339.

Grimes, M. D., Hansen, G. L., & Page, A. T. (1982). Black and white differences in gender role attitudes: An exploratory analysis. Paper presented at the annual meeting of the Southwestern Social Science Association, San Antonio, TX.

Gump, J. P. (1975). Comparative analysis of Black women's sex-role attitudes. *Journal of Counseling and Clinical Psychology, 43*, 858-863.

Hartman, M., & Hartman, H. (1983). Sex role attitudes of Mormons vs. non-Mormons in Utah. *Journal of Marriage and the Family, 45*(4), 897-902.

Hatchett, S. J., & Quick, A. D., (1983). Correlates of sex role attitude among Black men and women: Data from a national survey of Black Americans. *Urban Research Review, 9*(2), 1-3.

Hays, W. C., & Mindel, C. H. (1973). Extended kinship relations in Black and White families. *Journal of Marriage and the Family, 35*(1), 51-57.

Hawley, P., & Even, B. (1982). Work and sex role attitudes in relation to education and other characteristics. *Vocational Guidance Quarterly, 31*(2), 101-108.

Hershey, M. (1978). Racial differences in sex-role identities and sex stereotyping. *Social Science Quarterly, 58*(4), 583-596.

Jackson, J. J. (1971). And where are the men? *Black Scholar, 4,* 34-41.

Lewin, M., & Tragos, M. L. (1987). Has the feminist movement influenced adolescent sex role attitude? A reassessment after a quarter century. *Sex Roles, 16*(3/4), 125-135.

Lin, P. L., Mei, K. W., & Peng, H. J. (1994). *Marriage and the Family in Chinese Societies: Selected readings.* Indianapolis, IN: University of Indianapolis Press.

Lyson, T. A. (1986). Race and sex differences in sex role attitudes of southern college students. *Psychology of Women Quarterly, 10*(4), 421-428.

Marrone, J. G., & Rutnik, C. M. (1987, April, 9-12). Patterns of optimism and pessimism in perceptions of changing sex roles. Paper presented at the annual meeting of the Eastern Psychological Association, Arlington, Va.

Nelson, J. G., & Rutnikm, C. M. (1988). Reliability, validity and cross-cultural comparisons for the simplified attitudes towards women scale. *Sex Roles, 18*(5/6), 289-296.

Nobles, W. (1974). African roots and American fruit: The Black family. *Journal of Social and Behavioral Sciences, 30,* 52-64.

Rao, P. V., & Rao, V. N. (1985a). Sex-role attitudes across two cultures: United States and India. *Sex Roles, 13*(11/12), 607-624.

Rao, P. V. (1985b). Sex-role attitudes: A comparison of sex-race groups. *Sex Roles, 12*(9/10), 939-953.

Rogers, T., & Izutsu, S. (1980). The Japanese. In J. F. McDermott, Jr., W. S. Tseng, & T. W. Maretzki (Eds.), *People and cultures of Hawaii: A psychocultural profile.* Honolulu, HI: University of Hawaii Press.

Rosen, E. I. (1985). The New Bedford rape trial: New thought on an old problem. *Dissent, 32*(2), 207-212.

Scanzoni, J. (1975). *Sex role, life style and childbearing.* New York: Free Press.

Seginer, R., Karayanni, M. & Mar'i, M. M. (1990). Adolescents' attitudes toward women's role: A comparison between Israeli Jews and Arabs. *Psychology of Women Quarterly, 14,* 119-133.

Silver, N. C. (1988, April 21-23). Attitudes toward women among Black and White university students. Paper presented at the 34th annual convention of the southwestern Psychological Association, Tulsa, OK.

Stack, C. (1974). *All our skin.* New York: Harper & Row.

Stacey, J. (1983). *Patriarchy and socialist revolution in China.* Berkerly, CA: University of California.

State of Hawaii data book: A statistical abstract. (1990). Hawaii, Department of Business, Economic Development and Tourism. Research and economic Analysis Division, Statistics Branch.

Wicker, A. W. (1969). Attitudes versus actions: The relationship of verbal and overt behavioral responses to attitude objects. *Journal of Social Issues, 25*, 41-78.

Williams, J. E., & Holmes, K. A. (1982). In judgement of victims: The social context of rape. *Journal of Sociolgy and Social Welfare, 9*, 154-169.

Winnick, L. (1990). America's 'model minority'. *Commentary, 90*(2), 22-29.

Young, V. H. (1970). Family and childhood in a southern Negro community. *American Anthropologist, 72*, 269-288.

Article 5

Effects of Maternal Employment on North American Families

Felecia M. Briscoe
Judith Frankel
Dolores Stegelin

Introduction

In the past twenty-five years, one of the most crucial social changes in the North American scene has taken place through the increased entrance of mothers into the labor market. Women today enter and remain in the market, following the male labor market pattern. In 1950, 34% of women in traditional childbearing years were in the work force compared to 73% in 1988. Maternal employment is characterized by full-time, year-round work patterns. This pattern obtains for mothers of young children as well as those of older children. Single mothers are employed at a higher rate than married women, 88% versus 61-70%. The majority of women continue to be employed in traditionally segregated "feminine" occupations and are disproportionately underpaid (Weitzman & Fitzgerald, 1993).

Employed mothers are a very diverse group: Maritally, family type, life style, age-wise, racially, ethnically, and socio-economically. Effects of maternal employment on the various family members depend upon the unique nature of each family situation. However, all families are impacted by governmental policies and business practices as they relate to child care and other family concerns and benefits. Although public policy related to children and families has never been more visible, affordable child-care arrangements are still far behind the need.

Effects of Maternal Employment Upon the Mother

This section of the paper is based upon the work of Sears and Galambos (1993). Most of the research reported by them is concerned with the work environment. Most of these studies have evaluated the relationship between work conditions and amounts of stress felt by the working mother. These findings reveal a link between work conditions and stress. However, some conditions of work lead not to stress, but to a higher level of satisfaction. Both of these outcomes are possible.

Stress is most likely to occur when jobs combine high levels of demand without control over the conditions of work; have few clear expectations; provide little feedback from supervisors; are low status; yield low incomes; provide few opportunities for advancement; have poor environmental conditions; contain exposure to physical, chemical, or biological hazards; have low levels of complexity and job control; result in direct responsibility for the welfare of others; and have high levels of computerization that result in eyestrain, tension, and fatigue. When these conditions do not obtain, stress is less likely to occur.

On the other hand, work satisfaction may contribute to the well-being of employed mothers. For this to occur, congruence between the work role the woman is playing and her desire to play that role must exist—in other words, women who want to be employed and are employed in the positions that they desire and that meet their needs. Work satisfaction is also related to receiving appropriate rewards from employment, such as equality in pay, opportunity for promotion, high work status, and less work overload. Finally the nature of relations between co-workers impacts maternal work satisfaction. Higher levels of work satisfaction are found when women work with pleasant co-workers; have reasonable supervision; control critical aspects of the job; and are not sexually harassed.

Generally, the research does not distinguish clearly which specific work conditions are associated with marital functioning, and little is known about which specific aspects of work are related to marital relations for employed women.

The relationship between work and domestic roles for the employed mother can also lead to satisfaction or stress. If the roles are experienced as compatible and mutually supportive, rather than in conflict, then the woman feels satisfaction. If she has too much to do in each of her roles and too many demands are placed upon her in the workplace and at home, she will experience role strain and feel stressed. For the employed mother, juggling both roles without role strain is critical for role satisfaction. The nature of the support she receives in the workplace and at home for meeting this task will help determine whether she experiences role satisfaction or role strain.

Effects of Maternal Employment Upon the Father

Pittman and Kerpelman (1993) review the research on the role of fathers as it relates to family work in dual earner families. They conclude that much more research needs to be done on the allocation of family work, but say "...it remains that the balance of family work falls to women, even more so in families with children." Husbands and fathers do more domestic work if their wives are employed, but only minimally so. The primary factor that influences the amount of work that men do in the home is the amount of time *they* spend in paid employment. The more hours a husband is employed, the less involved he is in family work. The hypothesis that as a working woman's income approaches her husband's income, his family work time will increase is not supported by the research. Rather, research reveals that lower-income men take more responsibility for household chores than higher income men.

The financial need of the family affects the time spent in the labor force for women, while the state of the economy determines the time spent in the labor force for men. Men respond to strong economics by working longer hours, but women do not. Men's labor force responsibilities remain constant in the face of varying financial family need, but women's do not. Women respond to family financial need by seeking more hours of employment.

For men, the amount of time spent on *family responsibilities* is affected neither by family need nor by the state of the economy. Women on the other hand, respond to increased family work needs (such as the addition of a family member) by cutting back on employment and increasing family responsibilities disproportionately. Pleck (1977, in Pittman and Kerpelman, 1993) discusses the cultural buffers operating in the work and family domains. The result of these buffers encourages men to emphasize their work roles and women to emphasize their family roles. He states that gender-role identity limits the range of roles that a person will assume, and in this instance is the major determinant of who will do family work. Traditional gender-role ideologies continue to thrive in the United States. These gender-role stereotypes result in a disproportional amount of family work being assumed by women, while husbands continue to ignore most of the family work.

Women who work are more satisfied with their roles if they feel that their working role is supported by their husbands in both attitude and behavior. However, cultural buffers continue to affect working mothers in that they may have difficulty giving up some of their maternal roles, and thus give their spouses mixed messages about sharing child care. Greatest marital satisfaction is obtained by those couples who feel that the allocation of domestic and work roles is fair for both partners. However, it is often very difficult to accommodate the preferences of both parents, and social changes that would encourage such accommodations are slow in coming.

Effects of Maternal Employment on Children

Claire Etaugh (1993) summarized the research in this area since the mid-seventies. She finds that the effect on children differs somewhat with age and ethnicity of the child. The research on infants and preschoolers shows few or no differences between children whose mothers are employed and those whose mothers are not employed outside the home. Likewise, for elementary school-age children, maternal employment is not related to self-esteem, self-perceptions of competence, personal problems, or social and emotional problems. While maternal employment is not related to academic achievement for white girls, it may be negatively related to academic achievement for white boys. However, maternal employment is positively related to academic achievement for black children of both genders.

Recent research supports the position that maternal employment is not related to social adjustment for adolescents, in contrast to earlier research. In fact, adolescent girls with working mothers have higher educational and career aspirations, and show less sex-role stereotyping.

Etaugh (1993) states that the key factor affecting a child's response to maternal employment is the mother's attitude about her role. Those mothers who are satisfied with their roles, whether employed outside of the home or employed within the home, will have the best adjusted children. She concludes, "...the impact of maternal employment on the child can be understood by examining it within the larger context of work and family circumstances."

One of the major circumstances affecting family satisfaction is the support that the families receive or do not receive in meeting the daily demands of family life. An examination of public policies concerned with child-care issues will clarify some of the major concerns North American families face today.

Public Policy Related to Maternal Employment

Public policy related to children and families has never been more visible. Both at the state and federal levels, legislation that supports the needs of children and their parents is at an unprecedented high (Stegelin, 1992). Many forces have come together to create this new emphasis on family support. The women's movement has highlighted the need for quality child care that is affordable, licensed, and regulated. Maternal employment continues to rise, creating an even greater need for child care, particularly for infants and toddlers. Family support issues are not the mainstay of public policy and campaign efforts. Slowly but surely, the United States seems to be awakening to the fact that families need support in the day-to-day routine of work, parenting, and family-related issues. Those that seek public office in the United States now carefully include issues about family needs, and more systemic programs and plans for the support of working parents.

In North America, the young child of the 1990's is growing up amid a world of changing priorities. Social and economic forces that influenced their parents are eroded, and in their place are even more complex social forces. When reviewing the types of programs available today, it appears that three out of every ten U.S. children under the age of five are enrolled in day care homes, day care centers, or nursery schools. Most of these children (62%) are in programs that are publicly sponsored, licensed, or registered (Schweinhart, 1989). In spite of the accelerating impetus on issues directly related to children and families during the past two decades, the late 1980's found young children's care policy mired in a complex set of forces (Kagen, 1989). Kagen (1989), associate director of the Bush Center in Child Development and the Social Policy at Yale University and a leading authority, sums up the issue:

> By traditional standards, the task should have been comparatively simple. Armed with approved mandates and appropriated dollars, an unprecedented number

> of cities and states set off to implement high-quality, early childhood programs in the late 1980's. The time seemed ripe: Well-publicized research extolled the benefits of early intervention; demographics reflecting the massive movement of women into the paid labor force fortified the need for additional services for young children; and a consensus a bout definitions of good early childhood pedagogy and practice, not prevalent twenty years before, had emerged. (p. 434)

Emerging Parental and Child Care Policy Issues

A child care crisis confronts this nation. It grows more severe every day and will intensify further as North America approaches the new century. Policy changes addressing North American families' child care must take into account the various gaps in the existing systems. Many families cannot choose safe child care without financial assistance to cover the costs (Blank, 1992). As recently as 1970, only three out of ten preschool-aged children in North America had mothers in the work force. Today five out of ten do and the proportion will climb still further, to seven out of ten by the year 2000, if current trends continue. At the turn of the century, four out of five women in North America, ages 25-54, will be working. North America's patchwork child care system—already swamped by existing demands—is still ill-equipped to cope with stepped-up pressures. Unless North America acts now, the future will bring longer day care waiting lists and more children left in substandard day care or left waiting home alone because no affordable care is available.

Every day, millions of children—infants, preschoolers, and school-agers—are affected directly by the nation's child care dilemma. This is because the sole parent living with them, or both parents, are in the work force. The past few years have witnessed a surge in demand for child care for an especially vulnerable group, babies and one- or two-year-old youngsters. Because this nation's employment policies have not kept pace with changing economic realities, many parents, who would like to stay home with their infants, cannot afford to do so. They cannot afford the economic risk. Unlike other western nations, the United States does not have a parental leave policy that guarantees new parents a leave of absence and job security when they return to work. With the lack of such protection and with more and more mothers of infants having to work, more working families must seek infant care (Kammerman, Kahn, & Kingston, 1983). Fifty percent of mothers of babies one year old or younger are working. They find the costs of infant care especially unaffordable in the United States and the availability of infant care inadequate. The average wait in the United States for infant care at centers in high demand is nine months.

A Federal and State Action Agenda

According to Blank (1992), a proposed action plan for federal public policy related to child care should include the following:

- Congress should appropriate $925 million to fund the Child Care and Development Block Grant for FY 1993 and $50 million authorized to help states improve the quality of child care in the Licensing and Monitoring Grant Program;
- Congress should pass Senate Bill 911 which would ensure that full funding was available in 1997 to provide Head Start for all eligible children.

Blank (1992) also proposes that state government should follow up federal policy by accomplishing the following:

- Carefully implement the two new federal child care programs—the Child Care and Development Block Grant and the "At-Risk" Child Care Program.
- Supplement Head Start or support state-initiated programs that provide comprehensive services to preschool children and operate full days throughout the year.
- Put into place strong health and safety standards that are monitored carefully regardless of the sponsor of the child care program or the numbers of children served.
- Make sure all programs comply with state regulations by investing the necessary resources in monitoring and enforcement efforts.
- Adopt standards and policies that ensure quality care. These include standards that keep group sizes and child-to-staff ratios low and ensure an adequate and stable supply of trained early childhood teachers and administrators. They also include policies that promote the active involvement of parents.
- Increase the amount of good quality child care by establishing state grants and revolving loan funds to cover start-up and expansion costs and quality improvements, as well as recruitment and training efforts for new child care providers. These efforts should be targeted to those areas and communities in greatest need of financial assistance.
- Expand the supply of trained child care workers by establishing scholarship and loan forgiveness programs for individuals seeking early childhood development credentials. Significantly improve the quality and supply of training opportunities.
- Implement the child care provisions of the Family Support Act in a manner that ensures that families are offered high quality child care. Effective implementation must include adequate rates and payment mechanisms, meaningful standards, and child care counseling services.

Conclusion

If mothers in the paid labor force experience job satisfaction, the well-being of their children is not negatively affected and may even be enhanced. The job satisfaction of working women is affected by job conditions and role strain. Role strain for working mothers is reduced when congruence between employment and desire for that employment exist. Other factors that influence maternal role strain are domestic support and public policy. Cultural buffers thrust most of the domestic workload upon the working mother's shoulders. Public policy at this point does not address the need for child care experienced by millions of families. Blank (1992) suggests changes in federal and state child-care policies that would positively affect the lives of millions of infants, preschoolers and school-aged youngsters.

References

Blank, H. (1992). Emerging child care issues. In D. Stegelin, *Early childhood education: Policy for the 1990's.* Norwood, NJ: Ablex.

Etaugh, C. (1993). Maternal employment: Effects on children. In J. Frankel, *The employed mother and the family context.* New York: Springer Publishing Company.

Kagan, S. L. (1989). Early care and education: Tackling the tough issues. *Phi Delta Kappan, 79,* 433-439.

Kammerman, S., Kahn, A., & Kingston, P. (1983). *Maternity policies and working women.* New York: Columbia University Press.

Pittman, J. F., & Kerpelman, J. L. (1993). Family work of husbands and fathers in dual-earner marriages. In J. Frankel, *The employed mother and the family context.* New York: Springer Publishing Company.

Schweinhart, L. (1989). Early childhood programs in the U.S. today. *High/Scope Resource, 8,* 9-13.

Sears, H. A., & Galambos, N. L. (1993). The employed mother's well-being. In J. Fankel, *The employed mother and the family context.* New York: Springer Publishing Company.

Stegelin, D. (1992). Early childhood policy: An introduction. In D. Stegelin (1992) *Early childhood education: Policy issues for the 1990's.* Norwood, NJ: Ablex.

Weitzman, L. M., & Fitzgerald, L. F. (1993). Employed mothers: Diverse lifestyles and labor force profiles. In J. Frankel, *The employed mother and the family context.* New York: Springer Publishing Company.

Article 6

Social Functions of Gender in a Changing World in Russia

Maria V. Zolotukhina
Maria G. Kotovskaya
Nataliya V. Shalyguina

While it would be an inappropriate assessment to state that the subject of gender and ethnicity has not received coverage in the works of Soviet and Russian scholars, recent developments in the territory of the former Soviet Union, and Russia in particular, pose new, challenging questions in this field.

Research conducted by specialists from the Institute of Ethnology and Anthropology, Russian Academy of Sciences, as well as studies carried out by sociologists and psychologists of other establishments (Institute of Sociology, Gender Center, etc.), bear witness to an ever increasing interest in the issues of correlating ethnic identity and gender behavior, transmitting cultural norms and values derived from the ethnic component of family life on the one hand, and models and standards of conduct characteristic of the contemporary society in Russia and other newly formed states on the other.

A rich realm of women, family and gender studies as such has emerged fairly recently in this part of the world. Therefore, it seems rather natural that at present, serious in-depth research embraces principal basic aspects of the history and modern status of the sexes (first and foremost, women) in Russia.

An unprecedented degree of openness to the rest of the world, as compared to the socialist era, resulting in a strong, albeit often uncontrolled flow of Western life philosophy elements, primarily those of American lifestyle (notions of individualism and privacy that are frequently presented as opposite to notorious "Soviet collectivism") and being combined with existing norms (or their lack, so-called normlessness) gives birth to new specific values and expectations. This process, in our mind, justifies a call to undertake comparative studies.

The following does not in any way claim to be regarded as the "ultimate truth." In contrast, we would like to announce an invitation to further investigations. Allow us to start with a brief overview of the history of "mankind's half" in Russia, which has been to a great extent unfairly neglected, both in the sense of current treatment and subsequent historical reflection.

Speaking of the images and actual positions women enjoyed, the pagan times stipulated quite significant degrees of freedom for females and a due amount of respect towards them, accentuating such features as health, skillfulness in taking care of the household, being hardworking, and kindness. Many of the upper-strata women were educated ladies, active and influential in political involvement. As Christianity made its way throughout Russia, women became more and more secluded, which most vividly manifested itself in the famous code of morals and ethics for man and wife - "Domostroy."

Peter the Great, who oftentimes proved to be violently destructive to the patriarchal culture, brought about drastic changes to the fate of women. He demanded their presence in the life of the society, which required education and acquaintance with European trends and fashions.

Catherine the Great continued the cause: It was under her rule that the first woman-President of the Russian Academy of Sciences (and the only one, so far), Yekaterina Dashkova, served as an example to many ladies at the court. Education, even if rather superficial, became an inseparable element of nobility and women's image. Two distinct types of female models could be observed: that of attractive, enlightened femininity, and another one of ambitious manliness, and unconscious striving towards independence that took ridiculous forms at times.

The 19th century started with another phenomenon—the appearance of women-professionals, initially governesses and actresses, and the setting up of educational establishments for the daughters of nobility and, later, the petite bourgeoisie.

The prevailing image of the early 1800s was that of the romantic, almost mystical woman, brought up with humanist ideas. The Christian ideal of love, faithfulness, readiness to sacrifice and suffering for the sake of moral duty inspired young wives of Russian revolutionaries to give up everything so as to accomplish the most sacred commitment they had and follow their husbands into exile, to share all the hardships. Later on they became the symbol of a Russian woman for many generations.

An average fate of that time was to be a decent wife, trustworthy friend to her man, and caring and loving mother to her children.

In the second half of the century, there began to appear women who saw their vocation in abandoning families (or the very idea of having one) and devoting oneself to the great causes of liberating the society, or at least emancipating women. The predominant goal for those who had been concerned with the gender issue was to obtain the right to work on equal terms with men. It was through this that representatives of both sexes (quite a number of male public figures wrote and spoke on women's issues) envisaged the route to true gender equality.

It had been noted by a number of scholars that the percentage of women-revolutionaries had been steadily growing with the development of the movement itself.

Despite all the obstacles, many women had managed to obtain higher education by the turn of the century, whether within Russia or abroad. Family relations had become more egalitarian, which at times resulted in extreme forms of sexual liberation.

Such a brief sketch of women's history in Russia can hardly provide explanation for a widely cited truism that Russian women are unique; and if not for the revolution of 1917, their past and present could probably be no more specific than those of any other ethnic group.

Most of the deep, unexpected and unpredictable societal and political shifts brought about by the revolution had led to total elimination of certain strata and qualitative transformation of the others. Women of the intelligentsia and nobility, as well as those of the bourgeoisie, were famous for their unlimited devotion to ideals of the family and high commitment to civic duties. These women either perished during harsh post-revolutionary years, emigrated, or had to drastically reshape their inner worlds and actual behavior.

The type of a revolutionary woman "in a leather jacket" with a Mauser, for whom liberated familial and sexual norms served as a necessary prerequisite for their only calling—to commit heroic deeds in the name of the revolution—turned out to be rather short-lived. Its successor came in an image of a woman, physically (and morally) enduring, strong and healthy enough to labor to build communism and take proper—within the framework stipulated by the existing ideology—care of the family. Some had accomplished more than it seemed possible for a human being, some did not survive. All in all, there had evolved several age cohorts, not even generations. This was an entirely new phenomenon—"Soviet women"—a diverse, comprehensive, numerous stratum, characterized by yet one common feature: Emancipation that their Western counterparts had been longing for over a long time had been granted as an unrequested gift on the part of the omnipotent proletarian state. That was the deliverance very few Russian females had been actually asking for or may have even been thinking about. Due to the simple fact that human nature, both of men and women, changes more slowly than the decrees and orders of the ideological wizards, new tenets failed to find soil that would have absorbed them among the average, commonly believed norms of behavior. It ended in a discrepancy between traditional expectations, or at least partial divisions of spheres for relative subordination, and alien, rigid concepts that acknowledged no differences between the sexes, except in procreation.

Adjustment went on in a variety of ways; one should not forget that men had to alter their psychology as well. For many women, work turned out to be an unquestioned priority, often at the expense of their own health or families. Many had taken an enormous burden of responsibility upon themselves and learned how to cope with a "Soviet double standard" that did not take too long to appear: women were to be independent, strong and decisive at moments when their still patriarchal husbands permitted them to be. This type had become one of the most widespread, irrespective of the fact that it is frequently despised by subsequent female generations, and is apparently here to stay.

Another kind of role—though never an ideal—the reversed-roles image of an authoritative, powerful wife and a hen-pecked husband "under his wife's heel," is occasionally found in Russia. Control over one's mate is a desired accomplishment in the eyes of many women, but it must not ever be publicly advocated or admitted.

The mosaics of gender relations, together with ongoing changes, served as one of the reasons for a neo-traditionalist trend in public opinion and state policy (so far, on the theoretical level) that calls upon returning women to the place where they supposedly belong, i.e., the family. The underlying idea is to compensate for the allegedly lost decades, that are now assessed as unambiguously negative. A corresponding social program has not been elaborated, and so far this attitude has been aggravated by a growing number of unemployed women. The essence of this simplistic approach may be expressed in the words: Enough of emancipation, no one really needs it, let's decide for a woman that she should devote herself to running the household and taking care of the family.

However, survey data testifies to women's willingness and determination to make their own choices. As an example of this we would like to share some of the results of an interview of 200 young Russian females, age 16-25, and content analysis of 200 essays written by the representatives of the same age group to a youth magazine, "Pulse."

The majority of the respondents came from Moscow and the Moscow area, due to the fact that the contest announced by "Pulse" magazine intended to select young females to admit them to a several-month training program to assist in finding employment in future. One of our assumptions was that this sample represented a segment of the young generation that is rather open to change and the new developments of the transition period.

Most common responses to the question of how one envisages an ideal woman were: "the one who managed to withstand our reality...and remain a woman despite all hardships." One-third of interviewed respondents named femininity as the No. 1 desired quality. Being a real woman implied a whole range of other related traits: "Nature predestines her to love and be loved," "She is a tender and fragile creature," "She should be admired by everybody and bring joy to everybody," She is "sensitive, tactful, tolerant, necessarily well-educated and well-read." She "should have the gift of empathy, be merciful and be ready to sacrifice."

One may assume that we are witnessing a return to early 19th century models. However, surprising as it may be, this ideal woman must have the looks of Linda Evangelista. More than that, two world-renowned ladies appear to be most appraised models of femininity and beauty—Jacqueline Kennedy and Margaret Thatcher. The key to this enigma lies in the fact that in the opinion of young Russian females, they harmoniously combine elegance and femininity with characteristics that are no less essential for an ideal woman, namely, being energetic, assertive and able to communicate: "Today femininity and tenderness need to go together with being active, businesslike and following one's own principles"; "A woman must have her goal, enjoy herself...she should have a colorful personality...She knows how to control her emotions, how to deal with people and has got a sense of humor"; "a romanticist in her heart and a businesswoman at her work."

Psychologists who took part in this survey, claim that only 20% of young females tested act in full compliance with a so-called feminine or female model of behavior, i.e., first and foremost display being diplomatic, ready for compromises, reserved (not active) conduct, longing for support and protection.

The overwhelming majority choose both family and work as their life goals. Work more often occupies the second place, and career seems to be rather unimportant.

To "meet the requirements of the day" (and be loved), ideal woman should "be independent, hence she must work." The best way to accomplish this is to realize oneself through creative occupations which would secure yet another important element - she "will find herself in the center of attention."

Therefore, on the level of imagining and wishing there appears to be a quite clear vision of today's "Super Woman" with an emphasis on traditional feminine qualities and sphere of activity—home, family, children—combined with an integral set of features that are perceived as androgynous and almost necessary for an ideal female—smart, energetic, hard-working personality. One may suppose that the bridge between Woman-Human-Man is here; it is simple and harmonious, and the long search for the balance of the gender traits is found.

However, making personal choices with regards to one's own life and viewing an ideal mate makes it fairly obvious that the scheme is far from being complete and that simple. Judging by respondents' self-evaluations, they perceive themselves as adequate only in a certain unity (whether current or future) with the males, stating that they (females) are attractive, coquettish, seductive. Ability to "arrange one's personal life" is considered to be a criterion for being normal. On the one hand, a true harmony is deemed possible only through a male-female dyad, on the other hand, the world of men looks alien, or at least too different and, thus, subject to mistrust and caution.

Femininity should be recognized, ascertained and reinforced by men - this is precisely the way to accomplish a balance between equality (that may not be viewed as necessary as such) and inherent gender differences. Young females demonstrated the presence of a hidden superiority complex in their statements by stating that they in fact are smarter than men, exactly to the point of pretending not to notice their flaws and not showing off their intellect should they want a man to like them. Submissiveness may come later, once "he is conquered." Even a "real gentleman" must often need to be fought for. He is the one who acknowledges weaknesses in women and cherishes them. Young Russian females are so convinced of this idea that they are caught in the illusion that "such a man must exist somewhere"—a source of a popular stereotype of the ideal Western man. Interestingly enough, the Russian land failed to come up with "true knights"—Michael Douglas and Richard Gere were cited as ideal mates for an ideal woman. One of the reasons may be searched for in the fact that Russian men are frequently accused of being either too infantile, irresponsible, overdependent and inactive or rude and aggressive - a possible consequence of World War II, in the aftermath of which women had begun to treat men as some kind of "endangered species," and in the 1950's—1970's, mothers tended to spoil and over protect their sons.

A principal novelty in these seemingly traditional perceptions of a "real gentleman" is that he should provide protection and security (so many girls and women are longing for), and decide for "his woman" only for as long as she would want him to. Women are very concerned with finding a golden medium. But men should necessarily be courteous, gallant, polite and well-mannered.

So it is the woman who chooses what it is and when to be feminine, masculine and androgynous. For instance, whereas independence is an explicit desired trait of a man, it needs not be pointed out, and is even sometimes assumed, that female independence is not obligatory. Being kind and energetic is relevant with respect to both sexes. Physical and moral strength, decency were more often cited as preferred male features.

Not a single respondent has mentioned sexuality as a desired characteristic among males or females, while respondents that had been interviewed were much more willing to discuss sexual issues.

Summing it up, we may say that young Russian women, with all the confusion, uncertainty and illusions present, seem to be willing to integrate the values of the past—many of which had been forcibly forgotten or distorted—with new ideals and standards, some of which are still under formation, and others which had emerged over the past decades. Hopefully, a comprehensive and delicate balance based upon differentiated equality will be achieved.

Article 7

The Dowager Syndrome: Challenge to the Imagery of Women's Meek Status in Traditional Chinese Families

James C. Hsiung

I. Introduction

A comparative study of the power of empress dowagers in traditional China should properly fall within the bailiwick of our historians. It is, after all, an important topic for a number of reasons. First, the recurrence of powerful imperial matrons, from Empress Lü of the Han (2nd cen. B.C.), Empress Wu of the T'ang (reign 684-705 A.D.), to Empress Dowager Tz'ü Hsi (late 19th cen.) of the Ch'ing, offers a pattern of how the emperor's power was at times (perhaps more often than we realize) circumscribed, nay, even circumvented, from within the imperial household. Secondly, the pattern, if explored systematically, may shed new light on the extent of power actually wielded by Chinese imperial rulers. Thirdly, a systematic exploration of the role of the powerful dowagers in the imperial institution may throw a different light on the status of women in the elite (as opposed to peasant or merchant) families in traditional China. For example, instances of timid, hen-pecked emperors may well confirm the much more widespread stories about hen-pecked husbands within the literati class. The "hen-peck phenomenon," used here in the generic sense, would then bring into relief the question of the extent to which similarly ingenuous, upper-class women may have circumvented the formal "patriarchy" (Stacey, 1983) in traditional times. Last, but not least, a better grasp of the dowager syndrome may help us come to grips with the deeper cultural implications of Jiang Qing's role in the radical reign of terror that haunted Mao's China during his waning years (1966-1976). But, alas, despite the importance of the topic, there is a literal vacuum in the literature in this area. Other than scattered, disparate studies of Empress Wu (Fitzgerald,1968; Lin,1957) and Dowager Tz'ü-Hsi (e.g., Bland, Percy, & Blackhorse, 1912; Sargent, 1911; Seagrave, 1992), I know of no non-idiographic, comparative studies of the dowager syndrome across time.[1]

This paper is, by necessity, a ***think piece*** developed with limited resources by a political scientist venturing into a neglected terrain of the historians, and trying to make a headstart in a way that is coherent, non-desultory, and, hopefully, non-controversial.

Conventional Wisdom on Chinese Women's Status

The conventional wisdom on the status of Chinese women is best epitomized by the imagery of generations of meek, lowly, parasitic, and abused members of the patriarchal family unit. This imagery agreed with the self-view of radical feminist groups seeking women's liberation in Chinese homes at the dawn of the modern era. Sally Borthwick cites a fiery declaration from a radical Chinese women's magazine published in Tokyo back in 1907, to the effect:

> For the past several thousand years, women's position has been of the lowest, declining continuously, like living in the hell. . . In our view, this is because women have been harmed by the *old beliefs* of former days [emphasis added].

Works of feminine instruction, reflecting the "old beliefs," laid great stress on the virtues of accommodation, which Borthwick summarizes as: dutiful service to the elderly, unselfish affability to those of the same generation, lack of jealousy if a second wife were taken, willingness to treat a first wife's children as one's own (p. 64). No doubt, all this is true. But, our question is: Was all this equally true of women in "high places," in the imperial household especially?

We ask this question only half facetiously. As Albert R. O'Hara (1945, p. 261) points out, in considering the position of women in China, one should keep in mind that rules and customs "vary a great deal for different classes of women." The taxonomy offered by O'Hara includes the following: (a) slaves and laboring women; (b) wives of farmers and merchants; (c) wives of scholars and officials (i.e., members of the literati class); and (d) wives of nobles and rulers. In this study, we are concerned with women in the last two categories, first (d) and then (c), in that order.

As we apply this taxonomy, we realize why the conventional wisdom holds out the model of the fettered wives and why, on the other hand, the known records on some wives in upper-class families, including the imperial household, did not conform to the model, as we shall examine below.

Models of Ancient Eminent Women

In the lack of wider resources, one way for us to gain an insight into the role of women in elite Chinese families is to look at what is probably the only available collection of biographies of ancient eminent women, the *Lie Nü Chuan*, written in the first century B. C. by Liu Hsiang (translated in O'Hara, 1945). Some of the traits that can be gleaned from these biographies are very revealing. I am referring to what we can learn, about women's status in elite families, from the ordinary acts of these women—not the attributes for which they were deemed praiseworthy. In one specific area, germane to our interest here, we find the wife frequently consulted by the husband on important business concerning the home, himself, and even statecraft. Many of these "eminent women" were wives of kings or dukes or the like; and they were consulted by their husbands on matters of state (O'Hara: *chüan* I, 1; 6; *chüan* II, 3; *chüan* III, 2, in Part I). Others were wives of noblemen or pundits, who consulted them on important decisions such as whether to accept an invitation to serve in the court of a particular ruler *(Ibid., chüan* II, 13; IV, 15, etc.).

Thus, this practice of consulting the wife by an eminent husband (be he king, duke, or pundit) reveals at least two things worthy of note. First, it seems to show a much higher status enjoyed by women in families of the upper crust. Second, it indicates that the penchant of empress dowagers intervening in court politics in later dynasties was anticipated by this common practice of boudoir consultation in ancient times.

II. The Empress Dowager Syndrome

Dowager Tyranny

It may not be the first in Chinese history, but the earliest and most notorious recorded case of dowager tyranny was probably that of Empress Lü, wife of the first emperor, Kao-tzu, of the Han Dynasty (*Shih Chi, chüan* 8). Upon Emperor Kao-tsu's demise in 195 B.C., she became the empress dowager, as her son ascended to the throne to become Emperor Hui, at the age of 17. The young emperor had to depend on the mother and in effect surrendered much power to her. Empress Dowager Lü's first atrocious act was to persecute Mme.Ch'i, who was the deceased emperor's most favorite royal concubine, and whose son almost replaced Empress Lü's as the heir until the latter won the crucial succession battle. She banished Mme. Ch'i to braying rice with pestle and mortar, wearing prison garb. She then poisoned Mme. Ch'i's son to death. When Mme. Ch'i grieved, Dowager Lü had her limbs amputated, her eyes gouged, and had her made deaf and mute. The dowager kept Mme. Ch'i's limbless torso, dubbed "human vegetable," in a lavatory. As the tender-hearted young emperor was taken to view the "human vegetable," he knew what his dowager mother had done. Greatly perturbed and furtively resentful, it was said, he turned to lavishly wining and womanizing, never again tending to state affairs (T'ung, pp. 38-40). Emperor Hui died at the age of 24, whereupon Dowager Lü made a "false son"[2] his successor, the Shao Emperor. She became the Grand Empress Dowager [tai huang tai hou]. Wielding real power, she planted members of her own Lu family in powerful court positions, after purging the few important officials loyal to the Han house. Then, she had Emperor Shao murdered upon learning that he wanted to avenge the fate of his real mother, whom the dowager had killed. She put another "false son" of the late Emperor Hui on the throne (TCTC, *chüan* 13; T'ung, pp. 41-43).

Queen's Manipulation of the Emperor

Since an emperor had numerous royal concubines, whoever among them was able to bear him a son, thus a potential heir, would be a threat to the queen (or the emperor's most favorite concubine) if the latter should be unable to conceive. A sure (though bizarre) way for the latter to protect her position was to exterminate all the children begotten by [other] royal concubines soon after birth. This happened in the interior household of Emperor Ch'eng of the Former Han, who was infatuated with two sisters in his harem. One of them, Chao Fei-yen, was made the new queen after Queen Hsü, the former imperial consort, was outmaneuvered and banished. Neither Fei-yen nor her sister Chao-yi was able to bear a son for the emperor. To protect their own favored position in the emperor's presence, they conspired to kill all male issues of royal concubines, two even with the emperor's knowledge. As a result, Emperor Ch'eng died in the year 7 B.C. without an heir of his own. A nephew was made the next emperor, Ai, who died soon after, and was succeeded by a nine-year-old kin (reign name: P'ing). Taking advantage of the bizarre circumstances, an ambitious courtier and later regent, Wang Mang, was able to usurp power, making himself the new emperor, renaming the dynasty the Hsin. Although the interruption was only for a brief 18 years, followed by the rise of the Latter Han, the demise of the Former Han was the direct result of the Chao sisters' machinations. Their systematic infanticides in the imperial household deprived their spouse, the Cheng Emperor, of a male descendant who could inherit the throne, thus creating the chaotic circumstance that opened the gate to Wang Mang's usurpation.

Dowager Usurpation

The most blatant instance of outright usurpation by a dowager remains that of Empress Wu of T'ang. An iron-willed matron even at the time when her husband, Emperor Kao (r. 649-683 A.D.), was still living, Queen Wu killed her son, Crown Prince Li Hung, by requiring him to drink hemlock, for disobeying her. She had her second son, Li Hsien, made the next crown prince, but soon banished him for disobedience, too. Her third son, Li Che, became the Chung Emperor, after her husband deceased. She became the dowager, but soon removed her son, Emperor Chung, from the throne for showing partiality to the family of his wife, Queen Wei. Dowager Wu named her fourth son, Li Tan, the Jui Emperor, but almost immediately took over the throne herself, making herself the Empress Wu (literally, "Emperor Wu" in Chinese). She ruled for five years (690-695 A.D.) in her own right, as the "Sage Mother Holy Emperor" [sheng mu shen huang], until she was deposed by an overwhelming coalition of forces loyal to the Li House (TCTC, *chüan* 203; TCCS, *chüan* 178; Fitzgerald, 1968, pp. 113-146; T'ung, 1977, pp.207-302).

Queen-Staged Coups

While the term "dowager" appears in the title of this paper, our concern is much larger, extending to instances of power play, and abuse, by the wives of reigning emperors and incumbent crown princes. Our attention is drawn to cases where there is evidence that the wife either did her husband in or otherwise exercised undue influence over him, meddling in state affairs. Our ultimate interest is in the actual status of Chinese upper-class women, beginning with those in the imperial household. We will next turn to two examples of queens actually staging coups against their emperor husbands or members of the latter's clan.

The first is the palace coup staged by Chia Hou[3], royal spouse of crown prince Ssu-ma Chung, who became Emperor Hui of the Chin in 290 A. D. After Chia Hou became the new queen, she sought revenge for an old grudge against members of the imperial Ssu-ma clan, plus the clan of the now dowager Yang, who was the trusted consort of the deceased Emperor Wu but not the new emperor's mother. The new queen's plot was to set the imperial Ssu-ma clan against the dowager's Yang clan. She first had Dowager Yang's father and his associates arrested and executed on trumped-up charges of plotting a rebellion. After that, she turned to the targeted stalwarts of the imperial clan itself and, setting them against one another, had them eliminated one by one (Yin, 1990, pp.70-72). She then made sure that all powerful positions were occupied by members of her own Chia clan. All this happened while her husband, the emperor, did nothing to stop her, because, two years her junior, the emperor was not her equal when it came to a match of wits (*Ibid*., p.70; TCTC, *chüan* 82). What is of interest to us here is that, unlike in the other cases mentioned before, Chia Hou abused power not after the death of her husband, but while her husband was the reigning emperor. She staged the coups while she was the reigning queen, not an empress dowager taking advantage of a minor monarch, as in the other cases.

The second case involved the conspiracy between a queen and her daughter to kill the living emperor. It happened to Emperor Chung of the Tang, whose wife, Wei Hou, was power-greedy and dreamed of becoming a second Empress Wu. Her daughter, Princess An Lo, also ached to become the first "Crown Princess" in history, replacing the existing crown prince as the heir designate. After repeated warnings from loyalist aides, the usually indecisive Emperor Chung gradually began to be on guard. Sensing the emperor's vigilance was a threat to them, Wei Hou and Princess An Lo put poison in his food, killing the 50 year-old monarch in the Shenlung [holy dragon] Palace, in the year 710 A.D. (TCTC, *chüan* 209, p. 2975; Yin, 1990, p. 134f). She made Emperor Chung's fourth son (by a royal concubine) the new monarch, the Jui Emperor, but Dowager Wei Hou was in effect the ultimate power behind the throne. She was preparing to make herself the real emperor, very much after the fashion of Empress Wu, when she was overthrown by loyalists led by Prince Li Lung-chi (Yin, *Ibid*., p.135).

If other queens and dowagers were also power-greedy and acted in self-aggrandizement, Wei Hou distinguished herself as the queen who actually murdered her emperor husband, and with impunity.

Dowagers Outmaneuvering Rivals in Power Struggles

In the West, a female royal offspring may succeed to the throne as the ruling monarch, like Queen Elizabeth of England; but she did so through inheritance, not through winning power strives, as was the case with many an empress dowager in China. Besides, the Chinese dowagers or queens who maneuvered themselves into power were not imperial descendents, and were not necessarily related to the imperial family by blood, except when their son happened to be the crown prince or the next emperor. The fact that these Chinese women could, nevertheless, outdo men in palace power struggles cannot but be a testament to the status and freedom they must have enjoyed in the imperial household. This logical deduction seems to contradict what we normally believe to be true about the lowly and meek status of women in traditional China.

One typical example of how a dowager outmaneuvered her male rivals in the wrangle for ultimate power was the rise of Empress Dowager Tz'ü Hsi, in the Manchu (Ch'ing) Dynasty. Hailing from a middle-rung family in the Yehonala clan of the Manchus, and originally known as Lan Erh (Orchid), she was chosen as a palace maid and placed at the Yuan Ming Yuan Garden, the imperial summer palace, during the reign of the Emperor Hsien Feng (1850-1861 A. D.). She bribed a eunuch to lure the emperor to the usually deserted "Tree Shade Haven" [t'ung-yin shen-ch'u], where she was posted. By loudly singing southern Chinese folk songs from a hideout in a bed of flowers, she attracted the emperor's attention. Because of her beauty and wit, she immediately won the emperor's grace and was promoted to be a royal concubine, taking the name of Yi Bin. Two years later, in 1856, she bore the emperor a son, named Tsai Ch'un, the future Emperor T'ung Chih. She was made into the Yi Fei[4].

When the British and French forces invaded Peking in the 1860 joint expedition, the Hsien Feng emperor escaped to his imperial retreat in Jehol, leaving the harrying task of negotiating with the foreign invaders to Prince Kung, his brother. Hsien Feng brought an entourage that included Yi Fei and the young Tsai Ch'un. The following year, 1861, he died in Jehol, but not before he had appointed an eight-man regency that would assist and oversee the emperorship of the six-year-old Tsai Ch'un, who became the Mu emperor, better known by his reign title of T'ung Chih.

Yi Fei, now aged 27, became the Empress Dowager Tz'ü Hsi. She knew that the regency was a barrier to her political ambitions, and she had to get rid of the regents, all of whom were powerful courtiers in their own right. Her first move was to appoint Jung Lu, an old flame of hers, to head the Imperial Palace Guard, so that her safety would be absolutely assured. Upon return to Peking, she made sure that Prince Kung, who had all the reasons to resent the regency because, despite his political clout and experience, he was left out of it, would be on her side against the eight regents. With the support of Prince Kung plus other coopted officials, she had the regents arrested and executed one by one (Yin, 1990, pp. 277-281).

Tz'ü Hsi's victory in this decisive power struggle laid the foundation for her unchallenged political dominance in the next four decades. Until she died in 1908, she remained the ultimate power behind the throne, attending to state affairs "from behind the gauze screen," as historians put it. Without winning this battle, she would most probably not have been in the position to dominate the Manchu Dynasty over the head of T'ung Chih and, after his death at the age of 18 in 1874, of the succeeding Kuang-hsü emperor, whom she also had a decisive hand in putting on the throne (Bi, 1992). Once again, what is important for us here is that Tz'ü Hsi did not reach the pinnacle of power simply because she was the mother of the reigning emperor, but did so only after she had outmaneuvered a whole slew of political rivals, all males at that.

Hen-pecked Emperors; and Sexual License by Queens & Dowagers

The above history of the frustration and usurpation of imperial power, and even murder of one emperor, by queens and dowagers, is odd enough. We might further note, in this connection, however, that many Chinese emperors were known either to unduly spoil their women or to be plain hen-pecked. An incomplete list of hen-pecked emperors would include some of the principals already mentioned: Emperors Ch'eng of the Han, Hui of the Chin, Chung of the Tang. In addition, it would also include others like Emperor Wen of the Sui (589-618 A.D.) and Emperor Kao of the Tang (628-683 A.D.). The former was so "tamed" by his spouse, Queen Tu Ku, that he was deprived of the freedom to keep a harem of more than sixty women. Even then, the queen would allow none of them to dress up to look good, much less to compete for and win the emperor's "grace" at night. Queen Tu Ku had the emperor under her constant watch, including appearing with him at court (Yin, 1990, p.109f). It seemed that the Wen emperor was able to come close to some of his meagre palace ladies, like Lady Ch'en and Lady Ts'ai, only after the death of Queen Tu Ku (TCTC, *chüan* 180, p. 2649). Emperor Kao of the Tang, for his part, was a helpless victim mesmerized or intimidated by Lady Wu Mei, who was to become Dowager Wu in 683 A.D. and then Empress Wu in 690-695 A.D. (T'ung, 1977, pp. 282ff).

Furthermore, chronicles of Chinese imperial history occasionally sport instances of sexual license and promiscuity of queens and dowagers. Queen Chia of the Chin, wife of Emperor Hui (r. 290-306 A. D.), was one of the most notorious examples. She first had a liaison with the palace physician, Ch'eng Chü. Later on she became more profligate. Some reports alleged that she habitually transported young, stout males in "black coaches" from outside the palace to her boudoir to keep her company over night, only to be killed the next morning "to shut them up for good" (TCTC, *chüan* 83; Yin, 1990, pp.72-73). Another notorious example was Queen Wei of Tang, who had illicit rendezvous with a number of courtiers including Wu San-ssu, Hui Fan, and, after Wu San-ssu's death, Ts'ui-t'i, Ma Ch'in-k'e, and Yang Ch'un (T'ung, 1977, pp. 306; 313; and 321). All this lewdness happened before she and her daughter jointly murdered Emperor Chung in 710 A.D., as noted before.

Earlier we noted that Empress Tz'ü Hsi made her old flame, Jung Lu, the head of the Palace Guard. She was known to have other flames as well and, as a widowed dowager, she became pregnant at the age of 47 (Yin, 1990, p. 306). For her part, Empress Wu of the T'ang also was known to have kept a small male harem of her own. Its most celebrated member was a former exhibitionist named Feng Hsiao-pao (later known as Hsueh Hüai-yi), who was brought to the empress's attention (and bosom) by her daughter after he gained notoriety for indecent exposure while bragging about his sexual potency on the streets of Ch'ang-an, the capital city. Later on, two young and virile brothers, Chang Yi-chih and Chang Ch'ang-tsung, displaced Hsüeh as Empress Wu's favorite companions (TCTC, *chüan* 205, pp. 2937, 2945). Disgruntled, Hsüeh left the palace, and spread the word around about her harem. For that "crime," he was abducted back to the palace and executed by order of the empress (T'ung 1977, 294f; Fitzgerald 1968, pp. 129ff).

III. Implications of the Dowager Syndrome

We have kept to a minimum the details about the power play, and power abuse, by dowagers and younger imperial matrons of the "hou" (queen) and "bin" (royal concubine) ranks. But, the discussion thus far raises a number of important questions. In the first place, we do not doubt the existence of rigid, imperial house rules that were supposed to place constraints on the female occupants of the emperor's palace quarters. But, the lurid license of the palace ladies, as revealed in the cases above, is troubling in that it raises doubts on the emperor's ability to enforce discipline in the palace. Secondly, the seemingly treacherous palace ladies all seemed to have such a magic spell over their ruler, who at times seemed a willing victim. We are at a loss for an answer.

The only possible clue we can think of is the unwieldy size of the imperial harem, creating at least two problems. (a) The multitude of palace ladies made it necessary to delegate authority for enforcing discipline either to an internal female bureaucracy, of the kind discussed by Priscilla Ching Chung (1981), or to whoever, among the emperor's many consorts, happened to have his confidence, like the Chao sisters during the reign of the Ch'eng Emperor of the Han, thus making her, or them, extraordinarily powerful. In the event neither of these deputies could maintain efficient supervision on behalf of the emperor, then discipline broke down badly in the palace as a whole. (b) The emperor's harem was the hotbed of jealousy among the many women competing for the emperor's favor and attention. On his part, the emperor had reasons to feel "guilty" for physically not being able to give his multitude of women the attention they needed. This self-imposed sense of guilt may have spawned the kind of behavior that made him at times look like an inept, foolhardy victim of his own harem ladies.

In addition, there is a third, and more important, question raised by our discussion above, viz.: If the cases above reveal an unusual extent of freedom, and power, enjoyed by the ladies in the palace, was this phenomenon limited just to the imperial household? or was it found pretty much across the upper echelons of society (i.e., the official-literati class)? If the answer is in the affirmative, it would put an entirely different light on the status of women in traditional China, at least in the upper classes. Let us dwell on this last question a bit. There seemed to be both similarities and dissimilarities between the imperial household and the sub-imperial elite families.

Similarities and Distinctions in Imperial & Sub-Imperial Households

Among the similarities were: (a) polygamy, or what Olga Lang (1946, p. 48) calls "plural marriage," though its extent was much more pronounced in the imperial household, in which the mean size of the harem (with perhaps the sole exception of that of Emperor Wen of Sui) was said to be about three thousand ladies of various nomenclatures; (b) a close tie between a woman's personal status and the fortuitous circumstance of whether or not she had given birth to a son, hence potential heir to the family line; (c) boudoir consultation, or the husband's habit of consulting the wife on important matters concerning self, family, and the state; and (d) the oft-rumored "hen-peck" phenomenon.

The incomplete list given above of the emperors known to be hen-pecked is indicative of a common problem that was apparently more widespread among the male heads of sub-imperial households. Admittedly, it is hard to document this point from the written script, perhaps even harder than in the case of hen-pecked emperors, if only because the scribes, who were from the literati class, would less likely write about the problem among their own ranks. We can, nevertheless, find circumstantial evidence in novels, e.g., in *The Scholars* (Li Pao-chia, ch. 10); unofficial oral histories,[5] and the like. The popular novelist Lin Yutang (1935) developed a case for the wife-dominated Chinese husband in his famous *My Country and My People* (pp.137-171). In disarming candor, he even writes about "hen-pecked officials" often appearing at court "with bruised faces" resulting from wifely assaults fueled by jealousy (p. 142). Lin's thesis, however, was disputed by Marion Levy, Jr. (1949). But, if one examines their respective frames of reference, one will find that Lin was generalizing about the *elite* (i.e., officials' and scholars') families, whereas Levy's empirical universe was the common folks in China.

Among upper-class males, the hen-peck phenomenon was known as the "Chi-ch'ang phenomenon," named after Ch'en Chi-ch'ang (alias for Ch'en Chao), of the Sung Dynasty (960-1279 A.D.). It is said in the encyclopedic *Tz'u-hai* (1948, p. 1425) that Chen Chi-ch'ang was both a scribe and a knight, who did not succeed in officialdom, but was given to generous reveling with friends. He lived in the shadow of a "jealous and ferocious" wife, who would bellow and flail away her whip and staff until his reveling friends got scared and ran pell-mell away. The famous Sung poet, Su Tung-p'o, wrote a well-known poem about the Chi-ch'ang phenomenon, likening Chen's wife to a "roaring east-river lioness." In another entry (p. 401), the *Tz'u-hai* gives "the Chi-ch'ang phenomenon" the following succinct commentary: "Chi-ch'ang phenomenon: named after Ch'en Chao, alias Ch'en Chi-ch'ang, who was intimidated by his wife, surnamed Liu, known to be both jealous and ferocious. Henceforth, it is common to speak of all hen-pecked husbands as afflicted with the 'Chi-ch'ang phenomenon.'"

The grapevine has it that Dr. Hu Shih founded the informal "PTT Club," a fraternity of hen-pecked husbands (PTT is the acronym for *pa-tai-tai*, or hen-pecked). Many noted Chinese intellectuals, including Lin Yutang, Y. R. Chao, Liu Pan-nung, and Hu Shih himself, were said to be charter members. The club's membership was later extended to many celebrities in China (later in Taiwan), including the famous writer Hsu Chih-mo, one-time Education Minister Dr. Yi-ch'i Mei, former Defense Minister Dr. David Yu, long-time Legislative Yuan President Chang Tao-fan, Taiwan University President Fu Ssu-nien, and Dr. Monlin Chiang, the reknowned agronomist. The Club's officially stated purpose was to continue the "time-honored tradition" among Chinese scholars of "revering one's good wife as adversary."[6] Many men in mainland China admitted to me in private that the hen-pecked husband was a common creature in the post-1949 Communist period. Although it would be difficult to compare between the mainland and Taiwan, the prevalence of the problem, I would suspect, is probably at a comparable level across the Taiwan Strait.

The intellectual progenitor of the upper-class hen-peck tradition was probably Jen Huai, Duke of Kuan Kuo, of the Tang Dynasty (618-906 A.D.), whose motto was "the three 'awes' for the wife," which ran as follows: "(1) When she is young and beautiful, serene as a female Buddha, how can you not be awed [by her]? (2) As mother to your children later on, she protects your offsprings like a tigress. How can you not be awed? (3) At your old age, when she may pounce on you like a ferocious owl, how can you not be awed?"[7] I might add that the Chinese word *p'a* connotes "fear," "respect," "admire," and "be [over-]awed" as well.

Whether all these tales are true is not quite the point. What is more important, I think, is the attitude held by the upper-class Chinese males toward the wife, as reflected in these tales. One can scarcely detect, in these tales, the kind of male chauvinism and brutality that is flaunted in the conventional literature on Chinese "patriarchy."

Emily Ashern (1975) writes about Chinese men's fear of women's "power and pollution (due to the menstrual discharge)." "The *power* that women have", she explains, "is their capacity to alter a family's form by adding members to it, dividing it, and disturbing male authority; the *danger* they pose is their capacity to break up what men consider the ideal family" (p. 200, emphasis added). Since traditional Chinese culture emphasized not only the primacy of family, but equally its harmony, it only makes sense that this "power" that young, married women wielded, and hence their potential danger, instilled the kind of "fear" in elite men of their women, such as described by Duke Jen. Emily Ashern also observes a contrary trend to older women's progression toward menopause: They gain increasing power over the people around them through "the gradual accretion of influence and power," as their biological process brings on the end of menstruation (p. 201f). This "gradual accretion of influence and power" may have been one additional reason for what we in these pages call the "dowager syndrome" in the broad sense.

Chinese culture may be unique in many ways. But in one area, its uniqueness is often neglected. That is, it probably offers more humor about hen-pecked husbands than does any of the other cultures that I know. One typical joke is about a stag gathering, when someone invites all hen-pecked husbands to step to the left side, and all others to move to the right. In response, all men flock to the left. Only one steps to the opposite side. To an astonished audience, he explains: "My *old lady* always tells me that I should not go where there are too many people!"

Actual annals of hen pecks and hen-pecked husbands are hard to come by. But, the above is enough to suggest something, i.e., that among the sub-imperial elite families the wife may not be perceived and treated as a lowly, meek, and "parasitic" creature that conventional wisdom caricatures.

Notwithstanding their similarities, there were unmistakable distinctions between imperial and sub-imperial families as far as women are concerned. For one, the criterion for choosing wives was decidedly different. Women recruited for the imperial harem were more often than not picked primarily because of their looks,[8] whereas spouses admitted to sub-imperial elite families were, with few exceptions, chosen because of their potentials as a good mother, which made good education and personal virtues a mandatory requirement. This may explain why so many queens and imperial concubines were merciless, licentious, and unscrupulous. Another distinction apparently lay in the different ways in which chastity was valued and observed. The kind of license attributed to some of the queens and dowagers above seemed not to find parallels among women in sub-imperial, official-literati families. Liu Hsiang reputedly wrote *The Lie Nü Chuan* (see above) to impress upon the Han emperor what a "model" noble woman should be, and to persuade him to avoid, or get rid of, the less than scrupulous females in his harem, albeit to no avail.

Chastity was emphasized as one of the virtues of women, especially in the official-literati-class families (Asycough, p. 286). But the historical accounts about the licentious queens above scarcely instill confidence that chastity was observed with the same sternness in the imperial household as in the sub-imperial elite families.

In answer to the question we raised above, women in the sub-imperial elite families most probably enjoyed a status comparable to that received by queens, princesses, and dowagers in the imperial household. But, of course, they were more likely to be better educated and probably were held accountable to higher standards of personal virtue (Ayscough, 1937, p. 267ff).

Elite vs. Lower-class Families

We are led to the next logical question: Could the women in the elite families enjoy a higher status than that accorded to women in the lower-class families? All indications are that ladies in the elite households were treated with more tolerance, and in many instances even pampered by their men, as compared with the women in the "village" China that authors like Arthur Smith (1899) wrote about. The discrepant conclusions drawn by Lin Yutang (1935) and Marion Levy, Jr. (1949) are a case in point. In her classic study, Olga Lang (1946, pp. 193ff) interviewed wives in the lower social strata: peasants, coolies, artisans, clerks, shopkeepers, petty officials, etc. It is from the perspective of this level of Chinese society that she counseled against over generalizing about the "domineering wives," even though she admitted many such wives were found in old Chinese fiction - that is, literature portraying women in elite families. (Her interview sample did not include wives in what we would call the elite class.) Among the 194 wives in the lower social strata (chosen because each was the only one able to dispute the husband's power in a family in which the husband's mother was deceased), Lang found only 24 who were never consulted by the husband. In all other families the "ruling male granted his wife a certain degree of authority" (p. 194). Thus, even in the lower-class families, the wife was consulted by the husband, and enjoyed some "degree of authority" granted by the husband, in 87.6% of the cases that Lang studied. In another context, when her attention was turned to women in high places, she nevertheless did not hesitate to acknowledge that "queens and princesses were particularly violent in their treatment of their rivals" and in dealing with their "unfaithful" husband in this respect (p. 51). Implicit in Lang's discourse is an admission that upper-class Chinese women were not as meek and docile as the women in peasant, coolie, and other families in the same social strata.

Thus, we see generally identifiable lines of distinction separating three broad groups: the imperial households, the sub-imperial elite households, and the lower-class families. If these lines of distinction can be maintained, as I believe they can, then our next question is why? Why were upper-class women treated differently, i.e., enjoying more freedom and power than their counterparts in lower-class families? To go back to our main theme, why was the dowager syndrome possible in a cultural milieu in which women were purportedly downtrodden and dominated by men?

Origin of the Dowager Syndrome

In this paper, we have used the term "dowager syndrome" broadly to refer to (a) the power apparently enjoyed by queen mothers, plus imperial consorts of various grades, *hou, fei, bin*, etc.; and (b) the obviously higher status (and, with it, freedom and power) accorded to women married into the sub-imperial elite (official-literati) families. In both groups, as the discussion above shows, women seemed to enjoy better treatment, and more power, than conventional wisdom would have us believe on how women in general faired in traditional China. Now, it remains for us to explore the reasons for this dowager syndrome.

Thus far, we have avoided the epithet "Confucian." It is because we are dubious about the merit of making a blanket attribution of all Chinese women's troubles to Confucianism, as many writers are wont to do. In order to establish an air-tight case for Confucianism being the source of all Chinese women's troubles, one would have to prove, beyond any reasonable doubt, that women had enjoyed a decidedly better status before Confucianism was adopted as the state cult in 136 B.C. In fact, the available evidence shows that some of the major empirical findings about women's real status in later periods had existed since ancient times, i.e., long before China's Confucianization. For example, to the extent Liu Hsiang's *Lie Nü Chuan* (O'Hara, 1945) could be a guide, boudoir consultation goes back to pre-Confucian times. It continued till the modern age, as Lang's study attests (p. 194). The monopolistic succession by males to the family fief (and "sacrifices"), furthermore, also went back to the Spring and Autumn period or even earlier (i.e., pre-Confucian) (Shiga, p. 125). On the other hand, the practice of distributing property equally among male and female children is a family practice that straddled the pre- and post-Confucian periods (*Ibid.*) On another score, chaste widowhood had been an ideal for all women since time immemorial (i.e., pre-Confucian). Yet, despite that ideal, the queen mother of the Ching Emperor of the Han (r. 157-140 B.C.) was a remarried woman (T'ung, 1977, p. 51). This clearly attests to discrepancies between imperial-house and lower-class mores, dating back to the pre-Confucian period. Even after China's Confucianization, chaste widowhood survived in reality only till the Ming Dynasty (1368-1644 A.D.). In the ensuing Ch'ing Dynasty (1644-1911), chaste widowhood was expected of the wife of a scholar with official titles, but not of the common women (Lin, 1935, p.140). Here, to reiterate, we find discrepancies between ideal and reality (Pong & Fung, 1985), as well as between families in different social strata.

The moral of all this is: one has to be extremely careful in assessing the role played by Confucianism in determining women's status. The record is at best a spotted one. And, equally important, one has to keep an eye open for differences between women in upper- and lower-class families. With all things considered, the obvious conclusion is that, despite common beliefs to the contrary, Confucianism may or may not have made a difference with respect to the status of women in China. Certainly, its influence was not uniform across time and across social strata. It may, though, have left its distinct imprint in two ways: It set higher standards of virtue for women in elite (i.e., official-literati) families. Yet, didn't it set higher standards of virtue for all elite men, too? In addition, because of its emphasis on education, Confucianism probably created room for the better educated women, as found in the elite families, to feel their way through the gray areas between freedom by right and freedom by sufferance. Although equal access to education was a rarity enjoyed by women only in the upper class, the fact is that Chinese history was never known for want of blue stockings. The famed poetess Li Ch'ing-chao of the Sung, the great "literary wit" Hsieh Tao-yun of the Chin, and Su Hsiao-mei, the lengendary lady scholar, prominent daughter of Master Su Hsün, and talented wife of Ch'in Kuan, himself an accomplished scholar, of the Sung, are merely a few of the best known examples. Education gave a woman the wherewithal to speak with an equal voice in a men's world. Furthermore, education may also require the husband to be more tolerant and permissive than otherwise.

With the above disclaimer, we are now ready to discuss the possible link between Confucianism and the origin of the dowager syndrome. After Emperor Wu of the Han (r.141-87 B.C.) made Confucianism the "state cult" in the year 136 B.C., all Confucian classics were made the required scriptures to be closely followed and lived out by the entire nation. One of the texts was the *Hsiao Ching* (Classic of Filial Piety), purportedly written by Tseng Tzü, a Confucius disciple, recording the master's teachings. It expounds the basic Confucian tenet that "filial piety is the basis of virtue and the source of all instruction." As a result, filial piety was ground into the subconsciousness of the entire Chinese nation, from the emperor on down to the populace. The emperor, more especially, had to do what he preached. One immediate perceptible effect was the discontinuation, in the later years of the Han, of the practice of maintaining temples in honor of the reigning emperor (Ho, 1968, p. 17). For, while the emperor was the ultimate locus of authority in the land, he had his own seniors in the imperial household to whom he had to show filial piety. These included the emperor's uncles, aunts, elder brothers and elder sisters, etc., as well as matrons of the dowager generation.[9]

The political effects of the practice of the filial piety teaching were enormous in the Han, as well as in later ages. Many of the empress dowagers in the Han, as de Bary and associates (1960, I, p. 169) put it, "took advantage of this situation, forcing their sons to make moves which they did not wish to make by fuming, sulking, or even refusing to eat until they had their way." Hence, the genesis of the dowager syndrome.

For the Chinese nation at large, more or less the same phenomenon found its expression in the *de facto* change of the family from an otherwise perpetual patrifocal institution to a fixed-duration patrifocal institution, i.e., patrifocality being limited to the duration of the father's lifetime. Following the death of the *pater familias*, the surviving mother, if the grand mother was no longer living, would assume the ultimate authority of the family as the dowager. Since the Confucian filial piety teaching placed onerous duties on the son, a less than scrupulous dowager could abuse the filial piety code to get what she wanted. Thus, the dowager syndrome found its parallel in the sub-imperial elite families as in the imperial household.

The problem, however, was the more serious in the imperial household, for a number of reasons: (i) The women recruited into the palace as queens and princess were, as noted before, chosen primarily for their looks,[8] not for qualities like good education and personal virtues, in contrast to the women married into the sub-imperial elite households. Hence, the moral self-restraint, needed to check the impulse to abuse the power which a dowager may command by virtue of the filial piety code, was either weak or unknown to many of the empress dowagers. (ii) Jealousy, spawned by years of competition with hordes of other women in the imperial harem, found its first chance of venting, after the emperor's demise, in the form of power-hunger strikes, as it were. (iii) In order to make governing easier, it was wise for every emperor to rule by exhorting filial piety (known in Chinese as *yi hsiao chih t'ien-hsia)*, because this way he could be assured of ready and whole-hearted endorsement of all parents in the land and, thus, could count on them to help preserve social order by keeping their children in check. But, since the emperor had to practice what he preached, the filial piety code had his hands tied in dealing with the mother, the future dowager. More or less the same can be said of the emperor's relationship with a consort who had born him a son that was a potential heir to the throne: Filial piety conceded an extra place to the woman who helped the emperor meet his filial obligation to continue the family line. For all these reasons (and possibly more) combined, Chinese history thus distinguishes itself in the frequency with which it records instances of power play by empress dowagers and, occasionally, by a consort of a reigning emperor. These instances may suggest a different status enjoyed by women in the imperial household, in fact if not in theory.

The onerous burden of Confucian filial piety may explain the special status enjoyed by women in the sub-imperial elite families as well. The male head of the family, in the upper crust, was bound by the Confucian code to defer to the dowager mother in the absence of the father. But, before becoming the male head, and while the father was still living, filial piety required the son to defer to the mother as well as the father. The habit of deferring to a female, be it the mother or, later on, the dowager, was obviously transferable to another female, namely, one's wife, more especially if the latter had begotten him a baby son, someone to continue the family line. This may explain why women in the elite families enjoyed more freedom and power than women in lower-class families, in which Confucianism had taken understandably shallower roots. It may, too, explain why the so-called hen-peck syndrome was limited to the best-educated families, where the Confucian influence was the most deep-rooted. This bifurcation is best captured in a vulgar Chinese saying, to the effect: Lower-class husbands *ta* (beat, batter) their wives; upper-class husbands *p'a* (fear, respect) their wives. The initial exposure by most Americans to the Chinese family through the imported coolies and later laundrymen (purportedly the "wife-beating" class) in the United States may, not surprisingly, have reinforced the imagery of a [Chinese] nation indiscriminatingly dominated by men over women.

Concluding Remarks

We started with a brief examination of the roles played by palace ladies, including dowagers, queens, and royal concubines of diverse ranks. We then pursued the question of whether the obviously special status enjoyed by women in the imperial household was also found, with necessary differences, in sub-imperial elite families. Finally, we came upon the question whether the usual imagery of the lowly, meek, and fettered women was more truly tied to the lower-class families, albeit making up the majority of the Chinese nation as they did.

In seeking an answer for the origin of the dowager syndrome, we noted the impact of Confucianism, resulting from its inculcation of filial piety. We also noted, however, that, while Confucian filial piety was responsible for generating what we call the dowager syndrome, it also tended paradoxically to instill in Confucianized men a higher respect for (or else tolerance of) women, at least in the case of a family dowager, one's mother,[10] or one's spouse who had begotten a male offspring. Among the lower-class families, less influenced by Confucianism, on the other hand, the women enjoyed comparatively much less freedom and power, thus generally confirming the conventional imagery regarding the down-trodden women in traditional China. To the extent that this summation is empirically sustainable, the bottom line is that the true reality will probably go counter to the grain of conventional wisdom on the subject. Furthermore, it will also go against a common conviction among students of traditional Japanese women, in that Confucian influence is said to have reinforced the inferiority of Japanese women (Condon, 1985, p. 3).

While I will be the first one to dispute any claims of definitiveness for these findings, what we see emerging from this study is a huge *paradox*, as already explained. Moreover, most of the findings here are counter-intuitive. The paradox, though, points up a matter of consequence for policy. The Communist "family revolution" was launched as a frontal attack on the Confucian tradition that the Communist Party believed had created the two thousand years of injustice against Chinese women. While we agree in essence with the claim about the injustice, this study shows that whether Confucianism was to blame for the entire problem is questionable. If anything, the Confucian filial piety code, which contributed to the rise of the dowager syndrome, seemed to confer a higher status on women (from the empress dowagers on down) not only in the imperial household, but more especially in the sub-imperial elite families, the seat of the heaviest Confucian influence. The circumvention of men's patrifocal authority by the dowager and other women in these elite families, to reiterate, is an oft-neglected evidence of this paradox. Among the commonfolk families, where the injustice against women was the most acute, on the other hand, Confucian influence was much less entrenched. We are not questioning the merit of the Communist assault on traditional Chinese "patriarchy" (Stacey, 1983). But, we do think it appropriate to raise a question regarding the blanket fashion in which Confucianism was singled out as the "bogey" to be blamed indiscriminately for all the problems besetting the generally fettered Chinese women. Emerging from this study is a varying picture of traditional Chinese women's status**es**, a picture which is far from monolithic, but dependent on the specific social strata one addresses. It may be flattering for Chiang Ch'ing and her cohorts to be able to claim that Chinese women, after the socialist revolution, are now "holding up half of the sky" under Communist rule (cf. Barret, 1973). But, we think, it is empirically truer to say that *at times* in Chinese history, **some** traditional women were already holding up *more than half* of the sky, as our sample of empress dowagers alone amply demonstrates. In this sense, what we call the dowager syndrome does seem to offer a challenge to the validity of the static, undifferentiated view of all women being equally fettered while mired in a meek and lowly status in traditional China.

Endnotes

1. The only comparative study similar to this one, written by a sociologist, Wen-hui Tsai (1991), was not available to me. Another study, by Priscilla Ching Chung (1981), also a social scientist, looks into the roles and power of 92 "palace ladies" employed in a female, intra-palace bureaucracy, which paralleled the eunuch bureaucracy but regulated the lives of the female palace inhabitants of the Northern Sung Dynasty, 960-1126 A.D. Its principals were, therefore, different from the dowagers, queens, and other imperial consorts that this paper addresses. Besides, it is limited to a particular time period, and offers no comparisons across time.
2. "False son" is so-called because the dowager surreptitiously took the baby son of another royal concubine, after killing her, and reared and made him into Emperor Hui's son. The device was to ensure that the line of succession would be kept under Dowager Lü's control, and that she would be the Grand Empress Dowager, i.e., grandmother of the new emperor.
3. The Chinese word "hou" is a generic term which could mean the wife of a crown prince or a queen or empress, i.e., wife of a reigning emperor. If the "hou" or "tai hou [dowager]" should become an imperial ruler in person, like Dowager Wu of Tang, the title would change to "emperor" in Chinese (Empress Wu actually is "Emperor Wu" in the original). Chia Hou (literally, "Royal Consort Chia"; Chia being her family name) was so known when

she was the royal spouse of Crown Prince Ssu-ma Chung, but kept the title after her husband became the emperor. By then, of course, Chia Hou meant Queen Chia.

4. The title "fei" is second only to that of a queen (or *hou*), or one level above a "bin," or royal concubine of the basic grade.
5. Te-kong Tong, an authority on the late Hu Shih, would not write about it in his semi-biographical *Hu-shih Tsa-yi* [Random Memories of Hu Shi] (Taipei: The Biographical Literature, 1981). But Tong would orally confirm that Dr. Hu, perhaps the best known Chinese scholar of the 20th century, was hen-pecked in the presence of his wife, despite her bound feet, which bore witness to the last vestiges of the pre-modern Chinese tradition. This, however, did not prevent Hu from maintaining lifelong friendship with a number of tender hearts, some of Caucasian descent, as Tong relates in the book.
6. Chung Huan-ch'eng, "Origins of a Chinese Happy Family," *Meizhou Ping Xun*, a Chinese-language publication in New York, Feb. 1, 1993, p., 4.
7. *Ibid.*
8. Chia Hou of the Chin may be a rare exception. The young Chia Nan-feng was said to be a homely girl of "mediocre looks and dark skin," but was chosen as the wife of the 13-year-old Prince Ssu-ma Chung, in 272 A. D. The choice was made by his mother, Queen Yang, the gracious, persuasive spouse of Chung's father, Ssu-ma Yen, who was Emperor Wu. The homely girl's mother, a good friend of Queen Yang, had persistently lobbied for, and obtained, the latter's support for Chia Nan-feng over another candidate who was Emperor Wu's initial preference as his daughter-in-law (Yin, p. 67). Upon the death of Emperor Wu in 290 A.D., Prince Ssu-ma Chung ascended the throne, and Princess Chia became Chia Hou (or Queen Chia).
9. If the reigning emperor's dowager mother had been a concubine of the deceased emperor, for example, the latter's surviving queen and the nucleus of other concubines who had been close to the deceased ruler, as well as the dowager mother, would be the ones to whom the reigning emperor would feel obliged to defer, although not necessarily with the same affection or consistency. Hence, I used "matrons of the dowager generation" to suggest this complex relationship.
10. Because one's father may have more than one wife, one's own mother, if she was not *yuan-pei*, or the first wife, may not be the dowager after the father deceased.

References

Ayscough, F. (1937). *Chinese women: Yesterday and today*. Boston: Houghton Mifflin Co.

Ashern, E. (1975) "The power and pollution of Chinese women." In M. Wolf and R. Witke, *Women in Chinese history* (pp. 193-214). Stanford, CA: Stanford University Press.

Bi, C. (1992). *Hsi-shuo Tz'u-hsi* [The Drama of Tz'u-hsi: Biography of a Yehonala], (2d Ed). Taipei: Hankuang Cultural Publications.

Bland, J., Percy, O., & Blackhorse, E. (1912). *China under the Empress Dowager.* Philadelphia: J. B. Lippincott.

Borthwick, S. (1985). Changing concepts of the role of women from the late Qing to the May Fourth period. In D. Pong & S. K. Fung (Eds.), *Ideal and reality: Social and political change in modern China (pp. 245-281).* Lanham, MD: University Press of America.

Chung, P. C. (1981). "Power and prestige: Palace women in Northern Sung (960-1126)," In R. Guisso & Johannesen, *Women in China: Current directions in historical scholarship* (pp. 202-251). New York: The Edwin Mellen Press.

Condon, J. (1985). *A half step behind: Japanese women of the 80's.* New York: Dodd, Mead, & Co.

de Bary, W. J., Chan, W. T., & Watson, B. (1960). *Sources of Chinese tradition.* Compiled by W. J. de Bary, W. T. Chan, & B. Watson, with contributions by others. New York: Columbia University Press.

Fitzgerald, C. P. (1968). *The Empress Wu.* London: The Creesset Press.

Guisso, R., & Johannesen, S. (1981). *Women in China: Current directions in historical scholarship.* New York: The Edwin Mellen Press.

Ho, P. T. (1968). "Saliant aspects of China's heritage." In Ping-ti Ho and T. Tsou (Eds). *China in crisis*, Vol. I, Book 1: *China's heritage and the communist political system.* University of Chicago Press.

Lang, O. (1946). *Chinese family and society.* New Haven: Yale University Press.

Levy, M., Jr. (1949). *The family revolution in modern China.* Cambridge: Harvard University Press.

Li, B. J. (1974). *Kuan-ch'ang hsien-hsing chi* [The Parody of the Scholars]. A Ch'ing dynasty novel reissued by The World Publications, Taipei.

Lin, Y. T. (1935). *My country and my people.* New York: Reynal and Hitchcock, a John Day book.

Lin, Y. T. (1957). *Lady Wu: A true story.* London: Heineman.

O'Hara, A. S. J. (1945). *The position of women in early China.* Westport, CT: Hyperion Press.

Pong, D., & Fung, S. K. (Eds). (1985). *Ideal and reality: Social and political change in modern China.* Lanham, MD: University Press of America.

Sargent, P. (1911). *The great empress dowager of China.* New York: Dodd, Mead, & Co.

Seagrave, S. (1992). *Dragon lady.* New York: Alfred Knopf.

Shih Chi. (1989). *The Shi Chi* [Records of the Grand Historian], as annotated and rendered into *paihua* by Feng Tso-min. Taipei: Hsing-kuang Publications.

Smith, A. (1899). *Village life in China.* London: Fleming H. Revell Co.; reissued in 1970, with an introduction by M. Cohen. Boston: Little, Brown..

Stacey, J. (1983). *Patriarchy and socialist revolution in China.* Berkeley: University of California Press.

TCCS. *Tung-chien chi-shi pen-mo*.

TCTC. (1991) *The Tzü-chih T'ung-chien* [General Mirror for the Aid of Government], an authoritative work of history written by Ssu-ma Kuang (1019-1086 A.D.) under an imperial commission by Emperor Ying of Sung; reissued with vernacular translations, compiled by Chang Hung-ju [Zhang Hongru] and Shen Chih-hua [Shen Zhihua]. Beijing: Reform Press.

Tsai, W. H. (1991). "Women in traditional Chinese politics: The lives and careers of Empresses Lü, Wu, and T'zü-hsi." *Chinese Studies* (Taipei) 9, 2.

T'ung, H. (1977). *Chung-kuo Hou-fei Lie-chuan* [Biographical Accounts of Queens, Empresses, and Royal Concubines]. Taipei: The Crown Journal Publications.

Tz'ü-hai. (1948). *The Tz'ü Hai* [The Encyclopedic Dictionary] (Taipei: Chung-hua Book Co.), a 1948 reissue of a Ch'ing publication, compiled under an imperial edict.

Wolf, M., & Witke, R. (Eds). (1975). *Women in Chinese history*. Stanford, CA: Stanford University Press.

Yin, T. K. (1990). *Huang-hou te ku-shih* [Stories of imperial spouses]. Taipei: World Cultural Artifacts Publications.

Family Relationships

Part III

Article 8

Relationships among the Family Differentiation, Peer Relationships, Individuation and Self-Esteem of Korean Adolescents

Young-Ju Chun
Shelley M. MacDermid

Adolescence has long been considered a period during which concern with self-concept increases; also during this period, adolescents are thought to gradually individuate themselves from their families of origin and expand their network of intimate relationships to include members of the outside world, such as peers. From the family developmental point of view, the task of the family during adolescence is to provide an environment which facilitates the individuation process of the adolescent child, which in turn is positively related to the adolescent's psychological adjustment.

Adolescent individuation and self-esteem have most often been explored by focusing on family systems or on individual personality development (Bray & Harvey, 1987). Many studies have examined the relationship between family interaction and adolescent adjustment (Bartle, Anderson & Sabatelli, 1989; Gavazzi & Sabatelli, 1990; Gecas & Schwalbe, 1986). Most studies, however, have concentrated their focus on either parental behavior (parenting style) toward adolescents (Bartle et al., 1989) or global perceptions of adolescents about their families (e.g., perceptions of family conflict; Gavazzi & Sabatelli, 1990). While the former focus tends to disregard the bi-directional nature of parent-adolescent interaction and other dyadic relationships, the latter fails to acknowledge the possibility that various dyadic interactions between the family members may have different effects on adolescent self-esteem (Anderson & Sabatelli, 1992).

Most studies done in the U.S. have supported the view that adolescent individuation is positively related to psychological adjustment. For example, Flemming and Anderson (1986) found that adolescents' perceptions of fusion with their parents were related to lower self-esteem, mastery, health and college adjustment. Rice, Cole and Lapsley (1990) and Hoffman (1984) found significant positive relationships between adolescent individuation and psychosocial well-being. Wade (1987) showed that among adolescent girls, individuation problems were positively related to their attempts at suicide. These studies, however, may provide only a limited view of the relationship between individuation and psychological adjustment, ignoring macro-factors such as social, cultural and historical events.

In the present study, the interrelationships among family patterns of distance regulation (labeled 'family differentiation'), adolescent individuation and adolescent self-esteem were examined with Korean adolescents. Adolescents' perceptions of their dyadic relationships with each parent and their parents' relationship with each other (e.g., mother-father, father-adolescent, and mother-adolescent) were measured using "circular questioning" to provide richer and more precise information on family dynamics (Sabatelli & Anderson, 1991). Adolescents' perceptions of peer relationships also are measured to examine their links to adolescents' individuation and self-esteem.

The present study may challenge U.S.-based family research in two ways. First, the marital bond of parents may not be the primary dyadic relationship in functional Korean families that it appears to be in U.S. families (Teyber, 1983). Although Sabatelli and Anderson (1991) found that adolescent psychological adjustment is mostly influenced by parents' marital relationships, there are few comparable studies revealing the difference of the family dynamic patterns between eastern and western families. Second, family systems theorists and clinicians in the United States emphasize the importance of the developmental task of individuation for positive functioning of both the individual and the family as a whole (Anderson & Sabatelli, 1990). The present study asks if this also is the case in another culture which is more focused on collectivity rather than individuality. It is proposed that adolescents in different cultures go through somewhat different individuation processes, because of the different norms regulating families and individuals. In Korean culture, the significance of individuation is not thought to be as strong as it is in the U.S., and therefore, we expect to find that adolescent individuation is less related to adolescent self-esteem among Korean adolescents than has typically been the case in U.S. research.

Family Differentiation and Adolescent Adjustment

Prominent family systems theorists have conceptualized the interdependence between family and individual development processes. Murray Bowen (1978), in discussing family therapy, found that members of troubled families do not have separated identities which he labeled as "undifferentiated ego mass." In such families, all family members are emotionally reactive and not separated but fused (Nichols & Schwartz, 1991).

Minuchin (1974) noted emotional boundaries which regulate each subsystem within the family (Nichols & Schwartz, 1991). According to him, the boundaries in normal families are clear enough to protect an individual's autonomy while ensuring mutual support and intimacy. However, in abnormal families, there are two dysfunctional patterns of interaction: enmeshed families in which the boundaries are diffused and disengaged families in which the boundaries are too rigid.

Recently, Sabatelli et al. have integrated Bowen's (1978) and Minuchin's (1974) theories to establish a significant distinction between the constructs of "differentiation" and "individuation" (Allison & Sabatelli, 1988; Gavazzi & Sabatelli, 1990; Sabatelli & Mazor, 1985). "Differentiation" is seen as a family system property describing family patterns of distance regulation. Like Bowen, Sabatelli et al. note that all families demonstrate varying degrees of tolerance for connectedness (intimacy) and separateness (autonomy) through their interactions (Sabatelli & Anderson, 1991). The family's level of differentiation is seen as playing a significant role in the family's ability to adapt to social and environmental changes, developmental change for the family as a whole, and developmental change experienced by individual family members (Anderson & Sabatelli, 1990; Flemming & Anderson, 1986). In well-differentiated families, the system provides family members with developmentally appropriate autonomy while maintaining mutual respect and intimacy. In contrast, in poorly differentiated families, interpersonal boundaries are regulated in two extreme ways. That is, such systems show interaction among family members that either encourages separateness without enough intimacy or demands connectedness without a separate sense of identity (Allison & Sabatelli, 1988; Sabatelli & Anderson, 1991).

Meanwhile, "individuation" can be defined as the intrapsychic process by which a person comes to see him or herself as being separate and distinct within one's relational (familial, social and cultural)context (Anderson & Sabatelli, 1990).

Since adolescence, at least according to U.S. research, appears to be a time of gaining great autonomy and control, the issues of family differentiation and individuation may be more important during adolescence than during any other developmental stage. Hess and Handel (1985) asserted that in poorly differentiated families, adolescents' efforts to individuate are viewed as threats to the system's stability (Allison & Sabatelli, 1988). Family members who fear separation intensely dread letting go of one another because they may end up facing their own loneliness and emptiness (Wechter, 1983). Therefore, the successful resolution of the developmental task is thought to depend on not only the strength of the marital relationship and men's and women's functioning as parents, but also the availability of peer relationships to support the adolescent's individuation (Wechter, 1983).

Peer Relationships and Adolescent Adjustment

During adolescence, individuals often experience a lack of stability and uncertainty, which leads them to seek the comfort of being with others who are in the same transition. Also, adolescents use peer groups as a means of relinquishing their childish dependence on parents and achieving an autonomous sense of self rooted in their society (Brown & Lohr, 1987). Daniels (1990) asserted that adolescents who successfully achieve their developmental tasks acquire reasonable individuation from their parents, and depend more upon their peers. According to Seltzer (1989), peers are essential comparison objects against whom adolescents evaluate themselves, and depending on the outcome of the comparison, either "feeling good" or "feeling bad." Thus, peer support during this period is critical for adolescent adjustment (Collins & Gunnar, 1990). Considering the contribution of peers on adolescent social and psychological adjustment, it is a natural trend that more and more therapy program for adolescents involve intervention with peers as well as with the parent-adolescent relationship.

Recently, one of the most active areas of research on adolescents and peer groups has been the interrelationship of peer and family relationships (Collins & Gunnar, 1990). Earlier studies on families and adolescence considered peer groups as competing with parents for socialization of adolescents and hindering of successful transitions to adulthood (Bowerman & Kinch, 1958). However, some researchers argue that the shift toward a peer orientation does not necessarily mean a rejection of parents' opinions and values (Brittain, 1967; Sabatelli & Anderson, 1991). Instead, many researchers in the past decade found that parents have a greater influence on adolescents than do peers (Davies & Kandel, 1981; Loy & Norland, 1981; Reed et al, 1986; Smith, 1985).

Boys and girls seem to display different patterns of being influenced by family and peers. Sebald and White (1980) found that girls generally conform more to parental advice than boys, especially in the areas of dating and interpersonal relationships. Treboux and Bush-Rossnagel (1990), in their study of adolescent sexual attitudes and behaviors, found that male adolescents were more likely to be influenced by their friends than by their parents.

In the present study, functional aspects of peer relationships (i.e., peer support) are focused to examine adolescent individuation and self-esteem, on the basis of the increasing recognition of the influence of functional aspect on adolescent adjustment (Collins & Gunnar, 1990). It is proposed that peer support may facilitate adolescent individuation from his or her family of origin and therefore may be associated with higher self-esteem.

Therefore, it is hypothesized in the present study that family differentiation (measured separately by marital differentiation, father-adolescent differentiation and mother-adolescent differentiation) and peer support would be related to adolescent individuation, which in turn would be related to adolescent self-esteem as an indicator of psychological adjustment.

Methods

Sample and Sampling

The sample for this study consisted of students from four high schools in Korea (two girls' and two boys' schools). Two procedures were used for sampling. First, the researcher selected two high schools located in middle-to-lower and two schools from middle-to-upper class districts in an urban area of Seoul. Second, one first-grade class (9th-10th grade in U.S.) was randomly selected from each school, and all students in that class were invited to participate in this study.

Of the 198 adolescents who participated, 155 provided complete data and constitute the sample for this study (male 87 vs female 68). Demographic characteristics of the 87 boys and 68 girls are summarized in Table 1.

All four of the self-report instruments used in the present study were developed in the U.S. Since all of them were in English, they were translated and back-translated twice, and then pilot-tested to ensure that the Korean versions accurately reflected the originals. Respondents anonymously completed, in the presence of the researcher, a questionnaire focusing on family differentiation, peer relationships, adolescent individuation and adolescent self-esteem. The questionnaire took approximately 30 to 40 minutes to complete.

Table 1: Demographic Characteristics of the Sample

		Adolescents (N=155)		
		Male (N=87)	Female (N=68	
Size of Family	Three	= 5 (5.7%)	= 0 (0%)	
	Four	= 51 (58.6%)	= 25 (36.8%)	
	Five	= 22 (25.3%)	= 33 (48.5%)	
	Six	= 6 (6.9%)	= 7 (10.3%)	
	Seven	= 1 (1.5%)	= 2 (2.9%)	
	Eight	= 0 (0%)	= 1 (1.5%)	
	Missing	= 2 (2.3%)	= 0 (0%)	
Number of Friends	None	= 12 (13.8%)	= 3 (4.4%)	
	One	= 11 (12.6%)	= 4 (5.9%)	
	Two to Three	= 40 (46.0%)	= 45 (66.2%)	
	Four to Five	= 17 (19.5%)	= 12 (17.6%)	
	Six or More	= 6 (6.9%)	= 4 (5.9%)	
	Missing	= 1 (1.1%)	= 0 (0%)	
Perceived SES	Very Wealthy	= 1 (1.1%)	= 0 (0%)	
	Wealthy	= 27 (31.0%)	= 15 (22.1%)	
	Normal	= 58 (66.7%)	= 52 (76.5%)	
	Poor	= 1 (1.1%)	= 1 (1.5%)	
Religious Affiliation	Protestant	= 32 (36.8%)	= 24 (35.3%)	
	Catholic	= 10 (11.5%)	= 11 (16.2%)	
	Buddism	= 26 (29.9%)	= 18 (26.5%)	
	No Religion	= 18 (20.7%)	= 12 (17.6%)	
	Missing	= 1 (1.1%)	= 3 (4.4%)	
Marital Status	Intact	= 86 (98.9%)	= 67 (98.5%)	
	Separation	= 0 (0%)	= 1 (1.5%)	
	Missing	= 1 (1.1%)	= 0 (0%)	
Education	Father	Mother	Father	Mother
No Education	0 (0%)	1 (1.1%)	0 (0%)	0 (0%)
Primary School	2 (2.3%)	4 (4.6%)	1 (1.5%)	2 (2.9%)
Middle School	7 (8.0%)	12 (13.8%)	2 (2.9%)	5 (7.4%)
High School	22 (25.3%)	47 (54.0%)	17 (25.0%)	33 (48.5%)
College Graduate	42 (48.3%)	22 (25.3%)	36 (52.9%)	27 (39.7%)
Graduate School	14 (16.1%)	1 (1.1%)	12 (17.6%)	1 (1.5%)
Occupation				
Unemployed	1 (1.1%)	64 (73.6%)	0 (0%)	50 (73.5%)
Laborer	1 (1.1%)	3 (3.4%)	1 (1.5%)	2 (2.9%)
Clerical, Cook, Barber	1 (1.1%)	4 (4.6%)	0 (0%)	0 (0%)
Technician, Craftsman	8 (9.2%)	3 (3.4%)	2 (2.9%)	0 (0%)
Salesman, Small Business	18 (20.7%)	9 (10.3%)	11 (16.1%)	6 (8.8%)
Professional, Gov. Worker	26 (29.9%)	2 (2.3%)	23 (33.8%)	7 (10.3%)
Management, Military Official	22 (25.3%)	0 (0%)	26 (38.2%)	1 (1.5%)
Lawyer, Doctor, Businessman	10 (11.5%)	1 (1.1%)	5 (7.4%)	2 (2.9%)
Missing	0 (0%)	1 (1.1%)	0 (0%)	0 (0%)

Instrumentation

Differentiation In the Family System The Differentiation In the Family System scale (DIFS) (Anderson & Sabatelli, 1992) was employed to assess the level of differentiation in the reciprocal relationships within the family system. Each subscale consists of eleven items, each of which focuses on behavioral patterns of dyadic interaction. Each question is rated on a 5-point Likert scale from "never" to "always," and items are summed to form scale scores (after appropriate scale items are reverse coded). Higher scores imply a higher level of subsystem differentiation, or more tolerance for individuality in the context of intimacy and support (Anderson & Sabatelli, 1992).

The DIFS scale employs a "circular questioning" format to assess adolescents' perceptions of how various family members interact with one another (Sabatelli & Anderson, 1991). In the present study, adolescents' perceptions of six dyadic relationships (father/mother, mother/father, father/adolescent, adolescent/father, mother/adolescent, and adolescent/mother) were assessed. That is, six 11-items questionnaires were used. Items included, "My father shows respect for my viewpoint," "My mother shows respect for my father's viewpoint," "My father shows respect for my viewpoint," " I show respect for my father's viewpoint," "My mother shows respect for my viewpoint," "I show respect for my mother's viewpoint."

The potential range of each DIFS scale is from five to 55. The scoring of interactions between dyadic family members is done by multiplying the dyadic scores. For example, the score for the marital subsystem was calculated by multiplying the scores of father/mother and mother/father interaction (Sabatelli & Anderson, 1991).

DIFS scores have been negatively associated with adolescents' alcohol/drinking behaviors and anxiety (Bartle & Sabatelli, 1989). DIFS also is negatively correlated with adolescent anxiety and depression (Sabatelli & Anderson, 1991). For the present sample, the internal consistency reliability (alpha) for the six dyadic subscales ranged from .77 to .88 (See Table 2).

Peer Relationships The Perceived Social Support from Friends scale (PSS-Fr), a 20-item self-report instrument (Procidano & Heller, 1983), was used to assess peer relationships. Important dimensions of the quality of peer relationship such as peer support, interaction and nurturing as experienced by adolescents are assessed by this scale. The respondents are asked to answer "yes," "no" and "don't know" on each item. Items include: "There is a friend I could go to if I was just feeling down, without feeling funny about it later," and "My friends are good at helping me solve problems."

The PSS-Fr has been found to be correlated with psychiatric symptomology, anxiety level and self-disclosure (Procidano & Heller, 1983). Sabatelli and Anderson (1991) also found on their study with 60 college students that PSS-Fr is correlated with feelings of depression. In the present sample, the half-split reliability of PSS-Fr was .72 (See Table 2).

Individuation To assess adolescent individuation from the family of origin, the Intergenerational Fusion subscale (INFUS) from the Personal Authority in the Family System Questionnaire (PAFSQ; Bray, Williamson & Malone, 1984) was used. The INFUS consists of eight items, rated on a 5-point Likert-type scale, which measure the degree of persons' operating in a fused or individuated manner with their parents. Answers are rated from "strongly agree" to "strongly disagree." Higher total scores indicate greater individuation. Sample items include "My present day problems would be fewer or less severe if my parents had been different," and "I am usually able to disagree with my parents without losing my temper."

The INFUS has been correlated with parent-child coalitions, triangulation and detouring of parent conflict in families, in using in a clinical setting and with a non clinical college student population (Bray & Harvey, 1987). For the present sample, the internal reliability coefficient (alpha) was .69 (See Table 2).

Self-Esteem Rosenberg's (1989) well-known 10-item Self-Esteem (RSE) scale was used to assess adolescents' self-esteem. This scale measures an individual's global feeling of self-worth, and each subscale assesses the positiveness of one's attitude toward oneself. Items include: "I feel that I have a number of good qualities," "On the whole, I am satisfied with myself" and "I certainly feel useless at times." The answer choices are "strongly agree," "agree," "disagree" and "strongly disagree." Cronbach's alpha in the present study was .79 (See Table 2).

Table 2: Descriptive Information about the Measures

Scale	no. of items	Mean	S.D.	Possible Range	Observed Range	Skewness	Kurtosis	Cronbach's Alpha
Fa->Adol	11	35.07	8.49	11-55	14.5-52.5	-0.242	-0.614	0.88
Adol->Fa	11	37.16	6.69	11-55	15.5-50.5	-0.446	0.260	0.80
Mo->Adol	11	38.95	7.80	11-55	17.5-52.5	-0.623	0.078	0.86
Adol->Mo	11	37.31	6.12	11-55	21.5-50.5	-0.330	-0.118	0.77
Fa->Mo	11	37.32	7.61	11-55	12.5-54.5	-0.343	0.277	0.87
Mo->Fa	11	41.10	5.71	11-55	22.5-54.5	-0.352	0.269	0.80
Peer Support	20	7.69	2.98	0-20	1.5-14.5	0.148	-0.559	0.53[1]
Individuation	8	24.74	5.19	8-40	12.5-37.5	0.008	-0.222	0.61[2]
Self-esteem	10	22.48	4.78	10-40	12.5-36.5	0.117	-0.441	0.79

[1] Alpha rose to 0.72 after 5 items with low factor loadings were omitted
[2] Alpha rose to 0.69 after 2 items with low factor loadings were omitted

Results

Correlation and multiple regression procedures were used to test the hypothesized model for males and females separately, using marital differentiation, father-adolescent differentiation, mother-adolescent differentiation and peer relationship as predictors of adolescent individuation and self-esteem. GPA was used as a control variable in the present study. Also, because the relationship between individuation and self-esteem seemed to vary as a function of SES in the case of female adolescents, higher and lower SES girls were analyzed separately, using a median split (Med=.041).

As shown in a correlation table (See Table 3), for male adolescents, individuation was positively correlated to each dyadic family differentiation(marital, father-adolescent and mother-adolescent), but not to peer relationships. Also, individuation was negatively related to their self-esteem. For girls of high SES, relationships with both parents were positively related to their individuation, which was negatively related to their self-esteem. For them, peer relationships were related to neither individuation nor self-esteem. Girls of low SES, however, appeared to have no relationship; neither between family differentiation and their individuation, nor between individuation and self-esteem, but their peer relationships were negatively associated with their self-esteem.

Table 3: Correlations for Male and Female Adolescents

	Marsub	Fa-Adol Diff.	Mo-Adol Diff.	Peer Support	Individation	Self-esteem
		Male	Adolescents	(N = 87)		
Marsub	1.00					
Fa-Adol Diff.	0.46 **	1.00				
Mo-Adol Diff.	0.51 **	0.35 **	1.00			
Peer Support	0.11	0.24 *	0.15	1.00		
Individuation	0.37 **	0.44 **	0.35 **	0.04	1.00	
Self-esteem	-0.21	-0.25 *	-0.06	-0.09	-0.23 *	1.00
		Female	Adolescents	High SES	(N = 47)	
Marsub	1.00					
Fa-Adol Diff.	0.37 *	1.00				
Mo-Adol Diff.	0.32 *	0.50 **	1.00			
Peer Support	0.11	-0.12	-0.21	1.00		
Individuation	0.17	0.32 *	0.70 **	-0.15	1.00	
Self-esteem	0.11	-0.04	-0.24	-0.06	-0.40 **	1.00
		Female	Adolescents	Low SES	(N = 21)	
Marsub	1.00					
Fa-Adol Diff.	0.68 **	1.00				
Mo-Adol Diff.	0.54 *	0.56 **	1.00			
Peer Support	0.55 *	0.42	0.45 *	1.00		
Individuation	-0.26	0.26	0.29	0.01	1.00	
Self-esteem	-0.52	-0.38	-0.40	-0.46 *	0.04	1.00

The results also show that there are different patterns in terms of gender and SES (See Table 4). For male adolescents, father-adolescent differentiation was the strongest predictor of adolescent individuation. While the control variables, GPA and SES, were significantly related to adolescent individuation, no other family and peer variables except father-adolescent differentiation were significantly related to their adjustment. The predictors of marital differentiation, father-adolescent differentiation, mother-adolescent differentiation and peer support accounted for 31% of the variance in adolescent individuation ($F(6, 80)=6.08$, $P=.00$) and 24% of the variance in adolescent self-esteem ($F(7,79)=3.48$, $P=.002$).

Female adolescents seem to show different patterns of relationship between family differentiation and psychological adjustment in terms of SES. Among girls of high SES, mother-adolescent differentiation was the strongest predictor of their individuation, while the other variables were not significantly related to adolescent individuation. The predictors accounted for 51% of the variance in individuation ($F(6, 40)=6.88$, $P=.00$) and 26% of the variance in self-esteem ($F(7,39)=1.99$, P=non significant). For the girls of low SES, marital differentiation was the strongest, but negative predictor of adolescent individuation. However, father-adolescent and mother-adolescent differentiations were the positively significant predictors of their individuation. The predictors accounted for 66% of the variance in individuation ($F(6, 14)=4.588$, $P=.009$) and 42% of the variance in self-esteem ($F(7, 13)=1.357$, P=non significant).

More interesting is the finding that for the girls of high SES, adolescents' individuation was negatively related to their self-esteem, which was not the case among the girls of low SES. Independent of adolescent gender or SES, peer support was related to individuation and self-esteem.

Table 4: Regression for Male and Female Adolescent Individuation and Self-Esteem on Family Differentiaton and Peer Support

Individuation									
	Males (N = 87)			Females (N = 68)					
				High SES (N = 47)			Low SES (N = 21)		
Variables	β	beta		β	beta		β	beta	
Step 1									
GPA	0.78	0.20	*	0.39	0.11		0.63	0.18	
SES	-0.21	-0.21	*	0.17	0.02		-0.81	-0.30	
Step 2									
Marsub	0.002	0.19		-0.00	-0.05		-0.009	-0.87	**
Fa-Adol	0.004	0.32	**	-0.00	-0.02		0.006	0.62	*
Mo-Adol	0.002	0.16		0.01	0.70	***	0.005	0.50	*
Peer Support	-0.11	-0.07		0.06	0.04		-0.02	-0.01	
	R^2 = 0.31	F = 6.08	***	R^2 = 0.51	F = 6.88	***	R^2 = 0.66	F = 4.59	**
Self-esteem									
	Males (N = 87)			Females (N = 68)					
				High SES (N = 47)			Low SES (N = 21)		
Variables	β	beta		β	beta		β	beta	
Step 1									
GPA	-1.14	-0.31	**	-0.66	-0.18		-0.32	-0.08	
SES	-0.80	-0.15		-0.60	-0.17		-0.51	-0.37	
Step 2									
Marsub	-0.002	-0.15		0.002	0.20		-0.006	-0.47	
Fa-Adol	-0.001	-0.10		0.00	0.03		0.001	0.12	
Mo-Adol	0.001	0.12		0.00	0.03		0.00	0.08	
Peer Support	-0.16	-0.10		0.32	-0.23		-0.44	-0.30	
Individuation	-0.11	-0.12		-0.39	-0.40	*	-0.32	-0.28	
	R^2 = 0.24	F = 3.48	**	R^2 = 0.26	F = 1.99	+	R^2 = 0.42	F = 1.36	

+ $P < 0.1$ * $P < 0.05$ ** $P < 0.01$ *** $P < 0.001$

Discussion

The primary goal of this study was to test hypothesized relationships among family differentiation, peer support, adolescent individuation and adolescent self-esteem in the context of Korean culture. The hypotheses of the present study were based on theories and empirical studies developed in the U.S.; cultural differences therefore may account for some rejected hypotheses.

First of all, it is notable that father-adolescent differentiation was the most critical factor for male adolescent individuation, while mother-adolescent differentiation was the strongest predictor for female adolescents of high SES, and marital relationship of parents was the strongest predictor for girls of low SES. The result implies three things; 1) different dyadic patterns of distance regulation within the family have different impacts on adolescent individuation, and therefore, measuring different dyadic relationships rather than the global perception about the family is necessary for understanding family relationships exactly; 2) there is a different family interrelationship in terms of gender and SES; 3) the marital relationship may not be the primary dyad in the overall Korean families, which can be seen as dysfunctional from the American viewpoint (Sabatelli & Anderson, 1991; Teyber, 1983). No adolescents, except girls of low SES, reported marital relationship as significantly related to individuation.

Second, when examining the female adolescent of high SES and low SES respectively, it was found that different patterns of family relationships exist in terms of SES. For the girls of high SES, their relationship with their mothers was positively and most strongly related to their individuation, while for the girls of low SES, marital relationship of their parents was the strongest (negative) predictor of their individuation. This is to say that girls of high SES are more individuated when they have more "differentiated relationship" with their mothers while girls of low SES achieve more individuation as there is more disharmony between their parents.

Finally, the negative relationship between individuation of girls of high SES and self-esteem is the most exciting finding. That is, the female adolescents of high SES tended to report lower self-esteem when they were more individuated from their families of origin, and adolescents who have more intergenerational fusion with their parents tend to have higher self-esteem among the Korean female adolescents of high SES. This may be interpreted that girls of high SES are more dominated by traditional gender norm than girls of low SES. Or, this finding may be interpreted as that the theoretical base of family therapy developed in the U.S.'s context may be culturally biased, which has contended that psychological separation or individuation from the family of origin is the criteria of functional individual development and adjustment .

There are some limitations to the present research. Above all, adolescents who attend technical schools or work instead of attending school should have been included to make the sample more representative. Second, the present study was done based only on self-report questionnaires by adolescents. The value of assessing multiple family members' perspectives has been highlighted in recent studies (Anderson & Sabatelli, 1992). Inclusion of the method of interviewing, the process of observation and at least the self-report of the parents would make the data more valid. Third, the individuation instrument used in the present study (INFUS) seems to be problematic. High individuation is viewed as being achieved when there exist both moderate levels of individuality and connectedness, however, INFUS seems to overemphasize the individuality and less emphasize connectedness. Therefore, INFUS tends to offer only limited insight into the dynamic process of individuation. Finally, because this study was done only in the context of Korean culture, it is difficult to declare which and how much can be explained by the cultural variance which is only possible through direct comparative study between two cultures. Cross-cultural studies between American and Korean adolescents, or between American-Korean and Korean adolescents are needed to clearly distinguish between cultural variance and universal patterns which exist within families across cultures.

The present study was based on the proposition that family patterns of distance regulation, and peer relationships are interdependent with individual age-appropriate individuation, which in turn affects individual psychological adjustment. This study was partly successful showing the relationships among family differentiation, adolescent individuation and adolescent self-esteem. However, this study reminds us of the necessity in considering such issues as measurement unit, cultural difference, gender, and social class, when we work on family.

Reference

Allison, M. D., & Sabatelli, R. M. (1988). Differentiation and individuation as mediators of identity and intimacy in adolescence. *Journal of Adolescent Research, 3*, 1-16.

Anderson, S. A., & Sabatelli, R. M. (1990). Differentiating differentiation and individuation: Conceptual and operation challenges. *The American Journal of Family Therapy, 18*, 32-50.

Anderson, S. A., & Sabatelli, R. M. (1992). The differentiation in the family system scales: DIFS.*The American Journal of Family Therapy, 20,* 89-101.

Bartle, S. E., Anderson, S. A., & Sabatelli, R. M. (1989). A model of parenting style, adolescent individuation and adolescent self-esteem. *Journal of Adolescent Research, 4*, 283-298.

Bowen, M. (1978). *Family therapy in clinical practice*. NY: J. Aronson.

Bowerman, C. E., & Kinch, J. W. (1958). Changes in family and peer orientation of children between the fourth and tenth grades. *Social Forces,* 37, 206-211.

Bray, J. H., & Harvey, D. M. (1987). Intimacy and individuation in young adults: Development of the college student version of the PAFS-Q. Unpublished Paper.

Bray, J. H., Williamson, D. S., & Malone, P. E. (1984). Personal authority in the family system: Development of a questionnaire to measure personal authority in intergenerational family processes. *Journal of Marriage and Family Therapy, 10*, 167-178.

Brittain, C. V. (1967). An exploration of the bases of peer-compliance and parent-compliance in adolescence. *Adolescence, 2,* 445-458.

Brown, B. B., & Lohr, M. J. (1987). Peer-group affiliation and adolescent self-esteem: An integration of ego-identity and symbolic-interaction theories. *Journal of Personality and Social Psychology, 52, 47-55.*

Collins, W. A., & Gunnar, M. R. (1990). Social and personality development. *Annual Review of Psychology, 41*, 387-416.

Daniels, J. A. (1990). Adolescent separation-individuation and family transitions. *Adolescence, 25*, 105-116.

Davies, M., & Kandel, D. B. (1981). Parental and peer influences on adolescents' educational plans: Some further evidence. *American Journal of Sociology, 87,* 363-387.

Fleming, W. M., & Anderson, S. A. (1986). Individuation from the family of origin and personal adjustment in late adolescence. *Journal of Marital and Family Therapy, 12*, 311-315.

Gavazzi, S. M., & Sabatelli, R. M. (1990). Family system dynamics, the individuation process, and psychosocial development. *Journal of Adolescent Research, 5,*500-519.

Gecas, V., & Schwalbe, M. L. (1986). Parental behavior and adolescent self-esteem. *Journal of Marriage and the Family, 48,* 37-46.

Gecas, V., & Seff, M. A. (1990). Families and adolescents: A review of the 1980's. *Contemporary families: Looking forward, looking back*. NCFR: Alan Booth.

Hess, R., & Handel, G. (1985). The family as a psychosocial organization. In G. Handel (Ed.), *The psychosocial interior of the family* (3rd ed., pp. 10-24). NY: Aldine.

Hoffman, J. A. (1984). Psychological separation of late adolescents from their parents. *Journal of Counseling Psychology, 31*, 170-198.

Loy, P., & Norland, S. (1981). Parent and peer influence on adolescents' gender expectations. *Youth and Society, 13,* 175-187.

Minuchin, S. (1974). Families and family therapy. Cambridge, MA: Harvard University Press.

Nichols, M. P., & Schwartz, R. C. (1991). *Family therapy* (2nd ed.). MA: Allyn/Bacon.

Procidano, M. E., & Heller, K. (1983). Measure of perceived social support from friends and from family: Three validation studies. *American Journal of Community Psychology, 11*, 1-24.

Reed, F. W., McBroom, W. H., Lindekugel, D. M., Roberts,V., & Tureck, A. M. (1986). Perceived value similarity in the transition to adulthood. *Youth and Society, 17*, 267-285.

Rosenberg, M. (1989). *Society and the Adolescent Self-Esteem*. CT: Wesleyan, University Press.

Sabatelli, R. M., & Anderson, S. A. (1991). Family system dynamics, peer relationships, and adolescents' psychological adjustment. *Family Relations, 40*, 363-369.

Sabatelli, R. M., & Mazor, A. (1985). Differentiation, individuation, and identity formation: the integration of family system and individual developmental perspectives. *Adolescence, 20*, 619-633.

Sebald, H., & White, B. (1980). Teenagers' divided reference groups: Uneven alignment with parents and peers. *Adolescence, 15*, 979-987.

Seltzer, V. C. (1989). *The psychosocial worlds of the adolescent: Public and private*. NY: Wiley.

Smith, D. M. (1985). Perceived peer and parental influences on youths' social world. *Youth and Society, 17*, 131-156.

Rice, K. G., Cole, D. A., & Lapsley, D. K. (1990). Separation-individuation, family cohesion, adjustment to college: Measurement validation and test of a theoretical model. *Journal of Counseling Psychology, 37*, 195-202.

Teyber, E. (1983). Structural family relations: Primary dyadic alliances and adolescent adjustment. *Journal of Marital and Family Therapy, 9*, 89-99.

Treboux, D., & Busch-Rossnagel, N. A. (1990). Social network influences on adolescent sexual attitudes and behaviors. *Journal of Adolescent Research, 5*,175-189.

Wade, N. L. (1987). Suicide as a resolution of separation-individuation among adolescent girls. *Adolescence, 22,* 169-177.

Wechter, S. L. (1983). Separation difficulties between parents and young adults. *The Journal of Contemporary Social Work, 64*, 97-104..

Article 9

Contributions of Interpersonal Relationships to Well-Being in Adulthood: A Comparative Study of Four Life Transitions

Elizabeth L. Paul

In the past two decades, we have witnessed an intensification in research on the contributions of relationships to individual development and physical and psychological well-being. This attention is particularly apparent in studies of infants and children (e.g., Arend, Gove & Sroufe, 1979), and more recently in studies of older adults (e.g., Lee, 1985; Blieszner & Adams, 1992). The role of relationships at other points in adulthood, however, has received relatively little attention (with the exception perhaps of the marital relationship). The purpose of the present study is to explore adults' experiences of relationships and the associations of these varying relationship experiences with individual well-being. Furthermore, do associations between relationships and well-being vary across different transition points in the adult life cycle?

The scant research that exists on relationships in adulthood primarily concentrates on the marital relationship. Marriages in adulthood have predominantly been studied from two vantage points: the communications perspective and the family life cycle perspective. The communications perspective begins with the assumption that marriage and well-being are intricately linked and aims to determine interaction patterns that predict marital resiliency. From a family life cycle perspective, marriages are most often studied in relation to the transition to parenthood and the postparental or "empty nest" phase of the family life cycle in which adult children are no longer living in the parental home. An oft-asked research question regarding both family transitions is: what impact does the transition have on an adult's relationship with his/her spouse? (e.g., Krystal & Chiriboga, 1979; Harris, Ellicott & Holmes, 1986; Bozett, 1985; Cassidy, 1985; Bumagin & Hirn, 1982; Mancini & Bird, 1985). The assumption has been that the parenthood and empty nest phases of the family life cycle are typically experienced as difficult, or in the case of the postparental transition, even traumatic; however, empirical support for this hypothesis is mixed (Raup & Myers, 1989). As many studies have documented resultant improvement in the marital relationship as have pointed to deterioration.

This emphasis in adult research on a *focal* relationship (i.e., the marital relationship), has precluded attention to other salient relationships in adulthood. As a result, the simultaneous importance of other relationships (e.g., friends, children, extended family members) is virtually unknown; rarely are these relationships viewed as contributing to adaptation (i.e., well-being) in adulthood. This is especially surprising in light of the multiplicity of relational demands experienced by many adults (Brody, 1981; Cherlin, 1981; Hagestad, 1984; Richards, Bengtson & Miller, 1989). Recently, the gerontological literature has pointed to the importance of a variety of relationships in later adulthood, such as friends (Blieszner & Adams, 1992; Fiebert & Wright, 1989), siblings (Bedford, 1989; Matthews, Delaney & Adamek, 1989), children (Shehan, Berardo, & Berardo, 1984; Schnaiberg & Goldenberg, 1989; Clemens & Axelson, 1985), and grandchildren (Bozett, 1985). For the most part, the experience of these relationships in adulthood and their associations with adult outcomes has yet to be explored (see Bedford,1989, for a notable exception with regard to adult sibling relationships).

Another common vantage point on relationships in adulthood and other phases of adulthood is their service as supports during times of transition. The supporting role of relationships has been studied in such life transitions as: marriage (Surra, 1988; Milardo, 1982), parenthood (McCannell, 1988; Stueve & Gerson, 1977; Belsky & Rovine, 1984; Miller & Sollie, 1980), divorce/separation (Rands, 1988), retirement (Blumstein & Schwartz, 1983), caretaking for elderly parents (Robinson & Thurnher, 1979), and post-hospitalization of elderly adults (Johnson, 1988). As in studies of the transition to parenthood or the postparental transition, many studies of other transitions focus on changes in the marital relationship. If the role of more than one relationship is considered (e.g., familial and extrafamilial), often a structural social network approach is applied whereby the network composition (e.g., size, density) is studied, disallowing differentiation among relationships or indicators of relational affect or valence (e.g., Gottlieb, 1981). The assumption is that support is always good; thus, the larger the social network, the better.

Antonucci (1989) draws attention to the importance of relational affect or valence in studying relationships in pointing to a serious shortcoming in the social support literature: Bias toward the positive effects of social support. She states: "...social relationships are neither always positive nor always negative—it is important to approach the study of these relationships without directional bias. Whereas social relationships can have a positive effect on health and well-being (Antonucci, 1985), the reverse is also true" (p. 309). Relatedly, Hirsch (1981) argues that supportive relationships can be either limiting or expanding. Antonucci (1989) notes: "The expanding or limiting effects of social relationships are thus far understood in a very restricted sense. It remains for future research to explore the influences of individual life cycle and family stage on the expanding vs. limiting effects of social relationships" (p.311). For this reason, in addition to structural network indicators, relational affect or other subjective indicators are vital in the study of relationships in adulthood. As yet, the associations between structural and affective relationship indicators are not clear; however, current research on older adults' intergenerational family relationships suggests a weak (or nonexistent) association (Mangen, Bengtson & Landry, 1988).

Another criticism of the above-mentioned literature on the role of social support networks during transitions is that we do not know how the experience of one transition compares to other qualitatively different transitions (Lowenthal [Fiske], Thurnher & Chiriboga,

1975, 1990). Without such comparisons, how are we to understand variations across the life course? Fiske and her colleagues aimed to redress this issüe in their longitudinal study of four life cycle transitions, yet very few analyses of the role of relationships during these transitional periods were conducted.

Thus, in moving beyond the above-mentioned limitations in studying the associations between relationships and adult well-being, four steps must be taken:

1) the role of *multiple* relationships (including nuclear and extended family members and friends) must be explored;
2) affective dimensions of relational experiences must be used;
3) experiences of relationships must be considered in relation to adult outcomes such as well-being;
4) the associations between relationships and well-being must be compared across qualitatively different life transitions so that we can gain a more complete picture of the experience and role of relationships in various phases of adulthood.

Secondary analysis of the Fiske, Thurnher and Chiriboga *Longitudinal Study of Transitions in Four Stages of Life* (1968) allows a unique opportunity to apply the above-listed steps, particularly with regard to the experiences of relationships during various adult transitions. This data set is valuable for exploring the associations between relationships and well-being in adulthood because of the wealth of qualitative and quantitative data on relationships, individual development and well-being; the inclusion of four subsamples representing four normative transition groups spanning several stages of adulthood: high school seniors, newlyweds, empty nesters, and retirees; and the longitudinal design (five waves of data collected over a 10 year time period).

In the present paper, findings from a cross-sectional (using data from wave 1 of the Fiske et al study) comparison of the four transition groups will be presented addressing the following questions:

- Do mean affective experiences of several relationships vary across the four transition groups? (Specific relationships covered in these analyses include mother, father, spouse, children, and friends).
- Do indices of well-being vary across the four transition groups?
- Are affective relationship experiences associated with well-being in each transition group?

All analyses include sex as an independent variable, given the demonstrated importance of this variable in other adult relationship research involving comparable cohorts.

Method

Participants

Data were drawn from Fiske, Thurnher & Chiriboga's *Longitudinal Study of Transitions in Four Stages of Life* (1968), archived at the Henry A. Murray Research Center of Radcliffe

College. Participants in this study were 107 men and 109 women, selected from an urban area and representative of middle- and lower-class socioeconomic backgrounds. Participants were contacted five times over a ten year period (overall attrition rate was 26%). Individuals who were confronting one of four normative transitions were selected. Table 1 lists the four pretransitional subgroups represented in the sample and respective information on age range, cohort, and subsample size at wave 1.

Table 1

Age range, cohort, and sex composition of each transition group at Wave 1 (1968)

			N	
	Age range	**Cohort**	**Males**	**Females**
1. High School Seniors	16 - 18	1950-1952	25	27
2. Young newlyweds	20 - 38	1930-1948	25	25
3. Empty nest	39 - 61	1907-1929	27	27
4. Retirement	45 - 67	1901-1923	30	30

Measures

Relational affect. Data on relationships were extracted from the "social systems" section of the semi-structured interviews administered at each wave of data collection. Relational affect is an indicator of the overall emotional valence of participants' experiences in a variety of relationships. Participants were asked to describe their experiences in several relationships and to characterize them as involving primarily positive affect, primarily negative affect or mixed affect (ambivalent). In this way, participants were able to differentiate their relationship experiences where appropriate. Raters then provided final affect valence on a three point scale: (1) predominantly negative, (2) mixed, and (3) predominantly positive.

Intra- and extrafamilial mutuality. Mutuality ratings refer to participants' overall feelings of closeness, trust, and satisfaction in two groups of relationships: family relationships including parents, siblings, spouse, children and grandparents (intrafamilial mutuality) and friendships (extrafamilial mutuality). The scale used for these ratings ranges from 1 (reflecting an absence of trust, closeness and satisfaction in relationships) to 10 (indicating a high degree of closeness, trust and satisfaction in relationships).

Well-being. Following the suggestion of Baruch (1984) to use multiple indicators of well-being, five indicators of well-being were selected from the Fiske et al study for this secondary analysis :

- *Negative Adjective Checklist Index*: The sum of the Adjective Check List self ratings for items drawn from a principal components analysis reflecting negative self-concept. Items include: absentminded, affected, cruel, defensive, dissatisfied, dull, easily embarrassed, easily hurt, hostile, impulsive, jealous, lazy, rebellious, resentful, restless, sarcastic, self-pitying, stubborn, suspicious, touchy, tactless, undecided, unhappy, uninterested, unworthy, withdrawn, worried. The three-point scale ranged from 1=unlike self, to 3=like self. Thus, a high score indicates that the respondent rated many of the negative items as like him/herself.
- *Affective Balance Score based on Bradburn items*. The Bradburn items (cf. Bradburn & Caplovitz, 1969) are coded 1 for "not experienced" to 4 for "experienced often during the past week." The positive total is the sum of the codes for "on top of the world," "excited or interested," "pleased about accomplishment," and "proud." The negative subtotal is the sum of the codes for "very lonely or remote," "depressed," "bored," and "restless." The negative subtotal is subtracted from the positive total and a constant of 13 is added to eliminate negative numbers. Thus a high score is indicative of a high morale.
- *General Morale Index* is based on the sum of responses to "dissatisfied" and "unhappy" on the Adjective Checklist, the Bradburn overall happiness rating, and the rating for the present year on the life evaluation chart.
- *Symptoms*: Total count of positive (yes) responses to the 42-item Symptoms Checklist.
- *Loneliness*: Mean score from a loneliness scale comprised of 10 items using a 4-point scale. A high score reflects high loneliness.

Results

Results addressing each of the three research questions will be presented in turn.

1. Do mean affective experiences of several relationships vary across the four transition groups?

In presenting and discussing the findings associated with the first exploratory question, I will first provide results organized by variable, followed by a more descriptive summary or profile organized by transition group.

To assess differences between men and women and across transition groups, a series of analyses of variance were conducted with relational affect and mutuality scores as dependent variables and transition group and sex as independent variables. Following is a descriptive summary of the findings organized by variable. Means and standard deviations by sex and transition group are given in Figures 1 through 7.

Figure 1: Mean affect to mother by transition group and sex

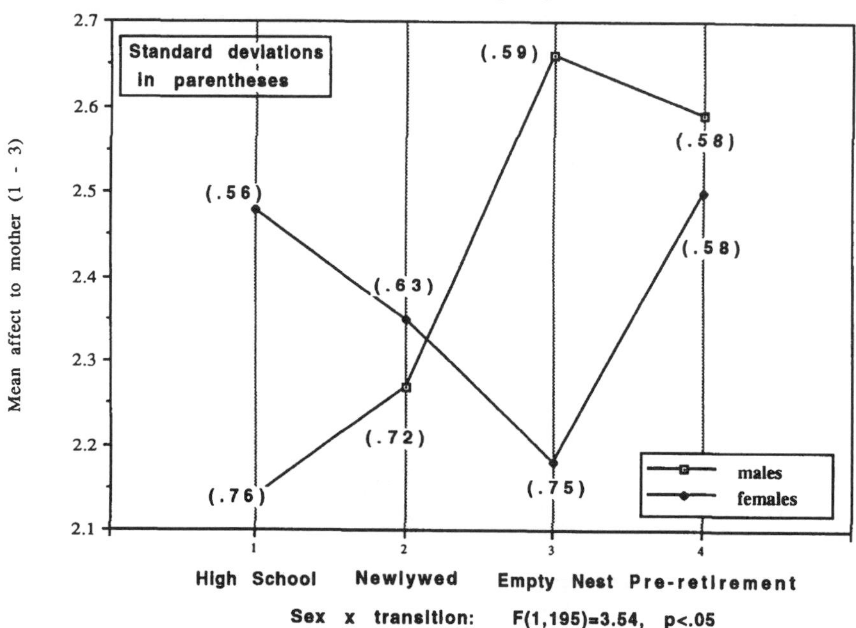

Figure 2: Mean affect to father by transition group and sex

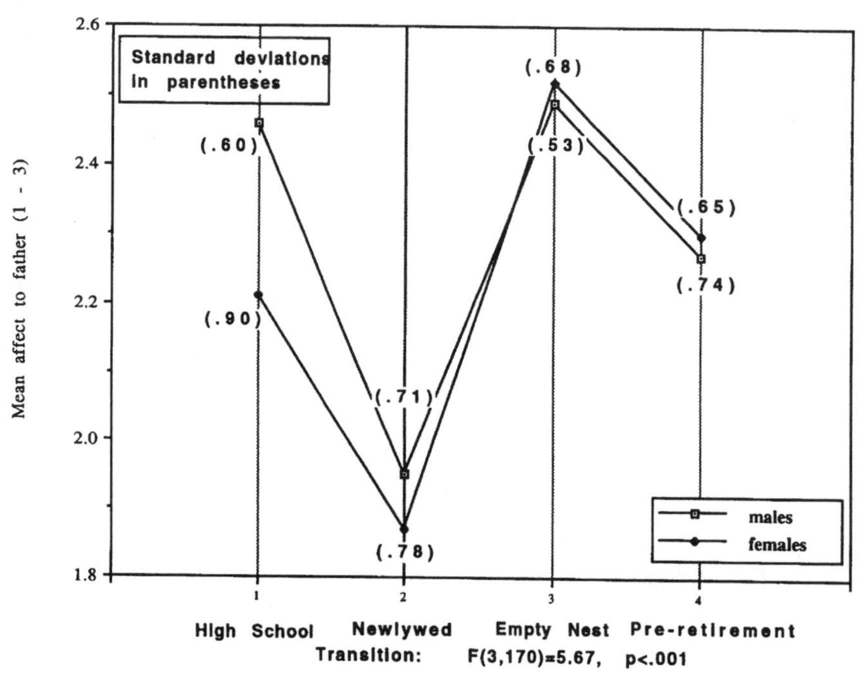

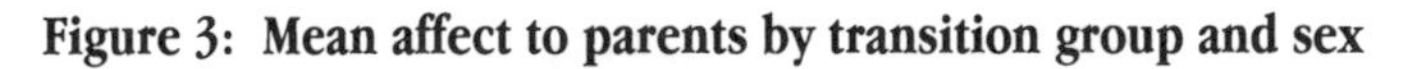

Figure 3: Mean affect to parents by transition group and sex

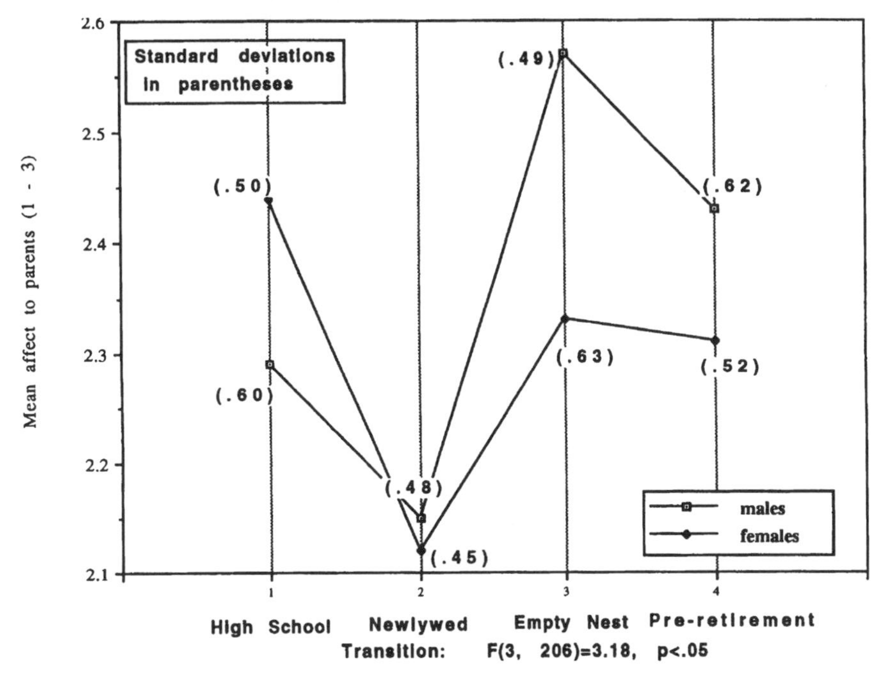

Figure 4: Mean affect to spouse by transition group and sex

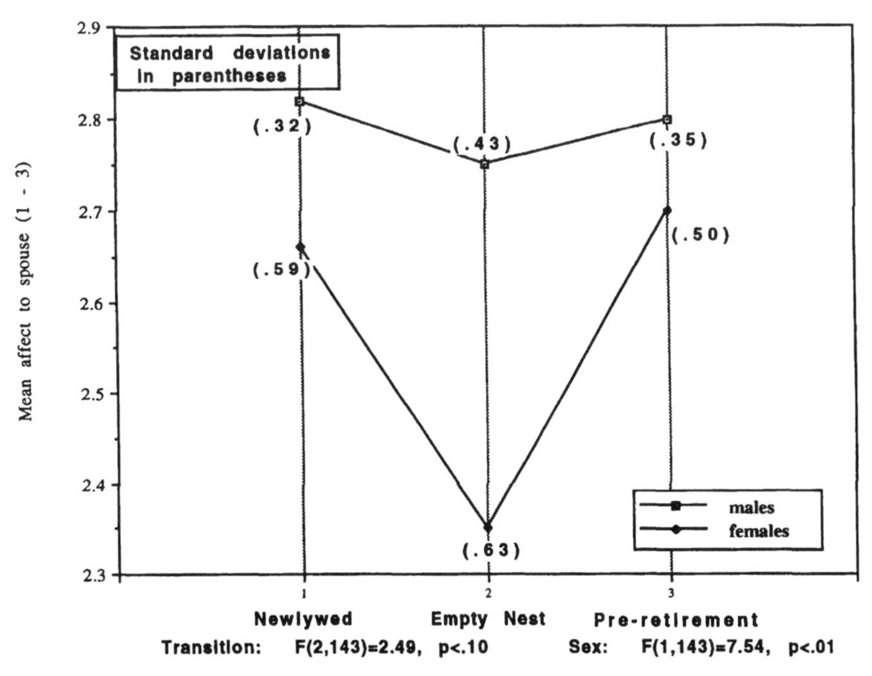

Figure 5: Mean affect to children by transition group and sex

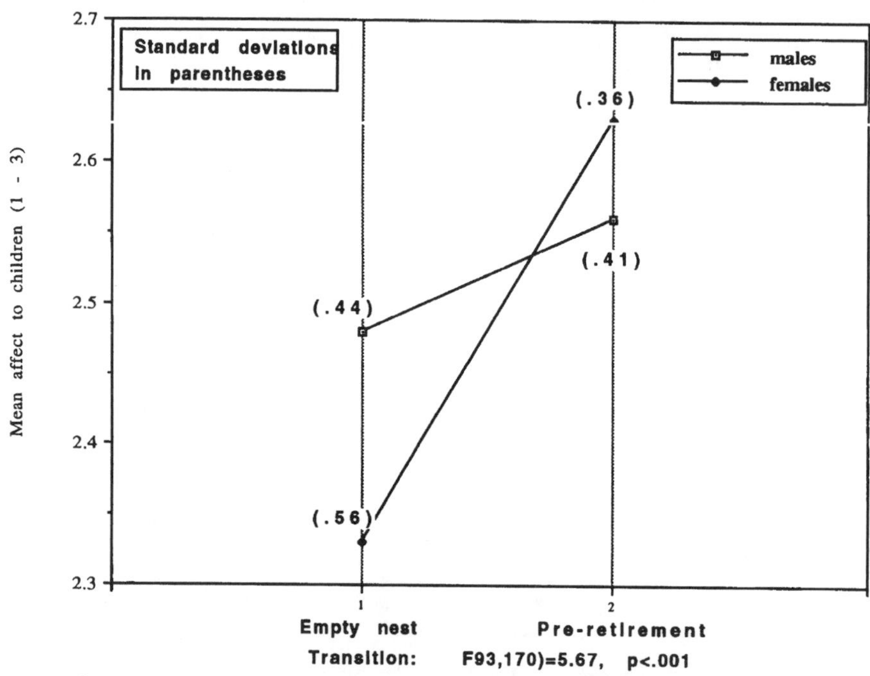

Figure 6: Mean intrafamilial mutuality by transition group and sex

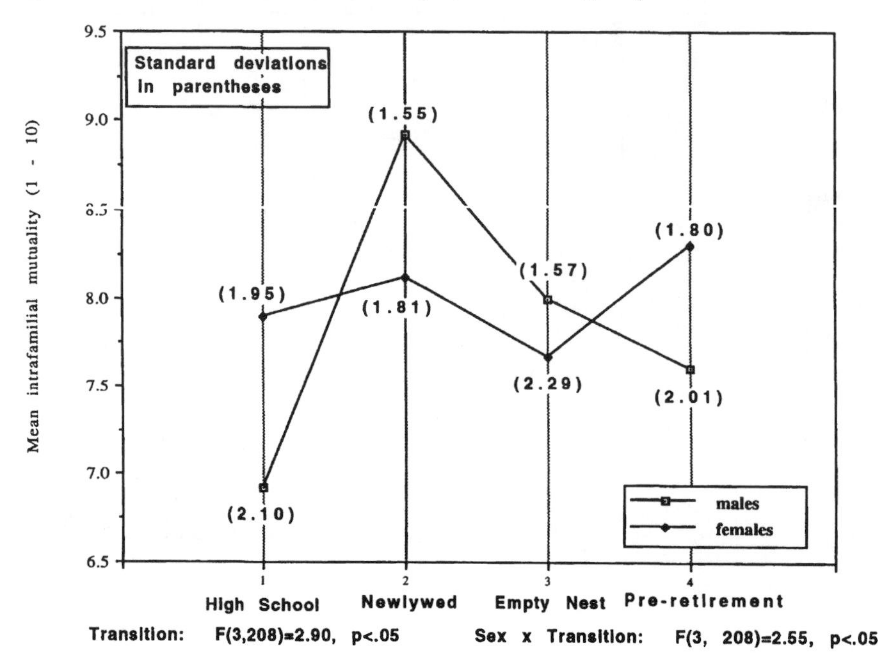

Figure 7: Mean extrafamilial mutuality by transition group and sex

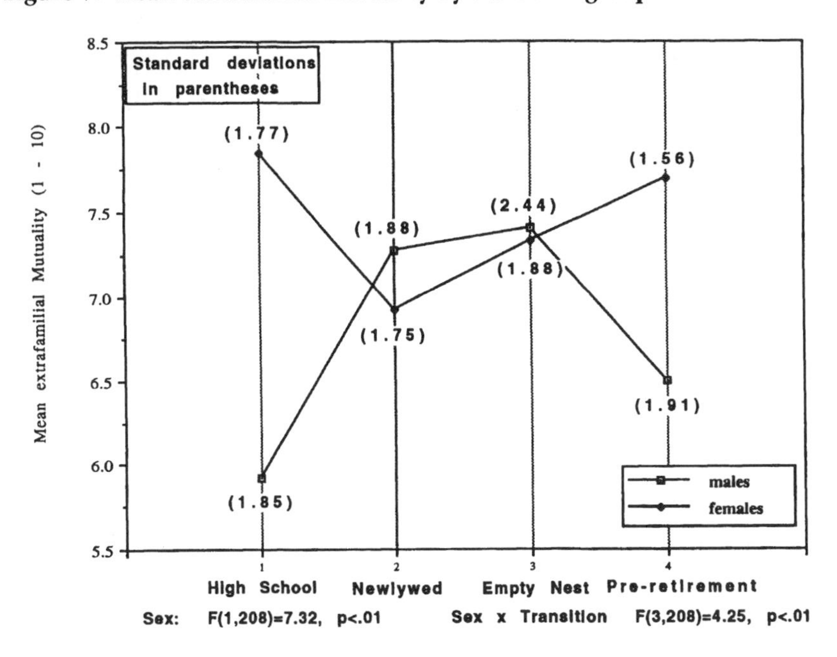

Extrafamilial mutuality. Males and females showed different patterns for extrafamilial mutuality across transition groups (Sex x Transition F(3,208) = 4.25, p<.006). The high school and pre-retirement transitions represented the lowest extrafamilial mutuality for males and highest closeness, trust and satisfaction with friends for females. In comparison, newlywed and empty nest males and females were relatively comparable.

Intrafamilial mutuality. Females showed a relatively comparable pattern of intrafamilial mutuality across transition groups, the highest point seen in pre-retirement. For males, high school seniors showed the lowest intrafamilial mutuality and newlyweds showed the highest. Empty nest and pre-retirement males were lower than newlywed males, but not as low as high school males (Sex x transition F(3,208) = 2.55, p<.05).

Affect toward parents. For both males and females, newlyweds had the lowest affect toward parents. The transition group in which females showed the highest affect toward parents was the high schoolers. The male high was in the empty nest group (Transition F (3,206) = 3.182, p<.025).

Affect toward mother. For the females, the highest affect toward mother was in the high school and pre-retirement transition groups. For the males, the highest affect toward mother was in the empty nest and pre-retirement groups. The group with the lowest affect for females was the empty nest transition group. In contrast, the male low was in the high school group.

Affect toward father. Males and females showed very similar patterns of means across transition groups (Transition $F(3,170) = 5.67, p<.001$). Males started out with higher affect toward fathers than females at the high school transition. The lowest affect toward father for both males and females occurred during the newlywed transition. The highest affect occurred during the empty nest transition.

Affect toward spouse. Males were consistently higher than females on affect toward spouse (Sex $F(1,143) = 7.54, p<.007$). Males also showed more consistency across transition groups in level of affect toward spouse. Females showed a decrease in the empty nest transition group, rising again to above the newlywed level in pre-retirement.

Affect toward children. For both males and females, affect toward children was higher in the pre-retirement transition group than in the empty nest transition group (Transition $F(1,96) = 4.18, p<.04$). Females showed a larger difference between transition groups, indicating higher affect toward children at pre-retirement. Males showed the opposite pattern, showing higher affect at the empty nest transition.

Men and women showed different patterns of mean affective relational experiences across the four transition groups. It is important to note that, on average, participants in this study indicated moderate to high levels of mutuality and affect in many of their relationships. Organizing these findings by transition group might help to elucidate these findings:

In comparing men across transition groups, a varying pattern of highs and lows results. In the high school transition group, males experienced low intra- and extrafamilial mutuality and low affect toward mother. No outstanding positive relational experiences were apparent in the high school transition group. In the newlywed transition group, males experienced high intrafamilial mutuality, and low affect toward parents, especially toward father. The source of their high intrafamilial mutuality appears to be either a result of their new spouse or perhaps from other family members such as siblings. In the empty nest transition group, males experienced high affect toward parents and children. Whereas affect toward parents was lower in the previous two transition groups, empty nest males found positive experiences with their parents. In the pre-retirement transition group, males experienced low extrafamilial mutuality and high affect toward mother. As in the high school transition group, pre-retirement males' friendships dropped in their provision of positive affect. Affect toward mother was highest in this transition group, however.

In comparing females across transition groups, a different pattern emerges. High school females experienced high levels of extrafamilial mutuality and high affect toward parents, especially mother. Affect toward parents, especially father was lower in the newlywed transition group. In the empty nest group, affect toward mother was lower and affect toward father was higher. Affect to spouse was low as well. In pre-retirement, extrafamilial relationships became important again, and affect toward mother and toward children was high.

2. Do indices of well-being vary across the four transition groups?

In terms of transition group differences on well-being, loneliness, general morale, affective balance and self-concept showed increases from low to high well-being across the four transition groups. Symptomatology showed a more varied pattern, differentiated for men and women. Women showed a consistently high pattern of mean symptomatology across the four transition groups. Males showed higher symptomatology only in the newlywed transition group.

Loneliness. Females and males showed a fairly comparable pattern of means starting with higher loneliness among high schoolers and declining over later transition groups. Females in the various transition groups showed a more consistent decline than males. Males showed a decline to the empty nest transition and then a slight increase in pre-retirement (Transition $F(3,195) = 10.88$, $p<.001$).

Symptoms Females, relative to males, showed a comparable pattern of high symptomatology across transition groups (Sex $F(1,195) = 4.44$, $p<.04$). Males had higher symptomatology than females in the newlywed transition group. The lowest symptomatology for males occurred in the empty nest and pre-retirement transition groups.

General morale. Males and females showed a comparable pattern of means indicating increases in morale in the newlywed and pre-retirement transition groups. However, males were lower in morale than females in the high school transition group. For males the lowest morale occurred in high school. In contrast, females' lowest morale occurred in the empty nest transition group (Sex x transition $F(3,195) = 2.88$, $p<.04$).

Affect balance. Males and females showed comparable patterns of means with lowest affect balance in the high school transition group and the high point in the pre-retirement transition group. Females showed slightly higher affect balance than males in the newlywed, empty nest and pre-retirement transition groups (Transition $F(3,195) = 3.39$, $p<.02$).

Negative adjective checklist index. Both males and females showed lower negative self-concept ratings in the newlywed and pre-retirement transition groups. Females showed lower negative self-concept in the newlywed transition than in high school, but males were similar in both transition groups (Transition $F(3,195) = 6.79$, $p<.001$).

3. Are affective relationship experiences associated with well-being in each transition group?

To assess associations between relational affect and mutuality and psychological well-being, Pearson product-moment correlations were computed for men and women separately in each transition group. Statistically significant correlations are indicated on Tables 2 through 5. Following is a brief description of the statistically significant correlations.by sex and transition group.

Table 2.

Associations between relational mutuality and affect and psychological well-being for high school males and females

High School Males

	Negative Self-concept	Affect Balance	General Morale	Symptoms	Loneliness
Mutuality:					
Extrafamilial					
Intrafamilial					
Affect:					
Parents			.59 **		
Father					
Mother			.65**		-.44*
Spouse					
Children					

High School Females

	Negative Self-concept	Affect Balance	General Morale	Symptoms	Loneliness
Mutuality:					
Extrafamilial					
Intrafamilial					
Affect:					
Parents					
Father					
Mother			.43*		
Spouse					
Children					

Note: * $p < .05$
** $p < .01$
*** $p < .001$

Table 3.

Associations between relational mutuality and affect and psychological well-being for newlywed males and females

Newlywed Males

	Negative Self-concept	Affect Balance	General Morale	Symptoms	Loneliness
Mutuality:					
Extrafamilial					
Intrafamilial					
Affect:					
Parents					
Father					
Mother					
Spouse					
Children					

Newlywed Females

	Negative Self-concept	Affect Balance	General Morale	Symptoms	Loneliness
Mutuality:					
Extrafamilial				-.50*	
Intrafamilial	-.51**	.65**	.67**	-.56**	-.56**
Affect:					
Parents	-.41*				
Father					
Mother					
Spouse		.62**	.55**		-.60**
Children					

Note: * p < .05
** p < .01
*** p < .001

Table 4.

Associations between relational mutuality and affect and psychological well-being for empty nest males and females

Empty Nest Males

	Negative Self-concept	Affect Balance	General Morale	Symptoms	Loneliness
Mutuality:					
Extrafamilial					
Intrafamilial					
Affect:					
Parents					
Father					
Mother					
Spouse			.48*		
Children					

Empty Nest Females

	Negative Self-concept	Affect Balance	General Morale	Symptoms	Loneliness
Mutuality:					
Extrafamilial					
Intrafamilial		.40*			
Affect:					
Parents					
Father					
Mother					
Spouse					
Children		.39*			

Note: * $p < .05$
** $p < .01$
*** $p < .001$

Table 5.

Associations between relational mutuality and affect and psychological well-being for pre-retirement males and females

Pre-retirement Males

	Negative Self-concept	Affect Balance	General Morale	Symptoms	Loneliness
Mutuality:					
Extrafamilial					
Intrafamilial					
Affect:					
Parents					
Father					
Mother			.41*		-.41*
Spouse					
Children	-.63**		.45*		

Pre-retirement Females

	Negative Self-concept	Affect Balance	General Morale	Symptoms	Loneliness
Mutuality:					
Extrafamilial	-.38*				
Intrafamilial	-.55**			-.38*	
Affect:					
Parents					
Father					
Mother					
Spouse			.50*		-.53*
Children	-.72**	.47*		-.62**	

Note: * $p < .05$
** $p < .01$
*** $p < .001$

High school transition group. Few significant correlations between relational affect and well-being were found for high schoolers. For males, affect toward parents in general was positively related to general morale. For both males and females, affect toward mother was positively related to general morale. For males, affect toward mother was also negatively related to loneliness.

Newlywed transition group. There were no statistically significant associations between relational mutuality and affect and psychological well-being for newlywed males. For females, extrafamilial mutuality (friends) was negatively related to symptomatology. Females' intrafamilial mutuality was associated with high well-being for **all** indicators of well-being. Affect toward parents was negatively related to negative self-concept. Affect toward spouse was positively related to affect balance and general morale, and negatively related to loneliness.

Empty nest transition group. For males, only affect to spouse was positively related to general morale. For females, intrafamilial mutuality and affect toward children were positively related to affect balance.

Pre-retirement transition group. For males, affect toward mother was positively related to general morale and negatively related to loneliness. Affect toward children was negatively related to negative self-concept and positively related to general morale. For females, extrafamilial mutuality (friend) was negatively related to negative self-concept. Intrafamilial mutuality was negatively related to negative self-concept and negatively related to symptomatology. Affect toward spouse was positively related to general morale and negatively related to loneliness. Affect toward children was negatively related to negative self-concept and symptomatology, and positively related to affect balance.

Of course, direct comparisons of these correlation coefficients can also be made using Fisher's z-transformation so that differences between transition groups in the magnitude of associations can be assessed.

Discussion

The aim of the present study was to explore the affective experiences of several close relationships at different transition points in the adult life course. Furthermore, associations between affective relationship experiences and psychological well-being were of interest. In past research on correlates of adult psychological well-being, the focal interpersonal relationship of interest has typically been the spousal relationship. The assertion in the present study is that adults are embedded in a broader context of important interpersonal relationships which might also be correlates of psychological health and well-being in adulthood. In fact, the network of familial and extrafamilial relationships which adults create might be expected to vary across the life course as various challenges and transitions involve the loss and gain of interpersonal relationships (e.g., getting married, having children, beginning and ending friendships, getting divorced). Furthermore, not only the constellation of relationship networks might change, but so too might the affective experiences of these relationships. Little is known for instance, about the affective experience of relationships with parents across different adult transitions.

Overall, these cross-sectional findings indicate the value of studying the experience of **multiple** close relationships in adulthood. Simply looking to the spousal relationship as the nexus of relational contributions to well-being in adulthood overlooks other important relationships. Furthermore, these findings suggest that adulthood is not a homogeneous experience; in fact, various adult transitions differentially implicate affective relationship experiences and well-being.

More specifically with regard to each transition group, the findings suggest that for high schoolers' well-being, the relationship with mother is especially important. Yet for males, the move out of high school seems especially challenging in that positive familial affect is important for well-being yet more often experienced as negative. These findings are interesting in that they challenge prevailing beliefs of the strong "peer-orientation" of adolescents and show instead the importance of family members as sources of well-being at this challenging time. The male high schoolers appeared to be in a potentially problematic "Catch-22" situation wherein they looked to family members as supports of well-being but experienced predominantly negative affect toward these relations.

Newlywed adults showed some similarities to the high schoolers but diverge from them as well. Newlywed males, though showing no significant associations between relationship experiences and well-being, appeared to be finding an important new relational niche with the advent of their marriage. Family of origin affect was again low, or more ambivalent or negative. For newlywed males, Aldous' (1968) boundary maintenance theory seems to be at play. They seemed to be emphasizing their strong new marital tie over former ties in order to consolidate their new identity which accompanied their new marital status. Newlywed females, on the other hand, showed many intra- and extrafamilial associations with well-being, indicating their multiple relational contributors to well-being.

When facing the empty nest transition, males and females seem to rely on different relationships for their well-being. Males experienced comparatively higher or more positive affect toward family but it was affect toward spouse which was significantly associated with well-being. In contrast, empty nest females showed more diversity in their relationship experiences, with lower or more negative affect toward spouse and mother, and more positive affect to father. Of importance to mid-life females' well-being, however, was affect toward children. Such differences between mid-life husbands' and wives' relational contributors to well-being raise interesting questions from a family systems perspective. What are the ramifications of such assymetry for marital functioning and satisfaction?

Finally, in the transition to retirement, males and females showed a bit more convergence both in affect valence and associations with well-being. Affect was more positive in pre-retirement males' and females' relationships with mother and children and showed significant associations with well-being. Thus, pre-retirement men seem to be disengaging from some aspects of their life (e.g., work) into their family relationships. On the other hand, for females, friendships were characterized by more positive affect and, along with the relationship with spouse, they were of importance to well-being. Perhaps pre-retirement women were enjoying a reprieve from heavy family responsibilities and were re-investing themselves in extra-familial relationships.

Thus, each transition appears to present a different set of relational challenges and resources to adults. The complex patterning of affect toward parents across the four transition groups is noteworthy, indicating the need for further research on this important continuing bond. This is an important finding in light of the prevailing view that family of origin becomes less important to North American adults as they develop. Reciprocally, adults' continuing relationships with their adult children are in need of study. Friendship also appears to have continued salience in adulthood.

Also of interest are the associations between relationship experiences and **specific** indices of well-being—substantiating Baruch's recommendation for using multiple indicators of well-being. A more indepth analysis is called for in teasing out these differential associations. For instance, how is it that during some transitions, relationships with parents are important for adults' general morale but during other transitions they are important for combating loneliness?

In need of further thought are the complex interactions found between transition group and participant sex. Possible interpretations include considerations of cohort differences as well as effects of social class in that this was a lower social class sample, known to be more traditional in sex role attitudes. Although these particular data are cross-sectional, developmental interpretations must also be considered. It is noteworthy that, although men and women diverged in relational experiences in earlier adult transitions with males appearing to be at a deficit, the pre-retirement females **and** males experienced predominantly positive affect in various intra- and extra-familial relationships which, in turn, were important for their well-being. Longitudinal analyses will help to discern possible developmental progressions.

Relatedly, it is important to note that findings reported in this paper are based on aggregates or means across individuals within transition groups. Scrutiny of the standard deviations associated with the means indicates often substantial within-group variability. In fact, in many cases, female subgroups had higher standard deviations than male subgroups. Thus, future analyses should examine the within-transition group variability in affective relationship experiences and associations with well-being.

A challenge for future research is the development of more differentiated relationship variables. Relational affect has served as a useful global indicator yet provides only limited information on important specific relationship properties. Furthermore, contemporary perspectives view positive and negative affect as distinct dimensions. Thus, the Fiske data are presently being recasted and recoded so that such relationship variables as closeness, conflict, satisfaction and contact can be included in the planned longitudinal analyses. Recoding enables the inclusion of additional important relationships mentioned by participants such as siblings, grandparents, grandchildren, cousins, and other extended family members and associates. Such is the value of rich, qualitative archival data.

The analyses reported herein provide a foundation for the consideration of relational contexts across several adult transitions and form the base for further longitudinal analyses of changes over time in affective relational experiences and their associations with well-being.

Longitudinal analyses based on these data (Paul,1993) are aimed at exploring transitions as processes, occurring over time. The present cross-sectional analyses reflect participants' experiences just prior to an expected transition. The longitudinal analyses address such questions as: Do relationship experiences and associations with well-being change as the transition progresses? For example, research on the marital transition suggests that there is a "honeymoon" period in which very high affect is experienced in the context of the marital relationship. Does this high affect subside over time? How does affect in this relationship change relative to affect in other relationships? Longitudinal case analyses have revealed differentiation of relationship experiences within multiple ties and flux in relational affect and associations with well-being as transitions proceed, especially for individuals in the high school and newlywed transition groups. Individuals in the empty nest and pre-tirement groups seem to experience more constancy in their relationships, however they typically experience flux in a small subset of relationships against this stable backdrop. For most individuals, sibling relationships continued to be prominent, some reporting more positive affect as the transition progressed. Similarly, relationships with parents remained an emotionally charged relationship for many participants. Future analyses, including individual-level analyses, on the entire sample will enable more thorough investigation of the experience and importance of relationships in adulthood.

Author's notes

This research used the *Longitudinal Study of Transitions in Four Stages of Life, 1968-1980* data set [made accessible in 1979 and 1981, raw and machine-readible data files]. These data were collected by M. Fiske, M. Thurnher, and D. Chiriboga and are available through the archive of the Henry A. Murray Research Center of Radcliffe College, Cambridge, Massachusetts (Producer and Distributor).

Funding for this research was received from the Midlife Research Program.

I am grateful to Junko Kaji, Kim Santagate, Amy Baumgartel, Nga Pham, and Niku Thomas for their assistance in data coding. Thanks also go to Dr. Jacquelyn B. James and Dr. Victoria H. Bedford for their insights regarding this project.

References

Aldous, J. (1968). Intergenerational visiting patterns: Variations in boundary maintenance as an explanation. *Family Process, 6*(2), 235-251.

Antonucci, T. C. (1989). Understanding adult social relationships. In K. Kreppner & R. M. Lerner (Eds.). *Family systems and life-span development*. Hillsdale, NJ: Lawrence Erlbaum Associates.

Arend, K., Gove, F. I., & Sroufe, L. A. (1979). Continuity of individual adaptation from infancy to kindergarten: A predictive study of ego-resiliency and curiosity in preschoolers. *Child Development, 58*, 958-959.

Baruch, G. K. (1984). The psychological well-being of women in the middle years. In G. K. Baruch & J. Brooks-Gunn (Eds.), *Women in midlife*. New York: Plenum Press.

Bedford, V. H. (1989). A comparison of thematic apperceptions of sibling affiliation, conflict, and separation at two periods of adulthood. *International Journal of Aging and Human Development, 28*(1), 53-66.

Belsky, J., & Rovine, M. (1984). Social network contact, family support, and the transition to parenthood. *Journal of Marriage and the Family, 46*, 455-462.

Blieszner, R., & Adams, R. G. (1992). *Adult friendship*. Newbury Park, CA; Sage Publications.

Blumstein, P., & Schwartz, P. (1983). *American couples*. New York: Morrow.

Bozett, F. W. (1985). Male development and fathering throughout the life cycle. *American Behavioral Scientist, 29* (1), 41-54.

Bradburn, N. M., & Caplovitz, D. (1969). *Reports on happiness: A pilot study of behavior related to mental health*. Chicago: Aldine.

Brody, E. M. (1981). "Women in the middle" and family help to older people. *The Gerontologist, 21*(5), 471-480.

Bumagin, V. E., & Hirn, K. F. (1982). Observations on changing relationships for older married women. *American Journal of Psychoanalysis, 42*(2), 133-142.

Cassidy, M. L. (1985). Role conflict in the postparental period: The effects of employment status on the marital satisfaction of women. *Research on Aging, 7*(3), 433-454.

Cherlin, A. (1981). A sense of history: Recent research on aging and the family. In B. Hess & K. Bond (Eds.), *Leading edges.* Washington, DC: National Institute of Health.

Clemens, A. W., & Axelson, L. J. (1985). The not-so-empty nest: The return of the fledging adult. *Family Relations, 34*(2), 259-264.

Fiebert, M. S., & Wright, K. S. (1989). Midlife friendships in an American faculty sample. *Psychological Reports, 64*(3, Part 2), 1127-1130.

Fiske, M., & Chiriboga, D. (1990). *Change and continuity in adult life*. San Francisco, CA: Jossey-Bass, Inc.

Gottleib, B. J. (Ed.)(1981). *Social networks and social support*. Newbury Park, CA: Sage Publications.

Hagestad, G. O. (1984). The continuous bond: A dynamic multigenerational perspective on parent-child relations between adults. In M. Perlmutter (Ed.), *Minnesota Symposium on Child Psychology, 17*, Princeton, NJ: Lawrence Erlbaum Associates.

Harris, R. L., Ellicott, A. M., & Holmes, D. S. (1986). The timing of psychosocial transitions and changes in women's lives: An examination of women aged 45 to 60. *Journal of Personality and Social Psychology, 51*(2), 409-416.

Hirsch, B. J. (1981). Social networks and the coping process: Creating personal communities. In B. H. Gottlieb (Ed.), *Social networks and social support*. Beverly Hills, CA: Sage Publications.

Johnson, C. L. (1988). Relationships among family members and friends in later life. In R. M. Milardo (Ed.), *Families and social networks*. Beverly Hills, CA: Sage Publications.

Krystal, S., & Chiriboga, D. (1979). The empty nest process in midlife men and women. *Maturitas, 1*, 215-222.

Lee, G. R. (1985). Kinship and social support of the elderly: The case of the United States. *Aging and Society, 5*(1), 19-38.

Lowenthal (Fiske), M., Thurnher, M., Chiriboga, D., & Associates (1975). *Four stages of life: A comparative study of women and men facing transitions.* San Francisco, CA; Jossey-Bass, Inc.

Mancini, J. A., & Bird, G. W. (1985). Six steps toward a happy midlife marriage. *Medical aspects of human sexuality, 19*(10), 163-177.

Mangen, D., Bengtson, V., & Landry, P. (Eds.) (1988). *Measurement of intergenerational relations.* Newbury Park, CA: Sage Publications.

Matthews, S. H., Delaney, P. J., & Adamek, M. E. (1989). Male kinship ties: Bonds between adult brothers. *American Behavioral Scientist, 33*(1), 58-69.

McCannell, K. (1988). Social networks and the transition to motherhood. In R. M. Milardo (Ed.), *Families and social networks*. Beverly Hills, CA: Sage Publications.

Milardo, R. M. (1982). Friendship networks and the transition to motherhood. In R. M. Milardo (Ed.), *Families and social networks*. Beverly Hills, CA: Sage Publications.

Miller, B., & Sollie, D. (1980). Normal stresses during the transition to parenthood. *Family Relations, 29*, 459-465.

Paul, E. L. (1993). A longitudinal analysis of midlife interpersonal relationships and well-being. Paper to be included in a volume edited by M. Lachman & J. B. James, University of Chicago Press.

Rands, M. (1988). Changes in social networks following marital separation and divorce. In R. M. Milardo (Ed.), *Families and social networks*. Beverly Hills, CA: Sage Publications.

Raup, J. L., & Myers, J. E. (1989). The empty nest syndrome: Myth or reality? *Journal of Counseling and Development, 68*(2), 180-183.

Richards, L., Bengtson, V., & Miller, R. (1989). The "generation in the middle": Perceptions of changes in adults' intergenerational relationships. In K. Kreppner & R. M. Lerner (Eds.), *Family systems and life-span development.* Hillsdale, NJ: Lawrence Erlbaum Associ-

ates.
Robinson, S., & Thurnher, M. (1979). Taking care of aged parents: A family-cycle transition. *The Gerontologist*.
Schnaiberg, A., & Goldenberg, S. (1989). From empty nest to crowded nest: The dynamics of incompletely-launched young adults. *Social Problems, 36*(3), 251-269.
Shehan, C. L., Berardo, D. H., & Berardo, F. M. (1984). The empty nest is filling again: Implications for parent-child relationships. *Parenting Studies, 1*(2), 67-73.
Stueve, C. A., & Gerson, K. (1977). Personal relations across the life cycle. In C. Fischer (Ed.), *Networks and places: Social relations in the urban setting*. New York: Free Press.
Surra, C. A. (1988). The influence of the interactive network on developing relationships. In R. M. Milardo (Ed.), *Families and social networks*. Beverly Hills, CA: Sage Publications.

Article 10

Changes in Norms and Behaviors Concerning Extended Kin in Taiwan, 1963-1991

Robert M. Marsh
Cheng-kuang Hsu

Students of the family and kinship in various societies have long been concerned with the strength of ties among extended kinrelatives of blood, marriage and adoption through one's father, mother, siblings, spouse and children. An analytical distinction is often drawn between **ideal** normative patterns and **actual** behavioral patterns of extended kinship. In the present study of the Taiwanese (Hokkien and Hakka) population of Taipei, we attempt to assess the strength of ideal and actual extended kinship ties.

Ideal, normative extended kinship ties: How do the Taiwanese answer the following questions: To what range of extended kin do we owe obligations? Should we maintain close relationships with extended kin? Give them economic or other forms of aid? Obedience? Respect? Do we have the same obligations to extended kin as to our parents?

Actual, behavioral extended kinship ties: There are various occasions which Taiwanese persons may or may not use to get together with extended kin. These include annual ceremonial occasions (New Year's, *pai pai* festivals, ancestor worship at the *Ch'ing Ming* festival) and certain **rites of passage** (marriage, child birth or *man yueh*, an elder kin's birthday or *chu shou*, and funerals). Thus we shall infer that ideal kinship ties among the Taiwanese are strong to the extent that obligations of several kinds are prescribed as being owed to a wide range of extended kin; and actual kinship ties will be regarded as strong to the extent that the Taiwanese frequently attend a variety of types of gatherings with extended kin.

Do ideal and actual patterns of extended kinship solidarity follow the same parallel course during societal modernization—both decreasing, both increasing, or both remaining unchanged? That both would follow the same course was a common assumption in earlier theory. Our data from Taiwan indicate that ideal obligations to extended kin declined, while actual behavioral ties to extended kin increased. We explore and attempt to explain this unexpected finding. Tracing changes in the strength of ideal and actual extended kinship ties in relation to broader social changes poses the difficult problem of combining systematic, representative samples of populations with the relatively long time spans required for significant societal changes to occur. The two common research strategies represent tradeoffs. The farther back in time we go, the more difficult it becomes to obtain representative samples of data on people's sense of their ideal obligations and actual behavioral ties to extended kin. Representative sample surveys can overcome this problem, but tend to have data from only a single point in time or at best a short time period. In the present study of the Taiwanese population of Taipei, the data come from two comparable representative sample surveys conducted 28 years apart; the first in 1963, when Taiwan's urbanization and industrialization were just on the verge of the significant rates of change that were to come, and the second in 1991, by which time Taiwan had become a highly urbanized, industrialized and relatively affluent society.

After considering theoretical arguments for why kinship solidarity might be expected to change in certain ways, and the historical background of kinship in Taiwan, we shall describe our research methods and findings. Finally, the implications of the findings will be discussed.

Social Development and Extended Kinship Solidarity

The strength or solidarity of extended kinship ties can be thought of as varying between two theoretical poles. At one extreme is an organized corporate extended kinship system, e.g., a traditional Chinese patrilineal lineage. Ideal extended kinship solidarity is high with mutual obligations prescribed among numerous kin. Actual kinship solidarity may be high only among the elite or economically more prosperous strata because poverty, high mortality (short life span) and other factors may restrict extended kinship solidarity among the mass of the population.

Modernization theory contends that "all social systems are moving fast or slowly toward some form of the conjugal family system and also toward industrialization" (Goode, 1982, p.176). For a society like pre-twentieth century China, whose ideal kinship pattern was the organized corporate patrilineage, Goode (1982) predicted that the change in extended kinship during industrialization would be toward a noncorporate kinship network. In the modern conjugal family system that emerges as both the ideal and the actual pattern, although the nuclear family's network of ties with extended kin is weaker than in the previous corporate patrilineal kinship system, the nuclear family is still part of a network of kin ties. Thus, even in a modern conjugal family system, "[a] majority of . . . families report that they engage in many types of exchanges with people in their kinship network, and these range from simple services to large gifts" (Goode, 1982, p. 109).

The implications of this line of thought for our Taipei data are as follows: Between the 1963 and 1991 surveys, Taipei, like the rest of Taiwan, experienced very rapid economic development, industrialization, and postindustrial modernization. These are among the most important conditions making for change in extended kinship solidarity. They make for change by increasing the amount of spatial and social mobility, by developing more spheres of life structured in nonkinship terms, and in other ways. Following Goode, we hypothesize that Taipei's rapid development has weakened especially the normative, ideal aspects of extended kinship solidarity. "Thus, the couple cannot count on a large number of kinfolk for help, just as these kin cannot call upon the couple for services. Neither couple nor kinfolk have many **rights** with respect to the other, and so the reciprocal **obligations** are few (Goode, 1963, p. 8)."

As for actual interaction with extended kin, the basis for an hypothesis is less clear. Goode, on a single page (Goode, 1982, p. 109) states, on one hand that interactions with kin "do not occur as frequently as in the past, "but on the other hand, "each family unit maintains contacts with a wide range of relatives." The conjugal family unit may be more independent of the extended kinship network than in the past, but if interaction with extended kin is less **obligatory**, more a matter of **choice,** it may increase, or at least not decline in frequency. This could happen under a variety of circumstances, such as the need to use kin contacts for migrant adjustments to life in Taipei, and the ease and cost of transportation and communication in overcoming spatial distance from kin.

Extended Kinship Solidarity in Taiwan

The source provinces from which the ancestors of the Taiwanese population came, Fujian and Guangdong, had extended corporate patrilineal lineages, as an ideal family pattern for all strata, if an actually approximated pattern only among the elite (Freedman, 1958, 1966). In the pioneer society of Taiwan, however, lineages were weaker. Large localized lineages generally didn't survive the move to Taiwan, where settlers came either as individuals or in small family groups. To the extent that lineages did survive in Taiwan, they were of relatively small size and minimum formalization. In eighteenth century Taiwan, the usual bases of social organization were the native place on the mainland, the community temple and a common surname (at that time, 20 per cent of the population were named either Chen or Lin). These factors, rather than powerful lineages, were the bases of mutual aid.

Land Reform in the 1950's deprived lineages of most of their economic underpinnings, though not necessarily of their ritual and other bases of solidarity (Cohen, 1969). In more recent times, Barrett (1989, p. 467) contends, "most lineages (if they existed at all) had little power over the sale or rental of land." Lineage segmentation occurred, in which a branch of a lineage established its own corporate estate. Ancestral halls *(tsungtz'u)* owned and managed by a lineage and used for the rituals of the whole lineage, were possible only for the wealthy and powerful lineages. Harrell (1982, pp.124-134) found that agnatic ties (between blood relatives) may be important in forming dyadic bonds, but they share this importance with ties of affinity, matrilineality, sworn kinship and simple friendship. There was no great solidarity among agnatic kin.[1] Thus, Taiwanese local communities continue to be defined more in terms of territoriality and ritual—the local temple and temple deity—than extended kinship.

Kinship ties are not absent, however. Even when the only common property of a lineage is a nominal—an ancestral tablet in the main room of one's home—it symbolizes the unity of the domestic line. Members of the lineage may gather and worship their ancestors on New

Year's Day, with each household bringing offerings. Members of the lineage help each other at marriages and funerals of fellow members (Suenari, 1986). Gallin notes that some but not all kinds of traditional rural lineage organization became weakened in Taipei. Kin based relationships continue to be significant for migrants to Taipei, "even though in the city these relationships function only on an individual rather than a group level" (Gallin, 1978, p. 281). Greenhalgh (1984) found that in urban Taiwan, although the extended kin group breaks up into smaller nuclear households, resources continue to flow between units of the larger *chia*, as members seek mobility and adaptation in the city.

The 1963 and 1991 Taipei Surveys

In 1963, the first author of this paper conducted a survey research project to study social stratification, class and mobility, work, family and kinship, and attitudes toward social issues in Taipei, Taiwan. In the sampling, the universe was defined as male Taiwanese household heads between the ages of 20 and 69, living in Taipei city. Taipei in 1963 was divided into 10 administrative districts, *ch'ü*, which were subdivided into 447 *li*, and the *li* into 7,391 *lin* (neighborhoods). The stages of the systematic, multistage area sampling were accordingly: (1) a selection of every eighth *li* in the city after a random number start; (2) within the 56 sample *li*, a selection of every third *lin;* (3) within the 317 sample *lin*, a selection of every fifth Taiwanese household whose head was male and between 20 and 69 years old. The sampling stages were carried out in the 10 district offices (*ch'ü kung so*) where registers are kept for all households. Interviews were completed with 507 respondents.

The 1991 survey used the same interview schedule questions and the same sampling design, but given the 28 year time lapse, we made no attempt to reinterview the same individuals. Between 1963 and 1991, the city of Taipei's population had grown from 1,027,648 to 2,719,659 and its area had expanded by administrative incorporation of adjacent area units from 67 to 272 square kilometers. The percent of the Taipei population that was Taiwanese rather than mainlander Chinese has risen from 61.7 to 73.1. Taipei Municipality by 1991 was divided into 12 *ch'ü* , 440 *li* and 9,818 *lin*. *Ch'ü* had between 18 and 56 *li*. We stratified *ch'ü* into those with fewer than 30 *li*, from each of which we drew two sample *li*, and those with 30 or more *li*, from each of which we drew three sample *li*. The target sample of each district (*ch'ü*) was proportionate to the estimated number of Taiwanese households in all Taipei who lived in that district. Every nth household in the sample *li* that had a male Taiwanese head between 20 and 69 years old was selected for the sample. This sampling interval varied across *li* due to variations in the proportion of Taiwanese households. The 545 people interviewed were living in 431 of the 749 sample *lin* in the the 34 sample *li*. In both 1963 and 1991, interviews were conducted in respondents' homes by students from National Taiwan University and other local universities. In summary:

	1963	1991
Number of *ch'ü* sampled	10	12
Number of *li* sampled	56	4
Number of *lin* sampled	317	749
Number of households sampled	642	1282
Number of completed interviews[2]	507	545

Having comparable survey data spanning 28 years—a generation—is of great value in the testing of theories about long-run processes of social change.

The Trend Toward Nuclear Households in Taipei

The standard classification of households units of coresidence whose members eat together includes three types of family units (*chia*): (1) the **nuclear** family of a married couple and their unmarried children; (2) the **stem** family of a married couple, one of their married children (usually a son) and spouse, and the unmarried grandchildren; and (3) the **joint** family of the parents, two or more of their married children (usually sons) with their spouses and children and any unmarried siblings of the middle generation. Large compounds permitted joint family households to exist in some parts of rural Taiwan. The greater cost of housing in crowded urban areas like Taipei reduced this possibility. It is useful to know what proportion of households in Taipei are exclusively nuclear[3], because while this need not preclude solidarity with extended kin, it may make it more difficult than when more households were of the stem or joint family type.

The per cent of the Taipei sample households that were exclusively nuclear significantly increased, from 58.2% in 1963 to 72.3% in 1991 (phi = .15**)[4]. Thus, by 1991, only 27.7% of the sample households had any extranuclear kin living with them. For some readers, the latter figure will attest to the continued importance of extended family coresidence in Taipei, but the trend is clearly toward the nuclear family as the most common type of household.

Norms Concerning Obligations to Extended Kin

Traditionally, the "six kinship ties" (*liu ch'in*) were those between husband and wife, parents and children, brothers, the children of brothers, the children of brothers' children, and the children of brothers' childrens' children. In addition to these, one also had mutual obligations to the immediate relatives on one's mother's and wife's sides of the family. It was this greater kinship circle, not the household alone, that constituted the importance of kinship in China. If one had none of the "six kinship ties" to rely on (*liu ch'in wu k'ao*), it was said that "one had nobody to turn to." In a corporate kin group like the patrilineage there were collective rights and duties which particular members of the extended kin group enforced over other members. Kin members would expect each other to conform to a relatively wide range of kinship obligations.

Our Taipei interview schedule refers to obligations as *ying-chin te tse-jen.* After asking what obligations people[5] have to their parents *(fu-mu)*, we next asked whether people have obligations to relatives *(ch'in-ch'i)* who are not one's parents.[6] Just under half of the 1963 Taipei sample (47.9%) and just over half (51.6%) in 1991 said people **do not** have obligations to other relatives (Table 1, row 1), a nonsignificant difference between the 1963 and the 1991 samples. The initial reaction of nearly half of the Taiwanese respondents was to eschew obligations toward non parental extended kin.

Table 1—Kinship Solidarity: Norms Concerning Obligations To Kin in 1963 and 1991, Taipei Sample

	% 1963	% 1991	Tau-c	Phi
1. Children have obligations to kin other than parents	52.1	48.4		.04
2. Children have obligations to "all" or "most" kin (rather than to "few" or "no kin")	38.7	30.1	-.04	
3. Specific obligations to kin				
A. Spontaneouly mentiond (open-ended)				
1. Non-economic aid, e.g., help with chores at home	23.5	20.7		.03
2. Economic aid	8.5	8.6		.00
3. Respect	7.1	9.5		.04
4. Emotional harmony	5.5	9.4		.07*
5. Maintain close social contact	4.7	7.3		.05
6. Other obligations	2.8	1.5		.05
7. Same obligations as to parents	2.6	1.1		.05
B. Pre-coded obligations				
1. Maintain close, intimate relationships	93.1	42.0		.54**
2. Respect	91.9	46.6		.49**
3. Obedience	66.7	20.9		.46**
4. Economic aid	51.9	16.1		.39**
5. Help them at work & at home	46.5	20.9		.27**
6. Same obligations as to parents	45.2	18.0		.29**
7. Other obligations	20.7	0.002		.34**
N on which percentages are computed	507	545		

Responses to parts A and B are based on questions to which multiple responses could be give, and the percents in part B sum to more than 100%.

*p<.05; **p<.01

For those who said there are obligations to extended kin other than parents, we first asked: "To which relatives do people have obligations?" The 52% of the 1963 respondents who said obligations were owed to kin specified the following kin: all relatives, i.e., those in one's patrilineage (*tsung tsu*), relatives through one's mother and affinal relatives through one's wife (13.1%); patrilateral and matrilateral kin (9.5%); patrilateral kin only (8.5%); unspecified "close relatives" (6.4%); relatives with whom you have good personal relations (2.4%); and various other sets of kin (7.0%); 5.2% said obligations were owed to kin, but did not indicate which kin. Among the 48% of the 1991 respondents who believe obligations are owed to kin, the following kin were named: "all blood relatives and relatives through marriage" (8.8%); various sets of kin we coded as a medium range of extended kin, e.g., close blood relatives, relatives with whom you have close personal relationships, blood relatives within three degrees of kinship, elders in the blood line, relatives through one's father and mother (21.3%); and various sets of kin we coded as "a few relatives," e.g., grandparents, or siblings, or father's and mother's brothers, or "relatives who have economic problems" (18%).

We re-coded these responses into four categories in order to make a comparison of the 1963 and 1991 **range of kin** to whom obligations are owed. The per cent who said obligations are owed to "all kin" or "most kin" (as opposed to "few" or "no kin") was 38.7% in 1963 and 30.1% in 1991, a nonsignificant decline (Table 1, row 2). Those who believe people owe obligations to extended kin have not significantly narrowed the range of extended kin to whom these are owed. Table 1 lists particular obligations to extended kin in 1963 and 1991, in order of the frequency of their support in the 1963 sample. In Part A we list the spontaneously mentioned obligations in response to the open-ended question, "What kinds of obligations do children have toward relatives?" The most common was: provide services to kin, e.g., help with chores at home, mentioned by 23.5% in 1963 and 20.7% in 1991 (a nonsignificant decline). This is coded "non-economic aid," to distinguish it from the next category, economic aid, e.g., give money, financial aid to kin, mentioned by nine percent of the respondents in both 1963 and 1991.

Each of the other obligations in Part A was mentioned spontaneously by fewer than 10% of the respondents in 1963 and 1991. This is noteworthy because in the interview schedule, the open-ended obligations to kin question came immediately after a pre-coded question, "Which of the following obligations do you think children owe to their parents?" Having just been asked about five specific types of obligations to parents-obedience, respect, maintain a close relationship, help with work and house chores, and financial aid—the tendency by most respondents not to draw on these in volunteering obligations toward other kin is all the more striking. Only one of the types of obligations to kin spontaneously mentioned changed significantly: maintaining emotional harmony with relatives increased significantly from 5.5% in 1963 to 9.4% in 1991 (phi = .07*).

Part B of Table 1 presents the responses to the precoded obligations to kin questions. When presented with specific kinds of obligations, the 1963 respondents were much more likely to agree that people have these obligations than they had been in the previous open-ended responses. In 1963, the ranking of obligations by per cent agreement was: maintain close, intimate relationships (93.1%), respect (91.9%), obedience (66.7%), economic aid (51.9%), help at work and at home (46.5%), the same obligations as to parents (45.2%) and miscellaneous other obligations (20.7%). **By 1991, support for every one of these precoded obligations had significantly declined,** often by a very large degree. The most marked declines in obligations toward relatives other than parents were: maintain close relationships (from 93.1% to 42%), obedience (from 66.7% to 20.9%), respect (from 91.9% to 46.6%), and economic aid (from 51.9% to 16.1%).

We can summarize the results of Table 1 by calculating ratios for the number of obligations mentioned relative to the total number of respondents. The 507 respondents in 1963 spontaneously mentioned a total of 277 obligations to extended kin (Table 1, panel 3A.1—3A.7); the ratio is 277/507, or 0.55 obligations per respondent. The comparable ratio for the 1991 respondents is 317/545, or 0.58 obligations per respondent. When respondents were asked if they agreed with each of the pre-coded obligations to extended kin (Table 1, panel 3B.1—3B.7), a total of 2,109 obligations were accepted by the 507 respondents in 1963, for a ratio of 2,109/507, or 4.16 obligations per respondent. The comparable ratio for the 1991 respondents was 898/545, or 1.65 obligations per respondent. Thus, while the number of spontaneously-mentioned obligations per respondent was equally low in 1963 and 1991 (0.55 and 0.58, respectively), the number of agreements with specific precoded obligations declined from 4.16 per respondent in 1963 to 1.65 in 1991. The chi-square for this difference—980.042 is significant beyond the .001 level.

We are thus faced with these findings concerning obligations Taiwanese think people have toward relatives other than parents: (1) The percent who think there are (unspecified) obligations to kin-about half the sample in both 1963 and 1991 has not significantly changed; (2) very few respondents spontaneously proposed any given specific type of obligation in either 1963 or 1991; (3) when asked about specific obligations, a much higher percent in 1963 agreed that the obligation exists, but this tendency declined so much by 1991 that the predominant picture is one where most of the Taiwanese of Taipei no longer expect people to meet these specific obligations to kin.

Extended Kinship Behavior

Having considered some aspects of **ideal** kinship patterns, we next turn to actual kinship patterns. Recall that the former refer to what people say they ought to do for kin, while the latter describes how they actually behave toward kin. Table 2 summarizes several areas of actual behavior relevant to extended kinship relationships. Although 34% of the 1963 Taipei sample had spent most of their life in villages or towns before moving to Taipei (24.3% in the 1991 sample), fully 42.2% of the 1963 sample and 58.3% of the 1991 sample had at some time during their life lived in a village or small town. Our first kinship behavior questions asked (1)

Do you still maintain contact with relatives who live in that village or town? During the previous year, (2) have you visited them in that village or town? and (3) have those relatives in that village or town visited you? We combined these three items into a Village Contact index, scored from 0 to 3, depending on how many of the three questions the respondent answered "yes" to. In Table 2, we see that somewhat more than two-thirds—68.4% in 1963, 69.3% in 1991—of the Taiwanese of Taipei had the high score of 3. Thus, among the considerable proportion of our Taipei respondents who used to live in a village or town, over two-thirds of them continue to keep in touch, and exchange visits, with kin from that village or town. The relatively strong tendency to maintain interaction with rural and small town kin was not significantly different in 1991 than in 1963. Ties with rural and small town kin have not become attenuated.

Table 2—Kinship Solidarity: Aspects of Behavior in 1963 and 1991, Ranked by Per Cent Solidarity in Taipei Sample in 1963

	% 1963	% 1991	Tau-c	Phi
I have a high level of contact (visiting back and forth) with kin in village or small town where I once lived	68.4	69.3	.03	
Attended marriage ceremony with kin during previous year	62.7	71.6		.09**
Attended festival (*pai-pai*) with kin during previous year	62.7	47.9		.15**
Attended New Year's celebration with kin during previous year	56.3	77.4		.23**
Attended funeral with kin during previous year	40.5	53.9		.13**
Attended ancestor worship ceremony with kin during previous year	39.2	75.0		.36**
Attended child birth ceremony with kin during previous year	34.1	30.1		.04
Attended birthday celebration with kin during previous year	32.6	44.4		.12**
Attended gatherings with kin five or more times during previous year	43.9	58.9	.20**	
Attended four or more types of gatherings with kin during previous year	39.1	61.9	.28**	
I have relied on kin in getting a job or promotion	9.6	17.5		.11**

**p<.01

Base Ns are 507 for 1963 and 545 for 1991 for all itiems except the first, where base N (263 in 1963, 339 in 1991) refers to those Taipei residents who have lived in a village or small town.

The next set of questions stated a number of occasions Taiwanese society provides which might be used to get together with extended kin, especially those not in one's immediate (nuclear family) household. These include **annual ceremonial occasions**—New Year's festivals (*pai-pai*) and ancestor worship--and certain rites of passage—marriage, child birth (*man-yueh*), birthdays of elder kin (*chu-shou*), and funerals. Table 2 lists these in order of their prevalence in 1963. We shall discuss them in that order, noting the degree of change by 1991.

The most common occasion for kin gatherings in 1963 was weddings, attended by 62.7% of the Taipei respondents. Such gatherings are, of course, centrally important in terms of kinship, for they signify and symbolize the linking of two different families (*chia tsu*), the incorporation of the bride into the husband's patrilineage, the commencement of a new family and, if accompanied by neolocal residence, of a new household. The prevalence of attending weddings with extended kin during the previous year increased significantly to 71.6% by 1991 (phi = .09*).

Equally frequent with weddings, in 1963, was attending pai-pai festivals with kin, done by 62.7% of the sample during the previous year. *Pai-pai* were originally festivals to worship a deity in a local temple such as Matsu, the Goddess of the Sea, who was worshipped by fishermen, and/or the daughters of Matsu—*erh Ma*, *san Ma*, etc. Each *pai-pai* festival is centered on a local temple and its deity, and is essentially a local community activity, organized each year by different worshipping groups. One would never invite only one's kin to a *pai-pai*, but these festivals are occasions one can use to get together with kin, along with local people.

The tendency of our sample to attend *pai-pai* with extended kin dropped significantly from 62.7% in 1963 to 47.9% by 1991 (phi = .15**). If one desires to maintain contact with kin, pai-pai dinners and festivals are now much less likely to be the means of doing so. The following are suggested as causes of this decline.[7] First, there has been a partial shift from the original religious meaning of *pai-pai* festivals—e.g., to celebrate Matsu's birthday—to more secular purposes—strengthening ties with one's network of business associates or friends, rather than with kin. One might spend lavishly to invite many people to an outdoor *pai-pai* dinner. During the presidency of Chiang Ching-kuo (1975-1988) the government tried to restrict *pai-pai*, claiming that people wasted too much money in those conspicuous displays (*lang fei*, spending money with nothing to show for it). To support its policy of the priority of economic growth, the government wanted a high savings rate, so it demanded that public employees stop offering *pai-pai* dinners for hundreds of guests, and also tried to dissuade the general public from this activity.

Another reason for the decline in the rate of attendance at *pai-pai* with extended kin by 1991 may be a heightened consciousness of the danger of contaminated food, left outdoors in summer heat for long periods of time. (Although school lunches are more sanitary than *pai-pai* food, students do at times get sick from them in Taiwan.) Finally, the sheer congestion that a *pai-pai* generates may deter some people from using it for a kin gathering.

Gallin contends that "economic development has also been accompanied by an elaboration of religious practices in rural and urban Taiwan. Participation in religious festivals (*pai*

pai), magical rituals and religious pilgrimages has increased" (Gallin 1985, p. 55). Although this statement refers to a period earlier than our 1991 survey, it is not necessarily inconsistent with our survey finding. As the population of Taipei has expanded, the absolute number of people attending a *pai-pai* or other festival could remain as large, or even increase, while the per cent of the population who attend with kin declines, as in our 1963-1991 comparison.

The third most frequent occasion for kin gatherings in 1963 Taipei was the Chinese lunar New Year's, the greatest of all Chinese festivals, held in late January or early February. Many ancient customs are associated with *Kuo Nien*, or passing the old year. All outstanding debts must be paid, everyone sports new clothing, and people present their relatives, friends and colleagues with little red envelopes stuffed with "lucky money" for the New Year. Cohen reports that in North China, lunar New Year's and the *Ch'ing Ming* festival (to be discussed below) were both occasions that "provided lineage-wide contexts for ancestor worship and associated feasting and visiting" (Cohen 1990, p. 519). The emphasis at New Year's celebrations was on "networking within a shared genealogically defined social sphere" (Cohen 1990, p. 521). The celebration of New Year's with members of one's extended kin has increased significantly in our Taipei samples, from 56.3% in 1963 to 77.4% in 1991 (phi = .23**). One general explanation of the several types of kin gatherings that have increased according to our data can be noted at this point. The Taiwanese are much more affluent in the 1990s than they were in the early 1960s. Although travel to get together with kin living elsewhere in the island may be more congested, it is less costly in relation to real income, and generally more rapid and efficient. With personal ownership of motor vehicles so high, it is subjectively more within the realm of possibility and expectations that people leave Taipei for holidays. Those who stay in Taipei report that the city seems almost empty of people. In fact, there is a large exodus from Taipei even on regular weekends now, and this is all the more true on longer holidays.

The fourth most frequent occasion for kin gatherings in 1963 were funerals, and attendance with extended kin at these has significantly increased from 40.5% in 1963 to 53.9% in 1991 (phi = .13**). This increase cannot be explained on demographic grounds, since the death rate in Taiwan for both sexes and all ages **declined** from 6.03 (per 1,000 population) in 1963 to 5.16 in 1989 (Directorate-General of Budget, Accounting and Statistics, Republic of China, 1990, Table 13). The rise in the attending of funerals with kin may, therefore, be an expression of the strengthening of the sentiments of kinship solidarity, a point we shall develop further below.

Ancestor worship *(chi tsu)* is the ancient rite performed in honor of one's ancestors. This is done mainly on *Ch'ing Ming* chieh, the "clear and bright festival," April 5 (April 4 in leap years). It is also known as tomb-sweeping day, and the traditional concept was that the larger kin group would gather at the lineage grave site, sweep it clean of debris, remove weeds, plant new trees, shrubs and flowers, and share in the offering of food sacrifices to the ancestors' spirits. "Lineage organization implied ancestor worship, a Confucian value of high order" (Freedman 1961-2, p. 325). According to Cohen, the *Ch'ing Ming* festival in north China was a "communal display of solidarity whereby each member family would send a representative to participate in activities centered on the lineage graveyard that involved both feasting and graveside ritual" (Cohen 1990, p. 521). Our surveys show a significant, and very marked increase in the attendance of the Taipei respondents at ancestor worship ceremonies during the previous year: from 39.2% in 1963 to 75.0% in 1991 (phi = .36**). Indeed, the magnitude of this change is one of the largest of any variable in our 1963-1991 comparisons.

The explanation of this marked **increase** in the traditional practice of tomb-sweeping and ancestor worship as an occasion for extended kinship interaction may be partly a matter of the active role of the Republic of China (ROC) in distinguishing itself from mainland China by state intervention in the preservation of traditional Chinese culture. While the communist regime on mainland China tried for decades to wipe out "superstitious, feudal" religious-based extended kinship practices like ancestor worship (Whyte & Parish 1984, pp. 223, 313-17), the ROC on Taiwan officially prided itself on fostering traditional Chinese culture. With regard to ancestor worship, the state took advantage of the fact that President Chiang Kai-shek died on the day of the *Ch'ing Ming* Festival, April 5, in 1975, to make that day henceforth one of double significance: a national mourning holiday for the Generalissimo, and for one's ancestors. The official *Ch'ing Ming* holiday was extended after 1975 from one or two days to three or four days. To implement its policy, the state now arranges more public transportation and other means for Taipei residents to journey to their ancestral grave sites, wherever these may be on the island. Some Taiwan specialists doubt that the increased interest in *Ch'ing Ming* festivities is due to the state's role. They argue that the Taiwanese do not give much credence to Chiang Kai-shek, and point out that the state's attempts to diminish *pai-pai* celebrations were not very successful. The alternative interpretation is that *Ch'ing Ming* ancestor worship is a renewed expression of identity, both ethnic (Chinese as well as Taiwanese) and family. Whatever the reasons, it is clear that while the highest rate of travel in Taiwan is still for lunar New Year's, the *Ch'ing Ming* Festival is crowding it now as the second heaviest in travel.

The significant increase in extended kin gatherings for ancestor worship is a clear instance, though by no means the only one, of what Goodkind (1991) calls "the deliberate, conscious social construction of tradition." Religious behavior in temples and other manifestations of Taiwanese folk religion declined during the 1960s and 1970s, but have been reviving since 1980. Ancestor worship can be said to be a phenomenon of modernization: precisely because social change has been so rapid, the Taiwanese need to "return to their roots." When the Kuomintang first moved to Taiwan in the 1940s, it systematically ignored Taiwan history and local customs. Nowadays, the Taiwanese feel freer to have nativistic movement-like revivals, such as ancestor worship. Some have pointed out that revivals of traditional religious customs enable the Taiwanese to stress their distinctness relative to mainlander Chinese. Goodkind seems correct in inferring that "modernizing forces themselves continue to allow new and unexpected species of traditions to bloom" (Goodkind 1991, p. 679).

But there is also a secular function subserved by kin gathering to observe Ch'ing Ming and ancestor worship. The lineage tomb and grave site may be outside Taipei, in a less polluted, pleasant, park-like setting. The kin group can use the occasion for a picnic and a diverting escape from crowded, polluted Taipei. And the increase in ancestor worship by 1991 may also be due to a tendency in modern Taiwan to shift somewhat from exclusive emphasis on the patrilineal lineage to more bilateral forms of kinship. As we shall suggest later, wives in urban Taiwan no longer must sever themselves so fully from their own parental lineage after marriage. Social interaction with the wife's side of the family has become more common in places like Taipei. Accordingly, the notable rise in kin gatherings for ancestor worship may reflect a more common practice of attending both the husband's and the wife's ancestral tombs.

Traditionally, the childbirth (*sheng ch'an*) ceremony, especially for a male baby, was as important as birthdays or funerals. The parents of the new baby would announce his birth by sending food to relatives and friends. Around the time the baby is one month old (*man yueh*) the relatives would come to see him, bringing red-wrapped gift money (*hung pao*). The per cent of our Taipei samples who had attended gatherings with kin for man yueh during the previous year was 34.1 in 1963, and declined non-significantly to 30.1 in 1991.

The least attended of the occasions for kin gatherings in 1963 were elder family members' birthdays (*chu shou*). The 32.6% of the Taipei sample who attended birthdays of elder kin in 1963 was exceeded by a significant increase to 44.4% who did this in 1991 (phi = .12**). Our interview schedule asked about only those special birthdays of older people who reach the age of 70 or 80 (celebrated on the person's 69th or 79th birthday, one year in advance, to make sure the monster, time, does not claim the person before the actual 70th or 80th birthday). These are *chu shou*, celebrating long life, as opposed to ordinary birthdays, *sheng jih*.

We have analyzed seven types of occasions on which Taiwanese can get together with their extended kin. For five of these--weddings, New Year's, funerals, ancestor worship, and birthdays—there was a significant increase from 1963 to 1991 in the percent who attended with kin. Only one type—*pai-pai* festivals—showed a significant decline as an occasion for meeting kin, and there was no significant change in the practice of meeting kin for childbirth ceremonies. For these areas of extended kinship behavior, the preponderant change, then, was toward a higher frequency of interaction with extended kin.

This can be seen in two other summary measures. We summed the number of these seven types of occasions each respondent had attended with kin during the previous year, and since some occasions could occur more than once a year, e.g., weddings, funerals, and birthdays, we also asked how many times one had attended all kinds of family gatherings during the previous year. Table 2 reports these as the per cent of the respondents who attended five or more times, which increased significantly from 43.9% in 1963 to 58.9% in 1991 (Tau-c = .20**); and the percent who attended four or more of the seven types of occasions, which also increased significantly from 39.1% in 1963 to 61.9% in 1991 (Tau-c =.28**).

The last item in Table 2 deals with a different context in which extended kinship ties may operate. The kinship basis of many urban economic activities in Taiwan—such as the small store run by a man and his wife—has been widely remarked in the literature. What is less clear is the importance of kinship in larger economic enterprises, in public organizations, etc.

We asked "Have you ever relied on your relatives (*ch'in-ch'i*) in getting a job or a promotion?" Only 9.6% of the 1963 Taipei respondents admitted doing this, but this rose significantly to 17.5% in 1991 (phi = .11**). While this aspect of what we are conceptualizing as extended kinship solidarity increased, our evidence suggests that depending upon kin to get a job or a promotion was a relatively uncommon pattern in both the 1963 and 1991 samples. It may be that not many respondents had relatives in a position to get them a job or promotion. This is not to say that one no longer needs *kuan-hsi* ("connections") to get ahead in Taipei. But people may be relying more on friends or newspapers to find jobs than was the case in the past.

Discussion and Conclusion

We have seen that ideal and actual patterns of extended kinship among the Taiwanese of Taipei have changed in **opposite** directions between 1963 and 1991. The **ideal patterns** that prescribe various obligations people have to their extended kin (other than parents) have generally declined significantly over the 28-year period. The Taiwanese in 1991 were much less likely to think they **should** have close relationships with kin, respect and obey them, give them economic aid, help them at work or with chores at home, or meet the same obligations to extended kin as are fulfilled toward parents. During the same time period, however, the behavioral indicators of solidarity with extended kin--what Taiwanese actually do--generally show an increased frequency of interaction with extended kin at gatherings for ancestor worship, New Year's, weddings, birthdays and funerals. Thus, ideal patterns of obligations toward extended kin have weakened while actual behavioral patterns of interaction with extended kin have become stronger. How are we to interpret or explain these apparently contradictory trends?

One interpretation of these trends might be that, whereas the ideal kinship ties include heavy obligations such as providing financial support and obeying relatives, the actual kinship ties we have studied are less onerous activities, such as simply being present together, making trips and putting up with relatives for visits. This would take the edge off our comparison between trends "going in opposite directions." Note, however, that even in this interpretation, despite the onerousness of the ideal obligations to kin, Taipei respondents did see these as obligations more in 1963 than in 1991. The substitution—if that is what is going on—of less onerous actual ties with kin for the more onerous ideal obligations is not inconsistent with what modernization theory predicts for kinship change.

Modernization theory does provide part of the answer. The solidarity of the patrilineage was more an ideal than an actual pattern for most of the Taiwanese population even prior to the urbanization and industrialization of the island. Goode (1963, 1982) argued that in a society like Taiwan, modernization would weaken traditional normative extended kinship obligations. As the conjugal or nuclear family becomes the ideal family pattern for more of the population, fewer obligations and rights can be expected to be observed toward extended kin. "Neither couple nor kinfolk have many rights with respect to the other, and so the reciprocal obligations are few" (Goode 1963, p. 8). Our Taipei data show that normative **obligations** toward extended kin have diminished since the 1960s.

The term for "obligations" used in both the 1963 and 1991 interviews was *tse-jen*, which, in Chinese, has an almost legal connotation--things you **must** do. It carries a more compulsory sense than *i-wu*, another term for duty and moral obligation. *Tse-jen* is certainly different from asking "what kinds of relationships would you **like** your children to have with their relatives?"

Thus, "obligations" toward kin have changed from fixed, formal musts and shoulds—what Durkheim (1895;1964) called rules with exteriority and constraint—toward being more voluntarily defined. It is as though the current notion is: If I wish or can afford to fulfill some action toward kin, I shall do it; but if I do it, it is because I want to, or the special circumstance makes it appropriate, not because of a uniform, externally defined obligation that I must fulfill toward kin.

Modernization theory is less satisfactory with regard to the changes in actual extended kinship behavior in Taipei. Goode recognized that different aspects of family and kinship may move in different directions as a society changes in the direction of a conjugal family system. For example, divorce rates in some societies, already high **before** industrialization, may decline during industrialization, while other societies' divorce rates rise during industrialization. But Goode nowhere explicitly predicted the combination of decreasing normative but increasing actual kinship solidarity that our Taipei data show. The closest he comes to this possibility is: "in spite of the perhaps lessened intensity of extended kinship ties, the ascriptive character of kinship greatly increases the chances of relatively frequent contact" (Goode 1963, p. 76). Many exchanges and interactions do occur from time to time, depending on how friendly kin are with one another and the kinds of needs they have. "But since these exchanges are not societally required and **do not occur as frequently as in the past**, both extended kin and the nuclear family unit have a weaker basis for social control over one another" (Goode 1982, p. 109, bolds added). What does "the past" refer to here? If it means rural or pre-industrial Taiwan, there are no data on attendance at family gatherings precisely comparable to our 1963 and 1991 Taipei data. If "the past" means simply 1963 in contrast to 1991, then Goode's assertion is flatly wrong, since actual interaction with kin in this study has become significantly more, not less, frequent.

How, then, are we to account for the increase in actual contact with extended kin among the Taiwanese of Taipei? This paper has suggested several specific reasons for the higher levels of sociability with extended kin in the 1990s than in the 1960s. Transportation and communication are more convenient for overcoming spatial distance from kin; there is more affluence and more leisure time and perhaps less of a compulsion to be at work to maximize income; one response to the very rapid pace of social change has been a desire to "return to one's roots" through greater contact with kin; the state in the Republic of China has emphasized kinship as a traditional Confucian virtue; and there have been other popular, deliberate efforts at the social construction of tradition in ways that encourage more contact with kin. Another reason is that as the sentiments of kinship change from obligation to choice, extended kin may become "ascriptive friends," i.e., one interacts with kin because one likes them as persons, in the same way as one associates with non-kin who are friends.

Finally, our Taipei data do fit one of Goode's ideal type characteristics of the modern conjugal family system: the descent lines of the father and mother are of nearly equal importance. There is a shift from patrilineal to bilateral kinship. Schak (1991, p. 1) has shown empirically for Taiwan that "in urban areas, Chinese kinship behavior—as distinct from kinship ideology—is better described as bilateral rather than patrilineal." The shift from an agricultural to an urban-industrial society has led to a greater reliance on and interaction with a man's affines (relations through his wife) and female consanguines (married sisters), rather than primarily relatives within the agnatic core of his patrilineage.

There are several reasons for this. When moving to Taipei, it may be the wife's kin who already live there and can provide help. Even if kin on both sides live in Taipei, new migrants can have a greater range of kin resources to tap than if they use only patrilateral kin. In a question not covered in this paper, we found a significant decline between 1963 and 1991 in the per cent of our Taipei respondents who thought it is important to have a male heir to transmit the lineage *(fu-tse chuan tsung chieh tai)*. Son preference has apparently declined in urban Taiwan. People recognize that daughters tend to keep closer kin ties than sons. Keeping in contact with one's mother's, wife's and married daughters' sides of the family is now seen in Taipei as at least as important as contacts with the patriline. The result is that the meaningful and effective range of kin with whom one can, on a more or less voluntary basis, interact has expanded. For these reasons, it is understandable that the actual rate of interaction with extended kin, even in modernized Taipei, has significantly increased over the last generation.

Endnotes

[1]Because Harrell's village was composed of wage laborers rather than peasants, its kinship patterns may be atypical of other Taiwan villages, but more comparable to the wage- and salary-earning population of Taipei.

[2]Given the intended sample N of approximately 500 in 1963 and between 500 and 600 in 1991, the ratio of the number of households drawn for the sample to the number in which interviews were completed was much higher in 1991 (1,282/545) than in 1963 (642/507). The response rate was lower in 1991 not because of a higher rate of contacted household heads who refused to be interviewed, but due to the higher rate of households not at home and who could not be contacted for an interview in 1991. The higher ratio of households in the sample

to complete interviews was deliberate, because we anticipated the "not at home" problem to be greater in 1991 than in 1963.

[3]Families may go through a cycle of growth from the nuclear form to the stem form and even to the joint form before dividing the family property and starting the cycle all over again (Cohen 1970). Although the individual may live in different forms of households over the life course, it is nevertheless worth knowing the distribution of household types at any given point in time. That a person may live for some part of his or her life in a stem or joint family household does not alter the fact that most households in Taipei at a given time are nuclear.

[4]Phi and tau-c are used as measures of statistical association between variables. Both vary between .00 and 1.00, with higher magnitudes indicating a greater difference between the 1963 and 1991 distributions of a given variable. The two ** after the association indicate that the difference between 1963 and 1991 in the per cent living in nuclear family households is significant at the .01 level. One * indicates that the phi or tau-c relationship is significant at the .05 level.

[5]The interview schedule asked what obligations children (*tzu-nu*) have toward kin. Since some obligations imply those expected of adult children—e.g., give economic aid to kin—we shall use the more inclusive term, people, rather than children.

[6]Because kinship ties to parents may be quite different from those to other extended kin, we are planning a separate paper on behavior, norms and attitudes toward parents in the 1963 and 1991 samples.

[7]The explanations and interpretations we offer for changes in this and subsequent aspects of kinship behavior are based on the fact that one of the authors was born in Taiwan and has spent most of his life there. He draws on his personal experience in Taiwan and especially in Taipei, and both authors draw on relevant scholarly publications. Respondents were not asked in the interview situation why they did or did not gather with extended kin for *pai-pai* and other occasions.

References

Barrett, R. E., (1989). The changing status of women in Taiwan. In H. H. M. Hsiao, W. Y. Cheng, & H. S. Chan, (Eds.), *A newly industrialized state* (pp. 463-492). Taipei: National Taiwan University Press.

Cohen, M. L. (1970). Developmental process in the Chinese domestic group. In M. Freeman (Ed.), *Family and kinship in Chinese society* (pp. 21-36). Stanford, CA: Stanford University Press.

Cohen, M. L. (1990). Lineage organization in north China. *The Journal of Asian Studies, 49*(3), 509-534.

Directorate-General of Budget, Accounting and Statistics, Executive Yuan, Republic of China. (1980). *Statistical yearbook of the Republic of China*. Taipei: Executive Yuan.

Durkheim, E. (1895; 1964). *The rules of sociological method.* New York: The Free Press.

Freedman, M. (1958). *Lineage organization in southeastern China.* London: University of London, Athlone Press.

Freedman, M. (1961-62). The family in China, past and present. *Pacific Affairs, 34*(4), 323-336.

Freedman, M. (1966). Chinese lineage and society: Fukien and Kwangtung. New York: Humanities Press.

Gallin, N. B. (1978). Rural to urban migration in Taiwan: Its impact on Chinese family and kinship. In D. C. Buxbaum (Ed.), *Chinese family law and social change in historical and comparative perspective* (pp. 261-282). Seattle, WA: University of Washington Press.

Gallin, N. B. (1985). Development and change in Taiwan and Hong Kong. In J. F. Williams (Ed.), *The future of Hong Kong and Taiwan* (pp. 47-64). East Lansing, MI: Michigan State University.

Goode, W. J. (1963). *World revolution and family patterns.* New York: Free Press.

Goode, W. J. (1982). *The family* (2nd ed.). Englewood Cliffs, NJ: Prentice-Hall.

Goodkind, D. M. (1991). Creating new traditions in modern Chinese populations: Aiming for birth in the year of the Dragon. *Population and Development Review,* 17(4), 663-686.

Greenhalgh, S. (1984). Networks and their nodes: Urban society in Taiwan. *The China Quarterly, 99*, 529-552.

Harrell, S. (1982). *Ploughshare village: Culture and context in Taiwan.* Seattle: University of Washington Press.

Schak, D. C. (1991). Bilaterality in urban Chinese kinship patterns: A Taiwan case study. Unpublished manuscript.

Suenari, M. (1986). Lineages in Taiwan and Korea: A case study of controlled comparison with variation. Paper presented at the Second International Conference on Sinology, Academia Sinica (December, 29-31).

Whyte, M. K., & Parish, W. L. (1984). *Urban life in contemporary China*. Chicago: University of Chicago Press.

Acknowledgement

This research was supported in 1963 by the (U.S.) Social Science Research Council and in 1991-93 by two foundations in the Republic of China—the Chiang Ching Kuo Foundation and the National Science Council. This help, and that of our universities—Brown and National Ising Hua—as well as the Academia Sinica, Taipei, Taiwan, is gratefully acknowledged.

Household Division of Labor

Part IV

Article 11

Division of Labor in Household Tasks Among Korean Immigrant Families

Shin Kim

I. Introduction

Since the 1965 revision of the U.S. immigration law, the number of immigrants from Latin American and Asian countries has been rapidly increasing, thereby ending the historical dominance of immigrants from European countries (Bryce-Laporte, 1980; U.S. Dept. of Justice, 1970-1988). As a part of such a trend in the immigration flow, the number of Korean immigrants has been dramatically increased. According to the 1970 census, about 70,000 Koreans resided in the United States. Since then, this number has risen sharply, with approximately 33,000 Koreans being admitted annually. In 1980, the Korean population numbered 354,529 (U.S. Dept. of Commerce, 1981). The 1990 census indicates the number exceeds 800,000. As one of the most rapidly growing immigrant groups, Korean immigrants are heavily concentrated in the five major metropolitan areas: Los Angeles, New York, Chicago, San Francisco, and Washington DC.

Unlike the past Asian immigrants at the turn of this century who came to the United States primarily as single males (Cheng & Bonacich, 1984), a great majority of the recent Korean immigrants came to the new land with their own family in the context of kinship-based chain migration (Hurh & Kim, 1988; U.S. Dept. of Justice, 1970-88). The immigrants are, therefore, likely to adjust in the United States as a family rather than as individuals.

One striking fact in Korean immigrant families is an intensive labor market involvement by wives. It is strong from the beginning and gets stronger as their length of residence lengthens (Hurh & Kim, 1984,1988). The wives' employment seems to be out of financial necessity. And, this necessity remains no matter how long they stay in the United States. A great majority of these employed wives works forty hours or more a week (see Table 1).

In Korea, married women generally stay home as full-time homemakers and married men are the breadwinners of the family. The heavy employment of married women in Korean immigrant families thus raises a number of questions regarding household tasks. Since certain household tasks must be performed regardless of the wives' employment (meals need to be prepared, clothes need to be washed, etc.), one interesting question is what happens to the level and method of household tasks when the wife works for pay outside the home. According to some studies (Blau & Ferber, 1986; Vickery, 1979; Strober & Weinberg, 1980), families with employed wives do not purchase more labor saving devices or commercial contracting (for example, restaurant meals instead of home cooking, commercial cleaning, etc.) than families with full-time homemaker wives. As for the frequency of household tasks, no difference again is found between the two groups except dishwashing (Hurh & Kim, 1988, ch. 5). If the families with employed wives neither use more appliance-intensive methods nor perform fewer household tasks, then, the question becomes the method of the sharing of household tasks among different family members.

Contrary to the common perception, a great majority (over 70%) of Korean immigrant families maintain a neolocal nuclear family—married couple with children. Family members in this type of family who can perform household tasks are wife, husband and teenage children. The absolute amount of time teenage children spend at household tasks is small. The basic question is, therefore, whether the husband shares household tasks in Korean immigrant families when the wife works. In addition, what are the factors which predict the division of labor between a couple.

TABLE 1 OCCUPATIONAL DISTRIBUTION OF EMPLOYED HUSBANDS AND WIVES AND THEIR HOURS OF WORK A WEEK

Hours of Wk A Week		Employed Husbands				Employed Wives			
		1	2	3	4	1	2	3	4
Less Than 35	N	2	5		5	9	3	1	2
	%	3.4	6.3		6.1	19.6	5.9	4.3	5.6
35 — 39	N	1			1	3	1	1	2
	%	1.5			1.2	6.5	2.0	4.3	5.6
40	N	21	4	5	21	27	2	7	11
	%	31.8	5.1	20.8	25.6	58.7	3.9	30.5	30.5
41 — 45	N	26	3	10	27	6	2	4	9
	%	39.5	3.8	41.7	32.9	13.0	3.9	17.4	25.0
More Than 45	N	16	67	9	28	1	43	10	12
	%	24.2	84.8	37.5	34.2	2.2	84.3	43.5	33.3
Total	N	66	79	24	82	46	52	23	36
	%	100	100	100	100	100	100	100	100

1: Professional/technical Occupations; 2: Self-employed small business;
3: Sales/administrative support occupations; 4: Service/manual occupations

II. Theoretical Frameworks and Hypothesis

Two economic perspectives offer the frameworks useful for the analysis of the above issue: neoclassical and radical-feminist approaches.

(1) Utility Maximization Model—Neoclassical Approach

As an economic model, this framework applies the rationalization principle to household decision making. A family (a couple) is assumed to allocate its scarce resources in such a way as to maximize the family's utility. A family maximizes its utility function subject to time and income constraints. Utilities are derived from consuming commodities, and household tasks are one of these commodities that directly enter a family's utility function. The difference between other commodities and household tasks is that the latter must be produced within a family combining market goods and time. Each family member is assumed to act altruistically, i.e. conflicts of interests are assumed away. The most efficient way a multi-person household can allocate time of its members is to follow the relative productivity of time of each member. Since everyone has a limited time, 24 hours a day, it is rational to assign each member to the task, market work or household task, at which the member is more productive than the others and to exchange the results (Becker, 1976, part 4).

One distinct possibility in this model is a complete specialization; one spouse at household tasks full-time, the other at market work full-time. If the wife has a comparative advantage at household tasks for whatever reason (be it socialization, on-the-job training or biological factors), then, the wife should perform the household tasks alone in exchange for the husband's breadearner performance. The relative productivity of one's time can be inferred from a market wage one commands. Since the husband's wage is typically higher than the wife's, it is the wife who should be the full-time homemaker (Becker 1976, ch. 2).

In the instances where a complete specialization is not feasible for financial or nonfinancial reasons, a rational outcome is a sharing of household tasks. The level of sharing must be dictated by one's relative productivity of time. One's relative contribution to family income is a better measurement than wage for a relative productivity of time because wage does not fully reflect institutional constraints workers may face in capitalism. These discussions lead to the following hypotheses:

> Hypothesis 1—Among the employed husbands, the greater (lesser) the husband's relative contribution, the less (more) he performs the household tasks.

> Hypothesis 2—Among the employed wives, the greater (lesser) the wife's relative contribution, the lesser (more) she performs the household tasks.

(2) Sex Segregated Dual Market—Radical-Feminist Approach.

This approach investigates the possible sources of conflicts within a family. A family is a social system with a material base, i.e., where production and redistribution take place. It is very likely that differences of interests exist among family members. These differences are resolved by power hierarchy within a family. In other words, who controls whose labor determines the production process within a family. A family is in the midst of a society, being shaped by it and also influencing the larger society. The United States' economic system is capitalism and the family system is a patriarchy. These two mechanisms interact and interlock reinforcing each other even though patriarchy preceded capitalism. The allocation of a scarce resource such as time between a couple depends on the relative economic power between two genders as in a neoclassical approach. Employment outside the home is a means of increasing one spouse's power within a family. The difference between this view and the neoclassical one is that the relative economic power is manipulated and predetermined by a patriarchal society in this approach. To continue the male dominance over female in a capitalistic system, females are segregated to a few predominantly female and low wage occupations. Once the male dominance in the labor market is accomplished, males are able to use this economic power to secure a favored position at home. Gender division of labor within a family is an effect of a dual labor market segregated by gender (Hartmann, 1976 & 1981).

This approach does not ignore possibilities of exceptions. There may be individual cases where the wife's earnings exceed that of the husband's. These are isolated cases and too rare to overcome the power of a patriarchal society. On the contrary, the wife may be pressured to conform or over-conform to the patriarchal hierarchy to maintain peace within an household.

In immigrant families from a society more patriarchal than the United States, the effect of a patriarchy is more prevalent, particularly when these traditional values are reinforced by their labor market experiences. As long as the Korean wives and husbands are confined to the secondary labor market, with little exposure to the primary labor market, this rigid division of labor at home will remain.

What does this view imply in the division of labor in household tasks among Korean immigrant families? First, it suggests that the relative contribution of wives will have no effect on the husbands' performance of household tasks. Secondly, the employment of wife does affect the time the wife spends on household tasks negatively because of time constraints. Husbands of employed wives, nevertheless, do not perform more household tasks than husbands of nonemployed wives. In other words, an asymmetry between genders exits. Thus the following hypotheses:

> Hypothesis 3—The relative contribution of the wife will have no effect on the husband's performance of household tasks while the relative contribution of the husband will have a negative effect on the husband's performance only.
>
> Hypothesis 4—The employment of the wife will have no effect on the husband's performance of household tasks.
>
> Hypothesis 5—The employed wife will perform fewer household tasks than the nonemployed wife.

Furthermore, this view of interlocking patriarchy and capitalism infers the source of this asymmetry. Since most of the women are relegated to secondary labor markets and the jobs in the secondary labor markets possess little autonomy, the gender segregated labor market reinforces this unequal division of labor at home. Most Korean immigrants, male or female, experience workplace segregation. This implies that not only actual performance but also expected performance will display the same pattern. With a segregated labor market along race lines, the sex segregation is an additional mechanism to confine the Korean immigrant wives to double burden roles. Economically speaking, this seemingly irrational decision making is not irrational but a rational outcome with an exogenous factor called a preference. The false consciousness, as Marx called it, is the source of the gender based asymmetry. Thus follow the following hypotheses:

> Hypothesis 6—In Korean immigrant families, the employment of wives will have no effect on the husbands' expected performance of household tasks.

> Hypothesis 7—In Korean immigrant families, the employed wives and husbands show no difference in their expectation of husbands' and wives' performance of household tasks.

III. Data Collection and Analysis

Data for this study were collected through interviewing 622 Korean adult immigrants (20 years or older) in the Chicago metropolitan area. They were selected randomly based on *The Korean Community Directory of Chicago Area*, 1984-85 and eight 1985 telephone directories of Chicago and contiguous suburban communities. The interviews took place from October 1 to December 10, 1986. The interview items used in this study were a part of a larger study of Korean immigrants' adaptation and mental health funded by the National Institute of Mental Health (Hurh & Kim, 1988).

Most of the respondents are married (90.4% of males, and 76.2% of females), and married respondents show an extremely high rate of employment. Virtually all of the married males (husbands) and 74.6% of the married females (wives) report being employed. Right from the beginning of immigrant life, Korean wives show a high rate of employment. As they stay longer, however, proportionally more of them are employed. The length of residence of employed wives is slightly longer than the nonemployed wives and more employed wives (36.4%) have teenage children than the non-employed wives (21.4%). But the two groups show no difference in their current age and in the proportion of those who completed college in Korea. The average age of wives is 38 years and about half of the wives completed college education prior to their immigration to the United States.

The husbands are 42 years old on the average and a higher proportion of the husbands of employed wives (69.5%) have teenage children than the husbands of non-employed wives (31.8%). Also a higher proportion of the former (58.6%) are found to have completed college education in Korea than the latter (46.2%).

Table 1 shows the current occupations and hours of work a week of the employed husbands and wives. If full-time worker is defined as 35 hours or more of work a week, most of the employed husbands and wives work full-time. The working hours are particularly long among the self-employed. The average for this group is 61.6 hours for husbands and 57.8 hours for wives. All other employed husbands work for 44.8 hours on the average and the wives for 41.8 hours. These findings indicate that although the husbands work longer than wives, the difference is actually quite small.

A high concentration of Korean immigrants in self-employed small businesses shows their experience of occupational segregation in the US. A high proportion of their customers are Koreans, African Americans, Hispanics and other racial minorities. A high proportion of other employed husbands and wives also report that the majority of their coworkers are either minority workers or racially mixed. This co-worker racial composition indicates workplace segregation. In short, a great majority of Korean immigrant workers are in the secondary labor market (Hurh & Kim, 1988).

In order to measure the respondents' degree of involvement in the household tasks, the following questions were asked: (1) "Among your family members, how do you divide household tasks?" and (2) "In your opinion, how should the household tasks be divided in principle?" The first deals with actual performance of a family member, while the second deals with the expected performance. Five items of household tasks were given: Grocery shopping, cleaning the house, laundry, dishwashing, and preparing meals. These items were selected because these are traditionally women's tasks in Korean families. The respondents rank their family members in terms of their relative performance of each of these items.

The performance score is calculated by adding up the points based on the family members' relative performance of the above five items. A member's score ranges O to 5 for each task, O to 25 points overall. For an illustration, the wife's performance score is calculated as follows: 5, the wife alone performs or is so expected; 4, the wife performs more than any other family member or is so expected; 3, the wife and other members perform equally or are so expected; 2, a family member performs more than the wife or is so expected; 1, two other family members perform more than the wife or are so expected; O, the wife does not perform at all or is not expected to do so. The score for the husbands or other family members is calculated in the same manner.

Table 2 shows that the wives in Korean immigrant families perform household tasks far more than the husbands regardless of wives' employment status and they are expected to do so. At the same time, it is observed that the employed wives perform household tasks slightly less to some extent than the nonemployed wives. The husbands of employed wives perform household tasks slightly more than the husbands of nonemployed wives and are so expected.

The others' (children, mother, etc.) performance is found to be even far more limited than the husbands' is.

TABLE 2. MARRIED COUPLES' ACTUAL AND EXPECTED PERFORMANCE OF HOUSEWORK BY TYPES OF RESPONDENTS IN KOREAN IMMIGRANT FAMILIES

		Types of Respondents			
		Employed Wives	**Non-Employed Wives**	**Husbands of Employed Wives**	**Husbands of Non-Employed Wives**
Husband's Actual Performance	X	6.6	4.5	7.5	6.2
	SD	4.5	4.4	4.1	4.4
	N	159	55	174	65
Husband's Expected Performance	X	8.1	6.6	9.3	7.6
	SD	4.2	-	-	4.5
	N	161	55	173	66
Wife's Actual Performance	X	18.7	22.1	18.8	20.3
	SD	4.3	2.7	3.7	3.5
	N	159	55	174	65
Wife's Expected Performance	X	20.1	22.2	19.4	21.1
	SD	4.5	4.5	3.9	3.2
	N	161	55	173	66

The regression result regarding the effect of husbands' relative earnings contributions is reported in Table 3. The relative contribution is measured as a fraction of family income contributed by one spouse. It is self-reported and, interestingly, both employed husbands and wives seem to inflate their individual earnings contributions to family incomes. The employed husbands' average contribution is 74% while the employed wives' contribution is 54%. The earnings contribution of the spouse who is not a respondent is calculated by one minus the respondents' contribution score. Since self-employed husbands and wives have no individual earnings distinguishable from family income, they are excluded for this analysis. In a series of regression analyses, the wives' relative contribution is found to be insignificant on both spouses' either actual or expected performance of household tasks. Thus, it is not reported. However, as demonstrated by Table 3, the husbands' relative contribution is significantly related to husbands' actual and expected performance; the higher the contribution, the less performance. The opposite sign of beta values is due to our coding system and method of calculating performance score. Once again, though, the husbands' contribution does not significantly affect the employed wives' actual and expected performance. These findings confirm hypotheses 1 and 3 but not hypothesis 2.

TABLE 3 REGRESSION OF ACTUAL AND EXPECTED PERFORMANCE SCORES ON RESPONDENTS' TEEN-AGE CHILDREN, OWN OR HUSBAND'S RELATIVE INCOME CONTRIBUTION, EDUCATION, LENGTH OF RESIDENCE AND AGE

	Types of Respondents			
	Employed Wives		Employed Husbands	
	Husband's Actual Performance	Husband's Expected Performance	Husband's Actual Performance	Husband's Expected Performance
Teen Age Children	.10	-.10	.17**	-.09
Husband's Relative Income	.26**	.22*	-.18*	-.15
Education	.04	.15	.05	.08
Length of Residence	.04	.11	.06	.01
Current Age	-.11	.28**	-.06	-.14
R Squared	.28	.37	.29	.22
N	98	99	167	167

* –significant at the level of .05
** –significant at the level of .01

TABLE 4 REGRESSION OF ACTUAL AND EXPECTED PERFORMANCE SCORES ON AVAILABILITY OF TEEN-AGE CHILDREN AND WIFE'S EMPLOYMENT IN RESPONDENTS' FAMILIES AND RESPONDENTS' EDUCATION, LENGTH OF RESIDENCE IN THE UNITED STATES AND CURRENT AGE

	Husband's Actual Performance	Husband's Expected Performance	Wife's Actual Performance	Wife s Expected Performance
Teen Age Children	.19**	.05	.04	.01
Employment of Wife	.17**	.20**	.04	.13*
Education	.02	-.02	.09	.05
Length of Residence	.05	.06	.02	-.04
Current Age	.09	-.16*	.08	.08
R Squared	.29	.26	.13	.16
N	237	237	266	267

* – Significant at the level of .05
** – Significant at the level of .01

Table 4 presents the regression results of the effect of the wives' employment on the actual and expected performance scores of the husbands and the wives. Only the result with the husbands as respondents is reported here because the same is found with the wives as respondents. The employment of the wife significantly increases husbands' actual and expected performance while decreasing wives' performance. Nevertheless, the strength of the relationship is weaker in wives. These findings disprove empirically hypothesis 4 and fail to disprove hypothesis 5. It must be noted, though, the significance level is much lower in the testing of hypothesis 5.

The results reported in Table 5 reveal a quite interesting fact. Both employed wives and employed husbands are asked to reveal their expectation of household division of labor. As in Table 5, even after controlling education and length of residence, sex is found to be significant only in the husbands' expected performance. This indicates that the employed wives are more traditional than the employed husbands in their expectations. This finding along with the ones in the Table 4 disprove hypotheses 6 and 7. In Korean immigrant families, the wives adhere to the traditional sex roles more than the husbands. As in the radical-feminist approach, it is expected because the wives are in double jeopardy: greater influence of a more patriarchal Korean society and greater segregation in the American labor market.

TABLE 5 REGRESSION OF EXPECTED PERFORMANCE SCORES ON RESPONDENTS' TEEN-AGE CHILDREN, SEX, EDUCATION, LENGTH OF RESIDENCE AND AGE

Respondents Employed Husbands and Wives With Employed Spouses		
	Wife's Expected Performance	Husband's Expected Performance
Teen Age Children	-.05	.009
Sex	.06	-.13**
Education	.07	.04
Length of Residence	.01	.05
Current Age	.09	-.20**
R Squared	.15	.21
N	427	427

V. Discussion and Conclusion

The preceding analyses reveal the following points regarding the division of labor in household production among Korean immigrant families. First, whether the wives are employed or not, they perform and are expected to bear the bulk of household production. Second, the employed wives nonetheless perform slightly fewer household tasks than the nonemployed wives. Third, the husbands of employed wives perform slightly more in a relative sense than the husbands of nonemployed wives, and they are so expected. The existence of teen-age children is a significant factor only on the husband's actual performance. Fourth, the relative contribution of wives to their family income has no significant effect on either spouses' performance. Fifth, the relative contribution of husbands has significant impact on the husbands' actual and expected performance, but not on the wives' performance. Sixth, the employed wives seem to have a more rigid and traditional view on the gender division of labor in household tasks than the employed husbands. As a study of an immigrant group, the data analysis reveals two additional interesting points. The respondents' education and length of residence have no effects on their actual and expected behavior while the respondents' current age and presence (or absence) of teen-age children are significantly related to some aspects of actual and expected performance.

What would the above findings suggest for the understanding of Korean immigrant families regarding the household tasks? As discussed above, the high employment of wives is a prominent feature of Korean immigrant family life. The majority of them are, however, employed out of financial necessity rather than the wives' careerism or preference. Naturally, the employed wives perform slightly fewer household tasks than the nonemployed wives but they seem to feel that working outside the home is not "the proper thing" for wives to do. Consequently, the employed wives are unable to transform the economic power into bargaining power.

The employed wives in Korean immigrant families are in the secondary labor market. Thus, this influence of patriarchal Korean society does not weaken as the Korean wives remain in the American labor market. It seems that labor market segregation along gender and race lines in the American labor market reinforces rather than changes the traditional sex roles imposed on Korean women by the patriarchal Korean society.

Even though the husbands perform more household tasks when the wives have to work for pay, this study reveals a general reluctance or resistance of the husbands to share the tasks. This, again, is an evidence of the non-changing nature of sex roles because of the segregated nature of Korean immigrant's labor market position. The fact that the husbands' relative contribution is a significant factor in explaining the husbands' share of household tasks implies the importance of economic power in a family's decision making.

One caveat is called for. This study is not a timebudget study where activities of each spouse in a block of time (usually fifteen minutes) are recorded. It is rather a self-reported qualitative study with either one of the spouses as respondents. Nevertheless, the significance of this study lies in two facts; its operational definition of the relative productivity of time, and its sample population.

As the Korean immigrants try to take root in the United States, they face the new hostile environment as a family unit. A Korean immigrant household's decision making on time allocation reveals the importance of comparative advantage in an asymmetrical fashion along gender. This study reveals a powerful interaction of patriarchy and capitalism. The picture depicted in this study is a Korean immigrant family's rational response given time, income, and societal constraints. The constraint superimposed by a patriarchy is called "preference" or "taste" in economics. Unlike the time constraint, this constraint is an exogenous factor in a cross-sectional study like this one, but is an indigenous factor in a time-series study.

References

Becker, G. S. (1976). *The economic approach to human behavior.* University of Chicago Press.

Blau, F. D., & Ferber, M. A. (1986). *The economics of women, men, and work.* Englewood Cliffs, N.J.: Prentice-Hall.

Bryce-Laporte, R. S. (1980). *Sourcebook on the new immigration.* New Brunswick, N.J.: Transaction Books.

Cheng, L., & Bonacick, E. (1984). *Labor immigration under capitalism.* Los Angeles: University of California Press.

Hartmann, H. (1976). Capitalism, patriarchy, and job segregation by sex. *Signs: Journal of Women in Culture and Society, 1*(Spring), 137-69.

Hartmann, H. (1981). The family as the locus of gender, class, and political struggle: The example of housework. (1981). *Signs: Journal of Women in Culture and Society, 6*, (Spring), 366-94.

Hurh, W. M., & Kirn, K. C. (1984). *Korean immigrants in America: A structural analysis of ethnic confinement and adhesive adaptation.* Cranbury, N.J.: Fairleigh Dickinson University Press.

Kim, K. C., & Hurh, W. M. (1988). The burden of double roles: Korean wives in the USA. *Ethnic and Racial Studies, 11*(April), 151 -67.

Strober, M., & Weinberg, C. B. (1980). Strategies used by working and nonworking wives to reduce time pressure. *Journal of Consumer Research, 6*(March), 338-48.

Uprooting and adjustment: A sociological study of Korean immigrants' mental health (1988). Final report submitted to National Institute of Mental Health.

U.S. Dept. of Commerce (1981). *1980 census of population: Supplementary reports (PC 80-51-3).* Washington, DC: Government Printing Office.

U.S. Dept. of Justice (1970-1988). *Statistical yearbook of the immigration and naturalization service.* Washington, DC: Government Printing Office.

Vickery, C. (1979). Women's economic contribution to the family. In Ralph E. Smith (Ed.) *The subtle revolution: Women at work (pp. 22-26).* Washington, DC: The Urban Institute.

Article 12

"But Does He Clean the Toilets?" Gender Roles and the Division of Domestic Labor Among U.S. Households

Judith A. DiIorio

The title of this article is derived from a classroom discussion that occurred a few years ago in a course I was teaching on the sociology of gender roles. We were talking about the division of domestic labor in U.S. households and I was telling the students that, according to most studies, American women are still doing most of the housework and child care, even when they are married and employed outside of the home. Many of the older, married women in this class nodded their heads in agreement; a few even spoke about their own overburdened lives and the feelings of unfairness these burdens created. But one young, white woman, whom I'll call Angie, was not persuaded and chose to voice her skepticism. Angie said that she and her sister had been raised by her father and he had always done most of the cooking and cleaning. "Of course, " she cautioned," he expected my sister and me to help but he still did a lot of it himself."

I was about to tell Angie that I found her household situation an interesting exception but an exception nonetheless when from farther back in the room, Darlene, a black woman of about Angie's age with two children of her own said, "Yeah, but does he clean the toilets? I don't care what you say—and I'm not saying it ain't true—but there ain't a man I know that's man enough to wipe his own piss off a toilet seat if there's some woman he can get to do it for him." Angie laughed and replied, "No, I do that."

It had been a pleasant exchange and one I had observed before when issues of housework and child care arise. Later, however, as I reflected on it, I realized that implicit in these students' rather trite remarks and examples were many issues that were far from trite: Why in most cases has housework remained the responsibility of women, and why does this fact surprise some students? Under what conditions, and for what reasons, will men assume more of the burden of housework and child care? When men do housework, do they and their wives still perform different tasks? Are there variations in the division of labor by race and social class? Does the age of the couple make a difference?

And, as I thought of these questions and remembered the diversity of household composition and family forms in the U.S. today, a few others came to mind: Is the division of household labor the same for married couples as for cohabitating ones? For gay couples as for heterosexual ones? For lesbians as for gay men?

I was suspicious that I would have difficulty finding answers to some of these questions— and I was right— so in what follows I will be considering what social scientists know, as well as what we don't know, concerning these issues. Before I examine the nature of gender roles and the division of domestic labor in contemporary U.S. households, and in order to underscore the importance of the questions I have raised about it, I first need to present you with a brief historical overview.

Domestic Labor and Gender Roles in the U.S.: A Brief History

The use of words like "housework" or "domestic labor" implies the existence of other kinds of work that are "not housework" or "not domestic labor" —of work located in places or social contexts external to family and household. Indeed, as members of an industrial society, when we think of *real* work we think of it as work that takes place in factories or offices involving people who are rarely members of the same family. We also assume that the difference between housework and "real work" is a natural one that has somehow always been a part of peoples' thinking; few of us realize that this distinction, and all that it implies about the relative value, difficulty and importance of productive activity, emerged quite recently as a result of the massive social changes wrought by industrialization (Boydston, 1990; Oakley, 1976).

Prior to industrialization, while the U.S. was an agrarian society, most products were made by kinship units and households for their own consumption or for exchange on the market. Virtually all work was "housework." Certainly, as is universally true, who did what specific tasks was gender-based. Adult men and older boys were responsible for clearing land, plowing and harvesting cash crops, smithery, and carpentry. Women, with the help of their daughters and domestic servants drawn from poorer families, were responsible for the care of young children, gardening, spinning of cloth, sewing and cleaning of clothes, milking cows, making of butter and cheese, preparation of food, and so forth. Males and females were expected to do different work, and, as is true in societies where men hold positions of greater authority, men's work was probably seen as more important than women's, but the location of work per se was not relevant to how people viewed or valued it, and both women and men were involved in the production of products for market as well as for household consumption (Jackson, 1992).

Industrialization drastically changed the organization of work and our thinking about it. Socialized production in sites external to kith and kin engendered a separation of "housework" from "work," private production from public production, unpaid labor from wage labor.

Theoretically, this division need not have also involved a separation of "men's work" from "women's work." As Adams (1986, p. 235) suggests, "when economic production was removed from the home, the husband-father had several alternatives: he could leave household management to his wife and restrict himself to making money; he could help-out with heavier dirtier tasks and play a supportive role in child rearing; or he and his wife could divide domestic and economic responsibilities equally." To this list we can add a fourth possibility: the wife could have made money while the husband-father managed the household.

Obviously, neither the third possibility, suggested by Adams, nor the fourth, added by myself, came to pass. The patriarchal power of husband/fathers that preexisted industrialization would have made the implementation of such arrangements, and the political realignments they would have engendered, unthinkable. Instead, depending upon the social class of the family and to some degree on the historical moment, the first and second patterns became characteristic of the ideals, if not always and for all households, the realities of American marriage and family life. Backed by the force of laws that "protected" women and children from many jobs, by demands for a family wage that would make it possible for families to survive with a single wage earner, and by cultural ideas and ideals about feminine fragility, morality and maternalism and masculine aggressiveness, competitiveness, strength and rationality, male working class trade unionists and middle class reformers of the 19th century helped institutionalize a "separate spheres" view of men's and women's proper roles (Barrett & McIntosh, 1980; Hartmann, 1976). Men were to run the public spheres of society and women were to run the domestic spheres. As husbands and fathers, men's responsibility was to be the breadwinner or provider seeing to the economic needs of the family, while as mothers and wives (and nothing else) women were to see to the emotional needs and moral development of family members and manage the household. A real man was one who could economically support his dependents (wife and children); a good woman was a full-time homemaker and mother laboring not for money but for love.

The sweeping social changes engendered by this not only brought about a separation of work and housework, they also greatly altered the nature of domestic labor, as housework itself became to some extent industrialized (Boydston, 1990). Domestic labor, both today and in the past, can be said to subsume three general sets of activities: production of goods and services for daily use by members of the household, child-rearing, and status-defining activities (Peattie & Rein, 1983, p. 46). The last of these general categories refers to those activities undertaken in an attempt to establish and display the type of "home" and family relations that symbolizes membership in a particular social class or status group. For example, the function of lawn work, entertaining, or interior decoration among the upper middle classes of this society has little to do with household needs and much to do with communicating social status. During the past two centuries, historical changes have contracted the first, and expanded the latter two. Many productive activities like making candles, cloth and bread that were previously performed by women, men and children in the household were taken over by factories. In addition, new technologies and appliances such as the washing machine, vacuum cleaner, irons and ovens eased the sheer physical effort involved in cleaning and cooking. On the other hand, the number of consumer goods that a good, middle-class family should possess dramatically increased, the standards of household cleanliness became much more demanding, and expectations of what children need and mothers should provide increased in complexity.

As a result, while the *content* of these general categories of household labor has changed over time, contrary to popular belief, the amount of time women spend in domestic labor has not lessened. In that sense, these new technologies and appliances have not been "labor-saving." As Staci Jackson (1992, p. 161) states

> The removal of work from the home and the application of labour saving technology would only have reduced the time spent in housework to the extent that the standards of comfort it was required to provide remained constant. Such standards are not, however, fixed and housework does not comprise a finite range of tasks. Hence as some chores disappeared, others took their place, and as others became less onerous, women were expected to undertake them more.

Housework may be physically less strenuous now than in the past but no less demanding of time and involvement. The modern U.S. housewife may have fewer children than her grandmothers did, but care of children involves more intensive work and concern with more emotional, social, and psychological needs than her grandmothers had to worry about. "Instead of scrubbing, polishing and scouring, a woman spends more time as consumer-shopper, chauffeur, family counselor, social arranger, hostess, as we move up the class structure, and in child care" (Rothschild, 1983, p. 161).

Furthermore, as the quote from Rothschild's work implies, the content and intensity of housework has depended historically upon the economic resources of the household and has therefore varied with the social class, race and ethnic status of its members. At one end of the class structure, affluent, white women could afford to pay less privileged women, often from socially disadvantaged racial or ethnic groups, to do much of their labor for them. At the other end, poor women of all races not only had to do their own domestic labor, but typically had to do it under more arduous and difficult conditions created by poverty and racism while, in addition, holding paid employment, often cleaning the homes of others (Jones, 1985).

About the only social fact that remained the same throughout most of the past two centuries is that, regardless of what housework and child care involved, it was primarily women's responsibility in this society to see that it got done. Whether married or unmarried, whether of Asian, Hispanic, African or European ancestry, whether affluent or poor, whether childless or the mother of ten, whether alone or with the assistance of other female kin, women shouldered the unpaid work required for the care of human life and the making of "homes" out of houses. If married, then she could expect some assistance from her husband in certain types of jobs—lawn maintenance, car repair, disciplining of children—but the bulk of the labor, especially with regard to the jobs that have to be done on a daily basis, she was expected to do. And justifying this division of labor were a set of beliefs about men's and women's proper roles. He was expected to provide for her and she was expected to care for him, his house and his kids. He worked outside the home and she inside. He performed the instrumental roles and she the expressive.

Until recently, few people in any generation of Americans would have thought to question or challenge the fairness or rightness of this social arrangement. It was just the way things were and were supposed to be. During the past three decades, however, two very significant societal changes have caused many to alter if not reject these beliefs and the gender roles they support. One such change involves the entry of women, particularly married women and women with young children, into the paid labor force. Historically, poor women and young women have held jobs, but only recently have a majority of all women done so. In 1920, 22.7% of all women between the ages of 16 and 65 were in the labor force, but by 1990, 57% were. In 1960, 31.9% of married women with children were employed outside of the home, but by 1990 this figure had jumped to 58.2% (Ries & Stone, 1992, pp. 320-321). Furthermore, for married women with young children, rates of labor force participation now stand at approximately 60%, with almost 38% working full-time (Ries & Stone, 1992, p. 322). Dual-earner families in which husband and wife both assist in providing the family with income now outnumber "traditional" families in which the husband alone holds paid employment and the wife is a full-time housewife. And if current trends continue, and they probably will, only a minority of women will be spending most of their adult lives as full-time homemakers and mothers. Sometimes as the primary wage-earner, more often as a secondary wage-earner supplementing their husbands' incomes, women are assisting with the economic support of their families and themselves.

In addition, the 1960's saw a resurgence of the women's movement which challenged the traditional roles of women and the ideologies that had justified them. In a series of writings beginning in the mid-1960's, modern feminists offered a critical view of the traditional roles women and men have played, claiming that these roles oppressed women by keeping them economically dependent on their husbands, isolating them in households, and forcing them to do the unpaid, drudge work of society (see Firestone, 1970; Friedan, 1963; Mainardi, 1970).

The Division of Domestic Labor Today

Given that the majority of women, including married women with children, are now in the paid labor force, what changes if any are taking place in the domestic roles they are expected to play? Do traditional patterns persist or are more egalitarian divisions being worked out? As women in married couple households assume at least some responsibility for the "economic-provider" role previously assigned to husband/fathers, are an increasing number of men in their roles as husbands and fathers sharing responsibility for housework and child care with their female partners?

Some sociologists have answered yes to this last question. Joseph Pleck (1977) developed a model of the "work-family role system" based on reciprocal relationships between the husbands' and wives' paid and unpaid work. According to this model, as wives exert more time and effort in paid work, husbands will increase their participation in household labor. His own research examining changes in the amount of time husbands' and wives' spent in domestic labor from 1960 to the late 1970's supported this hypothesis and indicated that a *role-convergence* had been taking place over this period such that when wives worked outside the home their husbands were spending more time in housework and child care and they were spending less (Pleck, 1981; 1983).

The majority of researchers, however, dispute the role-convergence view. Instead, the large and growing body of research looking at the division of domestic labor in contemporary U.S. households and based for the most part on surveys of who does what among married couples indicates the following: (1) The majority of women and men now accept a fairly egalitarian view of gender roles in the family (2) Despite these changes in attitudes, men still perform much less of the housework and child care than their wives or female partners, even when their wives are fully employed outside the home and (3) The division of domestic tasks in heterosexual couples continues to be sharply divided by gender.

Changes in Attitude

Traditional attitudes regarding gender roles and domestic labor are well known, were discussed earlier, and can be simply put as "real" men earn money and "good" women stay home. According to these conventional ideologies, a husband can and should assist with certain household chores but his real job is seeing to the economic provision of his dependents, and for him the home should basically be a place of sustenance, nurturance and rest. Wives, on the other hand, are to see to the running of the home (cooking, cleaning, shopping, washing and ironing), to the care of children and husbands, and to the family's social obligations.

In recent years, as women's participation in paid labor has increased, these traditional gender-role expectations have also begun to change. Films like *Mrs. Doubtfire*, television programs like *The Cosby Show* of the 1980's, the day-time soap operas, and many advertisements now depict families headed by a dual-earner couple with fathers who are deeply involved in the rearing of their children. Of course, like the earlier, more traditional family forms glorified in situation comedies such as *Leave It To Beaver* or *The Donna Reed Show*, these popular portrayals generally offer a romanticized and sentimentalized depiction of this "new" family life--seldom do we get glimpses of the economic struggles, stresses, conflicts, and violence that characterize social relations within many U.S. households--but the ideal is nonetheless a new one based on a more egalitarian view of gender roles.

But has this new ideal found its way into the minds and hearts of American men and women? According to attitude surveys, for a majority of Americans the answer is yes. In a 1982 study, over 80% of husbands and wives agreed that husbands should perform more housework when wives are employed (Ferber, 1982). Concomitantly, by the 1980s, 47.7% of all men, and 60.7% of men between the ages of 18-34 both approved of a married woman earning money, and disagreed with the idea that it is better if the man is the achiever outside the home (Wilkie, 1993). This latter study also showed that highly educated men and men whose wives already have full time employment are most likely to express more egalitarian views of the provider role.

What we say is not necessarily what we do

As social psychologists have known for some time, the attitudes or beliefs people hold are not always nor necessarily consistent with their behaviors. For example, individuals who are prejudiced do not necessarily discriminate against those they view as their inferiors, nor do individuals who are unprejudiced always refrain from engaging in racist or sexist actions. Apparently, another area of social life in which many live with a discrepancy between what they say and what they do pertains to gender roles and the division of domestic labor. Traditional views of what is right, natural, necessary and fair may be changing but many couples have yet to put these new ideas and ideals into practice.

Among all types of households headed by a heterosexual couple, the woman is still responsible for most of the housework and child care. Whether the couple is a dual-earner or single-earner (Berardo, Shehan & Leslie, 1987; Berk, 1985), married or cohabitating (Demo & Acock, 1993), has no children, young children or older children (Rexroat & Shehan, 1987), the amount of time men spend in housework and child care is significantly less than that of their wives and frequently less than what they themselves feel they should be doing (Hiller & Philliber, 1986). When women work outside of the home, what changes is not the amount of time husbands spend doing housework, which remains fairly constant at between 5-10 hours per week, but the amount of time they do, which, depending on the number and ages of their children and the number of hours they work outside the home, averages between 16 and 60 hours per week. Full-time housewives do spend significantly more time doing housework than wives employed outside the home but their husbands or male partners typically do not. Although some men with employed wives do make an equal contribution to housework, they are a distinct minority comprising no more than 10% of dual earner households (Blair & Johnson, 1992, p. 575) and probably no more than 5% of all married couple households (Coltrane & Ishii-Kuntz, 1992).

Table 1, drawn from a 1987 study comparing the amount of time dual-career husbands and wives (couples where both partners have a professional or managerial position) spend in housework to that of their same-sex counterparts in dual-earner (couples in which both have jobs but not careers per se) and single-earner households (couples where he works and she is a full-time housewife) helps illustrate this point (Berardo et al., 1987). Across all household types, on average, wives performed 79% of all housework that was done. As is to be expected, full-time housewives spent more hours doing domestic labor than did wives who were employed outside the homes but the latter still averaged between 16-22 hours per week. The hours invested by husbands in housework and child care, on the other hand, averaged between 4-6 hours per week and varied little with their wives' occupational status or the number of hours their wives spent in housework.

Table 1—Time Spent in Housework Each Week by Occupational Status of Husband and Wife[1]

Occupational Status of the Couple	Wives' Hours	Husbands' Hours	Others' Hours[2]	Wives' Proportion[3]
Dual–career[4] couples	16.6	5.7	6.5	.69
Dual earner couples:				
Husband has a career/wife has a job[5]	19.6	5.7	6.3	.69
Husband has a job/wife has a career	21.2	5.3	8.1	.68
Husband and wife have jobs	21.8	5.9	6.8	.71
Single–earner couples:				
Husband has a career	32.8	4.3	4.6	.82
Husband has a job	35.0	3.9	5.8	.83
TOTAL	28.9	4.7	5.9	.79

[1]Adapted from Berardo, Shehan and Leslie (1987, p. 386).
[2]Hours of housework contributed by babysitters, children, or paid domestic help.
[3]Wives' proportion of the total number of hours allocated to housework each week by family members.
[4]Career refers to a professional or managerial position.
[5]Job refers to a non–professional blue–collar or clerical position.

Hence, it still seems to be the case that despite some important shifts in women's economic roles and in women and men's attitudes regarding men's domestic roles, the primary burden of child care and housework falls on women's shoulders. As a result, many more women than men who are fully employed come home to a *second shift* and may end up working well over 70 hours per week (Hartmann, 1981; Hochschild, 1989).

Does the division of domestic labor vary with the race, social class or age of the couple? Yes, but not dramatically. Although there is support for the idea that, in general, African-American marriages are more egalitarian than those of white or Hispanic Americans (Scanzoni,1971; Ross, 1987), and that black husbands and fathers are more involved in child care than their white or Hispanic counterparts (Hossain & Roopnarine, 1993), the actual differences are not great. In addition, these findings have been based on studies of households where the father is present. Given the high proportion of African American families where the father is not in residence, overall it seems that black women are shouldering most of the responsibility for household maintenance and child care. However, when the father is not present in the home, black women are likely to receive assistance from extended kin, especially their children's grandmother (Wilson, Tolson, Hinton, & Keenan, 1990).

With regards to social class, findings are at best inconclusive. When the effects of increased education on the husband's participation in housework is compared with effects of increased income, the findings are conflicting. As either the wife's or husband's education increases, support for both the idea of shared housework and the actual behavior of sharing increases (Model, 1981; Haas, 1980) but as the income of the husband increases, relative to his wife's, the amount of time he spends doing housework decreases. Working class women and men do seem to hold to more traditional gender role attitudes than do middle class couples, but they have always had more difficulty conforming to them, due primarily to the need for a second income (Rubin, 1976), and when working class men have working wives, they appear to do as much housework as their middle class counterparts. In fact a recent study comparing the proportion of housework done by husbands in dual-career families across the class system, using data from the United States and Sweden, concluded that "class location is simply not a powerful determinant of the amount of housework husbands perform" (Wright, Shire, Hwang, Dolan, & Baxter, 1992, p. 276). On the other hand, if married to a full-time housewife, the working class male does less than his middle-class counterpart (Perry-Jenkins & Falk, 1994). It may be the case that the wife's social class position and her class position relative to that of her husband's are more important determinants of the division of domestic labor than the husband's social class position taken by itself. Women in middle class professional and managerial occupations on average appear to spend less time in housework than working class women, regardless of the social class of their respective husbands, but working class wives of middle class husbands spend the most (Berardo et al., 1987; Perry-Jenkins & Falk, 1994).

Age of the couple also makes a difference, with younger couples sharing more housework than older couples (Albrecht, Bahr, & Chadwick, 1979; Farkas, 1976). This finding could either be a result of changes in gender roles that accompany different stages of a family's life cycle or of generational shifts in gender roles. Since the birth of the first child dramatically increases the amount of time women spend in housework and child care (Berk & Berk, 1979; Rexroat & Shehan, 1987), it could be that younger couples share more of the family work because there is less to do and because her time investments are therefore more commensurate with his; on the other hand, it may also be the case that younger generations of Americans are bringing new sets of behavioral expectations to bear on their family arrangements and that they will continue to share more of the household labor than older generations of Americans regardless of their stage in the family life cycle (Coltrane & Ishii-Kuntz, 1992). Only longitudinal studies that examine the division of labor in young couples as they age can tell us for sure which is the more important factor.

His Chores/Her Chores

Not only are there quantitative differences in the amount of time husbands and wives spend in family labor, there are also qualitative differences with regards to the kinds of household tasks each performs. Although some activities, like the managing of household finances or going to the market, are increasingly viewed as joint or shared responsibilities, most couples continue to divide household tasks along fairly traditional gender lines. Outdoor work and work pertaining to heavy machinery such as car repairs, yard work, or external upkeep (if they own a house), continue to be done or seen to primarily by husbands. Cleaning, cooking, laundry, and care of the children, and social obligations are still done primarily by wives. This division of labor reflects significant differences in the intensity, frequency, and content of the domestic chores men and women do. Alice A. Kemp (1994, p. 275) describes these differences this way:

> The particular chores women perform, including child care, are the ones that are more immediate and cannot be postponed. Preparing meals, doing laundry, and looking after children are tasks that demand to be done not only each day, for the most part, but also at particular times, in response to the needs of others. In contrast, men's chores are not typically based on the daily needs of others. Their domestic work tends to include tasks that are more postponable, intermittent, and noncontinuous, so that men have more control over when they are done. Repairs, car maintenance, and yard work can frequently be done when it is convenient for the doer.

The one area of family work in which men have increased their involvement over the past two decades is that of child care, but again such involvement is likely to be the least when the children are infants and their care the most demanding, and often revolves around playing with the child or simply being accessible in case their children need something. Mothers, even when employed outside the home, continue to assume greatest responsibility for the general care and welfare of the children--seeing that they are clothed, fed, changed, taken to the physician when necessary and so forth (Jump & Haas, 1987; Lamb, 1987; Vanek, 1980).

To summarize this section on the division of labor and gender roles in the contemporary U.S. household, findings of recent studies continue to demonstrate the persistence of traditional patterns of behavior in the majority of U.S. families headed by a married couple. As Demo and Acock (1993, p. 330) suggest,

> In the face of enormous social change over the past three decades, and with the accompanying popular interest in how families have been reshaped by changing gender roles, by steady increases in female labor force involvement, and by growing diversity in family structure, women's domestic labor has remained at a constant and substantial level . . . the fact that women continue to do two to

three times as much nonwage family labor as their husbands or partners is compelling evidence that family labor remains gendered and that popular descriptions of changes in marital, family, and gender roles are overstated.

Why Don't More Men Do More Around the House: Attempts at Explanation

How then can we explain the persistence of these traditional patterns especially in light of the other changes that have been occurring in women's labor force participation and in gender-role ideologies? Why don't men do more of the housework, particularly when their female partners are themselves wage earners? We have already established that in the majority of cases it is not because they hold to traditional norms and values of the husband/father roles. Both principles of fairness and balance would appear to dictate a more equal or shared division of family work, but this simply doesn't seem as yet to be occurring.

So what are the reasons? Attempts to answer these questions and to explain the persistence of traditional gender roles can be classified into two general categories: male-resistance hypotheses and female-resistance hypotheses. Both focus on the factors that affect the negotiations and outcomes of marital interactions (microlevel processes through which a couple determines who does what) but the first stresses his perceived interests and power in determining these outcomes and the latter emphasizes hers.

Male-resistance theorists argue that the majority of adult men with female partners do not do more housework and child care because they do not want to and because they have the power to exert their wishes (Glazer, 1980; Hartmann, 1981; Polatnick, 1973). Theorists who offer this explanation claim that all men, regardless of their social class or race, derive material and symbolic benefits from traditional arrangements. Having a wife or female partner responsible for running his home and caring for his children frees him for other more extrinsically rewarding pursuits like a full-time job; frees him from the draining but necessary drudgery of seeing to his own basic needs; offers him greater leisure; and enhances his sense of masculinity by providing him with a domain to rule and a subordinate to service him.

Altering these arrangements means a loss of privilege for him, and who wants to lose privilege? He may be willing to assume a greater share of the domestic labor if his wife demands that he does and if she has the power to back up her demands, but in the majority of households, her power will be less than his if for no other reason than that he makes more money than she, and she is therefore more economically dependent on him. Indeed, the very fact that she is expected to bare primary responsibility for the care of young children means that it is precisely when she is most in need of assistance, when her children are infants and babies, that she is at her weakest in the relationship (Gillespie, 1972). In addition, and as further evidence of his greater power in the relationship, when he does participate in housework he does so selectively, choosing "nicer" jobs and leaving the mundane, repetitive, symbolically demeaning, never-ending work for her to do. He may "help" her with household chores but typically he doesn't assume responsibility for them. He may spend time with the kids but he doesn't clean the toilets.

Therefore, while the attitudes of both husbands and wives towards a fair division of household labor are changing, behaviors are not, because changes in his attitudes, without changes in her power, are not enough. Signs that these traditional patterns are under attack from within, however, are suggested by the higher levels of marital dissatisfaction reported by employed wives of house-lazy husbands and the increasing conflict over the division of household labor that couples now report (Hartmann, 1981; Huber & Spitze, 1983).

Support for this position comes from recent studies that have shown a relationship between the size of the economic contribution a woman makes to the household finances and the amount of time her husband spends in domestic labor (Coltrane & Ishii-Kuntz, 1992). Conversely, the more the husband's earnings exceed those of his wife, the less housework he does (Ross, 1987). Presumably the greater her contribution (not how much she earns per se but how much she earns as a proportion of total household income) the greater her power in the marriage and the more successfully she can press for a renegotiation of household and child care tasks. Furthermore, there is some evidence—as yet inconclusive—that when husbands' and wives' views of the way things should be differ, his attitudes have greater significance than do hers in influencing household patterns (Ross, 1987). If this is the case, than this would support the male-resistance hypothesis as well.

Given the U.S. society's cultural and institutional support for male-dominance in marital relations, the male-resistance explanation for the perpetuation of traditional patterns of household labor no doubt has much to commend it. Female resistance researchers, however, note that there is nothing inherently odious about housework or child care and that, to the contrary, much of it can be rewarding. They argue, therefore, that at least in part, the failure of most couples to divide up domestic labor more equally might be because women refuse to give it up rather than because their husbands refuse to take it on (DeVault, 1990; Ehrensaft, 1980; Thompson, 1989). Like the male-resistance theorists, the reasons female-resistance scholars put forward for the continuation of traditional gender-based divisions of domestic labor emphasize historical practices of sexism and sex discrimination but with twist. They argue that, since women have historically been excluded from equal participation in the public institutions of society and have instead been relegated to family roles, many women have come to see the home as the one arena of their lives that they control and resent any male intrusion into it. Furthermore, the intensive socialization for marriage and motherhood females in this society undergo (Pogrebin, 1980) results in a strong identification with these roles. The work of household maintenance and child care becomes valued as an expression of their womanhood. Much as men in certain male-dominated occupations fear a loss of symbolic-masculinity when women do their jobs, so women with a lot invested in their roles as mothers and wives may fear a loss of symbolic-femininity when their male partners try to share them. Granted her interests in maintaining control over this labor may be intrinsic rather than extrinsic in nature and may even undermine her occupational and economic attainment in the public world of work, but these facts do not necessarily detract from their importance as behavioral motivators.

Support for the female-resistance hypothesis resides in the fact that only a minority of wives who do most of the housework want their husbands to do more (Berk, 1985), and that many mothers do express concern about letting their husbands do more of the child care (Jump & Haas, 1989). In addition, wives who are more accepting of maternal employment, and who are therefore less supportive of traditional family roles as the sole or even primary source of a woman's identity, do have husbands who share more of the housework.

It seems that men do not insist on doing housework and may, if their power is great enough, resist doing so regardless of the attitudes they or their wives hold, but even when women's power relative to their husbands is great enough to influence the division of family labor, she tends not to demand it unless her gender-role attitudes are liberal (Hardesty & Bokemeier, 1989). As long as women see their primary roles as those of wife and mother, even when they work outside the home, they may not see their work roles as anything but extensions of their familial roles. Under this condition, they may want their husbands to "help" but not to share equally in domestic activities for fear of the loss of rewards and power they derive for their familial roles.

No doubt the relative power of the male and female partner and the gender-ideologies they hold all play a part in the division of domestic labor that is negotiated by U.S. couples. But as both of the above explanations imply, a complete explanation of the persistence of traditional gender-role patterns must also take into account the institutional forces that impinge on family life and that shape, constrain, and limit both what couples see as fair as well as what they see as workable. The fact that men are still economically advantaged does indeed make it more likely for both husbands and wives to see his occupational achievement as more important than hers and to respond to its demands by having her assume more of the domestic labor, enabling him to give his job whatever it takes. Even if she is employed outside the home, she and her husband are not likely to see her low wage job as anything more than supplemental, and she therefore gives her paid work less and her domestic work more than he does. As a result, all but the most privileged women in U.S. society are caught in a vicious cycle of paid and unpaid labor. Their responsibility for child care and domestic labor means that they typically must avoid the higher paying, more demanding jobs that would interfere with their familial responsibilities; yet, the low wages they therefore end up taking keep them dependent on their husbands and make it seem only fair that they do more of the housework to compensate (Glazer, 1980).

Furthermore, most businesses, schools, and organizations continue to operate as if families have full-time moms at home. The majority of work roles continue to be based on the assumption that those doing them have full time wives to see to the needs of their house and children so that they can make their profession or the company their first and foremost commitment. Men who reject this view and who are committed to spending time with their children report pressure to conceal this fact from coworkers and colleagues who might view them as less committed to their work as a result (Coltrane, 1989).

While women out of economic necessity and personal desire are entering the work force in increasing numbers, the public institutions of this society have made too few concessions or accommodations to this fact. The school day and the school year presuppose a mother at home by midafternoon and throughout the summer. Few work places are sensitive to the needs of working parents.

As a result of this institutional myopia, the majority of dual-earner households with children face greater burdens and stresses and these burdens are disproportionately being shouldered by American women. Dual-career couples in which both have relatively high-status, high-paying jobs can afford to relieve this stress by hiring others--typically poorer women--to clean for them, but this is not a feasible solution for the majority of households. Most couples must seek to absorb the additional burden in other ways that maximize perceived benefits. In some cases, depending upon their values and their economic resources, they do seek more egalitarian household arrangements, but even in these cases they do so primarily to minimize her role overload and maximize his ability to spend time with his kids rather than because of an ideological commitment to sex equality (Coltrane, 1989; Haas, 1980). In too many cases, she makes the greater sacrifices, absorbing a disproportionate share of the extra-work that her employment outside the home creates. Unfortunately, whether or not they adhere to the ideological principles at stake, many couples find it easier to slip into traditional patterns when the burdens imposed from the demands of public institutions are too great, and these traditional patterns, whether she works or not, mean that she continues to see to the domestic labor.

All the attitude change in the world may not be enough to alter the household division of labor without the type of institutional policies and practices that make such changes feasible and attractive. Now that increasing numbers of Americans believe that women have the right to work outside the home and that men should assume more responsibility for housework and childcare, now that so few American households reflect the traditional ideals of a stay-at-home-Mom and a breadwinner-and-little-else Dad, it is time that public institutions followed suit. Flexible work schedules, paid maternal and paternal leaves, on-site child care, publicly subsidized quality child care facilities, before school and after school programs, summer school programs, shared jobs, even wages for housework are all intriguing policy options that would offer families of all types a wider range of possibilities while relieving them, and women in particular, of the added burden of assisting their husbands in providing for the family without assistance in the care of their home and children. At present, the U.S. lags behind almost all the other industrialized societies of the world in offering these types of institutionalized benefits to working parents.

In addition, it might be time for members of U.S. society to rethink the standards we bring to bear on the meaning of "home." As citizens in advanced capitalist societies, we are all, men and women alike, bombarded most of our lives with images of what a real home should look like. Many of these images are sold to us by corporations seeking to sell products by playing on our status anxieties and concerns for the health and well-being of those we love and for whom we are supposed to care. So we buy more things and we work harder to keep them clean. We get more space and need more time to keep it neat. It could very well be that some of the stresses would be alleviated by less tolerance of consumerism and more tolerance of dirt.

Unanswered Questions

I began this paper by listing some questions about gender roles and the division of domestic labor in U.S. households that I thought it important to consider. Some of these questions I have tried to answer by reviewing the major findings of recent studies. Research seems fairly conclusive that women assume far more of the burden for the unpaid labor of housework and child care in their households than do their male partners even when they have full time jobs. We know that there have been significant changes in gender role attitudes among American women and men, but we also know that in the majority of cases behaviors have yet to catch up with beliefs. Furthermore, despite some shifts, the division of family labor continues to be sharply divided by gender. Apparently very few men who live with a female partner do actually clean the toilets.

Yet, as I tried to indicate above, we do not as yet fully know why these traditions persist among married couple households. And many other questions remain unanswered. To date, little is known about the organization of domestic labor in households headed by gay or lesbian couples. More research has been conducted on the sexual lives of such couples than on how the work of running homes and raising kids (should there be any) gets done, even though these latter activities consume far more of a couple's time and energy.

Too little qualitative work has been done on the nature and interconnections of social class and racial differences in the division of domestic labor. To be sure, as a variable social class has not been ignored in quantitative survey research on housework, and child care, but this work has not examined class differences in the "meaning" of housework and in the "standards" of child care as they relate to gender roles. Similarly, ethnic and racial differences in family organization and cultural ideals needs study in more depth. Faced with the extraordinary burdens created by poverty and racism, impoverished African-American families have been more likely than white middle class families to create family arrangements for multiple households in complex exchange systems of support and assistance organized around female kin (Stack, 1976). What this alternative family form means for the content and performance of housework has not been adequately addressed.

Similarly, the role children play in the division of domestic labor and how this role varies with the family form as well as the gender and age of the children needs more research. A few studies indicate that while, overall, children in most American households do little domestic labor (3-6 hours per week), teenage daughters do substantially more than other children (Demo & Acock, 1993). Most studies, however, have ignored the family labor of children and the way such labor may itself perpetuate the division of labor by gender that adults then recreate in their own homes.

No doubt other important questions about the nature, causes and consequences of gender roles and the division of domestic labor in U.S. households need to be asked and addressed. Perhaps you can think of some yourself.

References

Adams, B. E. (1986). *The family: A sociological interpretation*. San Diego: Harcourt Brace Jovanovich.

Albrecht, S., Bahr, H. M., & Chadwick, B. A. (1979). Changing family and sex roles: An assessment of age differences. *Journal of Marriage and the Family, 41,* 41-50.

Barrett, M., & McIntosh, M. (1980). The "family wage": Some problems for socialists and feminists. *Capital and Class, 2,* 51-72.

Berardo, D. H., Shehan, C. L., & Leslie, G. R. (1987). A residue of tradition: Jobs, careers and spouses' time in housework. *Journal of Marriage and the Family, 49,* 381-390.

Berk, R., & Berk, S. F. (1979). *Labor and leisure at home: Content and organization of the household day.* Newbury Park, CA: Sage.

Berk, S. F. (1985). *The gender factory: The apportionment of work in American households.* New York: Plenum Press.

Blair, S. L., & Johnson, M. P. (1992). Wives' perceptions of the fairness of the division of household labor: Intersection of housework and ideology. *Journal of Marriage and the Family, 54,* 570-581.

Boydston, J. (1990). *Home and work: Housework, wages and the ideology of labor in the early republic.* New York: Oxford University Press.

Coltrane, S. (1989). Household labor and the routine production of gender. *Social Problems, 36,* 473-217.

Coltrane, S., & Ishii-Kuntz, M. (1992). Men's housework: A life course perspective. *Journal of Marriage and the Family, 54,* 43-57.

Coverman, S. (1985). Explaining husbands' participation in domestic labor. *The Sociological Quarterly, 26,* 81-97.

Coverman, S., & Sheley, J. F. (1986). Change in men's housework and child-care time. *Journal of Marriage and the Family, 48,* 413-422.

Cowan, R. S. (1983). *More work for mother: The ironies of household technology from the open hearth to the microwave.* New York: Basic Books.

Demo, D. H., & Acock, A. C. (1993). Family diversity and the division of domestic labor. *Family Relations, 42,* 323-331.

DeVault, M. L. (1990). Conflict over housework: The problem that (still) has no name. In L. Krisberg (Ed.), *Research in social movements conflicts and change: A research annual, Vol. 12* (pp. 189-202). Greenwich, CT: JAI.

Ehrensaft, D. (1980). When women and men mother. *The Socialist Review, 49,* 37-73.

Farkas, G. (1976). Education, wage rates, and the division of labor between husband and wife. *Journal of Marriage and the Family, 38,* 473-484.

Ferber, M. (1982). Low-market participation of young married women: Cause and effects. *Journal of Marriage and the Family, 44,* 457-468.

Firestone, S. (1970). *The dialectic of sex.* New York: Morrow Quill.

Friedan, B. (1963). *The feminine mystique.* New York: W. W. Norton.

Gillespie, D. (1972). Who has the power? The marital struggle. In H. P. Dreitzel (Ed.), *Family, marriage, and the struggle of the sexes* (pp.121-150). New York: Macmillan.

Glazer, N. (1980). Everyone needs three hands: Doing paid and unpaid work. In S. F. Berk (Ed.), *Women and household labor* (pp.249-274). Beverly Hills, CA: Sage.

Haas, L. (1980). Role sharing couples: A study of egalitarian marriages. *Family Relations, 29,* 289-296.

Hardesty, C., & Bokemeier, J. (1989). Finding time and making do: Distribution of household labor in nonmetropolitan marriages. *Journal of Marriage and the Family, 51,* 253-267.

Hartmann, H. (1976). Capitalism, patriarchy and job segregation by sex. *Signs, 1,* 137-168.

Hartmann, H. (1981). The family as the locus of gender, class and political struggle: The example of housework. *Signs, 6,* 366-394.

Hiller, D. V., & Phelliber, W. W. (1986). The division of labor in contemporary marriage: Expectations, perceptions, and performance. *Social Problems, 33,* 191-201.

Hochschild, A. (1989). *The second shift.* New York: Viking.

Hossain, Z., & Roopharine, J. L. (1993). Division of household labor and child care in dual-earner African-American families with infants. *Sex Roles, 29,* 571-583.

Huber, J., & Spitze, G. (1983). *Sex stratification: Children, housework and jobs.* New York: Academic Press.

Ishii-Kuntz, M., & Coltrane, S. (1992). Predicting the sharing of household labor: Are parenting and housework distinct. *Sociological Perspectives, 35,* 629-647.

Jackson, S. (1992). Towards a historical sociology of housework: A materialist feminist analysis. *Women's Studies International Forum, 15,* 153-172.

Jones, J. (1985). *Labor of love, labor of sorrow: Black women and family, from slavery to the present.* New York: Vintage Books.

Jump, T. L., & Haas, L. (1987). Fathers in transition: Dual earner fathers participating in childcare. In M. S. Kimmel (Ed.), *Changing men* (pp. 98-114). Newbury Park, CA: Sage.

Kemp, A. A. (1994). *Women's work: Degraded and devalued.* Englewood Cliffs, NJ: Prentice-Hall.

Lamb, M. E. (1987). Introduction: The emergent American father. In M. E. Lamb (Ed.), *The father's role: Cross-cultural perspective* (pp.3-25). Hillsdale, NJ: Lawrence Erelbaum.

Mainardi, P. (1970). The politics of housework. In R. Morgan (Ed.), *Sisterhood is powerful: An anthology of writings from the women's liberation movement* (pp.501-510). New York: Vintage Books.

Model, S. (1982). Housework by husbands: Determinants and implications. In J. Aldous (Ed.), *Two paychecks: Life in dual-earner families* (pp. 193-206). Beverly Hills, CA: Sage.

Oakley, A. (1976). *Woman's work: The housewife, past and present.* New York: Vintage Books.

Peattie, L., & Rein, M. (1983). *Women's claims: A study in political economy.* Oxford: Oxford University Press.

Perry-Jenkins, M., & Falk, K. (1994). Class, couples, and conflict: Effects of the division of labor on assessments of marriage in dual-earner families. *Journal of Marriage and the Family, 56,* 165-180.

Pleck, J. H. (1978). The work/family role system. *Social Problems, 24,* 417-427.

Pleck, J. H. (1981). *Changing patterns of work and family roles* (Working paper No. 81). Wellesley, MA: Wellesley College Center for Research on Women.

Pleck, J. H. (1983). Husbands paid work and family roles: Current research issues. In H. Lopata and J. H. Pleck (Eds.), *Research in the interweave of social roles. Vol. 3: Families and jobs* (pp. 130-171). Greenwich, CT: JAI Press.

Pogrebin, L. C. (1980). *Growing up free: Raising your child in the 80s.* New York: Bantam Books.

Polatnick, M. R. (1973). Why men don't rear children: A power analysis. *Berkeley Journal of Sociology, 18,* 35-86.

Rexroat, C., & Shehan, C. (1987). The family life cycle and spouse's time in housework. *Journal of Marriage and the Family, 49,* 737-750.

Ries, P., & Stone, A. J. (1992). *The American women 1992-1993: A status report.* New York: W. W. Norton.

Ross, C. E. (1987). The division of labor at home. *Social Forces, 65,* 816-833.

Rothchild, J. (1983). Technology, housework, and women's liberation. In J. Rothschild (Ed.) *Machina ex dea: Feminist perspectives on technology* (pp. 79-93). New York: Pergamon.

Rubin, L. (1976). *World of pain: Life in the working-class family.* New York: Basic Books.

Scanzoni, J. (1971). *The Black family in modern society.* Boston: Allyn & Bacon.

Schooler, C., Miller, J., Miller, K., & Richtand, C. (1984) Work for the household: Its nature and consequences for husbands and wives. *American Journal of Sociology, 90,* 97-124.

Stack, C. (1974). *All our kin: Strategies for survival in a Black community.* New York: Harper & Row.

Thompson, L. (1991). Family work: Women's sense of fairness. *Journal of Family Issues, 12,* 181-196.

Vanek, J. (1980). Household work, wage work, and sexual equality. In S. Berk (Ed.), *Women and household labor.* Newbury Park, CA: Sage.

Wilkie, J. R. (1993). Changes in U.S. men's attitudes toward the family provider role, 1972-1989. *Gender & Society, 7,* 261-279/

Wilson, M. E., Tolson, T. F. J., Hinton, I. D., & Keenan, M. (1990). Flexibility and sharing of childcare duties in Black families. *Sex Roles, 22,* 409-423.

Wright, E. O., Shire, K., Hwang, S., Dolan, M., & Baxter, J. (1992). The non-effects of class on the gender division of labor in the home: A comparative study of Sweden and the U.S. *Gender & Society, 6,* 252-282.

Article 13

My Choice? Or My Obligation?

Chih-duen (Painton) Tse

Introduction

The following discussion will not be presented as a research study. It is, rather, a discussion based on my personal experience and observations acquired in the past eighteen years living in Western society with a background of eastern culture.

Personal Background

My parents were both born and raised in Southwestern China. They left for Taiwan following the Chinese Revolution in 1949. I was born in Taiwan as the second of five children. My father was a highranking military officer as we were growing up, thus, the children in my family experienced a very structured and well-disciplined childhood. I received my basic education and four years of college in Taiwan. Then I came to the United States to pursue a graduate degree. I met and married a Caucasian man during my graduate school years. While we were married we spent almost every holiday with his family, which consisted of his parents and a grandmother. Occasionally, we spent time with his uncles, aunts, and cousins. We had attended a few of the bi-annual family reunions where we were acquainted with those relatives whose names were mentioned occasionally in family conversations.

In the fourth year of our marriage we had a son, our first and only child. After the addition of a younger generation, the inlaws visited more often. My mother visited us from Taiwan, lived for extended periods, and was a great help for my dual career family. I also have two sisters and one brother residing in the United States, and we have visited each other frequently. It is not difficult to imagine the many different conflicts which have arisen in my intercultural marriage. When East meets West, harmonies do not always exist. However, the attitude used to handle the conflicts is often the key to determine whether the conflicts can be resolved with a happy ending. With the brief introduction to my intercultural experience, I would like to go into the subject of my discussion.

Choice or Obligation: Some Examples

According to recent statistics, U.S. immigrants from the Far East (i.e., Chinese, Japanese, Korean, Filipino, and Vietnamese) have increased from 10,000 per year in the 1950s to over 200,000 per year in the recent years (Borjas, 1990). The source also pointed out that the Far East immigrant population is one of the fastest growing minority groups in the U.S. These immigrants brought with them their cultural heritages, among which are dedication to hard-work, respect for their ancestries, avoiding being trouble makers, being great savers, obedient, etc. These were the most-mentioned virtues by the Western society. Nevertheless, there are less noticeable problems gradually being developed in these tradition-bound families. These problems frequently exist between generations and gradually endanger family relationships.

What are some of these problems? Perhaps many of us who have spent a good portion of our lives in both the Eastern and Western dominated cultures have had some painful experiences in this regard. The rules one should, or is expected to, obey in an Eastern family and a Western family setting are quite different. A few of examples can easily be found without much research:

- Your son wants to quit violin lessons so that he can spend the time practicing with his soccer team twice a week. You tell him that he has invested ten years in the lessons, and he is doing well, winning state recognitions for excellent performances. Every son and daughter in your friends' families is doing well in violin, and you can not afford to not be one of them. Your son says that he really has no interest in the lessons any more; he enjoys soccer much more than anything he is doing. He has followed your will for ten years and it is time for him to make his own choice for his own interests. He thinks that the investment put into the lessons is for you, not him. He has no trouble dropping the violin lesson while you cannot let go of it. Perhaps ten years ago he should have taken the piano instead of violin—another one of your decisions for him. Perhaps he wouldn't have minded taking drumming lessons at the time. But no! Kids in other Chinese families were all taking violin; it had to be the ONLY noble thing to do.

- Your daughter wants to go to an institute for performing arts to pursue her education. The decision shocks you! You always had plans for her to go to an Ivy League school. She has always been a straight "A" student. She has one of the highest ACT and SAT scores in her high school class and has received numerous honors and awards. You and your spouse have lived in minimal subsistence in order to save for your daughter's education. Now she wants to be an actress, an ACTRESS! You cannot even stand the thought of telling your friends about what your daughter does for a living while these friends' children are all physicians, dentists, scientists or accountants. Where can you place your pride?

- Your mother-in-law had moved in to live with you for a while. You, being a very nice daughter-in-law, welcomed her with open arms At first everything was running smoothly and your life was in peace and harmony. A week later, she began to think that she was the woman of the house and she should be in charge. One day she wanted to rearrange all the furniture, the next day she wanted to add a Buddha stand in your Italian-style dining room.

Then she told you that you did not know how to raise your own children. She told you that your cooking needed improvement. She complained that you have been wasting too much money on unnecessary things. Your house was messy. You didn't get up early enough. You didn't show enough respect for her... Suddenly, you became unfit to be the wife of her son, and unfit to be the mother of her grandchildren-

- Maybe you are a very successful person. You have done well in your career. Your spouse is also doing well and both of you have a combined income that would place you on the top of the middle class family category. Your children have excellent academic records that have earned you a great deal of respect among your friends. You live in a million dollar home located in one of the most prestigious subdivisions in town. Both you and your spouse have younger-than-your-age appearances with excellent health and are in excellent physical shape. It is hard to even think about what more you may need in your life, and you are very content with your lives. Your parents are both very old and need a lot of medical attention. You wish to have them living with you under the same roof so that you may look after them. However, the practical problem of their state of health has prevented you from having them in your home. With their consensus, you placed them in a nearby nursing home where 24-hour medical assistance was available. Frequently, on the weekends you pick them up so that they can spend a couple of days with you and your family. These are the best arrangements one could have and relieve your mind from having to worry about neglecting them Then one day a friend told you that a rumor about you has been spreading. People are talking behind your back about how you have abandoned your parents. They regard you as a cold-blooded, heartless person to your parents, even though you might have invited these people as guests to your dinner parties many times in the past. People are saying that you should have placed your parents in your house so that you can take good care of them. No one, certainly NO ONE, has considered the fact that your parents really cannot be left alone without any nursing attention. Well, if you argued in this regard, they might think that the RIGHT thing for you to do is to quit your job and be at home with your parents.

Perhaps you, your siblings, your friends, or someone you know, has experienced similar situations to those listed above. And perhaps they managed to iron out these obstacles in their lives without many painful results. For most people who are involved in problems like these, however, the problems are often much deeper than it sounds to an outsider. It is simply not easy to survive any one of these situations without being stung and left with a, or several, broken hearts.

Facts and Non-Facts: East Versus West

Western culture, just like Eastern culture, does have rules governing family relationships. Unlike many stories people have been told in eastern societies concerning the coldness and looseness of Western family structures, the people-to-people relationships in Western society are also centered around families. A family with five generations all living within a mile is not too rare for the agricultural states in this country. Households having a grandmother are not uncommon. Many of my caucasian friends have their parents live in the same city so that the grandparents would baby-sit, while the grown-up children would take care of their elderly parents' house chores whenever needed. Relatives visit each other often, and large-scale family reunions are commonly heard of. But, of course, the Eastern family and Western family relationships are different. We all know that they are different. In what ways are they different?

It is very difficult to generalize these questions into a few well-defined points. However, I think the differences between the Eastern and Western families probably originated from the basic concept of individuality. In Eastern cultures, men live in a world which is mastered by a central unity. The relationships between different levels of society segments are governed by the law of the universe. Individuals are partial entities and do not have many independent values. The basic element of the universe is the society, and each individual's behavior should be directed towards a common society goal. Families are just a minor strand of a large society. The strength of the society depends on the harmony of each family in it. And each individual in the family should just fit themselves into this harmony. No disruption is allowed.

Western culture, on the other hand, is centered around each individual in the society. No one *is of* partial value. Each individual represents an independent entity. A family is merely a group of individuals "temporarily" linked together, and no one in this group should be responsible for its unity. In fact, no one is expected to sacrifice for any common goal. If harmony is reached among family members, fine, if not, that is fine too. A person's responsibility stops at him or herself. No one will be given responsibility on others' behalf. Therefore, whatever you choose to do, or to not do, is entirely depended on your own free will. Once you have taken care of yourself, no obligation will fall on your shoulder.

Conclusion: When East Meets West

So, when East meets West, would they be compatible with each other? Can the two coexist peacefully? The examples illustrated above show that many problems can arise when people of the Eastern culture are living in the Western world. These problems, like all other cultural conflicts, require devoted sincerity from all parties involved. Tolerance, understanding, consideration, and compromise are the key virtues required to resolve these conflicts. A much more positive and constructive attitude would also be helpful to reconstruct the mutual trust among all parties in the conflicts. "When there is a will, there is a way." This good old saying exists in both Eastern and Western cultures and could lead the way to a final harmony.

Reference

Borias, G. J. (1990). *Friends or strangers: The impact of immigrants on the U.S. economy.* New York Basic Books.

The Elderly

Part V

Article 14

The Societal and Cultural Context of Retirement in Four Countries

Chikako Usui

Introduction

Over the last several decades, labor force participation among older men has declined dramatically in many industrially advanced countries, although the **rate** of decline has varied considerably across countries. Many scholars (Clark & Barker, 1981; Cowgill, 1986; Duggan, 1984; Fields & Mitchell, 1984; Koli et al., 1991) cite changes in economic conditions (e.g., high unemployment; obsolescence of skills among older workers) or social policy factors (e.g., retirement benefits, age of entitlement) as the cause for these trends. Others (Parns & Nestel, 1971; Bixby, 1976; Sheppard, 1976; Palmore, 1975; Palmore et al., 1985) stress the importance of subjective variables (e.g., health, attitudes toward retirement). However, few cross-national, comparative studies have examined the relative contribution of all these factors **simultaneously**, owing mainly to the lack of appropriate data.[1]

Here, I present data on aspects of retirement in four nations (the United States, the United Kingdom, France, & Japan) for 1981 and 1986. I also examine how retirement patterns are related to economic policy, and cultural and social psychological variables in each nation. The data suggest that some of the retirement patterns in all four countries are strongly correlated with economic and social policy factors. However, when one retires, and how to supplement one's retirement income are also strongly related to cultural and social psychological variables.

Three Perspectives of Determinants of Retirement

Three general classes of explanation have been advanced to account for the increasing proportion of the aged who are retired: (1) changing economic and demographic conditions in a society; (2) changing governmental policies that influence the well-being and other circumstances of the aged (e.g., Social Security in the United States); and (3) cultural orientations and individual attitudes toward work, leisure, and retirement.

(1) Economic and Demographic Changes

In contrast to an agricultural society where the work experience of the aged is valued, older workers in the industrialized society find themselves increasingly at a competitive disadvantage compared to younger workers (Cowgill, 1974; Graebner, 1980). The development of an industrialized, bureaucratized economy requires an educated, skilled, and mobile labor force, and the value of older people **as workers** tends to decline. Employers often seek to replace them with the more recently trained young so as to avoid retraining costs and to rejuvenate the workplace. In the event of plant closings, layoffs, and company reorganizations, older workers are more likely to lose their jobs, and once unemployed, they remain unemployed for longer periods (Atchley, 1991, p. 205). Even when experience, technical competence, and education are held constant, older workers are still laid off first (Parnes & King, 1977). Rum (1989) reports that job dislocation rates of older workers have increased significantly since 1970. Economic preferences in the firm for younger workers therefore steadily remove older workers from the labor force.

An important demographic change being witnessed in most industrially developed countries is a recent increase in the size of their older populations (Morrison, 1983, p. 14). Two hypotheses have projected the effects of this change of patterns of retirement. First, it has been argued that as the proportion of the aged increases, the pressure to keep workers employed longer will also increase, so as to ease the burden of social security taxation. Also, as life expectancy increases, people might be willing to spend more of their years working. Both of these would lead one to expect increasing delays in retirement as the size of the elderly population increases. An opposite view (Cowgill, 1974), however, argues that if the number of available jobs remains steady, an increasingly larger older population will lead to more job competition among the aged themselves, in a process sometimes called the "cohort crowding effect" (Duggan, 1984), and this in turn would serve to drive down the average retirement age. Although some predicted acute labor shortage in the near future as resulting from the reduction of the youth labor force, the expansion of the prime work force (age 35-54) is expected to offset such labor shortage (Morrison, 1983, p. 15).

(2) Social Policy

In addition to economy and demography, social policy is also frequently cited in explanations of the retirement patterns of older workers. Public, corporate, and private pensions, the associated levels of benefits, and other legal regulations play very important roles in shaping the retirement decision of older individuals. The more extensive the benefits, one assumes, the greater the number of retirees and the earlier the average retirement age. One may also assume that older workers will be more likely to retire as legal regulations governing eligibility for pension benefits are relaxed (e.g., flexible early retirement options for reasons of long service, poor health resulting in partial disability, or in response to involuntary unemployment) (Morrison, 1983; Quinne & Burkhauser, 1990; Zeitzer, 1983, p. 53).

(3) Cultural and Social Psychological Factors

Finally, it can be hypothesized that retirement decisions will also reflect cultural and social psychological influences. Cultural influences might include the degree to which "retirement" is a formalized status. In the US, to illustrate, the concept of retirement has matured, especially in the last 50 years, and it is accepted as good and proper (Conner, 1992). However, in Japan, people are more likely to think of themselves as being "old" than being "retired", the latter concept having come into widespread use only in recent decades (Martin, 1989; Inkeles & Usui, 1989).

Other cultural factors of possible significance include popular images of what it means to be old or retire; general values surrounding work and leisure; shared conceptions about what constitutes a good life; and the closeness of family ties and people's dependence on them. Significant national differences in any of these attitudes could conceivably explain variations in the rate of retirement across societies.

A number of studies (Atchley, 1991) have demonstrated the importance of attitudes and values in determining the patterns of retirement. Individuals with unfulfilled aspirations for hobbies and other leisure time activities, for example, are likely to retire earlier than others. Employing National Longitudinal Study data on US men aged 58 and 59 in 1966 and 1976, Palmore and associates (1985) examined both objective factors, such as being subject to mandatory retirement, and subjective factors, such as being subject to mandatory retirement, job attitudes, and attitudes about retirement. Their findings indicate that attitude towards one's job was the single best predictor of retirement age in a multiple regression analysis that included urban vs. rural status, wages, occupation, health, and being subject to mandatory retirement. Specifically, men who said "I would like to work even if I did not have to" and those who said "prefer work to leisure" remained in the labor force longer than their opposite numbers.

Clearly, no single factor or set of factors could be considered as the sole determinant of cross-national variation in retirement rates. The question then becomes one of the relative contributions of various factors.

Data

This study examines the relationship between the rates of retirement among older men and economic, social policy, cultural and sociological factors in the four countries. Thus, the hypothesis to be tested is macro-sociological. In accordance with the hypothesis, the data to be analyzed will be aggregate (primarily population) and cross-national (four countries in the sample) for 1981 and 1986.

Economic, demographic and policy data for this analysis were obtained from standard international source books. Data on retirement rates and attitudal informations were obtained from international surveys conducted by the Japanese Prime Minister's Office in 1981 and

1986 (Japan Prime Minister's Office, 1982, 1987). These Japanese survey data are based on personal (face-to-face) interviews of national samples of about 400 men aged 60 and over in each country. In 1981, the survey included US, UK, France, and Japan; in the 1986 survey, Italy and Denmark were added and the UK and France were dropped. In this paper, I report data for the initial four countries.

In this study, the retired are those males age 60 and over who have withdrawn from the labor force. According to this definition, elderly persons who are working full-time or part-time, those working while on pension, and those still seeking employment are not retired. Retirement rates (thus defined) vary considerably across the four nations: in France in 1981, 92% of the over-60 males were retired by the above definition; in Japan in 1981, by way of contrast, only 43% of the over-60 males were retired.[2]

Independent Variables

(1) Economic and Demographic Variables

The general level of economic development in each nation was measured as the gross national product (GNP) per capita in U.S. dollars, as obtained from the World Development Reports (The World Bank, 1980, 1983, 1987). Characteristics of the occupational structure of a society were indexed by the percentage of the labor force employed in agriculture. This measure is closely related to the percentage of self-employed and has been used previously by other investigators (Pampel & Weiss, 1983). Labor force (and unemployment) data are taken from the *Yearbook of Labor Statistics* (ILO, 1981, 1982, 1984, 1987).

Key demographic variables implicated in prior research include: (1) the percentage of population aged 60 and over; (2) the age structure, measured here as the ratio of the population aged 60 and over to the population aged 25-59; and (3) male life expectancy at age 60. These data were obtained from the *Demographic Yearbook* (United Nations, 1982, 1984, 1987) and the *Yearbooks of Labor Statistics* (ILO, 1981, 1982, 1984, 1987).

(2) Policy Variables

I characterize the structure of **public pension** programs in each country with several related measures: (1) formal pensionable age; (2) early retirement age (the earliest age at which retirement with pension is possible); (3) eligibility criteria for receipt of benefits; (4) percentage of wage replacement by pension (for an average couple); and (5) tax rates for old-age, disability, and survivors pensions. These data were obtained from *Social Security Throughout the World* (U.S. Department of Health and Human Services, 1982, 1987).

I also characterized each nation according to the percentage of older men receiving financial support from (1) public (government-sponsored) pension, (2) private (corporate) pensions, and (3) other private sources (savings, investments, support by relatives, etc.). These data were obtained from the Japanese Prime Minister's surveys (1982 & 1987).

(3) Cultural and Social Psychological Variables

Recent large scale surveys sponsored by the Japanese Prime Minister's Office in 1981 and 1986 provide information for respondents in four countries on attitudes and values regarding work, leisure, and retirement; these surveys also obtain data on income and employment status. Palmore and Maeda (1985) and McMallum (1988) have utilized these surveys and have demonstrated the usefulness and thoroughness of these surveys.

The survey data tap three key cultural or social psychological issues that might conceivably influence retirement rates: (1) opinions about how people should support themselves financially after they retire, (2) attitudes about the "appropriate" retirement age, and (3) reasons retired people give for why they chose to retire.[3]

Results

As anticipated, the data (Table 1) show significant variation in patterns of retirement across the four countries available for analysis. The proportion of males age 60 and over who were still active in the labor force (in 1981) was highest in Japan (57%), relatively high in the U.S. (33%) and significantly lower in the UK (13%) and France (8%); thus, retirement of the over-60 population is much more common in the two European nations than in either Japan or the United States. Between 1981 and 1986, there were slight declines in these proportions in Japan and the U.S., and a slight increase in France.[4] However, the overall patterns do not change despite these small trends. What, then, accounts for the country-to-country variation in retirement patterns?

Economy and Demography

Findings with regard to economic and demographic variables are given in Table 1. With the exception of unemployment rates, none of the economic indicators seems strongly related to aggregate retirement rates. GNP per capita (in 1981) was relatively high in all four nations and varied in a rather narrow range (from $9,110 in the UK in 1986 to $12,820 in the U.S.). The range of variation widened in 1986, but the ratio of most to least wealthy among these four nations was still less than two. More to the point, there is no consistent relationship between GNP per capita and retirement rates. Indeed, the rank-order correlation coefficient for the seven relevant entries in the table is .11, which is definitely not significant.

The same appears true of the proportion of each nation's labor force employed in agriculture. Japan and France have the highest levels of agricultural employment (7 to 10% of the total labor force in each country, depending on year), but are at opposite ends of the retirement continuum (France with the highest retirement rate, Japan with the lowest). Likewise, the U.S. and UK each have 3% of the labor force in agriculture but very different retirement rates. The relative size of the agricultural sector, in short, is not related to retirement rates among these four nations.

Unemployment, in contrast, does appear to be correlated with retirement rates in the aggregate. France and the UK have the highest rates of unemployment and the highest retirement rates among these four nations; Japan has the lowest unemployment and lowest retirement rate; the U.S. figures are "in the middle" on both factors. This suggests that men are less likely to retire where jobs are plentiful.

In general, demographic differences among these four societies are modest and therefore probably do not account significantly for differences in the retirement rate. The proportion of the population aged 60 and over varies only from 13% to about 30%. These figures are lower, however, in the two "low retirement" countries (Japan and the U.S.) and higher in the remaining two countries, indicating a modest positive relationship. The same might be said of age structure (ratio of the over-60 group to those aged 25 -59), except that the U.S. and France have nearly identical age structures but sharply different retirement patterns. Finally, years of additional life expectancy at age 60 vary in an extremely narrow range over these four countries and show no consistent relationship to retirement rates.

Table 1—Socioeconomic and Social Policy Conditions in Four Countries

	Japan		U.S.A.		U.K.		France	
	1981	1986	1981	1986	1981	1986	1981	1986
% male 60+ employed[1]	57	48	33	27	13	n.a.	8	11
G.N.P. per capita (US $)[2]	10,080	11,300	12,820	16,690	9,110	8,460	12,190	9,540
% in agriculture[3]	10	8	3	3	3	2	8	7
Unemployment rate[3]	2.2	2.8	7.5	6.9	10.4	11.9	7.4	10.2
%POP AGE 60+[4]	13.2	14.8	15.9	16.6	20.6	20.9	17.1	19.2
60+/(25-59)[3]	.26	.29	.37	.37	.47	.48	.38	.40
Life expectancy at age 60 (male)[4]	18.6	19.2	17.6	17.8	17.1	17.1	17.3	17.3
Pulbic Pensions:[5,6] Pensionable age	65	65	65	65	65	65	65	60
% wage replacement for a couple	61		66		45		75	
Payroll tax rates(total)	20.95	22.94	18.4	18.8	21.45	20.45	44.1	50.75
by employee	10.05	10.1	6.65	7	7.75	9	11.14	13.02
by employer	10.9	12.84	11.75	11.8	13.7	11.45	32.96	37.73
Early retirement age	60	60	62	62	62	62	60	none
Required conditions:	-Pension reduced by 20-80% if employed at age 60-64; reduced by 20% if employed at age 65-70 -35 years of contribution necessary forfull benefit: 25 years for early retirement.		-Pension reduced $1 for each $2 earnings above $5,500/year until age 72 (1981); above $5,400/year under 65, $7,320/year for ae 65-69 (1986). -40 quarters (10 yrs) of contribution necessary for full benefit.		-Basic pension reduced if earnings exceed +52/week (123.25) (1981); +70/week ($84.00) (1986). -Years of required contribution vary. -Early retirement possible only when replaced by unemployed person.		-No retirement necessary while on pension. -150 quarters (37.5 years) of contribution necessary for full benefit. -Early retirement possible if unemployed or replaced by unemployed person (1981).	

Sources: 1. Japan Prime Minister's Office (1982,1987). Figures are based on a nationsl survey and include only those who were actucally employed at the time of the survey. 2. The World Bank (1980,1983,1987). 3. I.L.O. (1981,1982,1984,1987). 4. U.N. (1982,1984,1987). 5. United States Department of Health and Human Services (1982,1987). 6. European Industrial Relations Review (1983).

Note: *ILO figure (ILO,1987). ILO figures includes those actually employed, paid and unpaid workers, and those who are looking for jobs. Therefore, the figure for actually employed and paid workers is likely to be lower than 11%. It could be as low as 4-5%. given high level of unemployment in France.

Social Policy

(A) Pensionable Age

Table 1 also shows the findings for selected social policy variables. The formal age for entitlement to a public pension (e.g., Social Security in the U.S.) is widely assumed to be a very important influence on individual decisions about retirement. As an account of cross-national **differences** in retirement rates, however, this one is clearly deficient, since all nations use the same pensionable age (65). (France lowered that to age 60 in 1983, but with no large effect on the retirement rate).

(B) Wage Replacement Rate

More important, perhaps, than the age at which one is eligible for a pension is the rate at which pensions replace earnings in various countries. Somewhat surprisingly, however, replacement rates do not seem strongly related to retirement rates. Replacement rates are very similar in Japan and the U.S. (61 and 66%), are highest in France (75%), and are very low in the UK (45%); yet retirement rates are quite similar in the latter two countries. Among these four nations, in short, the relative generosity of pensions does not seem to influence retirement.

Many of the men over age 60 in 1981 and 1986, of course, would have faced their retirement decisions at a much earlier time, when replacement rates in the different countries might have been very different. I therefore averaged the replacement rates for 1975 and 1980 reported by Aldrich (1982, pp. 3-11). These averages were below the 1980 levels, but still showed an identical pattern: The UK had the lowest average replacement rate, Japan and the U.S. were in the middle, and France had the highest rate (75%). Thus, the relative generosity of pensions is an insufficient explanation for the pattern of retirement in these four countries.

(C) Tax Rates

Another policy variable of some interest is the tax rate paid by employees and employers to support the old age pension and other programs. In most countries, contributions by workers and employers based on payroll percentages continue to be the main source of social security financing (U.S. Department of Health and Human Services, 1982, p. xiii). However, these rates do vary considerably across nations and might therefore influence relative aggregate retirement rates.

The expectation, of course, is the higher tax rates would encourage higher retirement rates, for three reasons: (1) Employers paying high contributions for older workers might encourage them to retire early to reduce their (the employers') financial burdens; (2) If workers pay high taxes to fund their own retirement, then there is an obvious incentive to retire (to stop paying the tax and start receiving the entitlement); and (3) High tax rates presumably mean more generous retirement packages.

Again, however, the data show a mixed picture. Social Security taxes are lowest in the U.S., somewhat higher in Japan and the UK, and astonishingly high in France. There are further differences in the mix between employer and employee contributions. Still, it is apparent that the UK and France have similar retirement rates and vastly different tax rates; Japan and the UK have similar tax rates and very different retirement rates. It can be plausibly argued that the heavy taxes imposed on French workers, and especially on their employers, combined with high unemployment in France, account for the high retirement rate observed in that country.

(D) Early Retirement Age

The early retirement age is either 60 or 62 in all four countries and so cannot be strongly related to retirement rates. The conditions on early (and normal) retirement, however, are much more variable and may well have some significant effects. For example, older persons must stop working altogether in order to claim full pension benefits at age 65 in Japan, the U.S., and the UK. In the U.S., one may work while on pension at age 65, but maximum earnings are restricted and earnings may be offset by reduced pensions until age 70 (age 72 until 1986). Similar restrictions apply to post-65 workers on pensions in Japan and the UK. One might expect these penalties for working after retirement to have led to similar rates of retirement in the three countries; the actual rates, of course, are very different. Oddest of all, French workers were permitted to receive full pensions **and** continue working (until 1983, when the law was changed); one would therefore expect the labor force participation of older men to be higher in France than in the other three countries, the reverse of the observed pattern.

(E) Required Conditions

Concerning the criteria for early retirement, we do find evidence that might explain the high retirement rates among French men, namely, that the most flexible early retirement options are those available in France. Variations in retirement rates in the other three countries, however, are apparently not sensitive to early retirement criteria. In the U.S., early retirement with a reduced pension is available at age 62; the Japanese system is similar. In the UK, a worker is permitted to retire at age 62 if his company replaces him with an unemployed person, a much more restrictive criterion than those of Japan and the U.S. Given this, one would expect higher levels of retirement among U.S. and Japanese men than among UK men, again opposite the observed pattern.

(F) Sources of Income in Old Age

So far I have considered only the replacement value of governmental pensions. However, individuals often supplement these pensions with private plans, thereby increasing the **de facto** replacement rate and, possibly, effecting aggregate retirement rates. According to Nusberg (1986, p. 28), for example, corporate and private pensions are much more widespread in France than in the other three countries, this despite a recent burst of interest among governments throughout Western Europe and North America in these plans. Also, retired individuals will often have access to economic resources other than those made available through pensions plans, and this too should be taken into account.

Table 2—Sources of Income among Men over 60 in Four Countries

	Japan		U.S.A.		U.K.	France
	1981	1986	1981	1986	1981	1981
N=	593	539	432	426	409	399
% receiving: Public Pension	64	76	78	82	83	73
Private Pension	10	7	29	36	46	54
Other Income*	47	49	68	75	31	21

Source: Japan Prime Minister's Office (1982, 1987).
* Other income includes savings, investments, assets, and help from children.

Data on sources of income among over-60 men from Table 2 indicate that proportions receiving governmental pensions were about the same in all countries (except for Japan in 1981, where the rate was somewhat low). Receipt of private pensions was much more variable: 54% in France, 46% in the UK, 29% in the U.S., and a mere 10% in Japan. This pattern tracks the pattern in retirement rates exactly, suggesting the availability of private pensions to supplement government pensions as a critical determinant of retirement decisions.

However, the differential availability of private pensions is apparently offset, at least to some extent, by the variable ability of the aged to draw on other sources of support, in particular income from savings and investments or help from children. These two sources combined were available to 47% of the Japanese men in 1981 (49% in 1986) and to 68% of the American men in 1981 (75% in 1986), but to only 31% in the UK and 21% in France. Thus, this "other support" tends to be most available where private pension plans are rarest, and vice versa. Summing across categories, much higher proportions of the American and the British samples had multiple sources of income than did the Japanese and the French. If we also take the replacement value of publicly supported pensions into account, it is clear that the elderly in the U.S., the UK, and France had roughly comparable income from public and private pensions yet differed greatly in their retirement decisions.

Cultural and Social Psychological Factors

Overall, two of the economic, demographic and social policy factors that I have examined show strong, obvious patterns: the rate of unemployment, and the availability of private pensions to supplement income from government pensions. Do cultural and social psychological variables, such as values, preferred modes of behavior, and general cultural orientations in the sampled countries fare any better?

Table 3—Major Causes of Retirement (Retired Men Only)

(percentages)

	Japan		U.S.A.		U.K.	France
	1981	1986	1981	1986	1981	1981
N=	593	539	432	426	409	399
Voluntary Retirement[1]	24	26	42	43	33	36
Health Limitations	28	31	22	20	17	42
Job Dissatisfaction[2]	5	5	0	1	1	1
Still Willing to Work	33	29	28	29	14	15
Other/N.A.	10	9	8	7	35	6

Source: Japan Prime Minister's Office (1982, 1987).
1. Includes responses such as "I retired because I want to enjoy a leisurely life." 2. Includes responses such as "I retired because my job did not suit me."

Table 3 presents survey data on responses of **retired men** concerning the major reasons for their retirement. Although no single response dominated, Americans showed the most positive response toward retirement, with more than 40% claiming they wanted to enjoy a life of leisure. Japanese men showed the least interest in voluntary retirement with the British and French in the middle. A very high proportion of Frenchmen reported poor health as the principal reason for having retired. It is well reported that health pressures play significant roles in one's decision to retire. Also, people often give health reasons because they see it as socially more acceptable (Atchley, 1991). It is not evident, however, why retired men in France report significantly higher health problems than those in other countries.

The results also show that many **retired men** in the U.S. and Japan still wanted to work; in contrast, less than 15% of the British and French retirees expressed any desire to do so. These results may suggest that work may be more socially significant and meaningful in relation to the individual pursuit of leisure in Japan and the U.S., thus accounting in some part for the lower rates of retirement found in those countries.

Table 4—Preferred Age of Retirement among Men over 60

(percentages)

		Japan		U.S.A.		U.K.	France
		1981	1986	1981	1986	1981	1981
	N=	593	539	432	426	409	399
55 or before		1	1	6	7	5	20
60		14	12	16	21	55	54
65		34	39	31	36	23	15
70 and over		39	42	22	19	2	3
Other		8	5	25*	17	13	4
N.A.		4	1	0	0	2	4

Source: Japan Prime Minister's Office (1982, 1987).
* This large percentage of "other" category in the U.S. may reflect the large number of respondents choosing the age 62 at which one can receive Social Security benefits.

Responses to questions about the preferred age of retirement were also of great interest (Table 4). Among Japanese men, three-quarters or more felt that the proper retirement age was 65 or older; in fact, the plurality of Japanese thought 70 or older was ideal. Similar, although definitely lower, percentages also characterized the responses of the U.S. men. In contrast, the majority of British and French men felt that age 60 was ideal; 20% of the French responded "age 55 or before." These aggregate responses regarding the ideal age at retirement match the actual retirement rates almost perfectly.[5]

Table 5—Preferred Source of Retirement Income (Men over 60)

(percentages)

		Japan		U.S.A.		U.K.	France
		1981	1986	1981	1986	1981	1981
	N=	593	539	432	426	409	399
Save While Working		60	57	64	66	42	39
Social Security		24	33	25	24	50	67
Family		12	9	1	1	0	1
Other/N.A.		4	1	10	9	8	3

Source: Japan Prime Minister's Office (1982, 1987).

Another relevant question asked was where an older person's income should come from. One possible response was, "One should save while working and not have to rely on the state or one's family." Another possibility was, "One should be able to rely on Social Security." Most respondents chose one of these two alternatives. In the U.S. and Japan, the majority preference was "save while working," whereas in the UK and France, Social Security was the preferred source of retirement income. Thus, reliance on self for retirement income appears to be associated with lower aggregate retirement rates, and reliance on the state with higher rates (Table 5).

Discussion

What can we learn from the four country data just presented? The present study suggests that the aggregate rate of retirement across nations may be attributable to a combination of factors, including the cultural and social psychological. Among the various economic and demographic variables considered here, the rate of unemployment seemed to be clearly related to the retirement rate; among the social policy variables, the availability of private pension plans had an equally clear apparent effect.

Social policies regarding retirement are often intended to increase or decrease the retirement rate and may indeed have such effects in some circumstances. In France, for example, more flexible options for taking early retirement, high wage replacement rates via public pensions, the heavy social security taxes imposed on employers, and high unemployment rates no doubt combine to produce the highest retirement rate of the four nations studied.

The availability of private pensions is also an important factor in the determination of retirement rates. In many countries, private pensions expanded in the post World War II years as they were increasingly incorporated into collective bargaining agreements. With the economic growth of 60s and 70s, many European countries, including France and the UK, have aimed to achieve a replacement rate of 60 to 70% of prior earnings, 20% of it from private pensions (Horlick, 1987, p. 13, & p. 24). In the U.S., one in four workers was covered by a private pension in 1950, and one in two in 1980; in 1940 only 4% of those aged 55 and over received income from a private pension, compared to 30% in 1980 (Sherman & Coleman, 1980; Tuma & Sandefur, 1988).

As to Japanese men, one may be tempted to conclude that their inadequate public or private pensions (Table 2) led to the low rate of retirement. But a number of observations do not fully support such a view. As a matter of fact, the lower rate of pensions does not necessarily imply that older Japanese men suffer from financial difficulties. Unlike what would be found in most other industrially advanced nations, about 60% of Japanese men over age 65 maintain multi-generational living arrangements. Consequently, cash income after retirement may be less important in Japan than in other countries.[6] In addition, a sizable proportion of older Japanese remains in the labor force because they perceive their work as conductive to the maintenance of good health in old age (Japan Economic Planning Agency, 1983; Osako, 1986). Work provides social activities, by linking individuals to social groups and by offering opportunities to pursue individual interests and leisure. Such attitudes are in sharp contrast to a common view in the Western countries of work as drudgery and of leisure as anything done outside the workplace.

The data analyzed here suggest that economic conditions, such as unemployment, and the availability of pensions are strongly related to the aggregate rate of retirement across nations. The results also show that retirement rates in each country are strongly correlated with attitudes toward work, leisure, and retirement. While the overwhelming majority of Frenchmen preferred to begin retirement at age 55 to 60, and the British around age 60, the majority of Americans preferred age 65, and the Japanese, 65, 70 or later. Nearly a third of Japanese and American men still wanted to work even after their retirement, while only 15% of the retired men in France and the UK expressed similar sentiments. Moreover, Japanese and American men were more likely to stress reliance on oneself (through savings) as a source of retirement income; French and British men were more likely to stress reliance on government pensions. A dominant theme found in this study is that many older Japanese and American workers continue to feel positive about their work, and thus continue working, even once they have passed retirement age.

It is noteworthy that both the United States and Japan have **raised** the official retirement age, the U.S. in 1983 and Japan in 1986 (Ricketts, 1986, p. 9). Given the data presented here, it seems obvious that this is one case of public policy responding to—rather than dictating—private preferences. Economics, demography, and social policy notwithstanding, one might also wonder how such a proposal would be received in the two other nations analyzed.

Notes

1. Important exceptions include Shanas et al. (1968) who compared three industrially advanced countries: the U.S., Denmark, and the UK; and Palmore (1975) (see also, Palmore & Maeda, 1985), who compared the Japanese retirement situation to those in other industrially advanced nations.
2. Since these surveys rely on personal reporting by samples of individuals, the data on retirement percentages among the aged are not strictly in agreement with those reported by the International Labor Organization. The ILO reports count those who are not working but seeking employment as working (economically active) (ILO, 1984: 3, 11). In the Japanese data these persons are counted as retired (economically inactive) persons.
3. Specific questions and responses were as follows:
    (1) "Where do you think older peoples' income should come from?" Response options were: (a) One should save while working and not have to rely on one's

family or government support. (b) One should be able to rely on Social Security. (c) One should be able to rely on support from one's family. A miscellaneous "other" category was also included.

(2) "In your view, when is the best age to begin retirement?" Response categories were: Age 55 or before, about age 60, about age 65, about age 70 or after, and "other."

(3) "What is the main reason that you retired and do not have a paying job?" Responses were coded into the following categories: (a) I want to enjoy a leisurely life. (b) My health does not permit me to work. (c) I cannot find a job that is suited to me. (d) I want to work. Again, a residual "other" category is also included.

4. As noted, the Japanese survey conducted in 1986 did not include France (or the UK). The 1986 figure for France reported in the table, 11%, was obtained from the ILO and, for reasons cited earlier, may not be fully comparable.
5. It might, of course, be argued that respondents are only trying to bring their stated "preferences" into line with what the employment data suggest they have already done in practice. Having no way to evaluate this hypothesis, I can only recognize it as a possibility here.
6. In 1982, nearly 60% of the Japanese elderly lived with their children, 17% lived with their spouse, and 11% lived alone (Japan Economic Planning Agency, 1983). Some assume that older people are forced to live alone in the US (and other Western countries), while they are forced to live with their children in Japan. Research on these issues (Atchley, 1991; Japan Economic Planning Agency, 1983) has shown, however, that older people in the Western countries prefer the independence of living alone, whereas it is considered appropriate and desirable for older persons to live with their children in Japan.

References

Aldrich, J. (1982). The earnings replacement of old-age benefits in 12 countries, 1969-80. *Social Security Bulletin, 45*, 3-11.

Atchley, R. (1991). *Social forces and aging* (6th ed.). Belmont, CA: Wadsworth Publishing Company.

Bixby, L. E. (1976). Retirement patterns in the United States: Research and policy interaction. *Social Security Bulletin, 39,* 3-19.

Clark, R. L., & Baker, D. T. (1981). *Reversing the trend toward early retirement*. Washington, DC: American Enterprise Institute for Public Policy Research.

Conner, K. C. (1992). *Aging America*. Englewood Cliffs, New Jersey: Prentice Hall.

Cowgill, D. O. (1974). Aging and modernization: A revision of the theory. In J. F. Gubrium (Ed.), *Late life: Communities and environmental policy* (pp. 123-46). Springfield, IL: Charles C. Thomas.

Cowgill, D. O. (1986). *Aging around the world*. Belmont, CA: Wadsworth.

Duggan, J. E. (1984). The labor force participation of older workers. *Industrial and Labor Relations Review, 37*, 415-30.

European Industrial Relations Review. (1983). Pension Provisions in Ten Countries, 13-18.

Fields, G. S., & Mitchell, O. S. (1984). Economic determinants of the optimal retirement age. *Journal of Human Relations, 19*, 245-252.

Graebner, W. (1980). *A history of retirement: The meaning and function of an American institution 1885-1978*. New Haven: Yale University.

Horlick, M. (1987). The relationship between public and private pension schemes: An introductory overview. In *Communicating public and private: The case of pensions* (Studies and Research No. 24). Geneva, Switzerland: International Social Security Association,

Inkeles, A., & Usui, C. (1989). Retirement patterns in crossnational perspective. In D. Kertzer, J. Meyer, & K. W. Schaie (Eds.), *Social structure and aging: Age structurinq in comparative perspective.* Hillsdale, NJ: Erlbaum.

International Labor Office. (1981). *Yearbook of labor statistics*. Geneva: ILO.

International Labor Office. (1982). *Yearbook of labor statistics*. Geneva: ILO.

International Labor Office.(1984). *Yearbook of labor statistics*. Geneva: ILO.

International Labor Office.(1987). *Yearbook of Labor statistics*. Geneva: ILO.

Japan Economic Planning Agency. (1983). *White paper of living conditions of the Japanese.* Tokyo: Minister of Finance.

Japan Prime Minister's Office. (1982). *International comparative survey of the life and perception of the aged.* Tokyo: Office of the Aged, Prime Minister's Office.

Japan Prime Minister's Office. (1987). *International comparative survey of the life and perception of the aged.* Tokyo: Office of the Aged, Prime Minister's Office.

Koli, M., Rein, M., Guillemard, A., & Van Gunsteren, H. (1991). *Time for retirement: Comparative studies of early exit from the labor force*. New York: Cambridge University Press.

Martin, L. G. (1989). *The graying of Japan* (Population Bulletin Vol. 44, No. 2). Washington, DC.: Population Reference Bureau, Inc.

McCallum, J. (1988) Japanese teinen taishoku: How cultural values affect retirement. *Aging and Society, 8*(1), 23-42.

Morrison, M. (1983). The aging of the U.S. population: Human resource implications. *Monthly Labor Review*, May, 13-19.

Nusberg, C. (1986). Early retirement in Western nations. *Aging International, 13*(4), 26-34.

Osako, M. (1986). Japanese workers resist early retirement. *Aging International, 13*(4), 33-34.

Palmore, E. B. (1975). *The honorable elders.* Durham: Duke University Press.

Palmore, E. B., Burchett, B. M., Fillenbaum, G. G., George, L. K., & Wallman, L. M. (1985). *Retirement: Causes and consequences.* New York: Springer Publishing Company.

Palmore, E. B., & Maeda, D. (1985). *The honorable elders revisited.* Durham: Duke University Press.

Pampel, F., & Weiss, J. (1983). Economic development, pension policies, and the labor force participation of aged males: A cross-national, longitudinal approach. *American Journal of Sociology, 89*(2), 350-372.

Parnes, H. S., & King, R. (1977). Middle-aged job losers. *Industrial Gerontology, 4*, 77-96.

Parnes, H. S., & Nestel, G. (1971). *Retirement expectations of middle-aged men.* Columbus, OH: Center for Human Resources Research, Ohio State University.

Quinne, J., & Burkhauser, R. (1990). Work and retirement. In R. Binstock, & L. Geroge (Eds.), *Handbook of aging and the social sciences* (pp. 307-27). New York: Academic Press.

Ricketts, J. M. (1986). Worldwide trends and developments in social security. *Social security Bulletin, 49*(9), 5-11.

Rum, C. (1989). Why older Americans stop working. *The Gerontologist, 29*(3), 294-99.

Shanas, E., Townsend, P., Wedderburn, D., Friis, H., Milhj, P., & Stehouwer, J., (1968). *Old people in three industrial societies.* New York: Atherton Press.

Sheppard, H. L. (1976). Work and retirement. In R. Binstock & E. Shanas (Eds.), *Handbook of aging and the social sciences.* New York: Van Nostrand Reinhold.

Sherman, S. R., & Coleman, J. R. (1980). Health care expenditures in nine industrialized countries, 1960-1976. *Social Security Bulletin, 50*(5), 5-22.

Stehouwer, J. (1968). *Old people in three industrial societies.* New York: Atherton Press.

Tuma, N. B., & Sandefur, G. D. (1988). Trends in the labor force activity of the elderly in the United States, 1940-1980. In R. Ricardo-Campbell & E.P. Lazear (Eds.), *Issues in contemporary retirement* (pp. 38-83). Stanford, CA: Hoover Institution Press.

United Nations. (1982). *Demographic yearbook.* New York, NY: United Nations.

United Nations. (1984). *Demographic yearbook.* New York, NY: United Nations.

United Nations. (1987). *Demographic yearbook.* New York, NY: United Nations.

U. S. Department of Health and Human Services. (1982). *Social security throughout the world.* Washington, D. C.: Government Printing Office.

The World Bank. (1980). *World development report.* New York: Oxford University Press.

The World Bank. (1983). *World development report.* New York: Oxford University Press.

The World Bank. (1987). *World development report.* New York: Oxford University Press.

Zeitzer, I. R. (1983). Social security trends and developments in industrialized countries. *Social Security Bulletin, 46*(3), 55-62.

Article 15

Social Policy and the Elderly in the Republic of Korea: The Need for a Social Development Strategy*

Howard A. Palley

Introduction

Korean Society in the 1990s

Since the 1960s, Korean society[1] has shifted from being a mainly agrarian, rural society to being an urbanized and industrial, newly modernizing society. Of the Asian modernized or modernizing societies, such as Japan, Taiwan, Hong Kong, Singapore and Thailand, which have Confucian ethical heritages, it appears that Korea is one of the most closely bound to the relational aspects of this heritage.

The Republic of Korea is a society of 44,000,000 people in which 98 percent of the population is literate and in which, in 1987, 78.1 percent of the labor force was in the secondary and tertiary industrial sector, and 69 percent of the population lived in urban areas (Choe, 1989). Per capita GNP in 1989 was $4,550, and in 1990 the average wage earner's monthly family income was about $1,235 ("Taiwan and Korea," 1990; *The Korea Economic Journal*, 1990).

In 1990 the Korean fertility rate was about 1.7 children per family and was expected to remain less than two children per family during the 1990s (Choi, 1990). On the other hand, life expectancy at birth in 1990 was 69.3 years for men and 75 years for women (Choe, 1989). In 1990, 4.7 percent of Korea's population was over 65 years old with the expectation that, by 2020, 11 percent will be over 65 years of age (Choe, 1989).

In Korea, modernization, accompanied by demographic changes, urbanization and industrialization have contributed to changes in family structure. Average household size for a family declined from 5.6 persons in 1960 to 4.2 persons in 1985. Moreover the proportion of three or four generation households in the population fell from 28.6% in 1960 to 16.2% in 1985 (National Economic Planning Board, 1988; Lee, 1988). These trends, plus other modernization trends such as increased nuclearization of families, are indicative that the availability of households which care for elderly relatives may also be shrinking.

---

*The research for this paper was primarily conducted under a Fulbright Research Award.

The Problem

Modernization increases strain in the family system. Traditionally, the Confucian ethical and relational system holds the eldest son responsible for the care of his elderly parents. (In modern Korea, it is possible for another son to assume this caregiving role). The second cardinal virtue of Confucianism requires the obedience of the son to the father. The third cardinal virtue requires the obedience of the wife to the husband (Koo, 1984). In reality, these obligations result in the daughter-in-law (the wife) being obligated for the care of the elderly in a three generation household (Koo, 1984). Informally, the daughter may be called upon to provide care and counsel to elderly parents although this role does not "fit" into the formal Korean relational system. This places tremendous role stress on married women as, increasingly, well-educated, middle-class women are seeking to balance other activities such as the raising of children and the maintenance of professional careers with the additional task of providing care for the retired elderly and, as longevity increases, the frail elderly. The work obligations of poor and working class married women are even greater, and the family care roles are "no less binding."

Moreover, the political structure's emphasis on economic development makes it difficult to moderate social stress factors through development of a social welfare infrastructure. The Democratic Liberal Party (DLP), the dominant political party in the Republic of Korea, has followed a political-economic model which emphasizes stimulation of economic growth and industrial development (*The Economist,* 1990). This political-economic orientation has resulted, in spite of the concerns of Korean gerontologists and other advocates of the aging, in a policy of minimal social services and income maintenance, and particularly no social services supporting in-home and community-based services for intact Korean families. This situation confronts women in a modernized Korean society who are informal caregivers for the elderly with conflicting and stressful obligations to—in-laws, children, employers, and husbands. In the American context, women in this situation have been referred to as members of "the sandwich generation."

Because of a growth oriented economic policy geared to an aggressive overseas marketing strategy, Korean political leaders have emphasized Confucian virtues regarding informal caregiving in the three generation family (essentially care by the daughter-in-law) as the basis of social policy. No public support for adult day care or in-home attendants for the frail elderly are provided through social programs where responsible relatives are available. Also, no publicly supported home care is provided for frail elderly relatives if responsible relatives are available.

According to such analysts as Tai Hyun Kim, a family relations specialist at Sung Shin University and Gene H.Y. Yoon, a gerontologist and psychologist at Yonsei University, modernization trends related to urbanization and industrialization have resulted in an increase in intergenerational friction as well as lower status for older people (T. H. Kim, 1990; Yoon, 1990). Young couples increasingly prefer residential separation, although most would accept responsibility for retired parents within their household (Koo, 1984). Widows are most likely to name their daughters-in-law as the persons who make them angry and mothers-in-law are most likely to be considered meddlesome by modern Korean daughters-in-law (Koo, 1981).

The Focus of the Study

This paper will examine The Republic of Korea's governmental strategy of intentionally not developing a supportive social infrastructure or a modern welfare state package of social service and income policies and programs for the elderly which would assist the elderly and informal caregivers (generally women). It will examine the reasons for the lack of government action (non-decisions) (Bachrach & Baratz, 1970) in the face of increasing imperatives of demography, as well as the segmentation and nuclearization of families accompanying modernization and urbanization. Another problem which does not seem to be adequately addressed by current social policies is the erosion of the status of the elderly in Korea today (Chung, 1982; Jacobs, 1985; S. K. Kim, 1990).

Methodology

This study is largely based on data collected in the Republic of Korea during the June, 1990-August, 1990 period; some preliminary data was collected during the July, 1988-August,1988 period. The research was based heavily on 33 interviews conducted with leading experts in the area of aging and social policy. Among those interviewed were administrators involved in providing direct services for the elderly, demographers, government administrators, political officials, interest group actors, and social scientists with a specialization in gerontology. Also relevant documentary analyses by experts and government documents have been reviewed. Material in Korean has been translated.

The interviews were based on a reputational method regarding expertise about gerentological problems and needs and/or social policy development and gerentological needs. Based on my preliminary visit and consultation with Korean colleagues, I identified an initial group of five experts to be interviewed. Each expert was asked to recommend two additional appropriate persons for interviews. Each interviewee was asked a series of questions regarding problems and needs of the Korean elderly, the adequacy of current social policies affecting the Korean elderly, and their views regarding prescriptive developments needed to ameliorate current and future social needs.

Who Are The Elderly?

In discussing programs for the elderly, we are generally referring to those persons 65 years of age or older. Yet we are not always discussing those persons in that age cohort. Korean average retirement age is 58. Also, the traditional celebration for advanced age for Koreans is the 60th birthday. Thus, problems of retirement and dependency may occur in ones' late 50's and early 60's.

Korean Development and the Needs of the Elderly

Older industrialized nations and recently industrialized nations have increasingly become concerned about a number of issues relating to the care of the aging. To a great extent, support of the aging in an income maintenance focus means social insurance "transfers" from current workers to retired workers. The cost of a national insurance system represents, to a great extent, the higher risks of illness and frailty which accompany increasing age. Another issue of caring for the frail elderly--in terms of chronic and acute illness--is informal caregiver stress and the unavailability of formal caregivers. Yet another crucial issue is the "cost" of sustaining social sector programs vis-a-vis the capital accumulation and subsidization of private corporate activity to "drive" an economic development strategy.

The primary drive for Korean economic development began in 1960 with the policies of Premier Chung Hee Park. Governmental support for such economic development and an "export strategy" has led to major improvements in Korea's standard of living. While in 1960, The Republic of Korea's GNP per person was about $675 in today's money, in 1990, the average income of $5,000 per household paralleled that of Portugal, and Korean children, due to a more nutritious diet, were, on average, 5 inches taller than their parents. These facts are the plus side of the ledger.

The negative side of the ledger which effects dependency and care for the elderly is that many Koreans still live in great poverty; the Korean Economic Planning Board reported in 1990 that over three million people, 7.7 percent of the population, live in absolute poverty--as measured by the government's poverty line. 3,256,000 Koreans had incomes of less than $67 per month and assets of under $452 (*The Korea Herald*, 1990, p. 3). This situation permits only a meager diet, while on the other side of the ledger, some very wealthy Koreans live in opulence "embarrassing" to Confucian ethical concerns with moderation but supported by a regressive and poorly enforced system of taxation (S. H. Kim, 1990).

Development, Modernization and Industrialization

Social and political modernization trends accompany economic development policies aimed at increasing material resources (Apter, 1987; Bendix, 1965; Jacobs, 1985). Such trends result in a "prismatic" contact with traditional culture producing new cultural developments which are not an imitation of the West (Westernization), but which adapt from the traditional culture and which may also represent significant departures from traditional modalities. The notion of a prismatic affect of economic development on the political and social structure of transitional (newly developing) societies was developed by Fred Riggs (1964). He notes that economic development was like a "white light" refracted in the prism of highly differentiated, transitional societies producing unique reactions with regard to political, economic and social structure as well as behavioral responses (Riggs, 1964; also see Harrison, 1988).

A study of "Asian Values and Modernization" points out a number of family changes which are occurring in east Asian nations as a consequence of modernization (Chen, 1977). There is in process a modification in the traditional extended family where several generations live together as a family unit and an increase in the number of modern nuclear families consisting of parents and unmarried children. Increasingly, fathers, and often mothers, are preoccupied with employment for the main part of the day in a separate establishment, and "because of a busy working life and social activities, parents nowadays spend less time with their children." (Chen, 1977, p. 34) This pattern leads to a widening generation gap. More broadly, modernization inevitably results in greater receptivity to changes in achievement orientation, consumerism and individualism. It also results in a greater stress on rationality, efficiency, flexibility and impersonality.

While only sometimes acknowledged, modernization and industrialization indeed challenge and modify traditional perspectives. Traditional Confucian society emphasized an ethical and moral perspective which deprecated material and ontological values. Values stressed were "honor, dignity, integrity and virtue or righteousness—not money, affluence or any physical conveniences." (Paik, 1991, p. 26; also see Chen, 1977). Modernization has fostered the belief that moral and spiritual power is "bound up" with material and physical power. According to Paik, this has transformed Korean consciousness from a fatalistic, passive mentality to an "anything can be done," economic expansionist mentality (1991, pp. 126-127). Economic goal attainment became an end in itself "and no attention was paid to what effect it would contribute socially." (1991, p. 133)

Economic and political leadership during this period has involved an alliance between business elites, "the Chaebol," as well as governmental elites. These alliances of elites are modeled in accordance with the Korean and Confucian tradition of vertical integration of decision-making. The values and decisional process described have resulted in a number of problems including authoritarianism, corruption and a social imbalance between the wealthy and the socially and economically weak. While having many dramatic positive consequences, the economic growth policies of Korea since the 1960s have had unfortunate side effects. Paik observes that the governmental elite led economic growth policy "... by necessity, brought about connivance between public administration and enterprises. Such connivance caused, without fail, structural corruption between public administration and enterprises. It was almost impossible for enterprises outside the protection and concern of public administration to aspire to grow." Paik characterizes this business elite, for which he uses the Japanese term "zaibatsu," as being involved with the decision-making process in public administration by securing acquiescence through political pressure as well as bribery and kickbacks and for not utilizing official channels but rather relying on informal ties relating to "geography, blood or acquaintanceship." (1991, p. 131, also see Yang & Ahn, 1991, p. 10). Moreover, such governmental policy for the benefit of "those who have" has been described as giving "rise to a number of social policy issues by bringing about the unbalanced distribution of wealth." (Min & Tacho, 1989; Paik, 1991, p. 132)

In some respects traditional Confucianism, which valorizes scholarship and deprecates entrepreneurial activity, had an anti-development bias. However, with modernization accompanying industrialization, the Confucian value of sustaining family esteem, not bringing shame upon the family, and scholarship have bolstered the level of literacy and technical competence which have helped drive the economic development initially of Japan and, more recently, the "4 tiger" nations of Korea, Taiwan, Hong Kong and Singapore. The form of aggressive, development-oriented Confucianism embodied in this movement has been termed the "new Confucianism" (Tu, 1984).

This analysis contends that while an economic development focus is well-developed in the Republic of Korea's public policies, the social development goal (human welfare) is not as clearly developed (Chenery, 1971, p. 46; Paiva, 1977, p. 329). Moreover, the lack of balance between economic development goals and social development goals contributes to the social and political tension of Korean society. This lack of balance is reflected in social policies for the elderly in Korea.

Modernization, The Family and the Needs of the Elderly

In a Confucian system, reverence for the elderly is an essential value. In Korean society this is conveyed in the formality and reverence of language describing people who have reached certain chronological milestones (Koo, 1984).

Modernization has brought certain dilemmas with it which are related to the well-being of the elderly. Rapid and recent urbanization is a characteristic of modernization. Because of the speed of this urbanization, new housing is often quite expensive and too small to accommodate the needs of elderly parents in multi-generation families. Moreover, according to Tai Chul Chung, Vice President of the Korean Senior Citizens Association, and Sang Nak Ha, a Board Member of the Korean Association of the Aged, many elderly parents are not anxious to move because it means their movement from long-standing social networks in rural village and regional towns (T. C. Chung, 1990; Ha, 1990). Also, increasingly Korean women in the middle class are well educated and professionally trained, and they are often loathe to be saddled with the strain of employee and child care responsibility (most Korean men take little responsibility for child care) as well as care of elders. Indeed, it is today noted with wry humor and with some seriousness that Korean women are loath to marry eldest sons who most often are responsible for parental care, because it means that the daughter-in-law becomes the caregiver of the son's parents.

Parental caregiving is often, in a Confucian system a "return" for the parents giving the son the parental equity. However, many elderly Korean parents have entered the home of their eldest (or other) son without making a significant economic contribution. This is because the Korean economy was generally impoverished by the Japanese during the colonial period, the economy was devastated in the Korean War period, and, following the war, the meager resources of many Korean families were heavily spent on education of their children. In spite of the sacrifice of parents for the well being of their children, many children view the care of parents and parents-in-law as necessary but burdensome. Also, the elderly often have little independence or autonomy in their sons' homes because of their financial dependence.

Current Programs and Future Prospects of Social Policies for the Elderly

A needs theory of social policy would hold that as the needs of the elderly and family caregivers increase, it would lead to the notion that a substantial commitment to development of health and social services for the elderly would soon take place (Sharkansky, 1971). However, given the political and economic constraints operative in the Republic of Korea, this analysis contends that only small initiatives are being made and that they are not commensurate with the expanding needs of family caregivers or the needy elderly--particularly the frail elderly. Only after sufficient incidence of caregiver stress and neglect and unhappiness of the elderly are burned into the political consciousness of the nation will Korean society address these issues. The social cost of this lack of policy will remain high for the elderly, and will place the burden of stress on both poor and middle class family caregivers that are both adapting to the demands of industrial society and seeking to maintain the obligations which are part of the traditional Confucian ethic. Such family obligations place a heavy burden on Korean women.

Social and Health Programs for the Elderly

The Korean Aging Policy Act of 1982 outlined the governmental approach to services and policies for the elderly. The primary approach of this policy is an emphasis on tax incentives, awards and honorifics to encourage families to provide care and shelter for elderly relatives. A number of other approaches were enumerated as policy goals, not necessarily as programs. These were: counseling, such as referral to voluntary or available institutional services; health diagnosis; special treatment for the elderly, such as free bus fares and reduced price train fares, recreational programs for the elderly, vocational development, occupational training and guidance, housing and social services. Outside of free and reduced fares and tax incentives by lowering inheritance taxes for children who provide living space in their homes for parents, little in the way of social services (in-home or community care) or institutional care is provided for the Korean elderly. In 1989, the City of Seoul sponsored two multi-purpose welfare centers for the welfare poor elderly without relatives. These centers provide social counseling and volunteer based home health visiting; the centers provide recreational activities as well as physical therapy and occupational therapy; bathing is provided, as is lunch in the center. A mobile visiting team includes a social worker, nurse and sometimes a house helper. The program is entirely funded by the City of Seoul for the poor "abandoned" elderly and also for the poor, unattached physically and mentally handicapped.

Also, there are two voluntary community care programs which have limited national and local government subsidies for the elderly. One is run by HelpAge Korea and one in 1990 was being organized by the Unchon Counseling Center. These programs target poor unattached elderly. HelpAge Korea selects 100 to 150 persons; 120 voluntary home helpers are trained to visit the elderly for two to two and a half hours. The problem according to Ki Dong Cho, Director of Help Age Korea, is that volunteers often "drop-out," leaving the elderly with a psychological loss (Cho, 1990). The national government is also financing a program to train 50 home visit nurses. Such nurses can be paid under Medicare by the National Medical Insurance Program for acute care conditions if the home visit nurses are registered to hospitals (Joo, 1990).

The elderly do receive benefits under the Korean Medicare Program. The Korean Medicare Program covers 90 percent of the population with the other 10 percent being covered by a means-tested Medicaid Program (National Federation of Medical Insurance, 1988; Anderson, 1989). Under the Medicare Program, both hospitalization and out patient charges require substantial patient co-payments (20 percent for hospitalization and up to 30 percent for outpatient charges). With the expansion of Medicare in 1988 and 1989, its services to the aged have increased. While in 1984, 7.6 percent of national medical insurance was expended on those over 65 years of age, by 1988 12.9 percent of total medical insurance expenditures were spent on this group (K. K. Chung, 1990). Moreover, in 1993 the national government was considering the expansion of Medicare to cover the treatment of the chronically-ill elderly in special chronic care hospitals. Little of this Medicare health care spending is targeted to early diagnosis and prevention. While the elderly are entitled to a free health examination every other year, the Korean government's expectation was that in 1990, of the two million citizens over age 65, only 217,000 (slightly more than 10 percent) actually would utilize this service (S. K. Kim, 1990). Moreover, overall national health and social services expenditures in South Korea in 1987 accounted for only 2.59 percent of the Gross National Product in 1987; of this amount only one percent was borne by the governmental sector (Lee, 1990).

Pension Income and the Elderly

Another important concern of many elderly Koreans is the lack of pension income which would allow a measure of financial independence. According to Jae-Gan Park, Research Director of the Korean Institute on Gerontology, the fact that the average Korean retirement age is about 58 years of age leaves a high number of non-earning years for many older Koreans (1990). The National Pension Act as amended in 1989 will apply to most Korean employees. Fully insured status but low benefits will occur after twenty years participation in this social insurance plan and will be payable at age 60 (National Pension Corporation, 1989). This plan provides for pensions on an actuarial basis for the currently employed, which will provide sizeable benefits for a number of the elderly by the year 2040. In 1990, only two percent of those over 65 received a public pension. By the year 2010 it is estimated that about 15 percent of the elderly will receive a pension, and when the 1989 insurance law is fully "actualized" in 2040 about 45 to 50 percent of the elderly will receive a pension (National Pension Corporation, 1989; J. G. Park, 1990).

Congressman Sang-Mok Suh, a key figure in the DLP, and the Director General of the Policy Coordination Office of the DLP, observed that a small, symbolic, non-contributory pension was a possibility about the time of the 1990 election (Suh, 1990). Unfortunately, it was not enacted. Moreover, the government was not embracing the issue of non-contributory pensions as a mechanism for enhancing autonomy and dignity of the elderly with the seriousness that elderly advocacy groups, gerontologists and welfare professionals felt the issue deserved (Y. Kim, 1990; Lee, 1990; Park, 1990).

Other Services for the Elderly

In 1990 there were 85 institutional homes for the elderly without families, housing 6,000 persons over 65 years of age. There were 18 public nursing homes (and four small private nursing homes) for the elderly, providing care for 17,000 elderly persons (Joo, 1990). The public nursing homes provided care only for those elderly without families or with families too poor to maintain them. While no unmet needs of the elderly data are available to indicate needs for such facilities, in 1989, 83,706 persons over 65 living alone, or in families incapable of supporting them, were deemed to be in need of housing (E. H. Choe, 1989).

Conclusions

The interface of such demographic factors as increased longevity and lower rates of reproduction; the effects of industrialization and consequent modernization trends, including the nuclearization of families and the weakening of the tradition of the eldest son serving as the family head, plus the problem of securing adequate housing in urban Korea all point to the need for a developed Korean infrastructure of social policies for the elderly, as well as other vulnerable populations. In spite of the efforts of Korean social service professionals and interest groups representing the elderly, little funding for resource development has been committed by the national government to this task. This inactivity contrasts with the development of a Medicare system which since 1989 has become universal, although it provides for substantial copayments for services rendered. It also contrasts with a substantial public sector involvement in developing an educational system.

The government's rationale for fostering "Confucianism" and family responsibility appears to be disingenuous. Korea's political leaders, at times, appear to be convinced by their own rhetoric that supportive income and social services would undermine the Confucian tradition of family care for the elderly—although such policies are being developed in Singapore and Japan (Chen, 1977). The political-economic drive of low income taxes and low taxes on equity transactions, combined with subsidies and incentives to encourage exports and a substantial commitment to the military budget, leaves few resources available for necessary services for the disabled and the elderly.

Given the current political-economic strategies and the laissez-faire rationale of maintaining the Confucian ethic, little impetus can be expected in dealing with the increasingly real problems of generally developing social policies focused on sustaining the quality of life of the elderly and their informal caregivers—daughters-in-law and daughters. Such policy development would require a refocusing of governmental strategy in terms of seeking to balance economic development with social development.

Some prescriptive recommendations for meeting the needs of the elderly and their informal caregivers include: (1) Income support after retirement. This initially would require non-contributory pensions and gradually more emphasis would be placed on contributory pensions. (Also, a serious policy of government-supported, paid, part-time work for the elderly might partially address this income problem.) (2) An infrastructure of in-home and community-based social services providing service to the elderly and their family caregivers would address important psychological and physical needs. (3) Development of government subsidized housing to either allow elderly couples a longer period of independent living and/or larger apartments for three generation households that would go beyond current tax-incentive features. (4) The development of a plan for government subsidized and regulated chronic care facilities or nursing homes for the seriously disabled elderly (as well as the non-elderly disabled)---a population which demographic trends indicate will be increasing.

Notes

[1]In referring to Korean society, this paper is discussing the Republic of Korea (South Korea).

References

Anderson, G. F. (1989). Universal health coverage in Korea. *Health Affairs*, (Summer), 24-34.

Apter, D. E. (1987). *Rethinking development: Modernization, dependency and post-modern politics.* Newbury Park, CA: Sage Publications.

Bachrach, P., & Baratz, M. S. (1970). *Power and poverty: Theory and practice.* New York: Oxford University Press.

Bendix, R. (1965). *Nation building and citizenship.* Chicago: University of Chicago Press.

Chen, P. S. J. (1977). Asian values and modernization: A sociological perspective. In S. C. Meow (Ed.), *Asian values and modernization*. pp. 22-28. Singapore: Singapore University Press,

Chenery, H. B. (1971). Targets for development. In B. Ward, J. D. Runnals, & L. DíAnjou (Eds.). *Widening gap: Developments in the l970's* (pp. 27-47). New York: Columbia University Press.

Choe, E. H. (1989). Current status of research on the Korean elderly: Demographic aspects and social welfare services. *Journal of Korean Gerontological Society, 9*, 113-137.

Choi, B. H. (1990). *Prospects of vital rates in Korea and the collapse of the family in the U. S. A. and Europe*, Seoul, Korea. (Manuscript in Korean).

Choi, S. J. (1989). *Aging in Korea: A new concern and challenge*. In Proceedings of the 9th Asian-Pacific Cultural Scholars Convention, May 29-31. Korean National Group, Asian-Pacific Parliamentarians Union.

Chung, C. S. (1982). Confucian traditions and values: Implications for conflict in modern Korea. In E. Phillips & E. Y. Yu (Eds.). *Religions in Korea*, pp. 99-116. Los Angeles: California State University, Center for Korean-American and Korean Studies.

Economic Planning Board. (1988). Population activities in Korea. Seoul, Korea: Population Division, National Bureau of Statistics, Economic Planning Board, The Government of the Republic of Korea.

Harrison, D. (1988). *The sociology of modernization and development.* London: Unwin Hyman.

Jacobs, N. (1985). *The Korean road to modernization and development*. Urbana, IL: University of Illinois Press.

Kim, S. H. (1990). The underground economy. *Korea Economic Report. 5*(July), 42-46.

Kim, T. H. (1989). Current status of research on Korean elderly. *Journal of Korean Gerontological Society, 9*, 168-176.

Koo, J. S. (1981). *Social integration and support systems of elderly Korean widows.* Paper presented at the International Conference on Aging, University of Hawaii, Honolulu, Hawaii, May 20-22.

Lee, H. K. (1988). *Public assistance for the elderly and the disabled: An analysis of the livelihood protection program in Korea.* In Proceedings of a Conference on Social Welfare Policies in Korea and Japan, Tokyo, Japan.

Min, J. S., & Tacho, B. H. (1989). *Korean's pension system and major policy issues*. Seoul, Korea: Korea Development Institute.

Ministry of Government Administration. (1981). Fundamental structure of the government of Korea. In *Organization of the government of Korea*. Seoul, Korea: The Government of the Republic of Korea.

Ministry of Health and Social Affairs. (1988). *Major policies and programmes in health and social welfare services, Seoul, Korea.* Seoul, Korea: The Government of the Republic of Korea.

Ministry of Health and Social Affairs. (1989). Old age welfare act. National Law No. 4178, December, 30. Seoul, Korea: The Government of the Republic of Korea.

Ministry of Health and Social Affairs. (1988). *Social welfare programs for the elderly.* Seoul, Korea: The Government of the Republic of Korea.

National Economic Planning Board. (1988). *Social indicators in Korea*. Seoul, Korea: The Government of the Republic of Korea.

National Federation of Medical Insurance. (1988). *Medical insurance in Korea*. Seoul, Korea: The Government of the Republic of Korea.

National Pension Corporation. (1989). *National pension act, amended in 1989*. Seoul, Korea: The Government of the Republic of Korea.

Paik, W. K. (1991). Merits and demerits of public administration in Korea's modernization. In G. E. Caiden and B. W. Kim (Eds.), *A dragon's progress: Development administration in Korea, pp.123-134*. West Hartford, CT: Kumarian Press.

Paiva, F. (1977). *A conception of social development*. Social Service Review, 51, 336- 377.

Riggs, F. W. (1964). *Administration in developing countries: The theory of prismatic society*. Boston, MA: Houghton Mifflin.

Sharkansky, I. (1971). Economic theories of public policy: Resource policy and need policy linkages between income and welfare benefits. *Midwest Journal of Political Science, 15*, 722-740.

Shin, S. J. (1988). Welfare policies and programs for the aged in Korea: Mainly of the aged at home. In *Proceedings of Social Welfare Policies in Korea and Japan*, Tokyo, Japan.

The Economist. (1990). Taiwan and Korea: Two paths to prosperity. *The Economist, 316*(July 14), 17-20.

The Korean Herald. (1990). July 6, 3.

The Korean Herald. (1990). August 5, 8.

Tu, W. M. (1984). *Confucian ethics today: The Singapore challenge*. Singapore: Federal Publications.

Yang, S. C., & Ahn, B. M. (1991). *Comparative analysis of North and South Korean ruling elites, 1948-1988: With special reference to their recruitment patterns*. Fifteenth World Congress of the International Political Science Association, Buenos Aires, Argentina, July, 22.

Interviews

Cho, K. D. (1990, July 10). Director, HelpAge Korea, Seoul, Korea, *Interview*.

Choi, B. H. (1990, July 5). Chief, Vital Statistics Section, Population Division, National Bureau of Statistics, National Planning Board, Seoul, Korea, *Interview*.

Chung, K. K. (1990, July 5). School of Public Health, Seoul National University, Seoul, Korea, *Interview*.

Ha, S. N. (1990, July 5). Board member, Korean Association of the Aged, Seoul, Korea, *Interview*.

Joo, K. S. (1990, August 3). Assistant Minister of Planning and Management, Ministry of Health and Social Affairs, Seoul, Korea, *Interview*.

Kim, S. K. (1990, July 18). College of Social Sciences, Seoul National University, Seoul, Korea, *Interview*.

Kim, T. H. (1990, August 3). Department of Home Economics, Sung Shin University, Seoul, Korea, *Interview*.

Kim, Y. (1990, July 23). Dean, College of Liberal Arts, Chung-Ang University and Director, Korea Institute for Welfare Policy, Seoul, Korea, *Interview*.

Lee, H. K. (1990, June 25). Department of Social Work, Yonsei University, Seoul, Korea, *Interview*.

Park, J. G. (1990, June 29). Research Director, Korean Institute of Gerentology, Seoul, Korea, *Interview*.

Suh, S. M. (1990, July 30). Member, National Assembly, Director General of Policy Coordination Office of Democratic Liberal Party, Seoul, Korea, *Interview*.

Yoon, G. H. Y. (1990, July 20). Department of Psychology, Yonsei University, Seoul, Korea, *Interview*.

Article 16

Interdependence of Older People in Changing Family Systems

Karen Altergott
Dinnie Chao

Introduction

The demographics of aging and the family have changed the population structures of nations around the world. The global diversity of multigenerational families results, in part, from fertility and mortality variations. Distribution of available family members in the multigenerational family depends upon geographic mobility imposed or enabled by societal structures or events. Functioning of the multigenerational family of which an older person is a member depends upon cultural roles, family variations and individual improvizations. Culture and belief systems influence multigenerational family systems. Taken together, demographic, economic, societal and cultural environments are changing interactively.

The aging family member is at the crest of a wave of social changes. Some scholars suggest that family organization and changes in individual lives follow technological and societal changes while others believe the family leads the process of societal reorganization. In either case, the interwoven realities of demography and family structure, economy and personal resources, society and role opportunities, culture and family life determine much about the way we age.

The core question this paper explores is: how is interdependence patterned in the complex multigenerational family systems around the world? Demography, societal forces and cultural patterns shape the possibilities, but diversity within nations, negotiated realities and innovations produce additional variations in interdependencies between the older person and families. We describe the conditions shaping multigenerational families, and raise questions about interdependencies.

Demography and multigenerational families

A great portion of the world's population is likely to be 65 and older in the next century, a fact that is neither positive or negative in itself. Whether the consequences are negative or positive depends on the social organization of families and societies. It must be clearly understood that this demographic aging is the result of both increased longevity and reduced fertility. As more adults survive into old age and fewer children are born into the populations around the world, the population structure 'ages.' Even Africa, with nations having some of the highest fertility rates, has had decreases in fertility in recent years and the life expectancy at birth has increased, for example, to 71 in Tunisia, nearly 64 in Morocco, and 61 in Kenya and Zimbabwe (U.S. Bureau of the Census, 1992). The increase in the numbers of elderly citizens is generally more rapid in developing nations, given dramatic changes in deaths and births (U.S. Bureau of the Census, 1992). In Western nations, the increase of those 65 and older from 2-4% to 10-12% took 100 years (Cowgill, 1981), but with the aging nations of the developing world, the population structure is likely to change much more rapidly.

But births and deaths vary within society. There are enormous variations in multigenerational family structures within nations, as well as population structure variations across nations. In demographic simulations of future populations at Cambridge University, Laslett and his students have projected distributions of possible generational structures for the U.S., England, and China (1989). Some family structures in each society risk having one middle generation missing. And, some nations have already had substantial numbers of older people reach old age without descendent kin, such as Korea where an increasing number of older widows are reaching old age without a surviving son (U.S. Bureau of the Census, 1992). Burton and Dilworth-Anderson have described three kinship structures commonly found within the U.S., varying based on familial patterns of fertility. These are: verticalized families with few in each generation but many generations; age-condensed with several generations of early childbearing; and, substitutional with roles emptied through death or low fertility and replacements of fictive or distant kin (1990). The patterns of multigenerationality vary with life expectancies, births, and family variations. Aging of populations has produced more potential for co-survival of multiple generations, but forces operating within each society have produced more variation in family structures than is commonly realized.

Another generational exploration has calculated the ratio of those 80 and older (roughly representing parents possibly needing care) to those 50-64 (representing offspring who may have a dependent parent). Several distinct patterns emerge across nations. For example, Sweden now has the highest ratio (57), and Japan is predicted to have the highest ratio in 2025 (91), based on demographic projections. Most industrialized nations now have a ratio at 20 or higher. Right now, developing nations have a ratio of 15 or less, but in the next thirty or forty years, this could rise to 48 (U.S. Bureau of the Census, 1992). Again, these demographic trends are neither negative or positive in themselves, but they reflect a need to reconsider intergenerational interdependencies in families and communities.

In addition to existence of kin, the geographic dispersion or concentration of kin affects the interdependencies of the multigenerational family. We have little insight into the structure of the intergenerational kin group in terms of membership and dispersion of kin. Shanas and her colleagues contributed to the understanding of the dispersion and interaction of kin in developed countries, where she repeatedly found that about 80% older people who were parents (or about 60% of older people in general) were likely to be located near at least one of their children and to interact often (Shanas, 1979). Recent studies in the U.S. show that fully

57% of those over 65 who live alone lived near one of their children in 1990 (U.S. Senate Special Committee on Aging, 1991). As Don Cowgill, demographer and gerontologist, often said, a study of the location of and the process of mobility of multiple generations would provide great insight into where kin are located and how they came to be near or far. Both in terms of cosurvival and family structure across the generations, and in terms of coresidence, the present and future hold many variations within as well as across societies.

The multigenerational family is not easy to define in any society. Families exhibit a remarkable diversity of multigenerational forms in the U.S. And, worldwide, "there is no historical precedent for a majority of middle-aged and young-old adults having living parents" (U.S. Bureau of the Census, 1992). To more fully understand aging and interdependence, we must understand the family systems that surround the individual. In many societies for which we know a great deal about household membership, we know very little about geographic distribution of family members or even numbers of kin alive. The impacts of variations in multigenerationality on interdependence have not been examined yet.

Economy and resources

The story of aging within multigenerational families is related to modernization and economic development of nations, as well as to developments in public health, private health related practices, and medicine, and to cultural transformation of beliefs and practices associated with modernity. Development or modernization has impacts on fertility, household formation, and mobility.

Cowgill's theory of modernization and aging suggested that aging populations, due to increased numbers of elders, health technologies, urbanization, modernization of productive technology, educational institutions, and developments in the work force such as retirement would lead to lower status of the aged in society (Cowgill, 1981). This theory has been challenged as ignoring political forces (Cherry & Magnuson-Martinson, 1981) that modify the position of the aged through policy or other actions. Bengtson and colleagues, in a reanalysis of Inkeles's study reported in *Becoming Modern*, found that neither national nor individual modernity had much impact on the ties of interdependence within the family (Bengtson, 1978). Further, in recent analyses of the impact of urbanization on older people in the U.S., there were no differences between metropolitan and non metropolitan elders in terms of living arrangements (Glasgow, 1988). Nevertheless, we can review how some of the components of modernization or economic conditions shape the multigenerational family in particular nations.

Fertility. Modernization is linked to the fertility reduction that is part of the aging of populations as well. Families in the West, including England, the United States, Germany, and France started to shrink after the industrial revolution in the nineteenth century. This occurred in the absence of highly effective contraception, and was initiated by middle class families who wanted to limit fertility, in part, to enhance the level of living of their families in the face of economic and social opportunities. This was probably at least as significant as another reason for fertility reduction: infant survival made it more likely that children born would be raised to adulthood.

In Japan, fertility began to drop in the pre-war period, started to rise during the war, as a result of the government's encouragement, and declined in the post-war period. Examining previous studies on fertility in Japan, Long (1987) summarized that in the 1950s and earlier a decrease in fertility mainly resulted from a desire for a higher living standard while the primary motivation since the 1960s has been a desire to provide higher education for children. The decline of fertility rate not only leads to smaller family size but also to births concentrated in the woman's late 20s to assure that the children will finish their education before her husband's retirement. According to the latest estimates by the Japanese Institute of Population Problems, Ministry of Health and Welfare, the average number of children per woman will be about 1.9 in the coming 25 years (Morioka, 1990).

Based on data from the 1982 One-per-Thousand Fertility Survey, a probability sample of rural brigades and urban districts in every province of China, Lavely and Freedman (1990) concluded that education and urbanization are negatively associated with marital fertility in rural and urban China. This preceded the practice of government family planning programs.

In many ways, these declines in family size, though variable, and the increasing opportunities that require mobility, change the nature of both the family structure and family operation throughout the world.

Mobility. Documented in the West during the 1960s and through occasional studies since then, geographic mobility has spread the multigenerational family thinner over space, at the same time declining fertility has reduced the number of members of each generation. This mobility, even more clearly than the fertility and mortality rate reductions, is a socially moderated process dependent on economic opportunities as much as on belief systems.

After the Second World War, Taiwan entered an era of rapid social change and economic growth, with a peak in the 1960s and 1970s. As industrial and agricultural production rose, the demand for manpower was high. With the practice of compulsory education as well as the progress of communication and transportation, more and more men and women started their career outside of their home or family business, with some of them migrating to another city (Coombs & Sun, 1981). This fostered dispersion of generations. This impact of modernization has not been systematically studied.

Increased mobility, stimulated by economic growth, may have reduced the intergenerational living in societies experiencing growth or dispersion of opportunities, but in many nations, stagnant economies are leading to shared housing. In the U.S. during the 1980s, many young adults remained or returned home, leading to a spate of articles on the not-so-empty nest. In 1989, almost five million adults aged 24-34 lived with their parents. This reflected 8% of women and 15% of men in this age category (U.S. Bureau of the Census, 1990).

Household membership. Many countries provide examples of how modernization influenced household membership. In addition, multigenerational households in the U.S. have never been as absent as some analysts have assumed. Given the way census data is usually reported, it is difficult to determine how many married elders live with offspring, since usually the categories provided are: alone (16% of men over 65, 41% of women), with spouse (74% of men, 40% of women), other relatives (8% of men, 17% of women), and non-relatives only (2% of both men and women over 65) (U.S. Bureau of the Census, 1990). We do know that older people provide the home in about half of the households that are shared with relatives (Schorr, 1980) and the proportion of older people sharing a household varies by race, class and marital status, but represents a significant minority of American families. Some evidence for multigeneration households can be inferred from the location of children in the same household as their grandparents. In the late 1980s, almost 5% of all children were grandchildren of the household head in the U.S. (U.S. Bureau of the Census, 1990). This does not include those grandchildren who live with grandparents in the middle generation's home, but gives some insight into the existence of multigenerational living. For the 5% of children living in the households of their grandparents, neither parent is present for one-fourth of the white children, one third of the black children and one-fourth of the Hispanic children while both parents are present for one fifth of white and Hispanic children and for about 4% of black children (U.S. Bureau of the Census, 1990). Clearly, much of the multigenerationality is due to single parents remaining with or returning to their parents. This is also reflected in the fact that one-third of the women aged 24-34 who live with their parents have at least one child with them as well.

Overall, the proportion of shared households for two adult generations has declined, but an argument remains between those who stress nuclearity, such as Laslett, and those who stress interdependence, such as Cowgill (1986). Long, in a study of the views of Japanese adults, found that most thought it was better for parents to live with married children, especially if the parent was frail or widowed (1987). Long suggested that the elderly person living alone or with a spouse is a temporary arrangement, preceded and followed by multigenerational living (1987). While nuclearity is preferred and numerically dominant as a household, how many people pass through an extended family experience sometime in their lives? How many would choose this if circumstances of one generation or another required?

Japan's industrialization resulted in shrinking of the household around 1955 (Morioka, 1990). Long (1987) reported that the mean household in the 1920s contained about 5 people and this was constant during and after the war. Since then, the family size had been reduced to a mean household of about three people in the 1980s. Also, conducting a study on demographic family changes in Japan, Morioka (1990) indicated that families started to shrink drastically from 5.1 persons in 1955 to 3.8 persons in 1975, but since 1975, the shrinking trend has gradually stabilized. However, these figures mask changes in fertility and intergenerational living.

Using data from surveys of the elderly, conducted in 1984 under the auspices of the World Health Organization, Martin (1989) concluded that about 75% of the elderly in Fiji,

Korea, Malaysia, and the Philippines live with their children, with the rate in Malaysia somewhat lower (69%). In Korea, the percentage of elderly people sharing the same household with their married children dropped from 71% in 1970 to 64% in 1980. In Korea, the percentage of the elderly living with their children or other married relatives dropped from 71% to 64% in 1980. In 1988, 48% of the elderly relied on their eldest son, 20% on all sons, 20% on all sons and daughters (Martin, 1990). There is also evidence of the decline in coresidence in Taiwan. Survey data indicated that 81% of the married female respondents aged 20 to 39 in 1973 lived or ate with their parent-in-law and it dropped to 69% for the samples in 1985. As in Japan, both older and younger generations in Korea and Taiwan have lower expectations of living with their adult children than the older cohorts (Cooms & Sun, 1981; Martin, 1990). However, these declining percentages are coupled with increasing numbers of older parents surviving, so the number of shared households is still high.

In 1982, the Chinese Academy of Social Sciences and some local institutions initiated the Five City Family Study. One of its findings was the high percentage of nuclear families in China. An average of 66% of all families in the cities surveyed were of the nuclear family type (Hareven, 1987). Hareven also reported the demographer Ma Xia's analysis of the third national census in 1982. The results showed that there was an increase in the percentage of one- and two-generation households (from 50% in 1930 to 81% in 1982) and a decrease in the percentage of three-generation households (from 50% to 19%).

The traditional Japanese household type was that of the stem family system, which emphasized the family's lineal linkage over generations. For each generation, one married son of the household head was made the successor to the headship and heir to the family property. Remaining in his parental home, he set up a new single household (Morioka, 1990). After the Second World War, the Japanese social system went under reform, and the family system was inevitably influenced. Koyama (1970), based on a result from his earlier study, reported that the ratio of the extended to the nuclear family in Japan had been 40% to 60% until 1955, but it dropped to 31% to 69% in 1964. The traditional concept and practice of intergenerational living has started to give way to those of the nuclear family system. Drawing data from two census years 1955 and 1985, Morioka (1990) concluded that, in Japan, nuclear family households have become most common, as a result of a decrease in stem family households and an increase in nuclear.

One variation in the general downward trend in multigenerational living is that the older parent in the East is more likely to live with a son and the older parent in the West is more likely to live with a daughter (Cowgill, 1981). These gender differences may mean that different forces are operating in each setting to influence multigenerational living. Also, particular situations, such as the high proportion of immigrants among the elderly in Israel, the presence of extreme inequality in some less developed nations, the high rate of female employment in Sweden and elsewhere, global mobility of young adults from less developed nations to more developed nations, and the rapidity of aging of some populations such as Japan and the Netherlands are factors influencing generations in some nations more than in others (Bagby, 1991).

Economic productivity. There is a trend toward retirement, or labor force exit in general, in later life in many nations. When economic productivity or accumulated resources in retirement are high for older people, intergenerational interdependence is likely. The lack of resources, pension or productivity on the older person's part may lead to reliance on offspring or to serious deprivation. The situation in nations like Hungary is particularly difficult. With pensions that were never very high coupled with an early retirement age, and the termination of part-time employment programs for pensioners due to economic reform, many older Hungarians are facing new and extreme economic dependency (Szeman, 1991). In the past, gardening for the market and bartering services such as home building or repair were common ways to make ends meet (Andorka, 1988). Now, it is difficult for older generations to find opportunities to support themselves and younger generations are often not in a position to provide resources for survival for their elders. In fact, under similar conditions of political and economic turmoil, Morawska reported declines in life expectancy, a bleak family economic situation, and an increasing proportion of older people in poverty in Poland (1989). The situation of older people is directly linked to the larger economy and when there is economic crisis, older people may experience most dramatic loses. The availability of either pensions, opportunities to work or sufficient resources in the kin network to support nonemployed members are important economic conditions for multigenerational families.

Countries vary a great deal in terms of how much of preretirement income is replaced by the public pension. Older people in Sweden receive relatively high income replacement, while other countries with pension plans that are not yet mature cannot grant as much economic security in retirement (Altergott & Duncan, 1988). This is one way the economy, policy and national agenda setting shapes families.

Society, roles and resources

In the 1700s and 1800s, European parents lost some of their ability to control young adults, as economic opportunities outside of parental control and migration to North America provided alternatives to family businesses or farms. This example of how frontiers, new opportunities, and new economic developments lead to dispersion of generations has been repeated many times in human history. As modernization and westernization took root in the East, Asia was under transformation both socially and economically. The control of older family members over the younger generation within the extended family has decreased while women's social and familial status has been greatly improved. Many younger people seek employment outside their home or family business, leading away from multigenerational living. At the same time, coresidence with parents helps younger couples solve such problems as housing expenses, costs of raising children, and balancing the mother role and the paid work role. The possible advantages of coresidence together with the traditional family values of intergenerational relationship sustain the extended family as a viable structure in the East (Hareven, 1987; Morgan & Hirosima, 1983). However, the ideal family pattern for the younger generation seems to be one with separate residence but sufficient proximity to ensure regular contacts with their parents (Hareven, 1987; Morgan & Hirosima, 1983).

Social roles also hold multiple generations together across household boundaries, however. And, role changes associated with modernity do not necessarily place older people at risk in their families. From the historic and traditional point of view, the Chinese culture emphasized strong familial relations, favored the extended family structure, demanded filial piety to parents, and took it for granted that sons provide support to elderly parents (Coombs & Sun, 1981). Freedman, Chang & Sun (1982) had similar findings. They maintain that couples in Taiwan who do not live with the husband's parents still manage to have close contact with their parents by means of paying visits and providing financial support. In 1973, 80% of couples living in the same area saw their parents several times a week or more, but in 1980, 64% did so. However, there was an increase (from 73% in 1973 to 87% in 1980) in the percentage of couples living in nuclear households that gave money to the husband's parents in 1980.

In the U.S., as economic resources in a family rise, older people are more likely to live alone. However, among Black and Hispanic families, increasing economic resources do not lead to quite as much independent living of older people (Goldschneider & Goldschneider, 1989). The Survey of Black Americans showed that African American generations more often share households because of mutual benefit.

Also, the role of older people in multigenerational systems in the West involves giving and receiving. American elders give financial support to offspring to buy houses, make major purchases and at other times. In 1990, 3.2 million were maintained by grandparents. Services are provided, such as childcare to grandchildren even across households. Two to three million children are watched by grandparents on a routine basis (U.S. Bureau of the Census, 1990).

In Australia, studies of adults conducted from 1981 to 1990 show that most younger adults would give financial help to parents (75%) and many would let parents live with them (43%). Most gave emotional support, help around the house, and care during illness, and one-fifth gave financial assistance to parents. On the other side of the relationship, most older people minded grandchildren at least some times (76%), one-third helped fund renovations, major purchases, and home ownership; some provided funds for education and even travel; most older people provided emotional support and care during illness (Edgar, 1991).

The pattern of help exchanged across households is repeated for nation after nation. Long, in studies of Japanese elders, found that those living separately from their children were not neglected or ignored. Based on the data from a 1975 survey, 23% of the middle-aged respondents living separately from their parents visited them at least once a week, 30% visited them once or twice a month, and 29% visited them at least once a year. Other research indicated that elderly parents, though living independently, turn to their children for financial, physical or psychological help.

Based on the Five City Family Project in China, Haveven (1987) reported that the elderly who do not live with their married children receive social, financial and other kinds of support from their children. These may be given partly out of the legal obligations of supporting parents and partly out of traditional filial piety. Thirty-five percent of the households in the cities surveyed sent remittances to parents. The older generation assisted their children in child care, housing or housework in most cases. But, among the respondents, the issue of old-age support was the problem most frequently mentioned by the respondents. They complain about the amount and type of support and the way it was rendered. Hoping to see their sons get married and live a better life, the elderly have lower expectations for financial support from their adult children. Within the household, power seems to have shifted to the young. From the elderly's point of view, most disputes and grievances between generations are endured, avoided, or ignored. This study demonstrated that the older generation seems to be in a vulnerable position depending on their children. Yet persistence of lineal family type in China indicates that there do exist mutual obligations among generations, especially the responsibility of old age support (Haveven, 1987).

Changes in women's roles have often been mentioned as influencing many aspects of the multigenerational family. Diamond examined the effect of outside employment on women's status, autonomy and control over their future and present lives among women on Taiwan (1979). And social changes have raised the age at first marriage and young people are given more freedom in choosing their marital partners. However, women's wages were usually under the control of the household head, and women's paid work was viewed as an extension of their domestic duties (Diamond, 1979). The younger generation in Taiwan contributed part of their income to the parents, which helped the family improve its living standards (Diamond, 1979; Thorton, Chang & Sun, 1984). Diamond reported that the majority of her sample of Taiwanese women textile workers in 1970 sent remittances home. Those who lived in the factory dormitories contributed about 46% of their income to their family, while those who live at home turned over 70-80% (Diamond, 1979). Examining the same figures for 1990 would be enlightening. Many authors, especially since the 1970s, have examined women's position worldwide and have documented, at times subtle, increases in women's status. Whether married or single, these changes may influence daughters' degree of interdependence with older parents.

Culture and family

Changes in generational and gender expectations have occurred in many nations, and these changes have been documented for decades. In the 1960s William J. Goode (1982) asserted that there was a worldwide trend toward companionate marriage as the core family relationship. As this emerged, a preference for separation of each new marital unit from older generations supposedly occurred. The emphasis on filial versus marital relationships is still undergoing changes in many nations. This, coupled with new opportunities and pressures for mobility, and with resources that maximize both privacy and maintained contact across households, produces more nuclearity in family structure. But, given these trends, how does the functioning of the multigenerational family change? To what extent does reduced control over marriage and over adult offspring disrupt intergenerational interdependence?

Parental control over marriage was never uncommon among Asian countries. With social, economical, and demographic changes, arranged marriages gradually became rare. One study described the earlier forms of marriage in Taiwan, one of which was taking in the future daughter-in-law at a tender age and having the son marry her when they were grown up. This form had disappeared many decades ago. Due to the financial independence of young people resulting from factors such as extended education and employment outside the home, the younger generation today is responsible for their own marriages (Thorton, Chang & Sun, 1984). In Taiwan most of the older generation have given their children the freedom to choose their marital partners. Thorton, Chang and Sun (1984) indicated that the percentage of women in Taiwan reporting that their parents decided their marriage dropped from 75% for the 1930s birth cohort to 15% for recent birth cohorts, whereas the percentage of women reporting that the decision was theirs increased from 5% to 33%.

In Korea, almost 90% of women who married between 1950 and 1959 had arranged marriages, whereas only 81%, 55% and 45% for the marriage cohorts of 1960s, 1970s, and the early 1980s respectively. Long (1987) indicated that in Japan there existed a clear trend from arranged marriage to marriage of one's own choice, with the high peak in the early 1960s when the economy started to grow rapidly. There were more marriages of one's own choice in the urban areas than in the rural areas. The more education a woman obtained, the more likely she was to select her marital partner. Arranged marriages were more prevalent in the upper and lower classes, but marriages of one's own choice have become the norm for the vast majority of middle class Japanese.

After the Marriage Laws in 1950 and 1980 were put into practice, a shift from arranged marriages to marriages of one's own choice has occurred in China and there is also a tendency to marry at a later age than before (Zhangling, 1990). As society underwent change, the age at which people are expected to be married increased (Diamond, 1979). Since the family in China allowed children to get married before they could be economically independent, the age at first marriage had been lower than that in the West (Barclay et al., 1976).

Marriage practices shape the nature of relationships in the multigenerational family. Older members may be more powerful in family systems with arranged marriage, but the length of time the younger generations are economically dependent may be longer as well. With marriage based on choice, older people lose control over another aspect of life besides economic opportunity. These two losses of control are linked: economic opportunities, and marriages based on choice, together result in relationships with elders that are also based more on mutual choice.

Data from Hendry's study (1981) of Kurotsuchi in Japan revealed that parent-child relationships are traditionally viewed as the most important in Japanese society. Children were indebted to their parents for their care and therefore were bound to look after their parents for the rest of their lives as a return for the care. By law and custom, children were to give absolute obedience to their parents. The concepts of filial piety have not been given up by the majority of the Japanese.

Traditionally, the family in the East was composed of the older generation, the younger married couple and their children, but since the postwar period, families in Asian countries such as China, Taiwan, Korea and Japan have favored nuclear family types (Freedman, Chang & Sun, 1982; Morioka, 1990; Long, 1987; Martin, 1989). Social and economic changes result in change in family systems, which may either lead to new family structures or adaptation of the old one (Morgan & Hirosima, 1983).

When investigating changing intergenerational family relations in East Asia, Martin (1990) reported that the fertility level of South Korea has fallen to 2.1 children per woman. Freedman, Chang and Sun (1982) reported that the history of coresidence with the husband's parents is positively correlated to marital fertility. Couples who always lived as a nuclear family ranked lowest not only in actual fertility but also in fertility preferences while couples who had been or are in the extended household ranked the highest in both.

Coombs and Sun (1981) examined the changes in attitudes and values about the family, using five island-wide surveys of Taiwanese wives from 1965 to 1976. In 1973, only 40% of the sample lived in stem or joint-stem types of household. Moreover, there was a significant decrease (from 94% in 1965 to 54% in 1973) in the percentage of women who expected to live with their sons when they were old, and a decrease (from 77% in 1970 to 52% in 1973) in the percentage of women who expect to be supported by children in old age.

Previous research indicates that it is very likely to have intergenerational conflicts in the family in every society, developed or developing. Intergenerational family relations in Asia are changing. It was a common phenomenon that the older generation exerted control over the household regarding economy and daily affairs. The younger generation could not be economically independent until fathers :transferred the family property or business to them. In China, all sons received equal shares of the inheritance, while in Korea all sons received shares but the oldest son got more. In Japan, the oldest son took all (Thornton & Fricke, 1987).

Evidence of disagreement between the dyad of mother-in-law and daughter-in-law are very common in East Asia, but the power has been shifting from the older generation to the younger generation. Within the household, the relationship between the wife and her mother-in-law is one susceptible to much stress and strain. Only when the two women get along with each other will the household run smoothly. In the past, women were very strict with their daughters-in-law in almost every aspect (Hendry, 1981; Yang & Chandler, 1992). During the past few decades in Japan, one of the factors of a young woman giving consent to marriage is whether she will be expected to live with her parent-in-law (Long, 1987). But with such demographic changes as extended education, extra familial employment, and improved social status, women become more independent. Older women in Japan do not treat their daughters-in-law as harshly as their own mothers did and are more likely to be nice to them in order to keep them (Hendry, 1987). This is also true in China (Parish and Whyte, 1978).

New families and multigenerational interdependence

Families around the world have new demographic structures; create and exist within societies at varying levels of development and economic opportunity; have different role structures and forms of organization; and cultural belief systems that influence family relationships. Yet, these large-scale national patterns do not determine the nature of family life within nations. Examining the impacts at both the national and kinship system levels would require somewhat different questions than in the past. The national context matters-the demographic and social structure as well as culture has an impact on interdependence. But the variations at the family level matter as well. Are the within nation or across nation differences more important in shaping the lives of families? Also, variations in values and practices exist within as well as across nations. A closer look at global variations in intergenerational interdependence will be fostered by a new type of comparative gerontology. We hope the future will bring more studies of aging that are multinational collaborative studies, and that both context and variations can be analyzed.

References

Andorka, R. (1988). Daily life of elderly persons in Hungary. In K. Altergott (Ed.), *Daily life in later life: Comparative perspective*. Newbury Park, CA: Sage Publication.

Bagby, B. (1991). Aging: Global trends and national perspectives. *Journal of Home Economics, 83*, 48-53.

Altergott, K., & Duncan, S. (1988). National context and daily life in later life. In K. Altergott (Ed.) *Daily life in later life: Comparative perspective*. Newbury Park, CA: Sage Publication.

Barclay, G. W., Coale, A. J., Stoto, M. A., & Trussell, J. A. (1976). A reassessment of the demography of traditional rural China. *Population Index*, *42*, 606-635.

Bengtson, V. L., Dowd, J. J., Smith, D. H., & Inkeles, A. A. (1975). Modernization, modernity, and perceptions of aging: A cross-cultural study. *Journal of Gerontology*, *30*(6), 688-695.

Burton, L. M., & Dilworth-Anderson, P. (1991). The intergenerational family roles of aged Black Americans. *Marriage and Family Review*, *16*(3-4), 311-330.

Chappell, N. (1989). Aging and the family. In G. Ramu (Ed.), *Marriage and the family in Canada today* (pp. 185-206). Toronto: Prentice Hall of Canada.

Cherry, R., & Magnuson-Martinson, S. (1981). Modernization and the status of the aged in China: Delcine on equalization. *Sociological Quarterly*, *22*, 253-261.

Choi, J. S. (1970). Comparative study on the traditional families in Korea, Japan and China. In R. Hill & R. Konig (Eds.), *Families in East and West.* pp. 338-347. Paris: Mouton.

Cowgill, D. O. (1981). Aging in comparative cultural perspective. *Mid-American Review of Sociology, 6*(2), 1-28.

Cowgill, D. O. (1986). Aging around the world. Belmont, CA: Wadsworth Publishing Co..

Coombs, L., & Sun, T. H. (1981). Familial values in a developing society: A decade of change in Taiwan. *Social Forces, 59*(4), 1229-1253.

Diamond, N. (1979). Women and industry in Taiwan. *Modern China, 5*(3), 317-340.

Edgar, D. (1991). Aging: Everybody's future. *Family Matters, 30*, 14-19.

Freedman, R., Chang, M. C., & Sun, T. H. (1982). Household composition, extended kinship and reproduction in Taiwan: 1973-1980. *Population Studies*, 36, 395-411.

Glasgow, N. (1988). The non-metro elderly economic and demographic status. *U.S. Department of Agriculture Rural Development Research Report, No. 70.*

Goldschneider, E. K., & Goldschneider, C. (1989). *Ethnicity and the new family economy: Living arrangements and intergenerational financial flows.* San Francisco, CA: Westview Press.

Goldstein, M. C., Schuler, S., & Ross, J. L. (1983). Social and economic forces affecting intergenerational relations in extended families in a third world country: A cautionary tale. *Journal of Gerontology, 38*(6), 716-724.

Goode, W., (1982). *The family* (2nd ed.). Englewood Cliggs, N.J.: Prentice-Hall.

Hareven, T. K. (1987). Reflections on family research in the People's Republic of China. *Social Research, 54*(4), 663-689.

Hendry, J. (1981). Marriage in changing Japan. New York: St. Martin's Press.

Hirschman, C., & Guest, P. (1990). Multilevel models of fertility determination in four south-east Asia countries: 1970 and 1980. *Demography, 27*(3), 369-395.

Koyama, T. (1970). Rural-urban comparison of kinship relations in Japan. In R. Hill and R. Konig (Eds.), *Families in East and West.* (pp.318-336). Paris: Mouton.

Laslett (1989). Personal communication.

Lavely, W., & Freedman, R. (1990). The origins of the Chinese fertility decline. *Demography, 27*(3), 357-367.

Lee, M. (1970). Consanguineous group and its function in the Korean community. In R. Hill and R. Konig (Eds.), *Families in East and West.* (pp. 202-210), Paris: Mouton.

Levin, I., & Trost, J. (1992). Women and the concept of family. Uppsala, Sweden: Uppsala University.

Long, S. O. (1987). *Family change and the life course in Japan*. Ithaca, New York: East Asia Program Cornell University:

Mancini, J. A., & Blieszner, R. (1989). Aging parents and adult children: Research themes in intergenerational relations. *Journal of Marriage and Family, 51,* 275-290.

Martin, L. G. (1988). The aging of Asia. *Journal of Gerontology, 43*(4), 99-113.

Martin, L. G. (1989). Living arrangements of the elderly in Fiji, Korea, Malaysia, and the Philippines. *Demography, 26*(4), 627-643.

Martin, L. G. (1990). Changing intergenerational family relations in East Asia. *The Annals*, 102-114.

Morgan, S. P., & Hirosima, K. (1983). The persistence of extended family residence in Japan: Anachronism or alternative strategy? *American Sociological Review, 48,* 269-281.

Morioka, K.(1987). A Japanese perspective on the life course: Emerging and diminishing patterns. *Journal of Family History*, *12*(1-3), 243-60.

Morioka, K. (Nov. 1990). Demographic family changes in contemporary Japan. *International Social Science Journal*, *42*(4), 511-522.

Parish, W. L., & Whyte, M. K. (1978). Village and family in contemporary China. Chicago: University of Chicago Press.

Schorr, A. (1980). ... thy mother and thy father....: A second look at filial responsibility and family policy. *SSA Publication*, No. 13-11953. Washington, DC: U.S. Health and Human Services.

Shanas, E. (1973). Family-kin networks and aging in cross-cultural perspective. *Journal of Marriage and the family, 35(3), 505-511.*

Shanas, E. (1979). The family as a support system in old age. *Gerontologist, 10*(2), 169-174.

Stopes-Roe, M., & Cochrane, R. (1989). Traditionalism in the family: A comparison between Asian and British cultures and between generations. *Journal of Comparative Family Studies*, *20*(2), 141-158.

Szeman, Z. (1990). *Old and hungry: Impoverishment of elderly in Hungary*. Budapest, Hungary: Institute of Sociology, Hungarian Academy of Sciences.

Thornton, A., Chang, M. C., & Sun, T. H. (1984). Social and economic change, intergenerational relationships, and family formation in Taiwan. *Demography*, *21*(4), 475-497.

Thornton, A., & Fricke, T. E. (1987). Social change and the family: Comparative perspectives from the West, China, and South Asia. *Sociological Forum, 2*(4), 746-779.

U.S. Senate Special Committee on Aging (1991). *Aging America: Trends and projections*. Washington, DC: U.S. Department of Health and Human Services.

U.S. Bureau of the Census (1992). An aging World II international population reports, p. 25, 92-93, Washington, DC: U.S. Government Printing Office.

Yang, H., & Chandler, D. (1992). Intergenerational relations: Grievances of the elderly in Rural China. *Journal of Comparative Family Studies*, *23*(3), 431-453.

Yuan, M. (1990). Trends in the Chinese family. *Peijing Review*, *33*(31), 30-32.

Zhangling, W. (1990). The family and family research in contemporary China. *International Social Science Journal*, *42*(4), 493-509.

Family Crisis

Part VI

Article 17

Marital Violence in Taiwan: A Cultural Perspective

Rita Jing-Ann Chou

Introduction

On November 8, 1989, a locally produced program entitled "Bruises That Fade Too Slowly" was shown on Taiwan television. The drama depicted a story of a battered wife and her family. At the end of the show, the phone number for the crisis line of the Women's Service Center in the Northern Division of Taipei City, the Carnation Hot Line, was given. For the next ten-odd days, the crisis line was flooded with calls. More than five hundred victims of marital violence, all women, called for help. The Center itself was so overwhelmed that it had to ask these women to come in for group rather than individual counseling, which the Center normally provides. This huge response, however, represented only the tip of an iceberg.

As in many other societies, marital violence is one of the major family problems in Taiwan. Marital violence not only degrades the quality of family life, but also leads to the dissolution of marriages. The very worst cases have ended in homicides. Although marital violence occurs within individual families, it is not enough, and may even be misleading, to simply look at it within the context of the family. A broader view is necessary to achieve a better understanding of the causes, the processes, and the interventions for marital violence. This research represents an effort to apply a cultural perspective to marital violence in contemporary Taiwan.

Research on Marital Violence in Taiwan

As far as the incidence rate of marital violence in Taiwan is concerned, statistical data are extremely scarce. The only data available come from two recently conducted official reports—Taiwan Provincial Women's Living Condition Survey Report of the year 1990, and that of the year 1992, based on surveys of 2,000 and 1,800 women in Taiwan respectively. According to the first report, among the 1,638 married women surveyed, 11.5% have been battered by their spouses "once in a while," 0.9% have been "frequently" battered, while 0.1% have been battered "to the extent beyond their tolerance" (Taiwan Provincial Department of Social Affairs 1991a, p. 34).

The report for the year of 1992 indicates that among the 1,496 married women surveyed, 16.4% have been battered by their spouses "once in a while," 1.2% have been "frequently" battered, and 0.2% have been battered "to the extent beyond their tolerance" (Taiwan Provincial Department of Social Affairs, 1993, p. 54). In other words, the most current data indicates that 17.8% of married women, or more than one out of every six married women, are victims of marital violence in Taiwan.

The gender construction of marital violence, which the above *Carnation Hot Line* incident implies, echoes findings from existing research. Although in Taiwan there are women who batter their husbands, the majority of marital violence has been committed by men (Chen, 1992a, p. 124). Male perpetrators, rather than female, have also caused considerably more severe injury (Chen, 1992a, p. 124). As a result, previous research and related publications have been inclined to focus on women as victims and men as perpetrators (cf. Chen, 1992a; Huang, 1992, p. 8), rather than vice versa, or men and women both as perpetrators and victims.

Studies on marital violence in Taiwan have been scanty. Liu (1987, pp. 382-384) conducted what seems to be the first research in this area by analyzing newspaper reports. Liu's study covered three large newspapers, *Central Daily News, China Times,* and *United News,* for the years of 1984 and 1985. A total number of 134 cases was found; among them, 24 women died because of the abuse and 46 were injured. Causes and methods of abuse were also discussed.

Chen (1992a) studied 55 battered wives who came looking for help in the Warm Life Association and the Women's Service Center in Northern Division of Taipei City. Chen's research shows that families with marital violence came from various socio-economic statuses. The educational background of the victims ranges from elementary school to college graduates, with the largest percentage (37%) having a middle or high school diploma. The batterers' educational levels cover from elementary school to master degree, with the majority (56%) being junior college or college graduates. These violence-plagued families are mostly nuclear families with two children, in which the batterers show extremely dominant attitudes and behavior. Violence usually started within one year after marriage. The direct causes of violence include conflicts in financial decisions and in childrearing, extra-marital affairs on the part of the husband, as well as the husband's suspicion of the wife's unfaithfulness. The result of violence caused eighteen percent of the victims being injured to the edge of death, with the rest sustaining lesser injuries.

The most recent research on battered women is currently being conducted by the author. This study takes place in "Safe Home," a women's shelter located in northern Taiwan, sponsored by the city government and run by a religious group. So far, data on 34 cases of marital violence have been collected, and part of the data will be applied in the following discussion.

Marital Violence as A Cultural Process

As indicated by Lystad (1989), theoretical perspectives on the behavioral causes of family violence can be grouped into three categories. The first category involves psychological needs and development as they relate to interpersonal violence in the family. The second category concerns the social statuses and structures that encourage marital violence. The third category deals with cultural attitudes and values that legitimize violence in the family. Although each perspective is valuable as an explanatory model for the cause of marital violence, a cultural perspective, because of its theoretical comprehensiveness and depth, is chosen as the fundamental framework in this paper.

Furthermore, this paper concerns itself not only with the causes of marital violence. The author intends to take two further steps for a more comprehensive understanding of marital violence in Taiwan. The first step is to find out the relationship between culture and the behavior patterns of the perpetrators and victims. The second step is to examine the roles that culture plays in intervention from outside the family.

The author proposes that marital violence, as it is now in Taiwan, can be viewed as a cultural process, which involves different cultural forces acting behind individual actors/agents. Conceptually, the process can be summarized by three stages. The initial stage is set up by the basic values and beliefs within the culture itself. As a society of patriarchy, traditional China manifested substantial power differences within the family structure. The most fundamental and dominant cultural value regarding the relative status between husbands and wives has been "male superiority and female inferiority." Along with other psychological and social factors, such cultural values set up the initial stage for marital violence.

The second stage covers the time period in which incidents of violence occur. It is of particular interest for the present research to see what cultural ideas and beliefs are based in justifying violence on the part of the abusers, and in accepting or tolerating the violence by the victims.

The third stage, which may or may not ever be reached, starts when the victim escapes, or tries to escape, from the vicious cycles of violence. It is a stage where other forces come onto the scene, that is, the possible social, medical and legal interventions guided by the current culture in Taiwan. Crisis lines, emergency shelters, psychological and legal counselling, and self-growth groups for battered women are only a few examples. To a certain extent, the nature of these interventions manifests a combination of both traditional cultural values and newly developed ideas and beliefs.

Culture and Causes of Marital Violence

Cross-cultural studies indicate that, due to its mode of production, gender division of labor, and social organization, the subordination of women reaches its highest degree in agrarian civilization (O'Kelly & Carney 1986, pp. 88-117). This has long been the case in traditional Chinese society. In understanding women's lower status in traditional China, however, we also need to look into the ideological aspects of this condition. In order to justify and to fortify women's inferior status, a system of specific ideologies and norms has been developed in traditional Chinese society.

Culturally speaking, this system of ideologies and norms governing women's status in traditional China began with the "Doctrine of the Two Principles," called *yin* and *yang*. Originating in the Spring and Autumn Age (770–481 B.C.E.), the cosmological idea of *yin-yang* was substantially developed during the Warring States Age (481–222 B.C.E.). The *yin* and *yang* represent two great forces in a most comprehensive form. They stand for heaven and earth, the sun and the moon, day and night, life and death, positive and negative, strong and weak, high and low, good and evil, and so forth. (Wong & Wu 1985, p. 19). Tung Chung-shu (176–104 B.C.E.), a famous scholar of the Han Dynasty, combined this cosmological idea with human relationships. According to him (Tung, 1968, p. 6), males embody the characteristics of *yang* and are thus noble and superior, and females are *yin* and thus humble and inferior. Within the family, the same principle applies to the qualities and status of husbands and wives. Therefore, the husband is superior to the wife, and the latter should assume no independence.

Following Tung's idea of *yin-yang,* specific norms were developed for women. The most basic norm regulating a wife's behavior resided in "treating one's husband as one's ruler or governor and following his ideas as one's principles of behavior." Hence, a wife was supposed to "be gentle, obedient, and humble and assume the role of the weak toward her husband" (Huang, 1991, p. 261). In addition to respecting and serving one's husband, a woman was also supposed to respect and serve her parents-in-law as best she could. On the other hand, men were encouraged to be dominant, to make decisions for the whole family, and to be in charge. While a wife was supposed to be faithful to her husband all her life, a husband was free to have concubines.

With the modernization process in the Republic of China, and the constitutional declaration of equality between genders, many women began to have more opportunities to pursue higher education, and to work outside the home. With higher education, paid employment, and outstanding career achievement, women in Taiwan today have become a group with mixed characteristics. The influence of modernization upon women's personal ideas of gender relations, however, is not equally distributed. While some women have adopted more equal ideas and ways in dealing with the opposite sex, some still embrace the traditional idea of female inferiority. Age, educational level, socio-economic status, family background, and personal experience all have much to do with the individual woman's perceptions of appropriate gender relations.

Taking contemporary Taiwan society as a whole, however, the cultural norms and values that guided gender relations in pre-modern China linger. Within the family, women with ideologically less modernized husbands and/or in-laws are jeopardized by the latter's rigid standard and expectation of an ideal wife/housewife and/or daughter-in-law. For many women, these lasting cultural norms and values regarding gender relations have become a source of substantial pressure. In a recent survey of 81 married women in the Taipei area, 55 (68%) indicated that the greatest pressure they experience comes from social pressure based on traditional cultural norms and social values, 16 (20%) from husbands, and 10 (12%) from parents-in-law (Fu-nu Hsin-chih Pien-chih-pu, 1991, p. 8). To put the latter two groups' responses in perspective, what they meant was actually quite similar to the first group. The only difference lies in that they experienced the pressure of traditional cultural norms and social expectations embodied in their husbands and in-laws.

The influence of traditional norms of gender relations on marital violence is shown in a number of ways. First, the patriarchal ideology of male domination and female subordination has cultivated a tendency for men to dominate in spouse relations. It has also helped in forming stereotypes of the roles of husbands and wives, and therefore, has shaped the "ideal" pattern of interaction between spouses—that is, "ideal" from the husband's point of view. Under certain circumstances, a tendency to dominate one's spouse can be easily transformed into actual physical coercion, and result in marital violence. Chen's study, for example, indicates that within 65% of the families experiencing marital violence, it was the husband who made almost all decisions on family affairs. And "all of the batterers showed a high degree of authority and dictatorship, asking their wives to constantly take heed of and satisfy their needs" (Chen, 1992a, p. 126). It seems appropriate to say, then, that the patriarchal ideology of gender relations in fact has provided a fertile ground for marital violence to happen in the first place.

Second, as discussed above, modern Chinese women in Taiwan have changed in many ways. Many of them are now double-burdened with work in and outside the home. More often than not, their time and energy do not allow them to contribute to their roles of wives and daughters-in-law as much as they would like to. To make the situation even more complicated, their concepts of being a good wife and daughter-in-law may not exactly coincide with expectations from their husbands and parents-in-law. Pressures on the women thus mount, and tensions between spouses rise. Again, the initial stage of marital violence has been formed.

The example of residents at Safe Home in Northern Taiwan further substantiates this argument. Since its opening in July 1992, Safe Home has taken in a total of 46 women who needed emergency shelter, including 34 victims of marital violence. Among these 34 cases, 26 have reported the educational background of both their husbands and themselves. Of these 26 cases, 11 women (42%) have an educational level higher than their husbands, 6 women (23%) have an educational level similar to their husbands, while the remaining 9 women (35%) have an educational level lower than their husbands.

This finding becomes quite meaningful when put against the norm of relative spouse educational levels in traditional China.

According to traditional Chinese culture, men should marry women with educational level not higher than themselves, so that the husband will be the leader of the family in every respect. Although there are men today who marry women with higher education, the traditional attitude on relative education levels between spouses still serves as a norm. As the status inconsistency theory points out, violence is more likely to happen when an individual's power or status is inconsistent (high in one aspect, low in another), or when norms governing status in the family are ambiguous or changing (O'Brien, 1971; Gelles, 1974; Rodman, 1972). It is therefore probably not coincidental that such a high percentage of battered women have higher education than their husbands.

Culture and Response Patterns Toward Marital Violence

How the abusers justify their violence and how the abused look at marital violence reveal attitudes toward gender relations in general, and marital violence in particular. Abusers often attribute the battery to their abused wives (Chen, 1992b, p. 48). Typical responses given by the batterers to inquiries from outside have been: "I am educating my wife," or "I am educating my wife for the nation," or "It is my right to hit my wife," (Chen, 1990, p. 13; Yang, 1993, p. 73; Yu, 1990, p. 20), or "Women need to be beaten to become obedient" (Kaohsiung City Bureau of Social Affairs: 1993, p. 1). Such remarks clearly indicate the patriarchal and patronage mentality of the abusers, and reflect some of the basic, traditional cultural values. Women are not treated as equals by the abusers. Instead, they are the ones to be disciplined and improved, much like ignorant children. And in the abusers' reasoning, the discipline is done for the benefit of the whole nation. In other words, according to the abusers, the society has authorized men to "educate" women so that women will conform to social norms.

How do victimized women look at and deal with marital violence? In Chen's study (Chen, 1992a, p. 131), more than half of the women (58%) regard the abusing behavior as "his habit." As for who should be responsible for the violence, 56% of the women said their husbands should, while 31% indicate both of them should. More than one third of the women felt guilty about the occurrence of violence (Chen, 1992a). Since being battered by one's husband is socially regarded more or less as a stigma, many women feel ashamed for the abuse and are afraid that the battery will be discovered by neighbors or strangers (Yu, 1990, p. 20). After the occurrences of violence, the majority of the victims either keep the problems to themselves (Hsin, 1987, p. 32) or go to their parents, siblings, or parents-in-law for help. Very few women report the incidents to the police or go to social agencies for assistance (Hsin, 1987, p. 32; Chen, 1989, p. 69). My current research on residents of the Safe Home also indicates that going to the public sector for help is often their last resort.

Since for many women, divorce is ideologically unthinkable, emotionally impossible, and legally impractical, they have to stay in a troublesome marriage. To endure the hardships of living with an abusive husband, many women have adopted the traditional idea of "fate" or "destiny" to explain their misfortune (cf. Hsin, 1987, p. 32; Chen, 1992a, p. 136, Chao, 1987, p. 4). By taking marital violence as something predestined and not to be changed or avoided, they become more willing and able to accept the abuse and free themselves from the inner struggles of defending, staying, or leaving. Ironically, the belief in fate brings some comfort, while prolonging the ordeal.

To explain why battered women are often unable to see alternatives while they are still enmeshed in the relationship, Walker (1979, pp. 49-50) described "learned helplessness," by which she meant that some battered women do not believe anything they do will alter any outcome. The behavioral pattern of those battered women in Taiwan who believe in predestination could be viewed as a Chinese version of "learned helplessness," or to be more precise, as "learned acceptance."

As a product of the traditional Chinese mode of thinking, however, "learned acceptance," seems to be losing its ground to other types of responses. An examination of what women in general think of what they would do when encountering marital violence indicates that change is under way. In the Taiwan Provincial Women's Living Condition Survey of 1992 (Taiwan Provincial Department of Social Affairs 1993, Appendix III), the following was included as a multiple choice question: "What are you going to do, if your husband treats you violently?" "I will (1) tolerate the abuse, (2) fight back, (3) ask others to mediate, (4) resort to legal actions, (5) other solutions:______." Answers to this question were tabulated according to the respondents' ages, educational levels, marital statuses, degrees of urbanization of place of residence, religious beliefs, and occupations. Tabulations of answers according to age and education are presented below:

		Percentage of Women				
Answer:	Total	(1)	(2)	(3)	(4)	(5)
Age:						
20-29	100.0	8.9	40.9	21.3	22.5	6.5
30-39	100.0	19.4	36.1	27.4	11.4	5.6
40-49	100.0	25.1	28.8	32.3	8.3	5.5
50-59	100.0	41.2	27.9	23.2	6.9	0.9
Education:						
Elementary School and Under	100.0	35.1	27.2	28.8	5.6	3.4
Junior High School	100.0	16.0	39.3	25.7	12.2	6.8
Senior High School	100.0	10.9	41.3	23.9	18.0	5.9
College and above	100.0	6.4	34.3	25.0	27.5	6.9

(Source: Taiwan Provincial Department of Social Affairs, 1993, p. 56)

A few observations can be derived from these results. First, the older a woman is, the more she tends to tolerate marital violence, and the less likely she is to fight back or to take legal actions against the violence. On the other hand, younger women not only tend to be less tolerant of marital violence, but also are more likely to fight back or go to the law. Second, the less education a woman has received, the more likely she is to put up with marital violence, and the less likely she will resort to legal actions. In other words, women with higher education tend to find marital violence intolerable, and are more likely to seek a legal solution.

Although the respondents may or may not be in an abusive marital relation, and their responses may or may not be exactly the same as what they would do in reality, the above analysis is significant in the following aspects. First, it indicates an intra-cultural variation on women's attitudes toward marital violence, a variation based on age and educational level. Second, it sheds light on the trend of social and cultural change. Marital violence will be less tolerated by women as time goes by. Third, it clearly reflects the impact of modernization on women's attitudes toward marital violence. Since the younger generations and the better educated have more exposure in modern ways of thinking, they have acquired a higher level of self-awareness. Besides demanding equality in gender relations, they often expect freedom from abuse from the other sex.

Culture and Social, Medical, and Legal Intervention

Traditional Chinese society was inclined to ignore marital violence. As long as no human lives or serious injuries were involved, it was considered a problem within the family and not a matter for external intervention. This attitude has been passed down to the general public, and its influence is manifested on two levels. On the individual level, since most people today still regard marital violence as a family problem, they often fail to render help in time, unless they are the victim's relatives or close friends. On the level of the whole society, the traditional concept has also made its impact on social, medical, and legal intervention.

In the medical aspect of intervention, it has been very difficult for women to get proof of medical examination on the injuries incurred in marital violence. Because physicians do not like the prospect that they may be required to appear in court as witnesses, many hospitals or clinics refuse to examine the injuries or they charge very high fees either to scare away the victims of limited means or to gain lucrative profit from wealthier ones. There are also hidden injuries that cannot be identified easily, which give the medical personnel a good excuse not to examine (Taipei City Bureau of Social Affairs, 1992, p. 4). If they are lucky enough to find a hospital or clinic which is willing to issue a document of medical examination, they still have to go through the humiliation inflicted by medical personnel (Fu-nu Hsin-chih Pien-chih-pu, 1991, p. 9). And very often the injuries are underestimated in the documentation.

In general, the police are usually not very helpful, either, although there are those who have assisted battered women. Partly because their workload is already too heavy, partly because "most policemen are unwilling to get involved with so-called 'others' family affairs," it is unlikely that the police will provide necessary help to the victims of marital violence (Taipei City Bureau of Social Affairs, 1992, p. 4; Pu-ping 1990, p. 25).

The legal and judicial system is another weak link in the mediation. First, there is no law to prohibit wife-beating husbands from approaching the victims or entering the residences. Victims, therefore, often are exposed to repetitive acts of violence. Second, judges often refuse to process cases of marital violence, on the basis that they are merely family affairs (Fu-nu Hsin-chih Pien-chih-pu, 1991, p. 11). Such behavior patterns of the judges obviously imply the impact of traditional Chinese culture. Third, the law requires that in order to get a divorce on the ground of spouse abuse, a battered woman needs to present at least three documents of medical examination. My research in Safe Home indicates that very often, even if a woman does have three such documents, her request for divorce may still be denied, if the judge thinks the injuries are not serious enough. It becomes, therefore, a dilemma. For those who have only one or two pieces of proof, their only chance of getting a divorce so that they can leave the abusers forever is to return home for more severe injuries. Fourth, divorce laws favor husbands. It is extremely difficult for women to gain child custody, or spouse and child support. For fear that they might lose their children and become penniless, many women hesitate in making decisions on divorce. As a result, they are stuck with an abusive spouse.

Social welfare agencies are the area of intervention most responsive to battered women's needs. They are also an area where there are clear signs of cultural and social change. First, there are professional social workers in the social welfare departments of the local county or city governments who help directly or refer victims of marital violence. Second, there are now crisis lines throughout the country to give immediate counselling and to refer women to other agencies for help (cf. Taiwan Provincial Department of Social Affairs, 1991b, pp. 191-294). Third, emergency shelters for a range of "unfortunate women" (including battered wives) are available in all areas except Kao-hsiung, Ping–tung and Peng-hu counties (Taiwan Provincial Department of Social Affairs, 1991b, pp. 293-294).

Historically and culturally speaking, the contemporary establishment of shelters for battered women indicates a significant break from the past. This is not to say that welfare institutions for women are new in Chinese society. In the Ch'ing dynasty (1661-1911 A.D.), for example, traditional Chinese society witnessed the founding of "houses for the chaste" (cheng-chieh tang) to take care of impoverished widows (Kao, 1988, p. 205). Yet, shelters for the battered women were absolutely unheard of in the past. What is most interesting is the difference in ideologies behind these different types of institutions for women. Houses for the chaste were established so that poor widows needed not remarry and relinquish their chastity (Kao, 1988). From a cultural perspective, this was a service to the traditional Chinese patriarchal ideology which dictated that a woman should always be faithful to her husband, alive or dead. Shelters for battered women, on the other hand, help the women to escape or to fight against the patriarchal tyranny at home, and to establish themselves as individual human beings with dignity. This then leads to a discussion of the basic ideology of the social workers in dealing with victims of marital violence.

To understand the fundamental principles of social workers in intervening in marital violence, I have interviewed ten social workers who work with battered women in different parts of Taiwan, in addition to my participant observations, interviews, and file-data analysis on Safe Home. Although the information gathered may not be sufficient to draw definite conclusions, at least a general trend is presenting itself. First is the principle of safety for the victims. When serious danger is involved, the woman is to be removed immediately from the batterers. Second is the principle of understanding. The social worker helps the abused woman to analyze her current situation so that she is able to have a better understanding of it. Third is the principle of self-decision-making. The victim makes her own decision on whether she should go back home, leave, or come to another solution. Based on the victim's own decision, the social worker gives recommendations on marital or legal counselling, vocational training, and other options.

These fundamental principles of social workers in working with battered women promote a notion that a woman no longer lives solely to meet the needs of the family. As an individual, she is to have her own personality and dignity. She is to have the right to make her own decisions and to be respected.

Conclusion: A Cultural Solution for Marital Violence

This paper has examined the current situation of marital violence in Taiwan. It also has proposed to understand marital violence as a cultural process. The impact of traditional culture is observed in the causes of, the responses toward, and the intervention with, marital violence. Yet, change is under way. Signs of cultural change are discerned in the various stages of marital violence. In short, the above discussion points out that cultural continuity and change are entangled in every stage of marital violence.

From a cultural perspective, what might be a solution for marital violence? In Chinese culture, is there a cultural solution for marital violence? The answer might reside in changing norms which govern gender relations, and in altering the society's general attitude toward marital violence. All social institutions, including law, social services, religion, and medicine, must be involved in this transformation. Certainly legislation and education will assume a leading role in this capacity. As a part of social norms, legislation based on equality of genders will enhance women's status and protect women from mistreatment. Legislation will also serve as a solid foundation upon which a culture of gender equality may flourish. Successful gender education, on the other hand, clarifies misunderstandings based on stereotypes of genders. In contrast with the traditional ideology of male dominance and female subordination, gender education shows that it is not only necessary, but also beneficial for both sexes to have equal standing. Finally, mutual respect and understanding between genders provide a more constructive framework and more flexible roles for gender interaction.

References

Chao, C. Y. (1987). Fa-yang Ch'uan-tung Mei-te. *Taipei Fu-chan Tsa-chi*. September 4.

Chen, J. C. (1989). Taiwan Hun-yin Pao-li te Chuang-kwan han Ch'u-li chih Tao, *Chien-kang Sh'ih-chieh, 37*(157), 68-75.

Chen, J. C. (1990). Tsung Taiwan Hun-yin Pao-li Mien-mao Tan Liang-hsing. Chia-ting Lung-li Kwan-hsi te Tsai Chian-tao. *Proceedings of Second Conference, Fu-nu Hsin-chih.*

Chen, J. C. (1992a). Taiwan Hun-yin Pao-li chih Pen-chih. Li-chen yu Yin- hsiang (Marital Violence in Taiwan: The Nature, Process and Effects) *Fu-nu yu Liang-hsing Hsueh-kan 3,* 117-147.

Chen, J. C. (1992b). Ju-ho Yu-fang ping O-Chih Hun-yin Pao-li. *Fu-nu Pao-hu Shou-cho—Hun-yin Pao-li Pien (Handbook of women's protection—on marital violence).* Bureau of Social Affairs, Taipei Municipal Government.

Fu-nu Hsin-chih Pien-chih-pu. (1991). Jang Pei-chu Pu-tsai chung-yen. *Fu-nu Hsin-chih, 114*, 7-10.

Gelles, R. J. (1974). *The violent home: A study of physical aggression between husbands and wives.* Beverly Hills, CA: Sage.

Hsin, N. K. (1987). Ta-chia Yi-ch'ih Lai Kuan-hsin tsai Chia-ting Pao-li chung Shou-kun te Fu-nu. *Woman ABC, 60*, 31-35.

Huang, Y. L. (1991). Chung-kuo Fu-nu Chiao-yu chih Chin-hsih. In Pao Chia- lin (Ed.) *Chung-kuo Fu-nu-shih Lun-chih.* Taipei: Tao- hsiang Ch'u-pan-she.

Huang, W. H. (1992). Shen-mo shih Hun-yin Pao-li? (What is Marital Violence?). *Fu-nu Pao-hu Shou-cho—Hun-yin Pao-li Pien.* Bureau of Social Affairs, Taipei City Government.

Kao, M. (1988). Wo-Kuo Cheng-chieh-tang Chih-tu te Yan-pien. In Pao Chia-lin (Ed.) *Chung-kuo Fu-nu-shih Lun-chih.* Taipei: Tao-hsiang Ch'u-pan-she.

Kaohsiung City Bureau of Social Affairs. (1993). *Hun-yin Pao-li yu Fu-ch'ih Kou-tung.*

Liu, K. P. (1987). *Nieh-ch'i Wun-t'i," Fu-Jen Hsueh-Chih, 19*, 375-391.

Lystad, M. (1989). Community prevention programs in family violence. In Leah J. Dickstein & Carol C. Nadelson (Eds.), *Family violence: Emerging issues of a national crisis.* Washington, DC: American Psychiatric Press, Inc.

O'Brien, J. E. (1971). Violence in divorce prone families. *Journal of Marriage and the Family, 30*, 692-698.

O'Kelly, C. G., & Carney, L. S., (1986). *Women and men in society.* Belmont, California: Wadsworth Publishing Company.

Pu-ping. (1990). Na-yi-yieh, Wo Yian-cheng-cheng Kan-che Ta Pei-ta. *Fu-nu Hsin-chih, 100*, 25-27.

Rodman, H. (1972). Marital power and the theory of resources in cultural context. *Journal of Comparative Family Studies, 3,* 50–59.

Taipei City Bureau of Social Affairs (1992). *Taipei city BOSA's welfare services for women—BOSA's service to victims in marital violence.*

Taiwan Provincial Department of Social Affairs. (1991a). *Taiwan provincial women's living condition survey report, 1990.*

Taiwan Provincial Department of Social Affairs. (1991b). *Fu-nu Fu-li Kung-tsuo Shou-tso.*

Taiwan Provincial Department of Social Affairs. (1993). *Taiwan provincial women's living condition survey report, 1992.*

Tung, C. S. (1968). Ch'un-ch'iu Fan-lu. In Sz-pu Pei-yao. *Ch'ing-pu, 12,* Chi-yi Pien. Taipei: Chung-hwa Shu-chu.

Walker, L. E. (1979). *The battered woman.* New York: Harper & Row.

Wong, K. C., & Wu, L. T. (1985). *History of Chinese medicine.* Taipei: Southern Materials Center, Inc.

Yang, M. Y. (1993, May). Ou-ch'i te Ku-shih, (The Story of Wife-Battering). Global Views Monthly.

Yu, M. N. (1990). Pieh-tsai An-yieh li Ku-ch'ih. *Fu-nu Hsin-chih, 92*, 20-21.

Article 18

Why are U.S. and Japanese Divorce Rates so Different? An Aggregate-Level Analysis

Lynn K. White and Yuko Matsumoto

Theoretical notions from Goode and Durkheim have been used to explain the general coincidence of industrialization and rising divorce rates. Neither theory nor research, however, has paid very much attention to those industrialized nations (such as Japan, Israel, and Italy) that have low divorce rates. In this paper we draw hypotheses about the structural determinants of divorce associated with high levels of industrialization and test them on aggregate-level data from 47 Japanese prefectures. We ask whether the same structural factors that explain aggregate divorce rates in the United States and Canada can explain divorce rates in this non-Western society and whether they can explain why Japan's divorce rate in 1980 was only 4.8 per 1000 married women compared to 22.6 for the United States.

Background and Prior Work

Theoretical Frameworks

Two general theoretical frameworks have been used to explain why divorce rates have risen in the industrialized West. The first, articulated most clearly by Goode, argues that industrialization has reduced the importance of family stability. The Durkheimian thesis, on the other hand, suggests that industrialized society lacks the integration necessary to sustain family ties. We review each theory briefly and then the empirical work that they have generated.

Goode's Thesis

Goode's classic thesis (1963, pp. 1-26) is that industrialization weakens the extended family and leads to the rise of the conjugal family because: 1) geographic mobility makes the extended family unwieldy; 2) social mobility reduces similarity and hence solidarity among family members: 3) the development of extrafamilial institutions covering such needs as security, finance, and education reduces the need for an extended family; and 4) the growing importance of achieved status makes family ties less important for individual welfare. Because the conjugal family as well as the extended family has lost many of its functions, he concluded that the conjugal family may well be intrinsically unstable, depending as it does on affection (Goode, 1963, p. 9).

During recent years, the fall of fertility and the growth of women's independent earning capacity have eroded still further the instrumental functions of the family. The rise of the conjugal family has been superseded by the rise of the primary individual. By a simple extension of Goode's reasoning, the marital union becomes even more intrinsically unstable.

Durkheim

Durkheim's work on the relationship between the individual and the community is directly applicable to understanding family stability. Social integration, or involvement in collective morality, reduces divorce through two mechanisms. First, those closely integrated with the community are more likely to follow community norms: They will be more likely to marry an appropriate partner, conduct their married lives according to the rules, and be reluctant to incur the stigma of divorce (Glenn & Shelton, 1985). Second, community integration reduces the excessive individualism that can lead to self-destruction through suicide or destruction of the dyad through divorce (Brodbar-Nemzer, 1986; Durkheim, 1951/1987).

Durkheim himself attributed the negative effects of industrialization largely to confusion about appropriate social norms arising from rapid social change. It is Wirth (1938) who spelled out how urbanization, high density, and residential mobility could undermine the moral fabric of a community: Where we do not know our neighbors and where the density of interaction is so great that we must protect ourselves against others rather than seek them out, then we are less bound up in the moral community.

Empirical Evidence from Past Studies

These ideas have been the basis for dozens of studies about the structural determinants of divorce. We review cross-cultural studies first, and then studies of North America and Japan.

Cross-cultural Comparisons

The literature shows only a few cross-cultural studies of divorce. An early study by Kunzel (1974) compares 15 European nations on indices of divorce and industrialization. Using simple cross-tabulations, he concluded that industrialization is empirically associated with lower age at marriage, lower fertility, and higher female labor force participation and that these factors, in turn, are associated with rising divorce rates. In a study of 48 tribal societies, Pearson and Hendrix (1979) found that measures of women's economic independence were linked to higher divorce rates. More recently, Seccombe and Lee (1987) used data on 88 societies to support the hypothesis that women's independence of the family is positively correlated with divorce. The conclusion from these studies has been stated succinctly by Lee (1982, p. 237): If women can survive independently of their husbands and can possess and accumulate resources of their own, they have less to lose from a divorce than if they are entirely dependent on their husbands. In a final piece in this tradition, Trent and South (1989) investigate the effect of sex ratios, socioeconomic development, religion, and women's status on divorce across 66 nations. They find a U-shaped relationship between divorce and both economic development and proportion of women economically active. Only when more than 39% of women are economically active is divorce positively related to women' economic activity.

National Studies

Most single-nation, aggregate studies of divorce are based on U.S. or Canadian data. Both theoretically and empirically, the primary independent variable has been residential mobility (Makabe, 1980; Glenn & Shelton, 1985; Trovato, 1986a, 1986b; Breault & Kposowa, 1987). The only longitudinal, aggregate study, however, found no relationship between changes in net immigration and changes in divorce rates in 292 non-metropolitan counties in the western United States between 1970 and 1975 (Wilkinson et al., 1983). Other variables that have been invoked with less success or regularity include urbanization, age at marriage, occupation, race, religion, age, unemployment, church membership, and socio-economic status (Reynolds et al., 1974; Weed, 1974).

Given the central role of female labor force participation in explaining cross-national and historical changes in the divorce rate, it is interesting that only one of the studies of national divorce rates included this variable. Makabe (1980) found a significant positive relationship, but her results were based on an N of 10 Canadian provinces.

We have identified three studies that examine aggregate variability in Japanese divorce rates. Using data from the 1955 Census, Kawashima and Steiner (1960) found no linear relationship between industrialization and divorce. In an informal analysis of prefectures with high divorce rates, Kurnagai (1983) reports that these are either highly industrialized or have a strong fishing industry, which has traditionally offered many women employment.

Brinton (1983) reported an exploratory study of the effect of cost/benefit structures on prefectural divorce rates from the 1975 Census of Japan. She finds that divorce rates are higher when smaller proportions live in extended households, fewer women workers are employed in family enterprises, and the ratio of female to male employees is higher.

The Problem

Both the Goode and Durkheimian theses seem reasonable when evaluated against U.S. experience: Industrialization, divorce rates, urbanization, family independence, and women's independence have all risen over the last 100 years. If we look farther afield, however, these hypotheses seem less self-evident. Japan is a highly industrialized nation with a well-developed tertiary sector; it is far more urban and densely populated than the United States. Its divorce rate has remained relatively flat over the last 40 years at a rate approximately one-fifth of that of the United States.[1]

One plausible explanation for the anomaly is that the Japanese family structure remains very different from North America on two of the dimensions identified in previous research: extended family and women's independence. Because of traditional norms and contemporary housing costs, the extended family remains a very common living arrangement (Morgan & Hirosima, 1983). In 1985,54% of married men 65-69 were living with a child and 32% of married men ages 30-34 were living with a parent. Women's participation in the economy is sharply restricted by traditional gender roles in the family and the emphasis in Japanese firms on continuous, lifetime employment. Much more than in North America, women are confined to temporary and part-time work (Lascocco & Kalleberg, 1988) or are working in family or home-based enterprises (Brinton, 1988, 1989).

Although both Japan and the U.S. are highly industrialized, wealthy nations, their economic development has taken different paths. Japan industrialized more recently than the U.S. and still retains a larger proportion in the primary sector than comparable industrial nations (Singlemann, 1978). It thus seems plausible that Japan's divorce rates have remained low because neither the conjugal family nor the primary individual has developed as far in Japan as in North America.

In this research, we identify three structural determinants of divorce suggested by theory and previous research—women's economic independence, family nuclearization, and residential mobility—and examine their ability to explain variance in divorce rates within Japan and the difference between the U.S. and Japan.

Study Design

Data for the 47 prefectures of Japan are taken from published volumes of the 1980 Vital Statistics and Census of Japan. Comparison data for the U.S. come from the 1980 Vital Statistics and Census of the United States.

Measurers

Divorce Rate.

An indirect standardization procedure is used to calculate an age-adjusted rate of divorce per 1,000 married women for each prefecture. The average age adjusted divorce rate for Japanese prefectures was 4.4 divorces per 1,000 married women, with a range from 3.0 to 7.6.

Family Nuclearization

We measure family nuclearization by absence of coresidence at two stages of the lifecourse: Percentage of men and women ages 3-34 not living in a household headed by their parents and percentage of men and women over 60 who live alone. Aggregate averages show that Japan had significantly higher co-residence patterns in 1980: an average of 73% of Japanese 30-34 lived apart from their parents compared to 95% of Americans, and an average 8% of Japanese over 60 lived alone compared to 25% of Americans. These two items are summed to produce an overall index of nuclearization.

Women's Independence

We use three indicators of women's economic independence: percentage of married women in the labor force, percentage of the female labor force that works independently, and ratio of females per 100 male professionals and administrators.

Although an average of 52% of married Japanese women are in the labor force (compared to 49% of married U.S. women), approximately one third of Japan's female labor force works in a family business or is self-employed out of their own homes. Their capacity to earn is not independent of family resources. To create a measure of women's independent labor force participation, we subtract women who are self-employed or who work in family businesses from the total number of employed women and divide this by the total female labor force. This measure taps the availability not simply of work opportunities, but of independent work opportunities. The average percentage of the female labor force that works independently is 61% in Japanese prefectures, compared to 95% for the U.S.

To measure economic opportunities of women relative to men, we measure the ratio of females per 100 males in professional and administrative occupations. In Japan, the average ratio is 49.8 female administrators and professionals for every 100 males: in the U.S. the ratio is 69.5. Because the Japanese Census has very little income data, median income by sex was not available.

Social Integration

We measure social integration by residential mobility: percentage of the prefecture who moved to a different residence among 1975 and 1980. Japanese residential mobility is about 40% less than that for Americans (28% moved in the average prefecture compared to 46% of the American population who moved across state lines).

Findings

Preliminary Analysis: Means, Outliers, and Multicollinearity

The means and standard deviations of each variable are presented at the bottom of Table 1. The figures for the total U.S. population are given in the row below for comparison. The Japanese averages show much lower percentage moving, lower family nuclearization, lower women's independence, and of course, higher divorce rates (see Table 1). On all measures except married women's labor force participation, there are sharp and statistically significant differences on these variables. These findings confirm that the extended family and community integration remain stronger in Japan than the United States, and that women's independence is lower. These findings provide preliminary support to the hypothesis that these variables may help explain the lower divorce rate in Japan. Multicollinearity, or high correlation among the independent variables can be a critical problem in aggregate analyses. When the correlations are too high, standard errors burgeon and estimates become unreliable.[2] The inter-item correlations and the multiple correlations among the independent variables are reported in the top of Table 1. The simple zero-order correlations demonstrate high levels of multicollinearity between residential mobility and family nuclearization and between residential mobility and married women's labor force participation. The same three variables appear to be problematic when we look at multiple correlations among the independent variables. The size of the correlations suggests that multivariate results must be approached with caution.

Table 1. Means, Standard Deviations, Zero-Order and Multiple Correlations for Japanese Prefectures, 1980. N=47.

	Divorce	FLFP	FLFP	Indep. Prof.	F:M Nuc.	Family
Mobility						
Divorce Rate	-	-.45**	.23	.32*	.65**	.62**
Married FLFP	-	-	-.59**	.43**	-.74**	-.81**
Independent FLFP	-	-	-	-.47**	.43**	.66**
F:M Profs.	-	-	-	-	-.15	-.34*
Family Nuc.	-	-	-	-	-	.85**
Rsq[a]	-	.71	.54	.32	.78	.85
Mean	4.35	51.64	61.18	49.79	80.70	28.42
S.D.	1.00	8.29	5.70	8.40	11.04	5.71
U.S. Total	22.60	49.17	95.50	67.86	119.95	45.65

* Sig. at $p < .05$.
**Sig. at $p < .01$.
[a]R sq is the squared multiple correlation when each independent variable is regressed on the other independent variables.

Bivariate Results

The bivariate correlations provide mixed support for our hypotheses. As predicted, divorce rates are significantly higher when family nuclearization, residential mobility, and quality of women's job opportunities relative to men are high. Percent of married women in the labor force, however, is associated with significantly lower divorce. This may be because this measure does not tap the quality of labor force opportunities.

Multivariate Analysis

Because of high levels of multicollinearity, the multivariate analyses add the intervening variables in backward stepwise fashion (see Table 2). Following Goode, we assume that geographic mobility precedes the nuclearization of the family and that both of these precede the rise of the primary individual, i.e., women's economic independence.

The first panel includes only the three measures of women's independence and it virtually replicates the bivariate results. As hypothesized, the female-to-male administrative ratio has a significant, positive effect on the age-adjusted divorce rate. Unexpectedly, however, the percentage of married women in the labor force retains its significant negative effect on the divorce rate even after the two measures of quality of work opportunities have been introduced. Together this set of three variables explains 55% of the variation in prefectural divorce rates.[3]

TABLE 2 OLS REGRESSION, AGE-ADJUSTED DIVORCE RATES PER 1000 MARRIED WOMEN, JAPANESE PREFECTURES, 1980, N=47.

	b	se
Percent Married Women in LF	-.078**	.016
Ratio F:M Profs and Administrators	.081**	.014
Percent FLF with Independent Jobs	.030	.023
K	2.478	
R^2	.550	
Percent Married Women in LF	-.030	.109
Ratio F:M Profs and Administrators	.068**	.013
Percent FLF with Independent Jobs	.025	.021
Family Nuclearization	.045**	.013
K	-2.640	
R^2	.653	
Percent Married Women in LF	-.013	.018
Ratio F:M Profs and Administrators	.071**	.012
Percent FLFP with Independent Jobs	-.008	.021
Family Nuclearization	.009	.016
Residential Mobility	.120**	.037
K	-2.236	
R^2	.724	

* Sig at $p < .05$
** Sig at $p < .01$

The second panel adds family nuclearization, a variable that has a significant, positive effect on age-adjusted divorce rates. As expected, when larger proportions of young adults and older adults live away from their families, divorce rates are higher. Control for family nuclearization does not change substantially the coefficient for ratio of females per 100 male administrators, but it does eliminate the significant negative effect of married women's labor force participation reported in panel 1. After family nuclearization is controlled, percentage of married women in the labor force does not affect divorce rates.

A post hoc hypothesis suggests that the negative zero-order effect is plausible in a society that puts so much stress on family communalism. In any society, women's employment has two contradictory effects: It increases family income, which generally reduces divorce rates, and it increases female independence, which is generally associated with higher divorce rates. The relative importance of the prosperity and its independent effects may vary across time and across societies (South & Spitze 1987). In a strongly communal society such as Japan continues to be, the prosperity effect may dominate. This explanation would account for the sharp reduction in effect after we control for degree of family nuclearization. Another possibility is suggested by the burgeoning standard error between panels 1 and 2. The quintupling of the standard error alerts us to the problem of multicollinearity due to the high ***negative*** correlation between married women's labor force participation and family nuclearization. Coresidence, especially the availability of grandmothers for childcare, appears to be an important enabling factor in Japanese wives' labor force participation. Again, this may signal that wives' labor force participation is part of a family economic strategy.

The last panel of Table 2 adds residential mobility, which has a statistically significant, positive effect. The control for residential mobility sharply reduces the effect of family nuclearization. Because of multicollinearity, however, we cannot divide the explanatory power of family nuclearization and residential mobility unambiguously. Given the powerful effect of family nuclearization in panel 2, it is reasonable to conclude that family nuclearization as well as residential mobility affect Japanese divorce rates.

Why is Japan's Divorce Rate So Low?

We now turn to the question of what these variables can tell us about the differences between Japanese and U.S. divorce rates. A simple approach to this question is to substitute U.S. figures into the Japanese equation reported in the last panel of Table 2. This procedure yields the estimate that Japan's age-adjusted divorce rate per 1000 married women would nearly double—rising from 4.4 to 7.8—if it had the same mean scores as the U.S. on these five variables. This exercise suggests that differences on these structural variables can explain a small part of the difference in divorce rates and that Japan's divorce rate would be substantially higher if it had the same levels of women's labor force opportunities and residential mobility as the United States. On the other hand, differences in mean scores on these variables explain only 18% of the difference (22.8 minus 4.4) between Japanese and U.S. rates. This suggests that the lion's share of the divorce rate differential is due to factors over and above simple-structural differences.

Summary

We began this analysis by asking whether the low divorce rate characteristic of Japan contradicted Goode's and Durkheim's theoretical ideas about why industrialization would be accompanied by higher divorce rates. Using data on 47 prefectures, we tested the hypothesis that women's economic independence, family nuclearization, and residential mobility would explain differences in divorce within a non-western society as well as differences between the two nations.

The results show that this set of variables explains 72% of the variance in the age-adjusted divorce rates of Japanese prefectures in 1980. Three variables play a critical role: divorce rates are higher when residential mobility is high, when family nuclearization is high, and when women's economic opportunities relative to men's are better. Instead of being contradicted by the Japanese data, both the Goode and the Durkheim theses are strongly supported within Japan.

When we turn to differences between countries, our hypotheses are only weakly confirmed. If Japan had the same mean scores on these five structural factors as the U.S., its age-adjusted divorce rate per 1,000 married women would nearly double, rising from 4.4 to 7.8. Although this moves us in the expected direction, these variables can explain only 18% of the difference between Japanese and U.S. divorce rates.

Conclusion

The United States and Japan are highly industrialized nations with very high GNP per capita, democratic governments, high life expectancy, low fertility, and almost universal high school graduation. Family law, due in large part to a post-war constitution written during U.S. occupation, is very similar. The apparent similarity in social institutions obviously masks some important differences. As a growing body of scholarship demonstrates, the structure and function of the Japanese and the North American family differ significantly (Cornell, 1984, 1989; Hendry, 1985; Long, 1987; Morgan et al., 1984).

Whereas U.S. culture value's self-fulfillment and personal satistaction (Bellah et al.,1986) and reason over tradition (Williams, 1970), Japanese cultural values are almost diametrically opposite. One recent review of Japanese culture suggests that four values are essential to understanding Japanese culture: the elevation of loyalty over reason, a stress on collective rather than individual goals, authoritarian familism, and an emphasis on accommodation of self to society (Iga, 1986). These cultural differences afect all social institutions, from modern industrial plants to the family.

We began this research with the question of whether this set of theoretically relevant variables could explain divorce rates in a non-western society. We end with the conclusion that these variables work similarly in Western and non-Western industrialized nations, but that they are largely inadequate to explain the differences. It may be that, complementary to the European marriage pattern that distinguished western Europe (and to lesser extent North America) from the rest of the pre-industrial world, that there is a North American divorce pattern. Although North American divorce rates rise and fall according to some general principles that seem to hold good as quite different cultures, they start on a base with a very high propensity to divorce relative to Japan and some other cultures. Differences in culture appear to overshadow the effect of any differences in women's status, family independence, or residential mobility.

This finding has two implications, one for understanding our own society and another for understanding other societies. High rates of women's labor force participation are often blamed for high divorce rates, with the implicit message that if women would have been content to stay home, the American family would have remained strong. Women's status has been suggested to be at odds with the family. Our data suggest that this is not necessarily true. In a strongly communal system, women's labor force participation can be a positive force for family stability. In any case, changes in women's economic opportunities explain very little of the difference between our high divorce rate and Japan's low divorce rate. We will have to look deeper than women's independence to explain why our divorce rates are so high.

Finally, as industrialization becomes more characteristic of nonwestern societies, in the Pacific Rim and around the world, it would appear that we need to consider more carefully the interaction between culture and economics. This analysis adds to the growing evidence that industrialization is not a totally homogenizing experience. Industrialization will not make them like us. More like us, perhaps, but still very different.

References

Bellah, R. N., Madsen, R., Sullivan, W. M., Swidler, A., & Tipton, S. M. (1986). *Habits of the heart: Individualism and commitment in American life.* New York: Harper & Row.

Breault, K. D., & Kposowa, A. (1987). Explaining divorce in the United States: A study of 3,111 countries, 1980. *Journal of Marriage and Family, 49,* 549-58.

Brinton, M. (1983). The determinants of group cohesion in contemporary Japan. In M. Hechter (Ed.) *The microfoundations of macrosociology.* Philadelphia Temple University Press.

Brinton, M. (1988). The social-institutional bases of gender stratification: Japan as an illustrative case. *Journal of Marriage and Family, 50,* 300-34.

Brinton, M. (1989). Gender stratification in contemporary urban Japan. *American Sociological Review, 54,* 549-64.

Brodbar-Nemzer, J. (1986). Divorce and group commitment: The case of the Jews. *Journal of Marriage and Family, 48,* 329-40.

Cornell, L. (1984). Why are there no spinsters in Japan? *Journal of Marriage and Family, 46,* 326-39.

Cornell, L. (1989). Gender differences in remarriage after divorce in Japan and the United States. *Journal of Marriage and the Family, 51,* 457-63.

Dietz, T., Frey, F. S., & Kalof, L. (1987). Estimation with cross national data: Robust and nonparametric methods. *American Sociological Review, 52,* 380-90.

Durkheim, E. (1951/1897). *Suicide: A study in sociology.* Glencoe, IL: Free Press.

Glenn, N. D., & Shelton, B. A. (1985). Regional differences in divorce in the United States. *Journal of Marriage and Family, 47,* 641-652.

Goode, W. (1963). *World revolution and family patterns.* New York: Free Press.

Hendry, J. (1985). Japan: Culture versus industrialization as determinant of marital patterns. In Kingsley Davis (Ed.), *Contemporary marriage: Comparative perspective on changing institutions* pp. 197-222. New York: Russell Sage.

Iga, M. (1986). *The thorn in the chrysanthemum: Suicide and economic success in modern Japan.* Berkeley: University of California Press.

Kawashima, T., & Steiner, K. (1960). Modernization and divorce rate trends in Japan. *Economic Development and Cultural Change, 9,* 213-240.

Kurnagai, F. (1983). Changing divorce in Japan. *Journal of Family History, 8,* 85-107.

Kunzel, R. (1974). The connection between the family cycle and divorce rates: An analysis based on European data. *Journal of Marriage and Family, 36,* 379-388.

Lascocco, K., & Kalleberg, A. (1988). Age and the meaning of work in the U. S. and Japan. *Social Forces, 67,* 337-357.

Lee, G. (1982). *Family structure and interaction: A comparative analysis* (2nd ed.). Minneapolis: University of Minnesota Press.

Lee, G. (1987). Comparative perspectives. In Sussman, M. B., & Steinmetz, S. K. (Eds.), *Handbook of Marriage and the Family (Chapter* 3, pp. 32-39). NY: Plenum.

Lewis-Beck, M. (1980). *Applied regression: An introduction.* Beverly Hills Sage.

Long, S. O. (1987). Family change and the life course in Japan. *Cornell East Asia Papers,* No.44. Ithaca: Cornell University China-Japan Program.

Makabe, T. (1980). Provincial variations in divorce rates: A Canadian case. *Journal of Marriage and Family, 42,* 171-176.

Morgan, S. P., & Hirosima, K. (1983). The persistence of extended family residence in Japan: Anachronism or alternative strategy. *American Sociological Review, 48,* 269-231.

Morgan, S. P., Rindfuss, R., & Parnell, A. (1984). Modern fertility patterns: Contrasts between the United States and Japan. *Population and Development Review, 10,* 19-40.

Pearson, W., Jr.,& Hendrix, L. (1979). Divorce and the status of women. *Journal of Marriage and the Family, 41,* 375-385.

Reynolds, R., Jr. (1974). An exploratory analysis of county divorce rates. *Sociology and Social Research, 69,* 109-120.

Seccombe, K., & Lee, G. (1986). Female status wives' autonomy, and divorce: A cross cultural study. *Family Perspective, 20,* 241-249.

Shelton, B. A. (1987). Variations in divorce rate by community size: A test of the social integration explanation. *Journal of Marriage and Family, 4,* 827-832.

Singlemann, J. (1978). The sectoral transformation of the labor force in seven industrialized countries. *American Journal of Sociology, 83,* 1224-1234.

South, S. J., & Spitze, G. (1986). Determinants of divorce over the marital life course. *American Sociological Review, 51,* 583-590.

Trent, K., & South, S. J. (1989). Structural determinants of the divorce rate: A cross-societal analysis. *Journal of Marriage and Family, 51*, 391-404.

Trovato, F. (1986a). The relationship between marital dissolution and suicide: The Canadian case. *Journal of Marriage and Family, 48*, 341-348.

Trovato, F. (1986b). The relationship between migration and the provincial divorce rate in Canada, 1971 and 1978: A reassessment. *Journal of Marriage and Family, 48*, 207-216.

Weed, J. (1974). Age at marriage as a factor in state divorce rate differentials. *Demography, 11,* 361-76.

Wilkinson, K., Reynolds, R., Jr., Thompson, J., & Ostresh, L. (1983). Divorce and recent net immigration into the old west. *Journal of Marriage and Family, 45*, 437-445.

Williams, R. (1970). *American society: A sociological interpretation* (3rd ed). New York: Knopf

Wirth, L. (1938). Urbanism as a way of life. *American Journal of Sociology, 44*, 1-24.

Endnotes

1. Urban measures are not strictly comparable across nations. The most comparable figures are for percentage living in U.S. central cities and percentage living in Japanese densely inhabited districts (DID). Using this comparison, Japanese prefectures average 45% living in DID compared to an average of 25% of the U.S. population living in central cities. Density is directly comparable: the average Japanese prefecture had a density of 5,896 people per square kilometer in 1980 compared to only 613 for American states.
2. Lewis-Beck (1980) suggests two warning signs for "too high" the correlation between any pair of independent variables is more than .80 or the R for each independent variable regressed on all other independent variables is close to 1.0. These latter criterion checks that no variable is a linear combination of the others.
3. Because of a small number of cases and highly aggregated data, ecological correlations are especially sensitive to outliers. To check the possibility that a few influential cases were producing study results, residuals were analyzed for each bivariate relationship and for

each stage of the analysis reported in Table 2. A standardized (z-scored) residual greater than plus or minus 3.0 was our criterion for judging when a case was substantially out of line. With a small number of cases, however, this may be an inadequate test because a single outlier could pull the entire regression line toward it to the extent that the outlier does not appear to be excessively deviant (Dietz et al., 1987). If this is the case, a visual inspection of a scattergram of residuals will indicate that the regression line has been pulled away from the general trend. These residual analyses were carried out for both the bivariate and multivariate analyses and the results appear to be robust. In two of the bivariate relationships (adjusted divorce rate on residential mobility and on family nuclearization), the prefecture of Okinawa (a Japanese island under U.S. military occupation for 25 years after WWII) was an outlier, having much higher divorce rates than predicted by its scores on the independent variable. Although there were no outliers at any stage of the multivariate analysis reported in Table 2, we re-ran the equations omitting Okinawa to test for sensitivity in this case. The pattern of results was identical. Visual inspection showed no evidence that the results were being skewed by outliers.

Article 19

Single Parent Adoption: A Challenge to the Stereotype of Deficiency in the Single Parent Home

Margo Sorgman

We are a new minority, we few women who choose to love children and enrich our lives as single adoptive mothers. No doubt we will suffer the fate of other minorities. We are and will continue to be ignored, maligned, stereo-typed, romanticized, tolerated, accepted, and finally understood. In the meantime, we are not individuated for we are rarely studied. Rather we are lumped together with other unmarrieds, which typically means the pregnant teenager, provocative, uneducated, sensuous to a fault, and irresponsible. Or we are linked with single mothers who achieved that status by circumstance, certainly not by choice. Above all, we are not seen as competent, content, powerful, and unique. And because we do not speak in our own voice, the distortions come at the very time when society needs alternatives that are viable and futuristic.

The image that comes to mind for most when the term single parent is invoked is the divorced woman who prefers the married state, a minority woman trapped in the city's core, a financially insolvent woman barely making ends meet, an invisible woman isolated from neighbors, a working woman whose primary obsession is finding quality child-care, and a beleaguered woman whose children yearn for the absent but much needed father figure.

These images are all too real for many single parents. One out of every five children under 18 is currently living with a single parent. While many single parent households arise from an increasing divorce rate, the recent 500% increase in never-married mothers (who now represent 20% of the mother-child families) will escalate. Of 100 children born today, 12 will be born to unmarried mothers, 40 to parents who will divorce before the child is 18, one to parents who separate, and two to parents who will die before the child reaches 18. Demographic projections confirm that the traditional two parent nuclear family will represent only 7% of the public school students by the year 2000 (Hodgkinson, 1985, p. 3).

If we look at these female headed families, 54% of the non-Hispanic whites live in poverty, with 70% among blacks. The proportion of single parent mothers who enter the labor force is currently 77%. While the median annual income for the two parent family is approximately $28,000, the median income in 1980 was $11,900 for white single mothers, and $8,999 for black single mothers. For single mothers not in the labor force the median income is $5,000 for white and $4,400 for black women. These women suffer financial deprivation of services and diminished standards of living resulting in the fact that "the major issue facing single mothers and their children in the USA today is poverty" (Burden, 1986). It is estimated that 90% of the poor in the 1990's will be minority women and children (Dornbusch, 1985, p. 326). This feminization of poverty is attributed to the financial upheavals concomitant with divorce, for the annual income of divorced women drops from $5,000-30,000, with an average of $15,000 per divorce (Eakins, 1983, p. 109).

The employment benefits for women go beyond the obvious financial rewards. These include improved health, heightened self-acceptance, greater satisfaction with life, freedom from emotional disturbance, greater longevity, increased marital satisfaction and higher levels of achievement for adolescent daughters. Employment has even been found to enable women to leave and stay away from abusive relationships. Burden (1986) noted that there are no significant differences between singles and marrieds in terms of job/family management, role strain, or number of child problems. She concluded that her study "refutes the literature which attributes greater problems with children to female headed families. Given adequate income and support, a single parent family can be as viable for children as a two parent family" (Burden,1986, p. 37).

Much of the research to date on single parents has focused on their transitory state (for 75% remarry six years after divorce), and deficient family structures. This has anticipated negative effects in relation to child abuse, juvenile delinquency, emotional and psychological problems, effects on poverty, welfare dependency, and maternal/paternal deprivation. Margolis noted that "low profile fathers are more responsible for delinquency than working mothers" (1984, p. 261). Since most data was collected on welfare mothers, impressions are skewed to that particular subset of the single parent mother population. Single adoptive mothers are not typically included in these studies.

Burden (1986) noted that there were no significant differences in job motivation, reported job performance or days absent from work between women and men. Women, single or married, scored at higher levels of job satisfaction which is vital since as many as 1/3 of all employees may be single parents at some point in their careers.

Life outside the home is a critical variable in most studies that look at mothers' self-esteem, satisfaction, optimism, and well-being. Eakins (1983) in her text on women returning to school, found that the children were positive and proud of their mothers, enjoyed greater degrees of freedom, and minimally resented the lack of time spent. Mothers became more patient, enjoyed their children more, had more to talk about, felt they were positive role models, and described interactions as less a duty, more a choice. The major problem identified was time constraints due to maintaining multiple roles, while trying to accommodate the inflexibility of the work place, unavailability of childcare (estimated to be available for only 10% of the working mothers), and the motherhood mandate embedded in society.

In her texts on *Ideologies of Motherhood*, Wearing (1984) described four archetypal mothers. First, there are the *Traditionalists*, who view women's roles as mothers at home, complementing their husbands, and with outside employment secondary to home life. These women believe that life is incomplete without a male, that children come first, that femininity is characterized as being loving, supportive, and attractive, with mothering the only life goal.

Second, was the *Ambivalent Traditionalists*, who typically feel that children need her, that mothering is a state in a woman's life, and that development of self is delayed for the children's sake. This group tends toward dissatisfactions with life, see themselves as individuals, reject nontraditional images, are married and have children later. Third, was the *Ambivalent Progressives*, who question the ideology of motherhood. These women may feel motherhood is either not necessary for fulfillment nor is inevitable. They believe mothers are not the primary caretakers, yet they have guilt relinquishing the role of mother. They feel self-esteem comes from their own abilities not from motherhood, and that the nuclear family is not ideal for child-rearing, although parenting is a part of a life plan. Finally, there are the *Radical Utopians* who reject social structures and view motherhood as a choice that is not inevitable or necessary. These women believe that women should have complete control over their bodies, motherhood does not lead to emotional maturity but may deter self-development, childcare should be shared, children are not property but individuals, and that states should provide assistance in caring. They are committed to abolishing sexism, feel men should be involved in care of children, see the family (in some instances) as repressive of women and children, prefer to bring up children in group contexts, want to restructure the workplace, and see themselves as individuals who have control over life options. They believe that parenting is not the primary identity, nor should it absorb the majority of one's time. These women see parenthood as a choice made more effective if adult needs are met and potentialities developed. They are optimistic about the future and socially active in changing conditions that lead to oppression. While fewer feminists would say that satisfaction is primarily associated with husbands and children, most "felt that in the long term perspective, the most meaningful activity was child-rearing" (Geissinger, 1984, p. 166).

In her book, *The Lesser Life: The Myth of Women's Liberation in America,* Hewlett (1986) details the rise of this cult of motherhood from the late 1940's as a new idea. This period of ultradomesticity convinced most that children should be raised solely by mothers. She contends that the idea of spending the better part of one's day in childcare has seldom occurred before in other cultures, or historical periods. Rather, mothers occupied themselves with other tasks and raised their children as a parallel activity.

The postwar generation encouraged mothers to take responsibility for the psychological and cognitive development of the child and to mold its total character and future potential. Any shortcomings in adult life were now seen as rooted in the failure of motherhood during childhood. She suggests "that cult is still with us and is reflected in the fact the United States does less than any advanced country to make life easier for working mothers. We have less maternity leave, less subsidized childcare and less job flexibility" (Hewlett,1986, p. 493).

The power of this motherhood cult is dramatically seen when one listens to the concerns of antinatalist women, the 10% of our child-bearing population who remain childless. While their decision not to have children is made mostly by husbands (33%) in contrast to wives (7%), the fact remains that 20% of all highly educated women (those with graduate training) remain childless (Hewlett, 1986, p. 77). While the social tensions are greatest during the fourth and fifth years of marriage, the stereotype of childless women is classic. They are perceived as selfish, immoral, irresponsible, immature, unhappy, unfilled, and unfeminine. Interestingly enough, childless women tend to agree that women desire children and envy those with them (Hewlett, 1986; Callan, 1986).

The stereotype of single parent families is equally pernicious. Single mothers' lifestyles, while typically less advantaged, usually are described in deficit language. Children have fewer toys and possessions, smaller homes, move about more often, and have less religious involvements. Their mothers have more abortions, send their children to daycare, and seek more medical help for problems. Lamb concluded that despite this negativism, the "single parent lifestyle has no systematically negative effect on the child's development" (1982, p. 341). In fact, Walton found that most of 134 families she studied tended toward more liberal positions in terms of their beliefs about sex roles (1985, p. 79).

As singlehood has increased 78%, society appears to be shedding the negative imagery that single women are "less feminine, loving and nurturing, sexually unattractive, are more selfish or having such strong, independent personalities and other qualities that cause them to be less likely to marry" (Cockrun &White, 1985, p. 551). The pathology of singlehood in the '50's is giving way to a current view that singlehood is one's choice of status and a mechanism for increasing one's happiness.

Satisfaction studies among singles reveal that college education, high occupational prestige, good income and vital support systems are critical to singles' happiness. Social isolation, found to be a major problem for single mothers, is seen as more acute for males, given their socialization toward groups and away from intimacy and self-disclosure. In contrast, women's rich networking abilities and capacity to disclose have been found to reduce loneliness. Overall, singlehood was found to be more satisfying for those who are voluntarily single (Stein, 1981).

These findings provide a context for four single adoptive parents. I studied myself and my friend Alice, and the two Janes. All of us were older mothers at the time of our first adoption. Our mean age was 36, which is older than the mean age of married adoptive parents at 29, but exactly the mean age of all single adoptive women. We are all professional women who have completed graduate school, a finding noted by Bachrach (1986) in his study. Our mean income is $45,000, which suggests we are well above the poverty level. As the research implies, our profile confirms findings that adopted children have older, and better educated mothers than children living with birth mothers. All of us are employed full time, as a university professor, a university administrator, and two teachers. This is compatible with the data that 51% of adopted children have working mothers.

We chose to adopt children who are Indian, Thai, and Mexican. While some studies suggest that adopted children are rated higher in psychological and school related behaviors and lower in social competence and school adjustment than nonadopted children, this is not the case for our children (Burden, 1986). These four school age children have been tested and found to have very high IQ's, independent natures, high levels of verbal acuity, maturity and sophistication well beyond their years. This is consistent with a finding described by Lamb (1982). Two of the children have had some school achievement problems, but these have been corrected through retention and medication. School problems, when they have occurred, are mostly due to the high levels of independence exhibited by these children. Sexist definitions of preferable female behavior may explain some of this.

Of the seven children between us, only one is a boy which confirms the reported preference of adoptive mothers for daughters. Our rationale for choosing international adoption was avoidance of the overwhelming abuse found among most American adoptive children, and also the availability of infants and agency support for single adoptive placements.

The international search for children resulted from two factors. First, the desire was to create a global family system. The goal for us was to expand our cultural dimensions recognizing that this runs counter to most adoptive practices stateside, which tends toward cultural/ethnic matching. Our commitment was to integrate Mexican, Thai and Indian cultural expressions such as holidays, history, historical characters and current events into our homes, with modest attempts at bi-lingualism. We became viable families who chose to connect and nurture children who, in return, bring rich cultural traditions. In so doing, we are forging multicultural practices, much needed in today's global society. The second factor was the discriminatory practices of adoption agencies which still prefer the two parent family and view single parents as homes for special needs or hard to place youngsters, those children who are handicapped, older, biracial, or with multiple siblings.

A major obstacle for each of us was the bureaucratic entanglements of the immigration process, which does not recognize an adoption as bonafide until one year after the court approval petition is filed. Secondly, citizenship is not awarded to such children upon adoption which diminishes the status of adoption to a torturous five year wait for citizenship.

All of us were supportive of open birth records, and in one case where geographic access is possible, communication has been established with the birth mother. All the children are aware and proud to be adopted youngsters. Such openness has not impaired the closeness with our children. This was found in the Geissinger (1984) study which reported that 77% of adopted parents support open records to some degree.

Our strong professional commitments are not surprising since women who have never married have been found to have greater work orientations than those formerly married. Never-married single women have been reported to have greater psychological well-being (happiness, morale, life satisfaction, less depression) than widowed women, followed by divorced and separated women. Education, health and income are seen as better predictors for happiness for never-marrieds than for those who have been married, probably because it makes possible the mobility and cultivation of varied interests and flexibility to maintain a more independent life-style. Our outlook is quite positive and our levels of happiness stable.

All of us have given thought recently to our future retirements and the possibility of reduction of work load. This is in keeping with never married career women, who exhibit the same type of career fatigue as their male counterparts. However, never-married women generally exhibit more positive attitudes about retirement than formerly married women. Our professional commitments have resulted in high levels of professional success, promotions, and mobility. In all, we would be described as exemplary professionals (Keith, 1985).

Contrary to popular assumptions, single women do not incur higher levels of job absenteeism than other employees, a finding noted by Hanson and Sporokowski (1986). Single mothers have less time to spend on community volunteerism and housework, but spend more than the typical one and half hours a day with children (Sanik & Mauldin, 1986). Concerns that intergenerational boundaries are compromised as mother and child become more like peers and partners is not characteristic among us. While we discuss our problems more openly and involve our children in many solutions, we do maintain an appropriate parent/child balance. This phenomenon is more evident in divorced families, when tensions have not been resolved (Glenwick & Mowrey, 1986).

While studies report that children raised by single mothers have lower educational, occupational and economic levels in early adulthood than more traditionally rooted peers, these studies have not included single adoptive parents in their samples (Brodzinsky et al., 1984). In our family systems, we have created intricate networks to insure participation of our children in a wide range of educational, social and recreational activities. Childcare and transportation systems do fail and upset the delicate balances we have established, but the overriding factor here is that we place a high value on these activities due to our levels of educational and professional aspirations.

Our commitment to education is most evident in the kinds of interactions we encourage. Much of our gaming is educative in nature and we are quite assertive in clarifying any school issues that arise. We are more involved in our children's education, as we are more likely to participate in weekend programming and summer activities in lieu of vacations. Since our children range between 10 and 19, it is too early to assess our impact on their adult years, but we would expect that educational, economic and occupational levels would not be compromised. All of us live approximately 1500 miles from our extended families. Therefore we rely on other support systems for services and problem solving. This had been found to be characteristic of single parents who seek help rather than remain besieged. In contrast to the 91% occasional dating pattern found for Air Force single parents by Bowen and Orthner, we range from occasional dates to never dating. But like the 9% in the Air Force sample who have never dated, we would like to do so (1986). While respondents in that study indicated that they would consider "unwed cohabitation" as an acceptable practice, three of us would be more reluctant to set up such patterns due to strong religious beliefs. However, like those in the study,we are more interested in establishing long term relationships than casual dating. This religious influence has resulted in second and third adoptions by three of us.

A unique characteristic we share, but one not reported in any of the few studies on single adoptive parents, is our nontraditional life experiences. We are the first in our peer, professional and family groups to adopt. Three have changed their religions and one left the convent. We are first generation daughters who have attained advanced graduate degrees, with four masters and two doctoral degrees between us.

The range of feminism within our group places us in the *Radical Utopian* category with one woman a scholar in gender issues and a director of a women's studies program.

While three tend to be Ambivalent Progressives, their impact has been great among their religious peers who value traditional family norms. All of us have experienced more acceptance within our neighborhoods because we are mothers than because we are single women. In fact, we feel being single women in married neighborhoods limits social interactions. While mothering establishes closer friendships, social interactions are still limited because of our single status. In most cases, we are more interactive with male neighbors due to our nonsexist participation in household chores such as painting, mowing, running, gardening, and remodeling.

In three cases, family support for our decision to adopt was considerable. We view this as critical in creating positive childhood environments since all of us experienced strong and endorsing support from colleagues and friends, our sense of well-being via the adoption process has been enhanced.

On the other hand, all of us have experienced societal biases against single parent adoption from agencies. This resulted in international and private agency placements where the current practice of matching special needs youngsters with singles was not a norm. None of our children are special needs youngsters, and three of us would not choose severely handicapped children due to our lifestyles and personal preferences.

All of us have experienced the strains between careers that require full attention and children with limitless demands. We know the frustration that arises when we must accommodate inevitable childhood illnesses. We know the hectic pace of lunch hours that are spent on errands. We live the stark reality that our single parent incomes can never provide us the range of opportunities that many two income families enjoy. There is the occasional anger and confusion when we try to be loving yet sometimes deny our children embraces out of personal pique.

In the end, we view ourselves as viable families that are stable, loving, humane and effective. Against all odds we meet the daily demands of managing multiple roles and, in the main, come out ahead. Our children are thriving and reaffirm their love for us regularly. We contribute to the life of our communities and are exemplary professionals. We feel joy and competence in our mothering. Still we have time for friends and family and seem to maintain our sense of delight and optimism. What we need from society is your willingness to acknowledge that.

References

Bachrach, C. (1986). Adoption plans: Adopted children and adoptive mothers. *Journal of Marriage and Family, 48*(5),243–153.

Brodzinsky, D., Schecgter, D. E., Braff, A. M., & Singer, L. M. (1984). Psychological and academic adjustment in adopted children. *Journal of Consulting and Clinical Psychology, 52*(4), 582-590.

Bowen, G., & Orthner, D. (1986). Single parents in the U.S. Air Force. *Family Relations, 35*(l), 45-52.

Burden, O. (1986). Single parents and the work setting: The impact of multiple job and homelife responsibilities. *Family Relations, 35*(l), 37-43.

Callan, N. (1986). The impact of the first birth: Married and single women preferring childlessness, one child or two children. *Journal of Marriage and Family,48(*5), 261-269.

Cockrun, J., & White, P. (1985). Influences in the life satisfaction of never-married men and women. *Family Relations, 34*(l), 551-556.

Dornbusch, S. M., Carlsmith, J. M., Bushwall, S. J., Ritter, P. L., Leiderman, H., Hastorf, A. H., & Gross, R. T. (1985). Single parents, extended households, and the control of adolescents. *Child Development, 56*(2), 326-341.

Eakins, P. (1983). *Mothers in transistion: A study of the changing life course.* Cambridge, MA: Schenkman Publishing.

Geissinger, S. (1984). Adoptive parent attitudes toward open birth records. *Family Relations, 33*(10), 579-585.

Glenwick, D., & Mowrey, J. (1986). When parents become peers: Loss of intergenerational boundaries in single families. *Family Relations, 35*(l), 57-62.

Hanson, S., & Sporokowski, M. (1986). Single parent families. *Family Relations, 35*(l), 3-8.

Hewlett, S. (1986). *A lesser life: The myth of women's liberation in America*. New York: William Morrow & Co..

Hodgkinson, H. (1985). *All one system: Demograhics of eucation, kndergarten through graduate school.* Washington, DC: Institute for Educational Leadership.

Keith, P. (1985). Work retirement and well-being among unmarried men and women. *Gerontonlogist, 25*(8), 410-416.

Lamb, M. (1982). *Nontraditional families: Parenting and child development.* New Jersey: Erlbaum Association.

Margolis, M. (1984). *Mothers and such: Views of American women and why they changed.* Berkley, CA: University of California.

Sanik, M.,& Mauldin, T. (1986). Single vs. two parent families: A comparison of mother's time. *Family Relations, 35*(l), 53-56.

Walton, S. (1985). Single parent families: New script, same action. *Psychology Today, 15*(3), 19-79.

Wearing, B. (1984). *The ideology of motherhood.* Sydney: George Allen and Unisin.

Family and Social Change

Part VII

Article 20

The Consequences of Urbanization and Westernization on Black Family Life in South Africa

Neels Bester

Introduction

In studying the South African society with its different ethnic groups, it becomes apparent that the South African economy is dualistic by nature. Dualistic, because parallel to a modernized industrial economy with its free-market system and its advanced technology which has primarily been developed by white people, there also exists a self-supporting, underdeveloped economy. The latter is characterized by primitive agriculture, low income and a lack of finances and technical skills, especially among Black people. This self-supporting agro-economy had originally been strongly embedded in the kinship system and the extended family of the indigenous Black society.

During the nineteenth century, after the discovery of diamonds and gold in South Africa, and the subsequent industrialization process, a process of urbanization took place. This process also had some effect on the traditional social structures of Black people in South Africa, which also implied a change in their kinship and family structures.

Urbanization of the Black Population in South Africa

Year	%
1911	24.7%
1936	31.4%
1970	45.9%
1980	47.8%
1985	55.9%
1991	61.9%

* Central Statistical Services, 1991, Pretoria

From Traditional Rural Life to Urbanization and Westernization

The above-mentioned changes that took place in South Africa affected Black as well as white people in different ways. Different groups experienced the changes to different degrees at different stages. Consequently, there is now less cultural uniformity among Black people than before. According to Rip (1960, p. 119), the political conquest of South Africa by the Europeans, accompanied by the Christian missionary efforts, education, administrative actions and the introduction of a new economic system, differentiated Blacks to such an extent that it is no longer possible to generalize regarding their habits and characteristics as a group. Some of them still live according to traditions which closely resemble those of the pure African lifestyle of the past, while others have changed considerably by adapting to the European standards of life with regard to occupations and perspectives. Between these two extremes, there lies the great majority who retain many of the old cultural characteristics while also increasingly participating in the "*new civilization.*" In the case of the latter, I would rather refer to them as the so-called westernized society. Furthermore, it is important to distinguish between the concepts of urbanization and westernization.

Other than urbanization, which basically means a physical presence in a city or town, westernization (in the South African context) means a drastic shift in values and perceptions (Hammond-Tooke, 1982, p. 32 & p. 34). Thus, urban man is not necessarily a completely westernized person. However, one must be careful not to generalize by stating that there are no fully westernized African urbanites. There are obviously those Black individuals who have achieved a consistency in their outlook and a global perspective which make them indistinguishable from middle-class whites.

Another important indication of whether a person is urbanized or not, may be found in the nature of the social ties that he or she develops (Mayer, 1961). It is probably true that most Black people have at least some roots in the rural areas, although they may have been born and bred in the urban areas. For example, the frequent practice of sending young children away from home to be brought up by a grandmother or to attend school away from the influence of the street gangs, is typical of Black parents. There are others who resist urbanization (the so-called migrants) and who, for example, attempt to strictly limit their interaction with townspeople, and who only try to associate with people from their own home areas and visit them in the home areas as often as possible (Hammond-Tooke, 1982, pp. 34-35).

On the other hand, the person who is born in the city, or who wishes to become completely urbanized, actively tries to establish ties with other urbanized people by joining certain associations, sports clubs, etc., which results in a change of values. The concepts of tribalism, chieftainship, kinship systems, belief in ancestors, and the whole range of traditional tribal values are often irrelevant to such a person.

It is important to take note of the fact that a relatively large number of Black urbanites still integrate the behavioral patterns of different cultures. For example, in his workplace, a person may operate according to all the values of the industrial environment, while at home, he may only choose friends from his rural home area, and when ill, still consults a traditional healer (*sangoma*).

The Changed Family Life of Urbanized and Westernized Blacks, Especially Regarding Child-Parent Relations

As discussed previously, industrialization, urbanization and westernization had a significant influence on traditional Black people in South Africa. Especially the family lives of Black people who have immigrated from the rural areas to the towns and cities have undergone remarkable changes.

First of all we must pay attention to the more visible characteristics of the traditional Black rural family and secondly, to the characteristics and problems of the average urbanized Black family.

Characteristics of the Traditional Black Rural Family

The traditional Black rural family is characterized by a self-supporting agro-economy and lives according to the tribal customs in a "stat" (kraal) with other families. These families are patrilineal by nature and under patriarchal authority with a polygamous system where a male may have more than one wife. Within this polygamous system each wife has her own dwelling and household, but is still dependent on the support of the extended group (Bruwer, 1956; Schapera, 1956; Steyn et. al., 1987; Vlok, 1984, p. 338).

Within the patrilineal kinship, rules of behavior are clearly defined. From a tender age, the Black child learns to behave correctly towards different people at different kinship levels, particularly with regard to the relationship with the father. The behavioral demands in this regard are normally those of respect for the elderly and a strict disciplinary position held by the father (patriarch). Social control plays an important part in the prescribed behavioral patterns of the family. Social control is reinforced by religion which is based upon the belief in and worshipping of ancestors. Absolute conformity to the traditional prescribed behavioral rules is very important. The parents are not the only ones responsible for the upbringing of the child. Usually a number of adults, especially women and older children, look after the child in the early years. When the child is older, any of the adults may discipline him/her, especially the patrilineal relatives.

As previously indicated, the migration of Blacks from rural areas to the cities and towns, brought about certain advantages, but also disadvantages for Black urbanites. As far as the theme of this paper is concerned, it is necessary to give an indication of the problems that are encountered by Black urban families. However, it is important to look at the factors which have influenced traditional Black family life, and the "problems" involved. From the perspective of traditional Black people from the rural areas, it is possible to talk of "problems", but from the perspective of western people, these may be regarded as "advantages" towards being modern. It also seems that established Black urbanites mostly experience them in the same context as whites.

Factors Which Have Influenced Traditional Black Family Life, and the Problems Involved

In their contact with white people and their Western culture during the eighteenth and nineteenth centuries, it was especially in the fields of religion, education, the economy, family role structures, administration and legislation that traditional Black family life was influenced.

Christian principles, which were introduced to Blacks by white missionaries mainly from Europe, did not, amongst other things, take into consideration the social structures of the traditional Black polygamous and extended family. It was polygamy in particular which was not acceptable in terms of the Christian monogamous principle.

As far as education is concerned, the predominantly white Western educational system is unfamiliar to Black children. As opposed to preparation for traditional adult roles being regarded as a self supportive family matter in traditional tribes of Black people, the Western educational values endeavor to prepare Black children—as is the case with white children—to become part of a modern, developed and industrialized economy.

To reiterate, there has been a transfer in the nature of the economic system from a homogeneous self-supporting, mainly agro-economy with the emphasis on traditional Black relationships, to a more differentiated western urbanized, industrialized economy of the whites in South Africa. Black immigrant families from the rural areas have to adapt to this new economic system.

Urban housing schemes only make provision for the needs of the white nuclear families; and not for the polygamous and extended families of traditional Black people. A shortage of housing does give rise to overcrowding and the development of slums and squatter camps. In the latter, a lack of social control has developed. The disintegration of the primary groups in Black society has resulted in this poor social control. It seems that, sociologically speaking, one may generally accept that in mass societies primary corporative groups can be replaced by informal friendship groups; that the focus can shift from communal prescriptiveness to the choice of the individual. In this regard Coetzee (1978, p. 9) refers to the existence of numerous organizations, which he calls "loose-knit" associative urban structures.

This so-called loose-knit situation in city life with its weakened communal structure and subsequent weakened social control; also naturally gives rise to weakened social control in the Black family and especially a lack of parental authority over children.

Other factors responsible for the weakening of communal structures and thus the weakening of social control, in other words the weakening of group responsibility, paternal authority, and of the relationships between the members of the Black family, were administration and legislation by the white government, such as influx-control. In this regard, Eloff already indicated in 1952(83) that administration and legislation negatively affected Black residents' rights, responsibilities, behavior and movements, because it did not recognize the tribal rights and principles of Black migrant people from rural areas. On the other hand, certain legislation provided some kind of protection to Black people, particularly Black women and children.

Furthermore, concerning the above-mentioned weakening of social control, there is a "loose-knit" situation regarding the previously traditional preparation for adult roles which has now become separated from traditional Black kinship. It is especially through urban school education that basic values among the youth could easily be changed to the existence of a sense of individualism and equal status between boys and girls. In line with the emancipation of women, this is one of the reasons why more urbanized and westernized Black women in South Africa , like most women of all other races in the country, are increasingly expecting more recognition of status and domestic help from their husbands. These expectations are increasing while still greater numbers of Black mothers, like white mothers and mothers of the other races, are employed, due to the present economic recession.

As a result of the increased joint labour force with regard to Black women, the so-called loose-knit situation mentioned earlier is becoming more serious. Most of these women have to work for an income because they are single parents. Like white families, the existence of Black single-parent families has increased. As a result of the absence of conservative Black traditional marital and family values, marriage and family disorganization is increasing. In this single-parent situation the children lack the experiencing of the paternal figure. More families become mother-dominant (mostly an employed mother) with less parental authority. As a result many children often find themselves in the streets of the townships without enough recreational facilities to keep them occupied after school. This situation also applies to children who are still members of a dual-income family.

What makes this whole situation more difficult, and that could also be applicable to unemployed, white urbanites in South Africa, are the increasing incidences of unemployment among Black urbanites, with the resulting increase in poverty.

As mentioned previously, a lack of social control and parental authority is noticeable among Black urban families. In the urban areas, where the traditional kinship group has weakened, it is only the parents leading a more nuclear-type of western family lifestyle, who are responsible for disciplining their children. They can not rely upon the support of the traditional kinship structure anymore. Up to this moment, conditions of the employment structure have hindered many Black parents from succeeding in their responsibility in child rearing. In addition, the absence of the working parents play an important part in the weakening of parental authority.

Quite an important factor regarding the lack of parental authority, especially the authority of the father is, as indicated by Steyn (1987, pp. 299-300), the influence of Western values and culture on Black urban children at school, and city life in general. Most Black parents have had little or no school education in their traditional rural homelands. As a result, there seems to be a great difference between the interest of children and that of their parents. No common interests, thoughts and insights seem to develop between parents and their children. The difference in school education also leads to the fact that the youth do not really take the authority of their parents seriously, because, as they experience it, their parents "know nothing."

The lack of parental control over children also leads to deviant behavior among great sectors of the Black urban youth. With their intimidating behavior, as well as their potential to be easily intimidated, this "lost generation" often becomes the victim of revolutionaries and radical political elements (Coetzee, 1978, p. 9).

Regarding revolutionary and radical political movements among Black youth, Hammond-Tooke (1982:39-40) describes the "politicized youth" as a new and frightening phenomenon on the South African scene, which not only opposes the "fat-cat" Black elite, but also very clearly opposes the parental generation, whom they regard as having failed to meet the challenge.

This politicized youth not only threatens parental authority, but unfortunately also behaves quite aggressively and, being easily intimidated by radical political groups, this group could seriously threaten the attempts by Black and white political leaders to effect the changes needed for a new democratic South Africa through negotiations.

The Future

Although there are certain advantages for Black people in South Africa regarding urbanization and westernization, there are, as indicated in this paper, quite a number of problems. To move toward a new balanced South Africa, a sound and balanced Black urban family life, formal negotiations as well as open communication in the future, should take place with all sections of Black opinion, which include among others, representative parent groups as well as representative Black youth leaders.

Furthermore, it seems necessary for the mass media to improve its contributions to make it easier for the Black youth to adapt to urban and Western values regarding parent-child relationships. Also, the agents for socialization, like the school, religion, and even the state, could play a more prominent role to make this adaptation easier. However, it is important that these values are not forced upon them in order to ensure rapid adaptations and changes.

Although it is not always possible to succeed due to a lack of money, community-development programs should provide for the creation of leisure and sport facilities for Black youth as far as possible, in order to keep them busy in a meaningful, constructive way after school hours, while their parents are working. Furthermore, it seems important that more Black young people should be more committed to, and become more proud of, programs regarding community development. In this way potential youth leadership could be identified.

In other words, I think that there is some potential to retrieve something of the weakened parental and social control of the Black urban youth and to motivate them to be part of a new orderly democracy in South Africa.

Bibliography

Bruwer, J. P. (1956). *Die bantoe van Suid-Afrika.* Afrikaanse Pers Boekhandel, Johannesburg.

Central Statistical Services. (1991). Pretoria.

Coetzee, J. H. (1978). *Die stedelike swartman in Suid-Afrika: Verlede, hede en toekoms.* Aktualiteitsreeks no. 16, Instituut vir Suid-Afrikaanse Politiek, Potchefstroomse Universiteit vir CHO, Potchefstroom.

Eloff, J. F. (1952). *'n Volkekundige studie van die aanpassing en ontwikkeling in die gesinslewe van die naturelle van Atteridgeville.* Ongepubliseerde M.A.-verhandeling, Universiteit van Pretoria.

Hammond-Tooke, W. D. (1982). The effect of urbanization on traditional values. In P. Smit, J. S. H. Gildenhuys, W. D. Hammond-Tooke, & P. C Schutte, *Uetstedliking in Africa* (pp. 30-40). Potchefstroom: Sentrale Publikasic-afdeling, Potchefstroomse, Universiteit vir CHO.

Mayer, P. (1961). *Townsmen or tribesmen.* Cape Town: Oxford University Press.

Rip, C. M. (1960). *The effects of cultural inertia and cultural diffusion on the structure and functioning of the Bantu family system.* UNISA. Unpublished M.A. dissertation.

Schapera, I. (1956). *The Bantu-speaking tribes of South Africa.* Cape Town: Maskew Miller.

Steyn, A. F., Van Wyk, D., & Le Roux, T. (1987). *Die gesin: Gister en vandag.* Academica, Pretoria.

Vlok, M. E. (1984). *Gemeenskapsverpleegkunde - 'n handleiding.* Kaapstad: Juta.

Editors' Note: We are grateful to the author for having traveled the longest distance in giving the above paper in Indianapolis. As in other papers presented in the symposia and this volume, it happened that the attention has been on the effect of industrialization bearing upon family life; and none has touched upon the subject of ethnic and racial strife that is prevalent everywhere, even in the United States, the leading advocate of universal human rights. We anticipate that future papers will address the effect of racism upon the family. We want to know about the progress of reconciliation between the races in South Africa. Empires rose and perished; fortunes were made and vanished. The family remains our first encounter and the last resort and hope for the future.

Article 21

The Muslim Family: The Essence of Family Modernization Changes in Family Values

John E. Sullivan

Muslim family values are defined in and derived from the *Qur'an*. Muslims believe the *Qur'an* to be the final revealed message to mankind. Since it is believed that this final Revelation is totally comprehensive, there is no need to look beyond this source for values, mores or standards for behavior for the system called "family."[1]

The forces of pre-modern, modern and post-modern influences have severely shaken the Muslim family system in America. "Family values" even became the undefined battlecry of both political parties during this country's last presidential election. The politicizing of family values left a bad taste in the mouth of many.

As societies moved through "eras of development," families have had to make tremendous adjustments:

> People in "premodern societies" had little need to struggle with the kinds of questions about identity and belief that bedevil most of us. The premodern mind, whatever its pains and sorrows, saw itself mirrored in every detail of its world. There were psychic anchors everywhere: in the myths that explained the cosmos; in the environment of signs, symbols and metaphors that gave form to thought; in the rituals and customs that shaped decision and action; in the social organization that assigned to every person a clear role and reason for being.
>
> Modern civilizations formed larger and more complex social structures, usually containing people of different cultural heritages. Increasing mobility and urbanization put more and more people in proximity to others with different beliefs and cultural traditions. Issues of pluralism began to invade daily life, and modern civilizations invented all kinds of rules and arrangements—civil rights, separation of church and state, ghettoes, apartheid—for managing difference. Religion, values and worldview ceased to be integral parts of the social environment and became matters of individual choice and conflict.
>
> Belief systems battled one another, and a great intellectual movement—the Enlightenment—attempted to establish a new universality based on reason. In the words of historian David Harvey, the Enlightenment "took it as axiomatic that there was only one

possible answer to any question"—an axiom from which it followed "that the world could be controlled and rationally ordered if we could only picture and represent it rightly," and that presumed "that there existed a single correct mode of representation which, if we could uncover it... would provide the means to Enlightenment ends."

In the Western world, the modernizing process also brought increasing individualism. The person became the chief container of value, replacing the premodern sense of self as part of a unified whole that extended from individual to community to cosmos.

A society enters the postmodern age when it loses faith in absolute truth—even the attempt to discover absolute truth. The great systems of thought like religions, ideologies and philosophies, come to be regarded as "social constructions of reality." These systems may be useful, even respected as profoundly true, but true in a new, provisional, postmodern way. Few expect that one truth ought to work for everybody.[2]

Throughout the years the Islamic response to the era of modernism has been varied. The following is an overview of these responses:

Modernization in Islam, is in its origin, a movement against blind imitation of the past (*Taqlid*). According to modernists, this called for the rational interpretation of the *Qur'an* so as to satisfy the present needs of society (*Ijtihad*).

The history of neo-*ijtihad* may be traced back to Ibn Taymiyya (d. AD 1328), a scholar from the Hanbali school of thought. "He was one of the most indefatigable writers and scholars of Islam who stood against uncritical acceptance of authority (*Taqlid*)." According to Iqbal the spirit of Ibn Taymiyya's teaching found a fuller expression in a movement of immense potential which arose in the 18th century.

The reform impulse developed but did not constitute an outright break from the past. However, as the interaction between Islam and the West increased during the late 18th and early 19th centuries, the "modernist movement" came directly under secularizing influences in the fields of science, economics and literature.

The original movement has become so distorted that the Modernists now claim that the traditions of the Prophet Muhammed (saw) are out-dated and they look upon them with scant respect if they run counter to their ideas. What they want is that Divine Law must conform with their values. Observes Schact:

> "The method used by the modernist legislators savours of unrestrained eclecticism. The 'independent reasoning' that they claim, goes far beyond any that was

practised in the formative period of (Islamic) Law. Any opinion held at some time in the past is likely to be taken out of its context and used as an argument. On the other hand, the modernist legislators are inclined to deny the religious character of the central chapters of the sacred law. They are apt to use arbitrary and forced interpretations of the *Qur'an* and traditions whenever it suits their purpose. Materially, they are bold innovators who want to be modern at all costs. Formally, they try to avoid the semblance of interfering with the essential contents of the sacred laws. Their ideals and their arguments came from the West, but they do not wish to reject the sacred law openly as was done in Turkey."

Such are the modernists who, under the influence of Western Society and in order to have material prosperity have gone to the extent of ignoring the very primary sources of law which, indeed, **was not the intention** of the early leaders of this movement, as they were only up against the finality of the schools (of thought) and the blind imitation of their followers. Ibn Taymiyya never conceived of a plan to undermine the foundations of Islamic Law. He was not a believer in complete departure from the past. What he formulated was a basis for the interpretation of Islamic Law without breaking with its historic past, but this movement in its advancement transgressed the limits, and deviated from the true spirit of Islam and its laws.[3]

Today in the so-called "Muslim World," modernism is out of favor. Movement towards traditional Islam has taken on a new life. Mislabeling this a "fundamentalist movement" will not slow this process.

From the outside, Islam often appears rigid and anti-development. Understanding why this is not the reality of Islam lies in more in-depth study of the "amazing capacity to absorb the change in life" inherent in Islamic Law. One would not expect to find this capacity within what is at the same time the immutable law of Islam. It is doubtful that any human construct could make compatible what appears to be contradictory principles. However, there are numerous examples within the *Qur'an* of marriages of concepts that could never be invisioned from man's narrow view of total Reality.[4]

The misguided attempt to coalesce the traditions of Islam with contemporary conditions is what doomed the modernist movement within Islam to utter failure. However, the exact opposite approach can work. This is because of the dynamic principle known as "the absorption of change within the law" which allows for contemporary conditions to **coalesce with** traditional Islamic values.

Examples of this profoundly dynamic principle on the micro-level of Muslim family values should clarify the Islamic perspective of the role of "modernism" in these values as defined by non-Muslim social scientists. Let's begin by looking at two Muslim family values to see how contemporary conditions may **coalesce with** these values.

Tawhid

Tawhid is the belief in the Oneness of the Creator. This belief includes the knowledge that all creation turns for guidance to a single direction, as in the more popular concept of "universe." Muslims are very comfortable relying on the Creator for guidance. To practice *tawhid* is to turn first to Revelation for any and all matters concerning our life in this world and the Hereafter. The significance of *tawhid* a family value is more fully comprehended when one understands that in Islam, worship equals obedience. Thus, that which one obeys is, in actuality, that which one worships. If the Muslim and his family are to be in harmony and at peace (homostatis) with the rest of creation, *tawhid,* must be valued, through practice. To value *tawhid* is to value harmony, peace and the natural state of homostatis.

Tawhid as a value and concept is the bedrock of the Way of Life (Deen), known as Islam. When *tawhid* is no longer valued enough to be practiced, there can be no family or society defined as "Islamic." *Tawhid* refers to the Oneness, the Singularity and the Uniqueness of the Creator. It means, therefore, that there exists only One Source of creation, sustenance and guidance for the creation. The Creator is the Cause of all causes, the Primal Origin.[5] As such, all of creation turns to this Single Source for guidance, standards, sustenance and law, indeed, for everything.

Education

The second family value for consideration is education. The concept/value of *tawhid* teaches there is only One Creator, one Source of creation. So, it follows that family values in Islam come not from the family, but from the Creator. Education as a "family" value stems from the fact that the first concept revealed to the Prophet Muhammed (saw) was "*iqraa*" (read, learn, comprehend).

> Proclaim! (Read, learn, comprehend) in the name
> of thy Rabb and Cherisher, Who created—
> Created man, out of a mere clot of congealed blood.
> Proclaim! And thy Rabb is Most Bountiful,—
> He Who taught (the use of) the Pen,—
> Taught man that which he knew not.
> Nay, but man doth transgress all bounds,
> In that he looketh upon himself as self-sufficient (*Qur'an* 96, pp. 1-7).

This ayah from the *Qur'an*, the first to be revealed, gives education its value and prominence in the Muslim family and in the Islamic society as a whole. Just as the best use of our mind as defined in Revelation is to use it to call to remembrance the Creator, the best source of learning (education) is Revelation. Beyond this, one must educate oneself in the sciences and any field of study that will benefit and promote life in this world and the Hereafter.

Muslim scientists, doctors, engineers and ditch diggers alike consider the inclusion of Revelation in the educational process to be a positive, highly functional approach to learning. Muslims do not accept the idea that this approach is in any way dysfunctional, "backwards" or at all pejorative. It is simply unatheistic.

Let me present a concrete example of the role of Revelation in education.

In the Islamic economic system there is no concept of interest. In fact, interest is against the law:

> O ye who believe! Fear ALLAH and give up what remains of your demand for usury, if ye are indeed believers.
>
> If ye do it not, take notice of war from ALLAH and His Apostle: But if ye turn back, ye shall have your capital sums: Deal not unjustly, and ye shall not be dealt with unjustly (*Qur'an* 2, pp. 278-279).

A young Muslim undergraduate student of economics at the University of Oklahoma devised a unique way to bridge the gap between Islamic economics and what he was being taught. He began turning in an extra assignment with the assigned homework. In addition, he would turn in formulas with a "zero" substituted for the figures given to calculate interest (*usury*). In this way he introduced the concept of "interest-free economics" to his professors. This led to a fruitful discussion of the Islamic economic system which is totally comprehensive. The principles of the Islamic economic system originate from Revelation (*Qur'an*).

This discussion of two Muslim family values brings us to the analysis of "how contemporary conditions may coalesce with these family values."

Contemporary Conditions and Tawhid

Regarding the value of *tawhid* we find that the successful removal of the Creator from our life threatens this Muslim family value. Replacing the Creator-as-Source with social constructs requires members of society to obey someone or something other than the Creator. This means it is not possible for this particular "contemporary condition" to coalesce with *tawhid* as a value. Once the Muslim turns away from the Creator, he/she is, by definition, no longer a "Muslim." The definition of "Muslim" is "one who submits to ALLAH." The Arabic word "Muslim" is at the same time a noun and a verb. Therefore, when the act of submission towards only the Creator (*tawhid*) ceases, the individual ceases to be a "Muslim" (verb: one who is **submitting** to ALLAH). This is why so many of the philosophies and concepts found in modernism and postmodernism are a **threat** to the very existence of Muslims.[6]

Modernists' and postmodernists' constructs vis a vis Muslim family values introduce far more than a "conflict of values" for the Islamic society. These ideologies/philosophies (ways of life) put Muslims in the position of making a choice that has ramifications beyond family and even society. It goes beyond even life in this world to affect the standard of living for the Muslim in the Hereafter.

Contemporary Conditions and Education

Contemporary conditions in education are changing so rapidly that it is difficult to remain "contemporary." This has become a major stressor for families. Stress comes from change, but the **speed of change** we are experiencing is what is producing the extremes in stress reactions we are witnessing in the "nineties." The education that is so highly valued in the Muslim family is defined as "acquiring knowledge which will benefit the person now **and** in the Hereafter."

The Muslim belief in the Hereafter is only considered to be functional when this belief actually influences ones' behavior in the "here and now." This dynamic is seen in the definition of education just cited.

During the Spring of 1993, the United States educational system had to cope with a recent Supreme Court decision banning prayer during graduation ceremonies. Citizens brought court cases to challenge this decision. School districts scrambled to make adjustments to avoid lengthy court battles. Apparently, education in this society is more of a co-value with religion than the Supreme Court suspected.

The atheistic movement or influence in education can not coalesce with this Muslim family value. The Muslim community's response to contemporary conditions in education has been to set up Islamic schools in the Masjids or to teach children at home. The only "condition" that would coalesce with the Muslim family value of education would be if educational institutions provided subject matter that prepared pupils for life now **and** in the Hereafter. This latter requirement means Revelation would have to be included as source materials since this is the only source of information (data) about the Hereafter available to mankind.

Postmodernism and Muslim Family Values

> Without quite noticing it, we have moved into a new world, one created by the cumulative effect of pluralism, democracy, religious freedom, consumerism, mobility and increasing access to news and entertainment. This is the world described as "postmodern" to denote its difference from the modern world most of us were born into.
>
> Prophets of modernism used to predict that, with progress, old beliefs would simply wither away. But that hasn't happened (what does seem to be happening)...is that belief itself is changing. People do not so much believe as have beliefs.

> A society enters the postmodern age when it loses faith in absolute truth—even the attempt to discover absolute truth. The great systems of thought like religions, ideologies and philosophies, come to be regarded as "social constructions of reality." These systems may be useful, even respected as profoundly true, but true in a new, provisional, postmodern way. Few accept that one truth ought to work for everybody.[7]

To say "there are no absolutes" is, of course, an absolute statement. Certainly, there are absolutes, just as there are "shades of gray." The above quotes on postmodernism provide excellent examples of how this ideology is leading societies far astray from the Muslim family value system. The ideologies spewing forth from postmodernism reflect a difference between living outside the framework of Revelation and living within its framework. The smokescreen that claims the difference is between "those who want progress and modernization" and those who don't, has people of good faith at each other's throats.

Revelation is the fountainhead of Muslim family values. It is very significant that Revelation is not a "social construct." One can readily see how "religions" are thrown in with ideologies and philosophies in the postmodern scheme of thinking as being little more than "social constructions of reality." This perspective is the natural outgrowth of man-made "religions" as humans have distorted Revelation over time. The Muslim family value of *tawhid* holds that Revelation is one and comes from a single Source. While the core message of Revelation has always remained the same, the details of Revelation changed as mankind evolved. Changes in details were modeled and taught by Prophets. "Religions" developed when what had been taught by Prophets was distorted by ommission and commission. In this sense, what we have come to know as "religions" are, in fact, "social constructions of reality." Modernists and now post-modernists seem unable to distinguish between Revelation and religion as a source of guidance.

The "social constructions of realities" called "premodernism," "modernism" and "postmodernism" are all time-bound. What will be the name given the next era? Will it be called "post-post-modernism"? From the Islamic perspective, the function of values has nothing to do with time. Just as certain creatures are provided particular instincts, humans are provided with certain values (via Revelation). The *Qur'an* refers to animal instincts as being a form of Revelation. Upon careful study of the *Qur'an* one finds references made to incidents "from the past" as well as incidents "from the future." Likewise, there are bits of information useful for the "here and now." To the Creator of time, all time is one.

Humans are not viewed as "moving through time" from the *Qur'anic* perspective. Rather, all things created, including time, are "moving through phases of existence." Muslim family values are seen as valid and functional no matter if they are premodern, modern, or postmodern "time." What makes Muslim family values valid is their source— Revelation from the Creator. These values are functional because one of the purposes of Revelation is to provide humans with guidance in this life that will benefit them in both this life and in the Hereafter.

Endnotes

1. Social scientists may find this statement disturbing until they understand that the *Qur'an* (Revelation) is totally comprehensive and considered by Muslims to literally be the "final word," explaining the workings of this world and the Hereafter on the individual as well as the societal level.
2. Maureen O'Hara and W. T. Anderson. *The family therapy networker*: "Welcome to the Postmodern World," (Pub. *The family therapy networker*, Washington, DC Sept/Oct), 1991, pp. 20-22.
3. Muhammad Muslehuddin, *Philosophy of Islamic law and the orientalists.* (Islamic Publications, LTD. Lahore, Pakistan, 1975) Introduction, pp. 16-18.
4. Izetbegovic, 'Alija 'Ali. *Islam between East and West.* American Trust Publications, Indianapolis, IN. 1984. *As of the date of this writing he is the President of Muslim Bosina.
5. To ALLAH is due the primal origin of the heavens and the earth: When He decreeth a matter, He saith to it, "Be," and it is. (*Qur'an*, 2, p. 117)
6. Any atheistic thrust (modern or postmodern) promotes a way of life that is diametrically opposed to Islam. Principles of the atheistic way of life do to Islam and Muslims what darkness does to light.
7. Maureen O'Hara and W. T. Anderson. *The family therapy networker*: "Welcome to the Postmodern World." (Pub. The Family Therapy Networker, Washington, DC Sept/Oct, 1991), pp. 20-22.

Article 22

The Changing Status of Chinese Women within the Family and Society

Minjie Zhang
Deborah Evans

Introduction

In historical and traditional China, men demanded submission and absolute loyalty from their wives in order to ensure that the family's heritage remained in the hands of legitimate male descendants. Marriage was a matter of perpetuating the family line, and wives were basically reproductive machines. This form of the Chinese family remained intact for over two thousand years.

During the twentieth century, the situation of Chinese women generally improved. The People's Republic of China (PRC) was founded in 1949, and its Marriage Laws of 1950 and 1980 gave women rights and equality within the family. Once Chinese women were legally freed from the bondage of traditional, orthodox roles, they left the confines of their homes to participate in production and state affairs. It remains, however, that China is a developing country, and there are still remnants of feudal ideologies in everyday life. Women have a distance to go before they can be truly satisfied with their position in family and in society.

Since 1978, the family's contract responsibility system has been implemented in rural areas. By the early 1980s, the people's commune system, which had been the basic unit of rural areas since 1958, was disintegrating. As the collective structure weakened severely, the family began to have a more important function in rural society. According to the principle of the family contract responsibility system, the land is distributed to each household and the family retains rights over all its produce. In other words, the new system is a family farming system (Zweig, 1987). The status of rural women within the family has improved because the value of their labor has been recognized by society.

During the 1980s, urban economic reforms were begun. Since implementation of these reforms, the situation of urban women has changed considerably as they now face many new situations and new challenges. Although urban reforms offer men and women equal opportunities to develop themselves, women generally start from an already disadvantaged position. Women must balance both career and family responsibilities. That is, women strive to be successful in work and keep their families happy and harmonious as well. Women carry double burdens. As the contradiction between work and family becomes sharper, women find it increasingly difficult to satisfy the demands of both job and family.

The Present Status of the Wife within the Family

In order to evaluate women's situation within the family, a focus on the wife's status is the key point in judging how much the condition of women has changed. For over two thousand years in Chinese history, women suffered great oppression within the family. Mao Zedong (1975) pointed out the following:

> A man in China is usually subjected to the domination of three systems of authority: [political authority, clan authority, and religious authority] . . . As for women, in addition to being dominated by these three systems of authority, they are also dominated by the men (the authority of the husband). These four authorities—political, clan, religious and masculine—are the embodiment of the whole feudal-patriarchal ideology and system, and are the four thick ropes binding the Chinese people (p. 44).

Under this oppression, a woman was subordinated to her father before marriage, to her husband after marriage, and to her son after the death of her husband. Generally speaking, in the old Chinese family, the husband had the absolute power to control his wife. After 1949, the new Chinese government adopted a number of policies and programs to redefine the roles of women and place them in a position of equal status with men in both public and domestic spheres. The traditional ethical code that held "the authority of the husband is supreme," and, "the husband governs the wife," has been replaced by a spirit of equality and cooperation. Today the condition of the wife within the family has changed immeasurably.

Wives' and Husbands' Equal Family Rights

Since 1950, the government of the People's Republic of China has issued a series of laws to improve the status of women. The most important of these laws are the Constitution and the Marriage Law. The Constitution issued in 1954 stipulated the following principle for women's rights in both society and family: "Women in the People's Republic of China enjoy equal rights with men in all spheres of life, including political, economic, educational, social and family life."

Marriage and the family have been a central concern of the government, and one of its first major pieces of legislation was the Marriage Law of 1950. The law established the right to marry the person of one's choice, prohibited polygamy, affirmed the equality of the sexes, and set out measures to protect the interests of women and children. In effect, the Marriage Law not only put an end to the traditional marriage code, but also encouraged marriages founded on mutual affection, respect for the aged and concern for the young. Three decades later the legislation was updated to take into account the great social changes that had taken place. The new Marriage Law of 1980, which came into effect in 1981, retains the basic spirit and provisions of the former law. The ninth article in this Marriage Law stipulates that "husband and wife enjoy equal status in the home" ("Marriage Law," 1994, p. 5). They also enjoy the following rights under the 1980 Marriage Law:

A husband and wife each has the right to use his or her family name.

Both husband and wife have the freedom to work, "to study, and to participate in social activities; neither party is allowed to restrain or interfere with the other."

Both husband and wife enjoy equal rights in the management of the property in their joint possession.

When one party fails to perform the duty to support and assist the other, the party in need of support and assistance has the right to demand that the other party pay the cost of support and assistance.

Both husband and wife have the right to inherit each other's property. After the death of a spouse, the other has the right to inherit the property. If the dead spouse has children and/or parents, they and the living spouse enjoy equal rights to inherit the property. The right is based on the personal relationship of the husband and the wife.

As both husband and wife enjoy the above rights, per the 1980 Marriage Law, they also bear certain obligations. Husband and wife are obligated to support and assist each other, to practice family planning, to rear and educate their children, and to support and assist both maternal and paternal aged parents.

Wife's Independent Economic Status within the Family

Legislation brought women equal rights with men within the family, but only when women go outside the home, take part in labor, and win economic independence can they possess actual equal status within the family.

In the countryside, it was estimated that in the late 1970s upwards of 80% of peasant women worked full–time or part–time in collective agriculture and therefore composed at least 40% of the total rural labor force (Johnson, 1983, p. 169). However, during the period of people's communes, men were still the mainstay of the rural labor force. This was because of the rigid working schedule set by the commune, and because the main responsibility for caring for the household and children fell to women. The "double burden" of outside work and housework was not alleviated by such inadequate services as irregular daycare (Johnson, 1983, p. 173). Also, an unequal wage system was not a great financial incentive for women to work outside the home, because they were not permitted to earn the same pay as men (Andors, 1983, p. 142). But the implementation of rural economic reform and, the family contract responsibility system gave women a new chance. Presently, because family income depends on the productive activities of its members, the wife must first of all be a social producer in order to enrich her family. Women are given a free hand to handle their business and they can decide for themselves what to do and when to do it. The wife's earnings become an important part of the family's income. Peasant women not only participate in agricultural labor on the land and in domestic sidelines, such as raising pigs, rabbits, hens or sheep, but also work in rural factories, rural fairs, or local markets. Increasingly, confident of their ability to perform, women are challenging men in traditionally male–dominated areas. Women find they can earn more money for their families and that as their income increases, so does their family's status.

The Changing Relationship between Wife and Husband

As women are increasingly involved in the labor force, improving their economic status, and bringing in more money, the woman's position within the family has changed. It has improved. Women now have more say, and the old scene in which the husband played the boss of the family is changing. Husband and wife have much in common, and their marriages are based on love and mutual regard. Slight age differences, corresponding educational backgrounds, equivalent jobs, and similar family backgrounds are the norm for contemporary marriages (Lin et al., 1992).

In May 1985, two women's magazines polled 997 Beijingers on their marriages. "Most marriages, it had been thought, were merely satisfactory relationships in which husband and wife managed to get along despite their differences. But as many as 53% of our respondents considered their marriages perfectly happy, and only 33% rated them just satisfactory. The percentages were the same for both women and men respondents" (Lin et al., 1992). However, there were marked differences in marital contentment among various age groups. Couples between 36 and 40 were the least likely to have found domestic happiness (only 43% of them) while about 60% of those either under 31 or over 50 had been successful. Why? This phenomenon may be attributed to the unstable social conditions that prevailed when those now between 36 and 40 were married. Many of them were married during the Cultural Revolution. Some married because marriage was what they wanted, but some were looking for something more, for a kind of sustenance beyond the scope of matrimony. The latter were bound to become disillusioned.

Changes have also taken place in the working hours of wives and husbands. The gap between their total daily working hours is narrowing, but not the hours for housework, which is still mainly a task for women in both city and countryside. Although family members are encouraged to share in household chores, domestic labor continues to make substantial demands on wives' time and energies. This reflects that women are not yet freed from housework. However, more couples are sharing equally in decisions, family expenditures, and housework, while supporting each other in social activities. The media has brought to public attention several cases where wives and husbands share domestic chores equally. For example in Shanghai city, out of "100 nuclear families [in] which both wives and husbands are employed, 25% said that [the] wife makes the final decisions, 45% said decisions were arrived at jointly, [and] 30% [said] the husband made the decisions" (Pan, 1987, p. 122).

In China today, most divorce suits are initiated by women, something unheard of traditionally, for previously only the husband had the right to renounce a spouse. "Statistics from Beijing People's Court show 60 percent of applications for 14,000 divorce cases are submitted by women." (Li, 1994, p. 16) There are three main reasons for the increase in the number of women plaintiffs. The first reason is that women have become more financially independent and no longer have to tolerate bad marriages. Second, diametrically different expectations on either side will give rise to despair and conflicts. There are very different demands in a family as a result of the husband and wife having different social status. Men are usually more career oriented than women and spend more of their mental and physical energies at work. Their home is often simply a place for rest and relaxation. Though women often do have important careers, as well, they still tend to play supporting roles in the family. In addition, society still expects women to be virtuous wives and good mothers, and upbringing has prepared them to play this role in the family. However, because women have often been dominated and inhibited for so long and have seldom felt respected and loved in their married life, they often need more love than husbands want to provide. Women are disappointed when they find their modest and meek lovers, who had been so attentive and caring before marriage, becoming indifferent afterwards. Thus marital breakdown typically begins with both sides claiming that they no longer love the other. Wives, especially, claim a lack of love as a motivator to apply for divorce. The third reason for the increase in women divorce plaintiffs is sexual incompatibility. Due to the influence of traditional concepts, some women have been taught since childhood to view sex as licentiousness, solely for reproduction, and the fulfillment of their wifely duty. Consequently, they have been taught to be passive and feel shameful about sex. Having been raised with this outlook, many women feel that they are no more than objects of their husbands' sexual appetite. Other women simply find the sexual component of their marriage "bland" and "dull." "In earlier times, people never uttered [a] word about sexual life. . . . Yet these days, people's ideas have changed and they regard sexual life as a serious matter in marriage" (Li, 1994, p. 16).

China's marriage law holds love between husband and wife as the core of the matter in divorce cases. To maintain the pretence of a happy marriage is bound to be painful to both parties, and may indeed have ill–effects on their children and even society at large. In certain cases, divorce is the only way of solving the problems of an inherently unsuccessful marriage, thus allowing the two parties the chance to set up new, contented families.

Conflict between the Demands of Work and Family

In the years since 1951 when the rights of women were formally proclaimed, the situation of Chinese women within the family has changed dramatically. The women's liberation movement in China has been part of the government's policies. However, under the socialist system, the course of women's liberation is still limited by subjective and objective considerations and many problems still remain.

Chinese women nowadays not only work outside the home but also assume a lion's share of the household work. These two burdens on women are tremendous. Women work outside their home in part because this is a government policy, but also because this is the wish of their families. In China, family income depends on how many family members participate in the workforce. For urban dwellers it is very difficult to get by on the husband's income alone. Most wives take part in social work, but their burden of housework is not eased. Women in rural households do 5.5 hours housework per day. In urban families, according to a 1988 survey, "female workers should do housework about 3.5–4 hours per day...This is 1.2 hours less than in 1980" (Lin et al., 1992). During the 1980s, over 70% of the families possessed washing machines, iceboxes, and even electric cooking stoves; with these labor–saving devices, the traditional domestic responsibilities of women have been reduced. Still, many wives complain that their housework is too time–consuming. Women are expected to work 8 hours every day; then, when they return home, they are expected do about 4 hours domestic work. As a consequence, few women have leisure time.

In recent years, Chinese women, in playing a dual role, work even harder than men. Once there was a push in China for women to return to the domestic sphere and let men work outside the home in order to regain a more even balance of responsibility, but this, of course, is no solution. If women leave outside work, they will be drawn back again to a subordinate position.

Conclusion

Socialist China has grown out of more than 2,000 years feudal and more than 100 years of semi–feudal and semi–colonial struggles. Though females have won equality with males as far as the laws are concerned, due to the influence of feudal ideology, women are still considered inferior to men in both family and societal affairs. Traces of the double standards concerning female chastity, the view of divorce as a social evil, and the conflict between traditional and socialist ideas about the preference for male children over female remain. Economic conditions and traditional practices have resulted in Chinese women being made to play the role of homemakers while holding down full–time jobs outside the home. Consequently, working women, especially young women with children, suffer under multiple burdens. Despite this, women in China are moving forward. The traditional and feudal family system has been radically changed by government policy and law, and adoption of the policy of reform and opening to the outside challenge the Chinese people to renew their conception of family. While moving forward, women help implement and offer a more beneficial society. The status of women within the family will continue to advance during the 1990s and society will only be the better for it.

References

Andors, P. (1983). *The unfinished liberation of Chinese women: 1949–1980.* Bloomington: Indiana University Press.

Johnson, K. A. (1983). *Women, the family, and peasant revolution in China.* Chicago: The University of Chicago Press.

Li, P. (1994). Will a family crises arise in China? *Women of China, 2,* 16–17.

Lin, P. L., Chao, W. Y., Johnson, T. L., Persell, J., & Tsang, A. (Eds.). (1992). *Families: East and West.* Indianapolis, IN: University of Indianapolis Press.

Mao, Zedong. (1975). *Selected works of Mao Zedong,* (Vol. 1.). Peking: Foreign Languages Press.

Marriage Law of the People's Republic of China. (1994). *Women of China, 2,* 5–6.

Pan, Y. K. (1987). The Chinese marriage and the family in cities. *Jinan, 12,* 122.

Zweig, D. (1987). Context and content in policy implementation: Household contracts and decollectivization, 1977–1983. In D. M. Lampton (Ed.), *Policy implementationin post–Mao China* (pp. 255–283). Berkeley: University of California Press.

Social Interventions on Family

Part VIII

Article 23

Using Self-Help to Rebuild Families in Transition: The Case of South-East Asian Refugee Families

Lina, Y. S. Fong

Self-Help

Social welfare programs based on "mutual aid," "self- organized," or "self-help" are growing so rapidly and are in such a process of change that they outstrip the tempo of data collection (Katz, 1965). The purpose and program of these groups vary considerably. They are generally organized by parents, relatives, or the clients themselves, who are suffering from or are concerned about a particular condition. Their broad aims include the provision of some forms of service or care for the clients and relatives, public and professional education, and the support of research. In nearly every instance these groups came into being to meet a concrete need or provide a concrete service that was, in the organizers' experience, not being adequately provided for by public efforts. The nature of these activities can be social, educational, therapeutic, and community- action orientated.

In organizing "mutual aid," the groups may be doing more than meeting an immediate need or social interest, perhaps supplying a channel for group participation, affiliation and identification that helps to overcome the anomic and isolating tendencies of the general society.

Goodman (1990) suggests that self-help also serves to supplement informal supports or to compensate for failures in family and friend relationships. Borkman (1984) theorizes that self-help increases confidence in experiential knowledge and lowers expectations of family and friends, thereby supplementing and eventually facilitating use of informal supports.

A cross-cultural study of these groups would no doubt yield important, fascinating information on the significance of self-help initiatives to the mental health of clients and their families and on the variables in the rise of grass-roots organizations under diverse social conditions. In fact, self-help has proved to be very helpful for families in cultural transition.

Families in Cultural Transition

The plight of refugees—women, children, men—cannot be understood without first examining the political, social, and economic reasons which have forced them onto the road of exile by the millions.

News of tragedies pours in at such a speed and in such profusion that we tend to forget that behind the news there are people whose suffering lasts longer than the short-lived attention given them by the mass media.

The world refugee map tallies almost perfectly with the world conflicts map, and illustrates the fact that the overwhelming majority of refugees come from and move between Third World countries. Out of the 12.5 million refugees officially registered by UNHCR and UNRWA in 1985, 83% have found sanctuary in the Third World. It is often through accumulation of setbacks, ranging from individual persecution, economic disorder and deprivation, political coercion and violence, liberation wars and wars of hegemony, natural disasters, and poverty, that people are driven by hunger and fear to leave their home country.

To the stresses and traumas inflicted on refugees before escape, during flight, and in refugee camps, one must add the difficulties, fears and anxieties that face the refugees during resettlement. They are faced with culture shock, a new/unknown environment, different rules and systems, language difficulties, host hostility, racial and cultural barriers and discrimination, survival adjustment and provision for education and work, often involving loss or degrading of status, e.g., from professional to menial, from an elite to an impoverished minority. Husbands cannot provide, women must work, children no longer respect the old ways. Drive and determination wane, discouragement sets in.

Specifically, the stresses and problems faced by refugee families in cultural transition include the following:

Most immediately, refugee families suffer from the disruption of their hitherto function, including the loss or lack of social ties and support that they used to have through their extended families, kinship network, and familiar community in the society and country they left (Fong, 1992). They are beset with worries and guilt over family members left abroad, or being dispersed in resettlement.

These refugee families undergo changing dynamics in the processes of cultural transition. They face the acculturative stress in choosing between identification with ethnic culture of origin and the culture of the host country. The resulting change and confusion in the role and function of family members is further accentuated by different rates of assimilation: (a) between parent and children; and (b) between husbands and wives. Wives who are not used to, and not equipped with skill and training to work are forced to work. Husbands are forced to take job at a lower status than they were used to in their home country, feeling a loss of power with their decreasing economic ability and status and the rising economic capacity of their wives. Children who acculturate faster at mastering the language and going to school in the host country often take on role reversal in helping to interpret and act as bridge for parents and grandparents, making parents feel a loss of authority that they are used to having (Dressler & Bernal, 1992).

The welfare of children whose parent(s) either deserted the family, or were killed at war, or who neglect them because they are too busy struggling for economic survival, are at risk. The elderly members of the family suffer from their diminishing power in the family. The weakening of the role of their children and family in taking care of them puts the care and social security that the elderly members used to be able to get from the family at stake (Fong, 1992).

Other refugee families with special needs include those with member(s); handicapped, disabled, widowed, or orphaned resulting from war and persecution. Many suffer from post-traumatic stress resulting from traumatic experiences of war, imprisonment, exile, abuse, prosecution, etc.. Others who find it difficult to handle the stress from multiple stressors, develop different forms of social, mental, and emotional disorders.

Self-Help for Families in Cultural Transition

Relevance of Self-Help For Families In Cultural Transition

From the global social support standpoint, world citizens across national boundaries have the responsibility to help refugee families as part of the global family to regain just and rightful living through relocation, and to help these refugee families to help themselves rebuild their families and communities through successful resettlement.

From the family and community level, the ethnic communities composed of ethnic families provide for social support and mutual help, one with the other. With the common disruption of extended family and kinship ties, this form of self-help has been a very helpful resource for families not used to the nuclear family form of functioning, or who are even further separated from their nuclear family members, resulting from different forms of oppression.

Then, within different sub-groups among the refugee populations, self-help can be organized to provide support for members of each sub-group, e.g., women, children, elderly, PTSD veterans or their spouses, etc. Individuals thus empowered through self-help groups from their respective sub-group can contribute to strengthen further their own nuclear family of origin.

In order to reach out to newly arrived immigrant or refugee families who are not yet ready to reach out to us, we must begin to establish links between formal helping systems and those informal systems the emigrant populations bring with them. By identifying central figures in helping networks, and extending consultation to them in the forms of training and education, the professional will be able to indirectly extend his expert services to larger numbers of people in newly arrived populations (Fong, 1992).

Resettled relatives and friends who, in turn, help newly arrived families, can also be encouraged to enter consultation relationships. The creation of workshops and informal discussion groups for receiving families is one way in which reinforcement, support, and guidance can be provided to those whose help is most valued and sought after by the immigrants.

Since most immigrants feel most comfortable expressing personal thoughts, feelings, and experiences in the company of primary groups it would seem relevant for professionals to create mutual aid groups consisting of networks of emigrants and their informal supports. In this way, resources known and available in one informal network can be shared with others. The confidence promoted through mutual help can also be expected to enhance the coping capacities of the emigre in addressing both the emotional issues as well as the concrete tasks involved in successful resettlement. Not only do self-help groups help to diminish the sense of alienation of emigrants, they also provide a sense of universality, of communication, and of sharing. They help to create a sense of not being alone, that there is somebody who cares, that there are people you can trust, and people who trust you.

Self-help groups send the message that you yourself know what is best for your own people. People want to participate in their own lives, their own recovery, and the decisions that affect their destiny. They are not so willing or feel it so necessary to turn these important matters over to authorities or experts or specialists.

Another dimension that emerges in these groups is hope. Refugees are survivors. Sometimes you don't know how long you are going to last, and you don't know what the future holds in store.

Related to this is the dimension of common belief systems and ideologies, providing cognitive antidotes, that unite all of the members with some common understanding about their condition or experience.

Aside from these dimensions of developing a sense of common identity, continuity, commitment, and hope, and sharing a belief system or ideology, the personable nature of the self-help groups provides a refreshing contrast to the impersonal, bureaucratic society in which refugee families live. The helpers at the grass-root level are people who care, who are available, and who can be reached at almost any hour. Moreover, they don't charge you, require you to give your insurance, and you don't need to make an appointment.

Another powerful element is the "helper/therapy principle" that operates with refugee associations. You learn the most when you need to teach it to somebody else. Getting actively involved in helping other people is enormously helpful for the person who provides help. Participation and involvement, helping other people is not only good therapy, it is good citizenship.

Another important characteristic of mutual aid groups is the relative ease in identifying the wealth of information they provide about their concern or condition. In our scientific, technical world, we have a tendency to underrate information that is not gathered and assembled by scientists, and yet the groups you represent are some of the best sources for information about the situations you face. While a scientist has a temporary concern, you have an all-abiding commitment. Whether they be traditional or historical or newly formed mutual aid groups, they need to be recognized for the wisdom and expertise they exemplify and represent, and be included in decisions that affect their lives.

This may involve a new kind of communication, a new openness, a new partnership or collaboration, between distinctive populations and those professionals or agencies concerned with their good and welfare.

The value of neighbors helping neighbors, reaching out and helping one another, harkens back to the barn-raising days of the founders of the country, where the ideas of mutual aid and support systems were more prevalent. Maybe the refugee and new immigrant groups will help bring back a revival of these values that are so important to all of us.

Critical Steps in Formation of Self-Help Groups

Self-help groups are distinctive in that the members become prosumers (Toffler's 1980's term for one who both provides and consumes service), experiential knowledge of the shared situation is valued, and a true parado (Rappaport, 1981) occurs, in that members are both self-responsible and give mutual help.

Goodman (1991) described perceived social support for caregiving and social conflict in measuring the benefit of self-help/support group participation. Borkman (1989) regarded self-help groups as grass-root efforts embedded in their local communities, valuable in their support of the autonomy and self-determination of mutual aid self-help groups.

Examples of Self-Help Projects Helpful To Rebuild Families In Transition

Refugee Self-Help Groups, together with references on available programs, funds, and resources that can be utilized by local service providers, local County and State human service agencies, and others involved in resettlement work, are listed in the Refugee Resettlement Resources Book (Brunch, et al 1980), and the Resource Guide For Refugee Women's Program Development, *Center for Applied Linguistics* (Center for Applied Linguistics, 1981).

The Fresno County Refugee Health Volunteer Project enables individuals, families, and community groups to meet their health care needs. It is a model approach to health care which builds on the strength and skills of the community (Kowe & Spees, 1987).

Renard (1990) and CAL (1981), in reviewing the current status of Indochinese Mutual Assistance Programs, describe the six kinds of MAAs that are found in the United States. They include: (1) cultural preservation/social activities—vital for preserving cultural integrity; (2)spiritual/religious services—vital for providing psychological base for smooth adjustment; (3) special constituency groups; (4) resettlement/social services; (5) business and economic development—to foster refugee self-sufficiency through the stimulation of small business opportunities and co-ops, as well as partnership and bridge-building with the American private sector; (6) advocacy and political action—advocacy to achieve refugee involvement in local, state and federal policy and planning, as well as in the policies and services of voluntary resettlement agencies. Shotts et al. (1981) recommend more emphasis should be placed on financial support for MAAs and particularly each State should be encouraged to contract with MAAs for the delivery of social services.

Finck, J (1983) described how the majority of the Hmong refugees in Rhode Island have become self-supporting despite a high local unemployment rate (only 6.6% higher than the local residents). Many refugees have started their own businesses and self-help groups.

Bui et al. (1981), in surveying the characteristics, composition, capacity building needs and future directions of sixty Cambodian, Laotian, and Vietnamese MAAs, evinced an interest in coalition building in these organizations.

Rogers (1990), described the use of self-help as an initiative for fund-raising as another abundantly clear historical evidence of self-reliance and self-help initiative by racial and ethnic groups in America.

Glasser and Suroviak (1989) described how the strengths of the guests to a soup kitchen, who are mostly drug addicts and ex- drug addicts, are mobilized to introduce effective education on prevention of AIDS through drug rehabilitation, the use of sterile needles for the drug user, and the promotion of sexual practices which are considered safe.

Tunnard (1989) described the Family Rights Groups, as an example of a self-help group for grandparents of minority children in public care.

Charping and Slaughter (1989) described the voluntary energy assistance programs as community self-help in action.

Mahalik and Kivlighan (1988), in using self-help for treatment of depression, found low superiority, high generalized self-efficacy, and an internal locus of control were related to success in the self-help depression treatment.

Goodman (1990) described a model telephone network program for caregivers of Alzheimer's disease victims, considering its impact in caregivers' use of informal supports as well as perceived social supports, mental health, burden, and information about Alzheimer's disease. Program benefits seen after the first three months (reduced psychological distress, increased support satisfaction, perceived social support satisfaction, and perceived social support) leveled off or declined during the second three months. Additionally, caregiver burden and social conflict increased during the second three months.

Using Self-Help to Rebuild Family and Community

The following describes how using social support and networking among refugee families within their ethnic community and with relevant institutions has been a powerful and effective way for enabling them to help themselves to rebuild their ethnic family and community.

Since the literature shows social isolation and family separation to be major causes of emotional problems, it is of utmost importance that the household as a unit of human capital, is valued and fostered ahead of individual interests.

In reaction to the life crisis of uprooting and separation, and to ease the disorganization of personal identity caused by such process, family units seek to mend or reconstitute their traditional structures as rapidly as possible. As soon as the refugees arrive in the United States, most of them make desperate attempts to get in touch with family members and acquaintances as soon as possible. With the strong emphasis on family loyalty and relationships, repeated efforts are often made by Indo-Chinese refugees to keep in touch with family members who remain in SEA, and to facilitate the escape for family members from Vietnam. Also, material goods are often made to family members in Vietnam regularly, at least to provide a feeling of relatedness.

Families split apart during evacuation and resettlement work hard at rebuilding a social network by incorporating distant relatives, friends, and even strangers who are refugees. Torn from one's homeland and family ties, one can adjust more easily in the company of others who have shared the experiences. Having literally been in the same boat seems to generate strong mutual support among refugees.

Some refugees make up for the loss of natural family members by creating "artificial" or "unofficial" families. Many of the unaccompanied minors were "adopted" by Vietnamese families; others were taken care of by "unofficial foster homes."

The loss of family support is particularly difficult for a sub-group of Vietnamese consisting of young, unmarried ex- servicemen, who, by and large, escaped from Vietnam at the last moment with the crowd, leaving their entire family network behind. Over the years, these people and others who are isolated and in need of family support develop support units that could be called "psuedo-families." Three or four of them will share an apartment, go to the same school, work in the same factory, and develop close relationships, reminiscent of the function allotted to extended families back in SEA. As more members are incorporated into the family unit, the economic burden is shared, the functions of the Vietnamese extended family are gradually restored.

This search for a support system and traditional community network gradually gives rise to a pattern of secondary migration. For example, growing Vietnamese communities in Texas, Louisiana, California, and the Washington, DC area provide evidence of this migration.

Aside from seeking to re-establish the traditional family structure, the refugees also seek to locate and build S.E. Asian communities in their new country. Being cut off from their families, villages, and countries, Southeast Asian refugees feel an urgent need to cluster together and to form community organizations as secondary sources of security. Therefore, the development of community-based fictive kinship networks e.g., mutual assistance programs, ethnic associations, etc., is very important in the helping strategy.

Living within an ethnic community would be crucial for development of a social support network. This can be illustrated by the way S.E. Asian refugees depend essentially on their primary group and immediate informal social network within families and between friends for health related help, support, and care of the persons who are ill. The informal support systems within various refugee communities have been important in assisting them finding jobs through their friends and relatives, and in achieving self-sufficiency by providing support that facilitates the social, cultural, and emotional adjustment of refugees. To resolve a personal or interpersonal problem, the Indochinese in their home countries relied on leaders in the community, elders in the family, religious leaders, and other community support mechanisms.

The new community pulls together all available S.E. Asian resources to form an identifiable ethnic support system: extended families, religious groups, friendship groups, and groups of professionals band together. Although growth may be inhibited initially by geographic distance, economic factors, and lack of clear leadership, the new ethnic community slowly begins to serve as a buffer between the old, familiar lifestyle and the new, modern one; as a forum for collective mourning of losses of the old, familiar lifestyle and consideration of acceptance of the new, modern one. They get together in small groups to share feelings of nostalgia for the old days, to commiserate over their present circumstances, and to exchange information.

Traditional activities involving S.E. Asian holidays, religious ceremonies, ethnic food and banquets, and mahjong clubs become rituals that restore normalcy to disrupted lives. There are about 1000 incorporated, non-profit refugee mutual assistance associations (MAAS) in the U.S. They operate primarily as social service networks, as temples, raise money to support resistance armies in other countries and act as freelance entrepreneurs, providing special services. Through MAAs, S.E. Asians can both maintain their ethnic community and integrate themselves into the new community. The refugees' attachment to the new community groupings serves to maintain their old identity until a newer identity and clearer status within the United States can be worked out. For example, where there are Hmong communities, there are Hmong Associations, consisting of heads of extended families, linking the community to the outside society. The strong bond and their own highly organized system of mutual assistance is their major source of strength for survival. Suspicion of community leaders has to be cleared; and leadership in the Southeast Asian communities encouraged in order for the refugees to maintain their communities and influence those who affect the ethnic communities. MAA help to develop a sense of belonging and a re-establishment of identity. Through MAAs, Southeast Asians can both integrate themselves into the new community, and maintain their ethnic community. The ethnic community provides support that facilitates the social, cultural, and emotional adjustment of refugees. By integrating the existing resettlement networks with mutual assistance associations, the process of acculturation becomes more culturally sensitive.

The support system in the refugee community plays an important role in determining the facility with which each family resolves the transitional issue. Many Southeast Asian refugees are in frequent contact with community educational and social service agencies for their youths.

It is obviously important to reinforce mechanisms of social support among refugees. Even being able to contact a sponsor—which tends to be disrupted with moves—has been found to be associated with better mental health. Being able to get connected with a similar but more established, immigrant group can also be a supportive bridge for the newly arrived S.E. Asian refugee families to eventually become more adjusted to the mainstream American society.

Self-Help with Subgroups Sharing Common Needs Among Refugee Families

Families

Self-help can be fostered within sub-groups sharing common needs among refugee families. Individual family members, being empowered through their respective self-help groups, can thus cooperate as a stronger force to successfully rebuild their own family, undergoing cultural transition.

Using Self-Help For Refugee Youth

For relocated children and adolescents, a self-help group provides them with mutual support that can be described as instrumental, emotional, educational and appraisal (House, 1981). It can provide a safe environment through which students, old and new, can meet and find that they are not alone in their fears and feelings of loss (Strother, J. & Harvill, R., 1986) and that they can accept themselves not as "oddballs" (Muro & Dinkmeyer, 1977). It provides an opportunity for them to discuss and appraise common areas of concern, to gather and disseminate information that is relevant for their cultural and social adjustment to the new educational setting and societal environment in general. Beyond informational and educational support, a self-help group provides emotional support, whereby empathy, caring and trust among members is promoted, to help to alleviate such common concerns of theirs as grief, depression, anger, or loneliness (House, 1981).

Examples of such self-help efforts with youth is their use of Orientation Groups for Relocating Youth, and Recovery Groups for those who have resorted to substance abuse to cope with the stresses related to their cultural transition.

Using Self-Help For Refugee Women

Refugee women are victims of accumulated disadvantages, but increasingly, they are beginning to assert that they are not just victims of circumstances beyond their control but creative and dynamic actors in their own histories.

The pivotal role played by refugee women, not only in the welfare of their own families, but in the entire refugee community, has been documented and reported in various mini-studies in different parts of the world, and reported by many field-workers. Many have witnessed their psychological and moral strength, their innovative and adaptive ability, and their abilities to lead the family, and to overcome the difficulties that come with family breakdowns. They manage to "make do with nothing," to secure as much as they can to meet the basic needs of their families. They demonstrate inner strength to assume new roles, despite overwhelming personal tragedy.

When recognized and encouraged to develop their potentials, refugee women have proved to be essential elements in the solutions to their own problems and that of the refugee community at large.

In the refugee camps in Thailand and Malaysia, where the counseling program for victims of violence at sea has been implemented, women have been encouraged to set up women's self-help groups, and community mutual aid associations.

The purpose of the group is to restore the self-confidence of women by giving them responsibility for the care and social well-being of the camp community.

In refugee camps in Africa, Central America, and South- East Asia the training of refugee women health workers has systematically improved the refugee women's access to health programs, and has been an important element in health-care programs.

In the Solumuna camp for Eritrean refugees, and in the Tendelti camp in Sudan for Chadean refugees, women "have proved themselves more than competent in taking over administrative work generally reserved for men."

Refugee policy-makers should realize that refugee groups which are in control of their own affairs seem to achieve much more, by giving them the opportunity to use their skills and acquire new ones.

The strength to assume new roles and responsibilities, and the courage to overcome distress in the face of an uncertain future, can be a source of liberation and positive change for many women refugees.

Through the experience of participation, women's consciousness and the ability to exert control over their own lives can be dramatically influenced. Establishing true partnership means recognizing and respecting their identity and their abilities in helping refugee women to help themselves whenever possible, and refugee women can be helped to form organizations of their own, where they can better identify their priorities and find solutions to their problems. An example in case is self-help groups for the treatment of female partners of Vietnam veterans.

While there is no development process without women's participation, there is also no solution to refugee problems without women's full contribution.

Using Self-Help For Elderly Refugee

Losses of aging can be mitigated by adequate personal and community resources, family respect, and closeness, and a past history of successful coping, the latter depending on a group's access to educational and economic opportunities in the larger society.

Using Self-Help For Refugee Torture Victims Suffering From Traumatic Stress Disorder

Another special group among the S.E. Asian refugee families is the refugee victims of torture ,suffering from post- traumatic stress disorder. This disorder has been conceptualized as an unintegrated emotional response to the horror of torture, resulting in the loss of feelings of safety and control, and sense of protection and invulnerability (Gressard, 1986). These victims have been apprehended violently, below the minimal international standards. The post traumatic stress disorder (PTSD) symptoms include: emotional numbness; avoidance and alienation from family, friends, and society in general; nervousness, shock, anger; frenetic overactivity or exaggerated startle response; recurrent intrusive thoughts and Ú; Ú and recurrent nightmares; Ú and psychosomatic manifestations; physical damage and even suicidal attempts; depression and depressive reactions that can develop into compulsive gambling or substance abuse; prolonged crying periods; obsessive reminiscence of past and others; survival guilt, and so on.

Post-traumatic stress disorder has proved very difficult to treat. The alienation and distrust these refugee victims of torture feel toward authorities, and helping professions, have kept them from voluntarily seeking treatment and from developing a trusting relationship with a professional practitioner when they do enter treatment. One early solution to the problem of getting help was the use of "rap groups." This form of self-help group served to meet the need of the refugee victims of torture for a sense of belonging with others who truly understood the events they had experienced. Many of these rap groups focused on a recounting of the experience of torture, recognizing that a reliving or revivification of the experiences was an important part of the healing process for PTSD. They also dealt with past and current issues of guilt and relationships. Recognizing the problems of using traditional group models, and observing the successes of the "rap groups," many professionals integrated the two. In these self-help groups, professional workers are not so much leaders as they are facilitators and instructors who understand the veterans' problems and who encourage the development of trust and support among group members.

Several therapeutic mechanisms are at work in such self-help groups. First, they serve as an island of support and understanding for the group members. This unique support they feel from each other leads to an exploration and reconsideration of the feelings they have denied or repressed around their experience of torture. The realization itself that they are not the only ones who have encountered problems is healing.

Second, such self-help groups provide the refugee victims of torture, who generally have difficulty in forming meaningful relationships with an opportunity to form meaningful relationships with the one group whose members they can trust. This renewed ability to form relationships is often transferable to other important people in their lives, promoting further adjustment.

A third important benefit of self-help groups is the exploration of guilt feelings. Survivor guilt and guilt in response to actions taken during experience of torture are powerful contributors to the poor adjustment of these refugee victims. The self-help groups provide these victims of torture with a safe environment to express their feelings to a nonjudgmental and accepting audience; thus allowing them to re- examine their guilt feelings, assess their value and accuracy, and explore alternative ways of dealing with them. Once their guilt is alleviated, group members can often move on to other issues which they had not been able to face as long as guilt was the dominant emotion (Egendorf, 1975).

The self-help groups also promote the expression of such other feelings as anger. The victims of torture usually have unexpressed anger towards society, authority figures, and family members who cannot understand what they have experienced. The group allows them to explore these feelings. Constriction of affect is another problem which can be alleviated by a setting which allows the victims of torture to bring forth emotions that have been repressed since the torture.

Since most victims of torture find it easier to discuss their experience with other victims than with professionals without such experience, it is often advisable to use a victim of torture as a co-counselor in self-help groups. This also is a gesture to demonstrate that they are worthy of trust. This co-leader has proven to be an invaluable resource for introducing the professional counselor to the lore and language of the refugee torture experience, and a guard against members' effort to deceive the professional counselor.

In general, the self-help groups have proven to be one of the most effective treatments for victims of torture suffering post-traumatic stress. Overall, they "help each member to realize that self-inflicted pain must stop—that they must get on with the process of daily living." Moreover, they provide a challenge for counselors working with these groups. They must face the anger and suspicion of the refugee victims of torture, and they must be able to cope with their own reactions to experience of torture. Working with such groups also demands a special knowledge of post-traumatic stress and the refugee experiences of torture.

Conclusion

To successfully rebuild families in cultural transition, the fostering and nurturing of self-help, at global level, family and community level, and among sub-groups that share common concerns, is a necessary and worthwhile investment, alongside culturally relevant and competent mental health and resettlement professional services.

References

Borkman, T. (1989). *Self-help groups at the turning point: Emerging egalitarian alliances with the formal health care system?* Paper presented at the Association for Voluntary Action Scholars, Seattle.

Brunch, J. (Ed.). (1980). *Refugee resettlement resource book: A Guide to federal programs and national support projects to assist in refugee resettlement.* Department of State, Washington, DC: Office of Refugee Resettlement.

Bui, D. D. (1981). *The Indochinese mutual assistance associations: Characteristics, composition, capacity building needs and future directions.* Indochinese Refugee Action Center, Washington, DC.

CAL (1981). *A future for us all.* Washington, DC: Center for Applied Linguistics.

Dressler, W., & Bernal, H. (1982). Acculturation and stress in a low income Pueto Rican community. *Journal of Human Stress*, *8*(3), 32-38.

Egendorf, A. (1975). Vietnam veteran rap groups and themes of postwar life. *Journal of Social Issues*, *4*, 111-124.

Finck, J. (1983). *The Indo-Chinese in America: Progress toward self-sufficiency.* New York: United States Committee for Refugees, Inc.

Fong, L. Y. S. (1992). Strengths and problems of S.E. Asian refugee families, In P. L. Lin, W. Y. Chao, T. L. Johnson, J. Persell, & A. Tsang (Eds.). *Family: East and West (pp. 15–24).* Indianapolis: University of Indianapolis.

Glasser, L., & Suroviak, J. (1988). Social group work in a soup kitchen: Mobilizing the strengths of the guests. *Social Work With Groups, 11*(4), 95-109.

Goodman, C. C. (1991). Perceived social support for caregiving: Measuring the benefit of self-help support group participation, *Journal of Gerentological Social Work, 16*(3/4), 163-175.

Goodman, G. (1990). Evaluation of a model of self-help telephone program: Impact on natural networks. *Social Work, 35*(6), 556- 152.

Gressard, C. F. (1986, May). Self-help groups for Vietnam veterans experiencing post traumatic stress disorder. *Journal For Specialists In Group Work.*

House, J. S. (1981). *Work, Stress & Social Support.* Reading: MA: Addison-Wesley.

Katz, A. (1965). Self-help groups. In (Eds.), *Social Work Dictionary*. New York: NASW.

Mahalik, J. R., & Kivlighan, D. M., Jr. (1988). *Journal of Counseling Psychology, 35*(3), 237-242.

Muro, J. J., & Dinkmeyer, D. C. (1977). *Counseling in the elementary and middle schools.* Dubuque, IA: Brown.

Rappaport, J. (1981). In praise of paradox: A social policy of empowerment over prevention *American Journal of Community Psychology, 9*, 1-25.

Renard, D. A. (1990). Mutual assistance associations: Refugee self-help groups play key role in America. *Perspectives On Refugee Resettlement*, N8, March.

Rogers, A., & Tartaglia, L. J. (1990). Constricting resources: a Black self-help initiative. *Administration In Social Work*,14(2), 125-37.

Shotts, K. F. (1981). Indo-Chinese mutual assistance association: Time for a new role. Texas, unpublished manuscript.

Strother, J.A., & Harvill, R. (1986, May). Self-help groups for relocated adolescent students: A model for school counselors. *Journal of Specialist in Social Work*, 121-127.

Toffler, A. (1980). *The third wave.* New York: William Morrow.

Tunnard, J. (1989). Local self-help groups for families of children in public care. *Child Welfare*, *58*(2), 126-130.

Article 24

Elderly Chinese Immigrants and Service Advocacy in Cleveland, Ohio

Julian C. Chow
Li-tao C. Hsieh

Introduction

The 1987 Amendment to the Older Americans Act (OAA) specifies that the focus of services should be provided to low-income, minority individuals with particular attention to cultural differences among these groups (Administration on Aging, 1987). Asian American elderly, however, have been disadvantaged regarding receiving OAA programs (Lee, 1986; Lee et al., 1991). Twenty years after the 1971 White House Conference on Aging and 10 years after the 1981 mini-White House Conference on the Pacific/Asian Elderly, our understanding of the Asian elderly and the services provided to these groups has *NOT* improved significantly. One major reason is the lack of research on the Asian elderly living in this country.

Recognizing the lack of information in both public and private services about the Asian elderly, the purpose of this article is two-fold: First, to address the issue of intra-group differences by profiling the Chinese elderly and their needs in the city of Cleveland, a mid-west metropolitan city in the United States; second, to document how a local initiative effort can be organized in order to address some of these issues, and to develop culturally sound services for the Chinese elderly and their families through the OAA public funding support.

Research on Asian American Elderly

Despite the fact that Asian Americans were the fastest growing ethnic group in the United States during the 1980s, the government has had little interest in obtaining information concerning Asian Americans. Not until the 1980 census were "Asians" included as a separate racial group for reporting (Kim, 1983). It took another decade (1990) for the Current Population Survey (CPS) to desegregate Asians from the "Other" racial category and to include them as a separate group among white, black, and Hispanic in selected reports (O'Hare & Felt, 1991). The lack of accurate information about Asian-Americans has largely handicapped researchers, service providers and planners in adequately addressing the service needs and issues that Asians face in their daily living situations.

The Asian elderly, in particular, are mostly victimized by lack of public attention. While Lum (1983) has appropriately described the Asian elderly as being in "quadruple jeopardy"—poor, minority, old and non-English speaking—the stereotypic labels of the "model minority," the belief is "that Asian-American aged do not have any problems, that Asian Americans are able to take care of their own, and that Asian-American aged do not need or desire aid in any form" (*The Asian American Elderly*, 1972), still the predominant misconceptions of the Asian elderly living in the United States. As a result, few programs are designed to assist the Asian elderly (Cheung, 1989; Fujii, 1976; Lum, 1983). Furthermore, studies have repeatedly found that the service utilization of the Asian elderly is extremely low, as the services are inappropriate and ill-suited to serve their needs and cultural background (Cheng, 1978; Cheung, 1989; Fujii, 1976; Lee, 1986; Lum et al., 1980; Wu, 1975).

Chinese Elderly in Cleveland

Compared to other cities like New York and San Francisco, where large populations of Chinese Americans are located, the Chinese population in the greater Cleveland area is relatively small. According to the 1980 census, there were 2,400 Chinese in the Greater Cleveland area. In 1990, the Chinese population had grown to 4,363, an increase of 82%.

The demographic composition of Chinese in Cleveland differs from national trends. The census showed that 10% of the Chinese population in Cleveland was elderly (60 years old and over). The overall average of Chinese elderly 60 years old and over in the United States in 1990 is 7%. Therefore, the larger percentage of Chinese elderly in the Chinese community in Cleveland requires more service needs to be met.

The 1980 PUMS[1] showed that 84% of the overall Chinese population in Cleveland was foreign-born. According to long-time local residents and community leaders, however, it is estimated that the percentage of foreign-born elderly may be higher than the reported 84%. They have observed that many families with elderly members have immigrated to Cleveland in the last decade. Nevertheless, it appears that the Chinese elderly comprise a significant portion of the Cleveland Chinese population, and that they are more likely to be foreign-born than the average Chinese elderly in the nation.

While the tendency to "lump" multiple nationalities and ethnicities together and to classify them as a definite ethnic group for reasons of simplification is strong, in actual service delivery and planning purposes there should be a disaggregation effort in order to examine the intergroup differences within the population. The fact is that immigrants coming from different parts of China would have differences in language usage, health care beliefs, dietary habits, and family resources, just to name a few. More importantly, the immigration history can be very different for those Chinese elderly who migrated to the United States at an old age as compared to those who come at a younger age.

At present, the Chinese elderly in Cleveland can be qualitatively divided into two groups: The Chinatown-connected Chinese elderly and the non-Chinatown-connected Chinese elderly. The non-Chinatown connected Chinese elderly are composed of retirees, most of them being scholars, professionals, businessmen, and newly arrived elderly family members from Taiwan, Hong Kong, Mainland China, and South East Asian countries. They tend to live in the suburban areas and use Chinatown only for eating in the Chinese restaurants and shopping for Chinese groceries. Among the Chinatown-connected Chinese elderly, there are two major divisions: Old Overseas Chinese (in Chinese, we call them Lo Wah Kiu) and Newly Arrived Elderly Family Members. It is the focus of this paper to discuss the needs of the Chinatown-connected group.

Old Overseas Chinese

Lo Wah Kiu refers to the group of foreign-born Chinese who came to the United States before 1965, and who are now quite old. The majority originated in the rural area of the Kwangtung province. As a group, the Lo Wah Kiu are known for their proverbial frugality. They dress and live modestly. Even those who have been successful economically still live in less-than-comfortable houses. They do not see any necessity to involve themselves in the American society. On the contrary, they believe in the maintenance of Chinese customs and the Chinese way of life in America—eating Chinese food, speaking Chinese, socializing with Chinese-speaking, older immigrants, and raising their children in the Chinese way (strict discipline with emphasis on filial piety). However, poor parental and family relationships can often be found among these elderly.

Not all overseas Chinese elderly are successful, however. Also, many of these elderly are less fortunate and can barely make their living on a daily basis. This group of elderly may be widows, widowers, or bachelors. Many of these elderly, now in their eighties, are those who were denied family formation and citizenship rights due to the exclusionistic immigration policies during the first two decades of the century (Lum, 1983). They stayed in the Chinese enclave and made their living in several "Oriental" businesses, such as hand laundries or restaurants. Some of the elderly in this group, though they have been living in the U.S. for over half a century, are still illiterate and cannot speak English.

Because of their experiences as being the targets of discrimination in the United States, this group of elderly are the most alienated and disadvantaged. Although many of them should be well-qualified for assistance, their names, perhaps, have never appeared on any of the public or private service agencies' clientele profiles. Isolation, loneliness, and lack of resources are just a few of the many difficulties with which these groups of elderly must deal. Many of these elderly are living in poverty and in substandard housing conditions. Because of malnutrition, most of them suffer from medical illness and disease.

Case Example #1: Mrs. Wong

In her 80's, Mrs. Wong represents the type of Chinese elderly who require the most help: inner-city resident, poor, living alone, illiterate, unable to speak English, and retired without employment benefits. She needs assistance to apply for Social Security widow benefits, help regarding housing and legal matters, medical care, and counselling for family relationships.

Case Example #2: Mr. and Mrs. Lee

Mr. and Mrs. Lee are former Chinese restaurant owners in their 80s. They moved from their son's home in New York City, electing to live alone rather than to suffer from the differences in lifestyle and having to deal with the role-reversal associated with living with their son's family. They requested assistance in applying for government-subsidized senior housing. As they spoke limited English, they had no idea what the process entailed.

Newly Arrived Elderly Family Members

Since the immigration reform in 1965 which emphasizes family unification, the number of Chinese immigrants has increased substantially. Many immigrants, after they become citizens of the United States, will apply for their parents' immigration, who then apply for the immigration of their other children, all for family unification. Ikels (1986) has observed that since 1977, 51-61% of relatives sponsored by adult citizens of Chinese ancestry to immigrate to the United States were parents. Ong (1987), in his study of the Chinese immigrant cohorts during 1983-1985 in three Chinatowns, found that the median age at the time of entry for this group was 61; 59% of them were 60 years old or older; two-thirds were females; and one-third were widowed.

Studies have shown that the newly arrived foreign-born elderly have great difficulty in adjusting to life in the United States (Chan, 1983; Chan, 1988; Chen 1979; Weeks & Cuellar, 1983; Ikels, 1983, 1986; Wu, 1975). When the immigration experience comes in the later years of one's life, the conflict of cultural values is substantial. These elderly commonly describe themselves living in the United States as being "blind, deaf, crippled, and dumb." Coping with an entirely "strange" environment, getting bored in the quiet residential areas, confronting the different expectations of themselves and their children, and hoping to retain their dignity after losing their social role are only a few of the many obstacles that these elderly have to face immediately after their arrival.

Case Example #3: Mr. and Mrs. Chang

Mr. and Mrs. Chang, in their early 60s, well-educated, having had a close-knit family relationship, came to join their children based on the traditional family value that adult children should take care of their parents.

Mr. and Mrs. Chang are confused by the treatment they have received since their arrival. Through their previous visits, they realize that living together with their children was an option far from ideal. There were differences in lifestyle, conflicts of daily habits, and differing opinions in child-rearing. However, when they migrated here and a separate residence was arranged for them, they felt acutely rejected. Visits from children and grandchildren are never frequent enough. Loneliness and poor self-image (especially due to language barriers and transportation difficulties) overwhelm them. For example, one day they took a wrong bus and wandered for four hours before they arrived home at 10 p.m. This caused their son, and all the people concerned, a great deal of worry. In their effort to make adjustments, the Changs are enrolled in an English-as-a-second-language class. They also want desperately to take driving lessons, but this was discouraged by their children for safety reasons.

Case Example #4: Mr. and Mrs. Woo

Mr. and Mrs. Woo, in their 80s, are refugees from Vietnam under the sponsorship of their daughter, Pat. Both Pat and her husband work full-time, and they have a teenage son. Accommodating her parents adds a great deal of physical pressure, financial stress, and family tension. A main source of problems involves the matter of cooking. Cooking Chinese food has become a daily responsibility for Pat, and shopping at the Chinese grocery store has become a major weekend event that requires substantial time and effort. Services that we have provided include assistance with SSI and Medicaid applications, and providing housing information and counselling to the primary caregiver. Half-a-year later, Mr. and Mrs. Woo have moved to a one-bedroom apartment that is 10 minutes away from their daughter's home.

America is a country of immigrants, and all ethnic groups have gone through stages of adjustment to the new environment. Adjustment is a difficult process, particularly for older immigrants, whose needs and views are different from those of the young. They are vulnerable to suffering from the cultural values conflict in their adjustment to a new country. Traditional Chinese values of aging portray a positive image of the elderly. Filial piety, respect for the aged, and support of the aged, are societal values that promote caring relationships between children and older parents (Cheung, 1989).

However, due to the influence of the new culture, the extended family caring structure is difficult to maintain. Having children may not guarantee future care and security for the parents. The parents' position as elders may not entitle them to a significant social or economic position. While a large portion of Chinese adult children still deeply hold the traditional values of respect and care for their parents, individualism and a nuclear family structure are emphasized. As a result, the problems of the Chinese elderly are beyond individual and family resources, and require public coordination and support.

There have been many unrecognized service needs among Chinese elderly persons because they may not want to rely on others, refuse to accept assistance, do not know how to ask for services, have difficulty in speaking English, or are unaware of the availability of social services. The language barrier is a major reason for their refusal to ask for services. Also, a strong sense of family responsibility arouses a feeling of shame when asking for external help.

To insure accessibility of services for the Chinese elderly and other groups, outreach efforts should be incorporated into service delivery. Crucial to service delivery is the need to provide a bilingual and bicultural professional staff, to coordinate and implement social services. It is important to accept the Chinese clients' values rather than to impose "new" values upon them. Our focus must be on building up the family support system, and fostering communication and understanding among the different generations. Chinese elderly are peer-group oriented. They like to spend time with other Chinese persons, and to join activities within the Chinese community or Chinese associations. The emphasis would be socialization toward independence rather than the encouragement of dependency (Cheung, 1989; Ikels, 1983; Lee, 1986).

Chinese Initiative Program: A Local Effort

Throughout its history, there have been no bilingual services available to the Chinese elderly in Cleveland. As a result, many of these elderly have never been served due to the aforementioned barriers such as language difficulty, lack of information, inaccessibility, and culturally-insensitive and -inappropriate services. A grass-roots initiative approach has been used in response to this shortcoming situation in the late 1980s.

In early 1990, due to the recent increase of the elderly population, a group of Chinese elderly, most of whom are Chinatown-connected, organized the first Chinese senior citizens association in Cleveland. The association was originally formed to provide self-support and social gathering activities for the Chinese elderly. Some board members of the association, however, recognizing the insufficient attention and resources available to the Chinese elderly, have also actively played an advocacy role and have demanded further support from the city and the state government. They have successfully approached and generated interest at the Western Reserve Area Agency on Aging (WRAAA), the official funding agency of the Older Americans Act of 1965 (OAA) in the Cleveland area. During the same period, the WRAAA was funded by the Cleveland Foundation for a Minority Targeting Project in outreaching to the traditionally underserved elderly population. The result has been the development of the Chinese Initiative Program (CIP), under the support of WRAAA.

By successfully lobbying to the needs of the Chinese elderly, the WRAAA has assigned a planner and a consultant to the project, both of whom specialized in minority targeting and outreach. The WRAAA has also allocated a special budget to hire a Chinese researcher to conduct an in-depth need assessment study of the Chinese elderly. The researcher then became a staff member of the CIP. Two social work interns were also assigned to assist in program planning and development of the project.

A first effort of the WRAAA has been to call for assistance from the Chinese activists in the community. With their support, an Ad Hoc Steering Committee was formed as a planning and advisory body to the CIP. The Committee includes representatives from various local

Chinese associations, Chinese residents, service providers, a lawyer, planners, and researchers. The Committee was aimed at identifying resources and providing direction of services to the Chinese elderly in Cleveland. Four task force groups—health care, social/legal services, nutrition, and planning—have been organized. Each member of the task group has carefully studied his or her area of interest and provided detailed recommendations to the Committee.

In order to implement the overall plan in a strategic fashion, the appropriate prioritization of services became necessary and crucial. It was believed that the Chinatown-connected, old overseas Chinese who are not only the most disadvantaged groups but also the most visible group, should be the target population. It was further decided that among the four task force groups, the nutrition project, which would be funded directly under the auspices of WRAAA, should be pursued as the top priority.

The Chinese Senior Citizen Association, responsible for the nutrition task group, has been working closely with the WRAAA to develop the special congregated meals nutrition program. The project was conceptualized as a grass-roots, local initiative generated by the Chinese elderly themselves. After about a year of planning and organizing effort, a Chinese nutrition meals program was implemented at a Chinese restaurant in the winter of 1991. This is the first such program of this kind for any Asian-American elderly in the history of Ohio and received high publicity in the state and local communities. Fifty Chinese senior citizens enjoy their culturally-specific meals on a daily basis (Western Reserve Area Agency on Aging, 1992). The success of the nutrition project, although it is still in its infancy stage, can be utilized as the foundation for the planning of other services. The strategy is becoming clear that by serving the old overseas Chinese as a core function, additional culturally-sound programs could then be developed in order to outreach and to connect to the larger Chinese elderly community, including the newly arrived senior citizens.

At the time of this writing, a proposal for subsequent funding has been underway which includes the further support of the nutrition program, a transportation escort for the non-Chinatown elderly, and a comprehensive needs assessment study for the development of a senior citizen cultural center. Funding has also been identified for the hiring of an Executive Director who will be responsible for project coordination, concrete service provision, and further development of the CIP to include a full scope of programs and services available to the Chinese elderly in the Cleveland area.

The commitment of the WRAAA, and the enthusiasm of the people who have been volunteering their professional and personal time over the past few years, have been key to the success of the CIP. The CIP holds a unique status in the history of the Chinese community in Cleveland. It represents the first time ever that the Chinese community has organized to work together to demand public funding support for their own needs from mainstream American service agencies. It also represents the cooperation of the grass roots approach with the support of a public agency. While the first step has now been taken, there is still a long road ahead.

References

Administration on Aging. (1987). *Older Americans Act of 1965, as Amended.* Washington, DC: Government Printing Office.

Asian American Elderly, The (White House Conference on Aging, 1971). Washington, DC: Government Printing Office.

Chan, F. (1988). To be old and Asian: An unsettled life in America. *Aging, 358,* 14-15.

Chan, K. (1983). Coping with aging and managing self-identity: The social world of the elderly Chinese women. *Canadian Ethnic Studies, 15,* 36-50.

Chen, P. (1979). A study of Chinese-American elderly residing in hotel rooms. *Social Casework, 60,* 89-95.

Cheng, E. (1978). *The elder Chinese.* San Diego, CA: San Diego State University, Center on Aging.

Cheung, M. (1989). Elderly Chinese living in the United States: Assimilation or adjustment? *Social Work, 34,* 457-461.

Fujii, S. (1976). Elderly Asian Americans and use of public services. *Social Casework, 57,* 202-207.

Ikels, C. (1986). Older immigrants and natural helpers. *Journal of Cross-Cultural Gerontology, 1,* 209-222.

Ikels, C. (1983). *Aging and adaptation: Chinese in Hong Kong and the United States.* Hamden, CT: Anchor Books.

Kim, P. (1983). Demography of the Asian-Pacific elderly: Selected problems and implications. In R. McNeely & J. Colen, (Eds.). *Aging in minority groups* (pp. 29-41). Beverly Hill, CA: Sage Publications.

Lee, J. (1986). Asian American elderly: A neglected minority group. *Journal of Gerontological Social Work, 9(4),* 103-116.

Lum, D. (1983). Asian-Americans and their aged. In R. McNeely & J. Colen, (Eds.). *Aging in minority groups* (pp. 85-94). Beverly Hill, CA: Sage Publications.

Lum, D., Cheung, L., Cho, E., Tang, T., & Yau, H. (1980). The psychosocial needs of the Chinese elderly. *Social Casework, 61,* 100-106.

O'Hare W., & Felt, J. (1991). *Asian Americans: America's fastest growing minority group.* Washington, DC: Population Reference Bureau, Inc.

Ong, P. (1987). *1983-85 Chinese immigrants in three Chinatowns.* Los Angeles, CA: Asian American Studies and Graduate School of Architecture and Urban Planning, University of California, Los Angeles.

Weeks, J., & Cuellar, J. (1983). Isolation of older persons: The influence of immigration and length of residence. *Research on Aging, 5,* 369-388.

Western Reserve Area Agency on Aging. (1992). *Final report: Minority targeting project.* Cleveland, Ohio: Author.

Wu, F. (1975). Mandarin-speaking aged Chinese in the Los Angeles area. *The Gerontologist, 15*, 271-275.

[1] At this time, the 1990 Public Use Microdata Samples (PUMS) census data regarding the Chinese elderly is not yet available.

Article 25

The Effects of Nutrition on Family Dynamics

Patricia A. Cook
Nancy E. O'Dell

There have been dramatic changes in the diets of most people in the technologically advanced sections of the world, much of it due to the changes in family structure in the past forty to fifty years. During World War II, women went to work outside the home in larger numbers than at any other time in history, and when the war ended, women stayed in jobs outside the home. In the early 70's slightly over 40% of the women with children worked outside the home. By the beginning of the 80's, the percentage had risen to over 50%, and it has been gradually but consistently rising since then. Because "Mother" worked outside the home, there were fewer meals prepared that took large amounts of time. Women who were tired from working all day looked to the faster meal for their families in the evening; also, the affluence attendant to double pay checks contributed to the ability to buy "non-critical" types of food. People were eating, not just for the necessity of staying alive and healthy, but for the fun and pleasure of eating. Junk food became a staple. Other factors such as the proliferation of television, made additional contributions to the snacking habits of the modern family. For whatever reason, the dietary habits of the United States have taken severe turns for the worse, and one of the areas significantly affected, according to many researchers, has been in the field of behavior.

Not only the diets, but the family structure itself has changed dramatically, to the point that textbooks today make reference to the "typical family" as being non-existent. Children are being referred to psychologists and psychiatrists and to temporary health facilities for rehabilitation in ever increasing numbers. While medical research has lengthened the lifespan of the average person, discomfort and illness, both physical and mental, have kept pace. One of the reasons proposed for this malaise is the worsening diet of average adults and the children. We are what we eat. It may be that simple. But this platitude may be more profound than it would appear on first hearing. The philosopher/physician Hippocrates some 2000 years ago advocated the use of a variety of foods and the changing of diet as a method of curing illness. This is particularly ironic inasmuch as neither the average physician trained in the United States today nor the typical family counselor takes a course in nutrition or diet as it affects health or behavior.

We became interested in foods and drinks as they affect learning and behavior and family interaction twenty years ago, when we went to a conference in Ohio dealing with delinquent youth. From the testimony of a corrections officer who demonstrated the lowest rate of recidivism in Ohio, to the admonishment of psychiatrist Abram Hoffer, who stated that a large number of the people suffering from mental illness in typical hospitals could be helped by nutritional changes, we heard of techniques and methods of working with behavioral and learning problems in a new way. While we do not claim, nor did the physicians, corrections officers, or clinicians at the Ohio conference claim, that nutritional changes will cure every ailment, this approach offers another tool—something else to try—in working with children at risk and with families seeking approaches toward better relationships and fewer crises. It is important to realize that this approach offers a **drug-free** method—a solid plus in today's society.

Now, as we begin to talk about foods and their implications to health and family interaction, we must start with the ingestion of sugar. Let us define sugar for this discussion. Sugar, as we will use it for this presentation, refers to sucrose, especially the refined version—granulated, white, "table" sugar. Surveys have revealed that the average American consumes almost 150 pounds of sugar per year. While some people immediately protest that they do not eat that much sugar, they may fail to realize that sugar is in ketchup, salad dressing, bread, chewing gum, most cereals, most canned goods—indeed, in most processed and packaged foods, as well as in colas, malts, ice cream and most soft drinks. Sugar is, of course, the main ingredient in candies and cookies and is high in cakes and pies and doughnuts.

One hundred and fifty pounds of sugar is significantly higher consumption than our grandparents had, and as the consumption of sugar has increased, so has the incidence of diabetes, heart trouble, arteriosclerosis, and high blood pressure. One researcher, Dr. Emanuel Cheraskin, (Cheraskin & Ringsdorf, 1976) at the University of Alabama, found sugar to "attack" the white blood cells (WBC), the body's immunological protection system. Cheraskin found that the typical WBC requires about four hours to "recoup" from what he calls the sugar attack. What this says for practical purposes is that the person who has a doughnut and coffee with sugar is more likely to catch cold, and more likely to sustain such a cold than the person without the sugar intake.

We find that sugar "triggers" some children into a form of hyperactivity (Smith, 1976). What we don't seem to realize is the amount of sugar in foods to which we don't actually add sugar......the typical piece of chewing gum, for example, has a 1/2 teaspoon of sugar. Bubblegum has even more. We have seen children practically swinging from the light fixtures after chewing one piece of bubble gum. We assume you are aware of the family problems created by the presence of a hyperactive child. They are a trial to everyone, **including themselves.** We had one child tell us that he felt as if he were "running inside" —surely not a pleasant feeling for anyone.

Sugar is also often considered a contributor to anemia. Sucrose is said to contain "naked calories." That is, it brings energy, but no nutrition. Since it does not bring nutrition with it, but requires Vitamin B-12 for metabolizing, it then robs the body's other sources of Vitamin B-12 for its own use. As Vitamin B-12 lowers in the body, the resulting condition is a form of anemia. Instead of prescribing extra iron in such cases, many nutritionists advise the physician to lower the sugar intake of their patients (Mark, 1989).

One of the most insidious problems contributed to by the large intake of sugar is that of hypoglycemia, or low blood sugar. Now, it seems contradictory to say that eating sugar contributes to **low** blood sugar, but that is a major theory in this area. The pancreas is a gland which helps the body regulate the utilization of sugar. The enzyme produced by the pancreas is called insulin. The usual theory proposed is that as the ingestion of sugar increases, especially up to 150 pounds per year, the pancreas over-reacts, dumping too much insulin into the bloodstream. The insulin then lowers the sugar level, frequently to a point of hypoglycemia, or, literally, low blood sugar. When the blood sugar is too low, such symptoms as headache, stomach ache, irritability, disorientation, blurred vision, depression, and many others can occur. A woman rose from her chair during one of our presentations (Cook & O'Dell, 1990) and told us her story—she was chronically depressed......didn't want to get up in the morning......felt terrible most of the time. She went to her physician, who knew that the woman and her husband had been wanting to start a family, but had not been successful. The physican advised that they be patient. Some time went by, and the woman did, indeed, become pregnant. Surely she would be happy? No, she was still depressed. Her physician told her the depression came from the hormonal changes in her body, and to be patient. The baby was born, and the woman was even more depressed, even though the baby was healthy and care was uncomplicated. She was told that she was now suffering from post-partum blues, again undergoing hormonal changes. Two years went by, and the woman was unhappy and unpleasant (her own description). She went in to a clinic for a check-up and was told that any woman with a two year old child had a right to be depressed. This was not funny to her, and she began to despair of ever feeling well again. She finally went into a hospital for a series of tests, which provided no answers. The staff recommended a hysterectomy. She was twenty-eight years old. She and her husband decided, however, regardless of her age, that life was not full as it was, and they agreed to the hysterectomy. Before the surgery, she met an old family friend, a physician, and stopped to talk with him. She told him the story, and he said the problem sounded like low blood sugar to him. He asked if she had ever had a glucose tolerance test. She replied that she had undergone every test in the book, but she did not recognize his description of the glucose tolerance test - the GTT. For this test one takes no food or water from midnight. Early in the morning a blood sample is taken and analyzed; then the patient is given some glucose - pure sugar - to drink, and the blood is sampled again. Blood samples are taken five to six times during the next few hours. The blood sugar will usually rise with the intake of glucose, then will begin to drop as the hours go on without additional food. The technicians and physicians who are knowledgeable about hypoglycemia know to study the level to which the blood sugar drops, the quickness of the descent, and the condition of the patient during the episode. Some physicians look only at the score and will say that the person is fine if the blood sugar drops no lower than 50 or 60 (a clinical measurement of glucose in the blood), but the most knowledgeable take into account the other factors as well. These physicians feel that the person is experiencing low blood sugar if the blood sugar drops to 75 or below, or if they experience a dramatic drop rather than a gradual one, or if they feel rotten - - any or all, or a combination, of these factors. Now, our friendly woman who was telling us the story, said that her blood sugar dropped to 50, and that she felt terrible, and that the drop was not gradual, but precipitous. She was put on a hypoglycemic diet, had reached the grand age of 33 at the time of this telling, and reported that she felt wonderful.

We hope you are connecting these dietary descriptions to the dynamics of the family. Family life with a hyperactive or anemic child is not easy. One may be wild, the other lethargic. Neither is frequently pleasant to be around, and discipline, in the usual sense, doesn't change the behavior. Children or adults in the throes of low blood sugar can make life miserable for themselves and for those around them.

We have had families tell us that they can't, or won't, or don't speak to each other in the mornings or maybe in the late afternoons, when people are getting up from fasting all night or when they are coming in from school or work, because everyone is so crabby. We suspect low blood sugar in such cases.

There is no medication for hypoglycemia, just the changing of habits and the diet mentioned in the story we just recounted. Primary recommendations include avoidance of sugar–candy bars, malts, milk shakes, gum, sugared cereal, pies, cakes, and caffeine, which also lowers blood sugar. We recommend having sandwiches ready for the late afternoon arrivals and juice quickly available for the early morning grouch. A viable substitute for sugar is fructose, a natural fruit sugar which much of the literature recommends as less demanding on the pancreas. A severe or "brittle" hypoglycemic should avoid all types of sugar as well as caffeine, just as the diabetic does. Stress also lowers the blood sugar, so we advise easy, stress free lives! Another aid is to eat small but frequent meals, again sugar/caffeine free. The frequent snacking of nutritious foods—nuts, fruit, celery, vegetables—can help maintain a stable, appropriate blood sugar level.

Now, sugar is not the only substance which can be harmful to people. The substance we look to after we check for sugar intake is milk. Some nutritionists say that cow's milk is for calves. We have seen children become almost hyperactive from milk; we have seen some become lethargic. Some people get rashes, red ears, flushed cheeks. Dark circles or puffy areas under the eyes are other signs of a milk sensitivity. Many of the children we have seen have had chronic running noses and sniffles or congestion. Milk is suspected of contributing significantly to upper respiratory problems, including earaches and ear infections. Some children seem to have diarrhea, some are constipated, from milk. One child, whose mother wrote a remarkable book about him (*Fighting for Tony*, by Mary Callahan) was classified incorrectly as autistic. When Tony's mother, a nurse, took all milk and milk products from his diet, Tony became a normal little boy.

We just mentioned the main corrective approach to milk sensitivity: removing milk and milk products such as cheese and ice cream from the diet. Another approach is to give a commercially prepared enzyme along with the milk product; this approach seems to work well when it is the lack of the enzyme which is causing the problem. Dr. Doris J. Rapp, (Rapp, 1986) an allergist in New York, uses a type of treatment in which she desensitizes the child by introducing small amounts of the product into the system in the manner of people's taking allergy shots to build up the body's ability to resist the allergen or sensitivity trigger. She does the same thing with milk. Yet we must remember that it is very important for everyone, especially growing children, to obtain enough calcium in their systems.

While there is some debate as to whether or not cow's milk metabolizes into usable calcium, most nutritionists think that a supply does translate into calcium. If that source is reduced, another source of calcium must be provided. Other sources of calcium are green, leafy vegetables and orange juice. While Dr. Cheraskin and other researchers maintain that such natural sources are best, they will recommend tablet supplements if the natural sources are rejected.

Another aspect of behavior as it relates to children and family dynamics is one called cerebral allergy, or addictive allergy. The theory is that we can become addicted to a substance to which we are actually sensitive. A quick story illustrates this phenomenon: a three year old boy named Jeremy was brought to us because his behavior was so terrible that he was more and more difficult to live with, and he was about to be dismissed from his preschool class. He was the typical "Jekyll and Hyde."—lovable and sweet one minute—throwing a tantrum the next. After talking with the parents for almost an hour, we learned that Jeremy's favorite drink was orange juice. Indeed, his family was happy that he seemed to LOVE orange juice, rather than begging for soft drinks. We heard that he drank orange juice at breakfast, as a ten o'clock snack, at lunch, as a four o'clock snack, at dinner, and at bedtime. As we plotted a time-study of tantrums and other variables, we found that he was most obstreperous shortly before juice times. We suggested the possibility that he was craving something in the juice, possibly citric acid. After he drank some juice, we surmised that his addiction was temporarily satisfied. We recommended to his parents that they remove all foods/ drinks containing citric acid from his diet, keeping notes about his behavior. Citric acid is in many foods and drinks, so such a task would not be easy. They were willing to try almost anything, however, and this didn't seem too difficult. They called us ten days later and said that they had had a terrible week and a half. The youngster had thrown tantrums almost around the clock. On the eleventh morning, however, he had arisen a different child. The compulsive, explosive behavior was gone. This lasted several days, and they decided it would be "safe" to have dinner with his maternal grandparents at a local restaurant. The child was wonderful all during dinner, the mother reported, but on the way home he "exploded," rocking back and forth in the car and crawling over everyone. At home, she went immediately to the telephone and called the restaurant, asking the manager to name the ingredients in the food Jeremy had eaten. When the manager came to the description of a "natural fruit punch," the second ingredient was citric acid. The family began a continuous diet with Jeremy that was closely monitored for citric acid. They did well until the Christmas holidays came, and Jeremy became slightly agitated again. We asked if the pre-school (where he was still in attendance) gave the children peppermint candy canes as prizes, and were informed that they did. Peppermint contains citrus acid.

The point that we hope to have made is for you to consider diet as a useful tool in changing a child's (or adult's) behavior. Look for clues such as times of day of persistent, objectionable behaviors, the food/drink ingested, family histories. Talk with a nutritionist. It is our firm belief that people are meant to feel well, and to be pleasant. Grumpiness, grouchiness, headaches, and stomachaches are not natural. It may be possible to change some negative behaviors and unpleasant family interactions by something as simple as a change in diet.[1]

References

Cheraskin, E., & Ringsdorf, W. (1976). *Psychodietetics*. New York: Bantam Books.

Cook, P., & O'Dell, N. (1990, October). *Biochemical aberrations and dietary interventions, or what they eat is what you get.* Paper presented at state (Indiana) convention of Council for Exceptional Children (CEC).

Mark, V. H. (1989). *Brain power*. Boston: Houghton Mifflin Company.

Rapp, D. J. (1986). *The impossible child*. Buffalo, NY: Practical Allergy Research Foundation.

Smith, L. (1979). *Feed your kids right*. New York: McGraw-Hill.

Endnotes

1. We make a statement at our presentations that some of these references are getting old....the ones we continue to use, however, have become classics in their field, and we haven't found any articles or books that give the information any better. We usually present a booklist at our presentations, and we make a point to have some very recent additions.....the information is really the same, however. The topic stays controversial, but we find new information available to support the old.

About the Editors

Phylis Lan Lin is Director of Asian Programs and Professor of Sociology at the University of Indianapolis. Professor Lin holds a Ph.D. in Sociology from the University of Missouri—Columbia in 1972. Her professional publications are in the areas of medical sociology, organizational behavior, and marriage and the family. She is the author and co-author of 12 books and numerous articles. Recently, she co-edited *Families: East and West* and *Marriage and the Family in Chinese Societies: Selected Readings*. Among her leadership roles, she has organized and chaired *International Symposium on China* and *International Symposium on Families: East and West*.

Wen-hui Tsai is Professor of Sociology at Indiana University-Purdue University at Fort Wayne. Professor Tsai received his Ph.D. in Sociology from the University of California at Berkley in 1974. He has published 19 books and over 70 articles on topics related to comparative sociology and cross-cultural studies, including *In Making China Modernized* (1994), *Comparative Social Structures between China and Taiwan* (1992), *Social Change* (1992), *Sociological Theories* (1992), and *Marriage and the Family* (1989).

About the Authors

(1) **Phylis Lan Lin,** Ph.D., is a Professor of Sociology in the Social Sciences Department, University of Indianapolis, Indianapolis, Indiana, USA.

(2) **Vera S. Maass**, Ph.D., is a Psychologist and Owner of the Living Skills Institute, Inc., Indianapolis, Indiana, USA.

(3) **Salvatore Imbrogno**, Ph.D., is a Professor of Social Work in the College of Social Work at Ohio State University, Columbus, Ohio, USA.

(4) **Tsun-yin Luo**, Ph. D., is an Associate Professor in the Department of Social Psychology, The World College of Journalism and Communications, Taiwan, Republic of China.

(5) **Felecia M. Briscoe**, Ed.D., is an Assistant Professor of Education at the Concord College, Athens, West Virginia, USA.

(5) **Judith Frankel**, Ph.D., is an Associate Professor in the Department of Educational Foundations, University of Cincinnati, Cincinnati, Ohio, USA.

(5) **Dolores Stegelin**, Ph.D., is an Associate Professor at the University of Georgia, Athens, Georgia, USA.

(6) **Maria V. Zolotukhina**, is a Fellow at the Institute of Ethnology and Anthropology of the Academy of Sciences of Russia in Moscow, Russia.

(6) **Maria G. Kotovskaya**, is a Fellow at the Institute of Ethnology and Anthropology of the Academy of Sciences of Russia in Moscow, Russia.

(6) **Nataliya V. Shalyguina**, is a Fellow at the Institute of Ethnology and Anthropology of the Academy of Sciences of Russia in Moscow, Russia.

(7) **James C. Hsiung**, Ph.D., is a Professor of International Politics, Department of Political Sciences, New York University, New York, USA.

(8) **Young-ju Chun**, is a Doctoral Candidate in Sociology, Purdue University, West Lafayette, Indiana, USA.

(8) **Shelley M. MacDermid**, Ph.D., is an Assistant Professor in the Department of Child Development and Family Studies, Purdue University, West Lafayette, Indiana, USA.

(9) **Elizabeth L. Paul**, Ph. D., is an Assistant Professor in the Department of Psychology, Trenton State College, Trenton, New Jersy, USA.

(10) **Robert Marsh**, Ph.D., is a Professor of Sociology in the Sociology Department, Brown University, Providence, Rhode Island, USA.

(10) **Cheng-kuang Hsu**, Ph.D., is a Research Fellow at the Institute of Ethnbology, Academia Sinica, Taiwian, ROC.

(11) **Shin Kim**, Ph.D., is an Assistant Professor in the Department of Economics, Chicago State University, Chicago, Illinois, USA.

(12) **Judith A. Dilorio**, Ph.D., is an Associate Professor in the Department of Sociology and Anthropology, Indiana University–Purdue University at Fort Wayne, Fort Wayne, Indiana, USA.

(13) **Chih-duen (Painton) Tse,** Ph.D., is a Group Leader/Principal Development Scientist at Miles, Inc., Granger, Indiana, USA.

(14) **Chikako Usui**, Ph.D., is an Assistant Professor in the Department of Sociology, a Fellow at the Center for International Studies, and an Associate Faculty in the Graduate Programs in Gerontology, University of Missouri–St. Louis, St. Louis, Missouri, USA.

(15) **Howard A. Palley**, Ph.D., is a Professor of Social Policy in the School of Social Work, University of Maryland at Baltimore, Baltimore, Maryland, USA.

(16) **Karen Altergott**, Ph.D., is an Associate Professor in the Child Development and Family Studies, Purdue University, West Lafayette, Indiana, USA.

(16) **Dinnie Chao**, is a Doctoral Candidate in Child Development and Family Studies, Purdue University, West Lafayette, Indiana, USA.

(17) **Rita Jing-Ann Chou**, Ph.D., is an Associate Professor of Anthropology in the Department of Anthropology, National Taiwan University, Taiwan, ROC.

(18) **Lynn K. White**, Ph.D., is a Professor of Sociology in the Department of Sociology, University of Nebraska–Lincoln, Lincoln, Nebraska, USA.

(18) **Yuko Matsumoto**, is an Associate Professor in the Department of Sociology, Seitoku University, Saitama, Japan.

(19) **Margo Sorgman**, Ph.D., is a Professor of Education in School ofEducation, Indiana University–Kokomo, Kokomo, Indiana, USA.

(20) **Neels Bester**, is an Associate Professor and Head of the Department of Sociology, Vaal Triangle Campus of the Potchefstroom University, South Africa.

(21) **John E. Sullivan**, MSW; ACSW, is a Family Therapist at St. Vincent Hospital, Indianapolis, Indiana, USA.

(22) **Minjie Zhang**, is a Research Fellow and an Associate Professor at the Zhejiang Academy of Social Sciences, Zhejiang, People's Republic of China.

(22) **Deborah Evans**, is a Senior at the University of Indianapolis, Indianapolis, Indiana, USA. She will graduate in December 1994 and plans to pursue graduate studies.

(23) **Lina Y. S. Fong**, Ph.D., is an Associate Professor in the Kent School of Social Work, University of Louisville, Louisville, Kentucky, USA.

(24) **Julian C. Chow**, Ph.D., is an Assistant Professor of Social Work in the School of Social Welfare, University of Albany, Albany, New York, USA.

(24) **Li-tao C. Hsieh**, DSW, is a Project Director at the Model School of Applied Sciences, Case Western Reserve University, Cleveland, Ohio, USA.

(25) **Patricia A. Cook**, Ph.D., is a Professor of Education in School of Education, University of Indianapolis, Indianapolis, Indiana, USA.

(25) **Nancy E. O'Dell**, Ph.D., is a Professor of Education in School of Education, University of Indianapolis, Indianapolis, Indiana, USA.

(Afterword) **Carl R. Stockton**, Ph.D., is a Professor of History and Dean for Extended and Special Programs, University of Indianapolis, Indiana, USA.

Name Index

Subject Index

D

  changing, 29, 215-226
  different, 19
  modern conjugal, 142
  patriarchy, 150

Afterword

We have come to expect thoughtful and highly diverse writing in this continuing series focused upon the family. The monographs in this volume have been collected under the auspices of the Asian Programs of the University of Indianapolis, and, as before, both the subjects and the writers are comprehensibly global in representation and scope. Although a distinctive microcosm may be seen under the particular lens of each writer, each piece contributes toward universal understandings of families, whatever the geographic context.

Reading through the collection, one often finds new insights through the eyes of these gifted observers and analysts. Sometimes one can quibble about conclusions, and wish to have a dialogue with the writers, if only to explain, clarify or magnify, particularly passages that appear to be controvertible or, owing to this particular reader's want of background, sometimes confusing. When that happens, we can happily assume that the writing has achieved the felicitous objective of critical engagement.

There are some pieces to which we shall return for further reflection; there are others which will serve as valuable reference points. This useful work should have a place of prominence in our library shelves. As an historian, I am reminded again of the crucial centrality of the family in the human story; as a human being, prodded to think of its role in the unfolding story of the future. If understanding can affect that story, then this work will have achieved much. On the whole, it leaves us sanguine about our prospects as a human family, in all its glorious diversity.

Carl R. Stockton, D.Phil.
Professor of History and
Dean for Extended and Special Programs

Chinese Studies

(The following books are published under the auspices of the Asian Programs, University of Indianapolis. The views expressed in each book reflect only those of the author.)

1. Phylis Lan Lin, Winston Y. Chao, Terri L. Johnson, Joan Persell, and Alfred Tsang (Eds.), *Families: East and West*, Indianapolis, IN: University of Indianapolis Press, 1992. 241 pp.
   ISBN NO: 1-880938-006 (paperback) $21.00
2. Wei Wou, *KMT-CCP Paradox: Guiding a Market Economy in China*, Indianapolis, IN: University of Indianapolis Press, 1993. 177 pp.
   ISBN NO: 1-880938-007 (paperback) $31.00
   IABN NO: 1-880938-007 (hardcover) $39.00
3. Yu-ning Li (Ed.), *Images of Women in Chinese Literature*, Indianapolis, IN: University of Indianapolis, 1994. 232 pp.
   ISBN NO: 1-880938-008 (paperback) $25.00
   ISBN NO: 1-880938-012 (hardcover) $39.00
4. Phylis Lan Lin, Ko-wang Mei, and Huai-chen Peng (Eds.), *Marriage and the Family in Chinese Societies: Selected Readings*, 1994. 372 pp.
   ISBN NO: 1-880938-010 (paperback) $35.00
5. Phylis Lan Lin and Wen-hui Tsai (Eds.), *Selected Readings on Marriage and the Family: A Global Perspective*, 1995. 362 pp.
   ISBN NO: 1-880938-013 (paperback) $35.00

Send your order to:
Asian Programs
University of Indianapolis
1400 Hanna Avenue
Indianapolis, IN 46227-3697
FAX (317) 788-3275